"Podell traveled the world having more hair-raising misadventures and harrowing escapes than Indiana Jones. He survived them all to write this delightful book. . . . perhaps the broadest range of human cultures ever portrayed in a single book. And he puts these intriguing experiences in the context of major events and world history. It sets a new standard for adventure travel books."
—Will Lutwick, author of *Dodging Machetes*

"An engaging and colorful storyteller. . . . Even if your desire for exotic travel never takes you out of your reading chair, you'll find Podell a fascinating companion."
—*BookPage*

"*Around the World in 50 Years* is [Albert Podell's] jokey, politically incorrect, thoughtful, and continuously engaging chronicle of the 102 separate journeys he took to accomplish his self-inflicted and likely unprecedented mission of visiting every recognized country on earth. . . . Mr. Podell can be a sensitive tourist and a shrewd observer. . . . Still, the rewards of Mr. Podell's book are less his geopolitical insights than his endearing appetite for adventure and the pleasures he unerringly finds at the ends of the earth."
—*The Wall Street Journal*

"Outdoor adventurer Albert Podell has written what they used to call a 'ripping yarn' about his lifelong quest (successful) of visiting every single country on Earth."
—*The Sacramento Bee*

"In this lively travelogue, Podell proves himself a worthy raconteur as he recounts his adventures. . . . An informative and sobering look at the world's many cultures and the importance of travel."
—*Publishers Weekly*

"Even the most jaded armchair traveler will enjoy these breezy anecdotal vignettes from Podell's fifty years of journeying. . . . This is absolutely not a travel guide but rather a shout-out to those who crave adventure from someone who persists with good luck and no fear of the unknown."
—*Library Journal*

"Albert Podell tells of his adventures with gusto, bravado, and humor in *Around the World in 50 Years*." —*Portland Book Review*

"This book is well written and you feel like you personally know Podell with his spirited voice and his witty comments in parentheses. . . . It was captivating to read about countries and specific landmarks that you don't learn about in geography class." —*TeenInk.com*

"Al Podell is a son of a bitch. I say that admiringly, incredulously, and enviously. A fast-paced action romp." —*DailyXY.com*

"He shares some amazing and very unique stories about countries most people have probably never heard of." —*ThereLiesFreedom.com*

"For people who think themselves adventurous, this could be a good eye-opener." —*ZWorstBlog.blogspot.com*

"A vast array of compelling stories." —*TheCultureTrip.com*

"It's a great book . . . a spellbinding work." —*ModernDayOzzieandHarriet.blogspot.com*

"A fascinating and entertaining read." —*TravelingOverEducatedHousewife.com*

"Outright packed with action. . . . *Around the World in 50 Years* stands alone among travel books I've read. Never have I read such a travel book that covers such a vast amount of land, people, and adventures. If you're a travel fan, this is a must-have for your bookshelf." —*MasculineBooks.com*

"There is so much here you won't find in any other text: plain, honest truth from Al, the slightly crazy, staunchly opinionated, and mildly debaucherous friend we feel we know quite well by the last page." —*SavvyGirlTravel.com*

"Podell's passport would be a more fascinating read than many a thriller, but the stories behind each stamp in his mad quest to touch every corner in the world are even better. This is a great book by an even greater traveler."

—Peter Allison, author of *Whatever You Do, Don't Run: True Tales of a Botswana Safari Guide*

"The fastest and most thrilling adventure book ever."

—Tracie Max Sachs, five-time World Cup speed-skiing champion

"This fascinating book is filled with adventurous curiosity and constant drama, and written with delight, humor, and compassion."

—James Fulton Hoge, Jr., former editor of *Foreign Affairs* and publisher of New York *Daily News*

"Swashbuckler, philosopher, humorist, Al Podell has lived, and written, a splendidly rollicking adventure." —Trevor Morrison, Dean, New York University School of Law

**ALSO BY ALBERT PODELL**

*Who Needs a Road? The Story of the Longest and Last Motor Journey Around the World*

*The Survival Guide for the Adventurous International Traveler*

ALBERT PODELL

# AROUND THE WORLD IN 50 YEARS

## MY ADVENTURE TO EVERY COUNTRY ON EARTH

THOMAS DUNNE BOOKS
ST. MARTIN'S GRIFFIN
NEW YORK

THOMAS DUNNE BOOKS.

An imprint of St. Martin's Press.

AROUND THE WORLD IN 50 YEARS. Copyright © 2015 by Albert Podell. Foreword copyright © 2015 by Harold Stephens. Parts of chapters 2–5 and 7 initially appeared in *Who Needs a Road?* and are used here with the permission of Wolfenden Publishers. All rights reserved. Printed in the United States of America. For information, address St. Martin's Press, 175 Fifth Avenue, New York, N.Y. 10010.

www.thomasdunnebooks.com

www.stmartins.com

Designed by Jonathan Bennett

All photos are by Albert Podell unless otherwise noted.

The Library of Congress has cataloged the hardcover edition as follows:

Podell, Albert.
   Around the world in 50 years : my adventure to every country on earth / Albert Podell.—First edition.
      p. cm.
   ISBN 978-1-250-05198-1 (hardcover)
   ISBN 978-1-4668-5293-8 (e-book)
   1. Podell, Albert—Travel.   2. Voyages around the world.   I. Title.
   G440.P73P64 2015
   910.4092—dc23

2014033858

ISBN 978-1-250-09422-3 (trade paperback)

Our books may be purchased in bulk for promotional, educational, or business use. Please contact your local bookseller or the Macmillan Corporate and Premium Sales Department at 1-800-221-7945, extension 5442, or by e-mail at MacmillanSpecialMarkets@macmillan.com.

First St. Martin's Griffin Edition: July 2016

10  9  8  7  6  5  4  3  2

*To*
*my beloved mother and father,*
*may they rest in peace,*
*and may they forgive me*
*for having assured them*
*that this journey was*
*"nothing to worry about."*

# CONTENTS

# CONTENTS

We will either find a way, or make one.

—HANNIBAL

I did not wish to take a cabin passage, but rather to go before the mast and on the deck of the world, for there I could best see the moonlight amid the mountains.

—HENRY DAVID THOREAU, *Walden*

Yes, Al, there is a certain publicity value to your being killed on this quest, but most publishers want a living author who can do TV and press interviews, so, on balance, it's a bit better to stay alive. If you can.

—TONY OUTHWAITE, LITERARY AGENT

One of the many spectacular rock formations in the desert of Saudi Arabia near Al-Ula, north of Jeddah. Saudi Arabia stopped issuing visas to tourists many years ago, but I was able to slip in as part of an archaeological group.

# AROUND THE WORLD IN 50 YEARS

# FOREWORD

## Harold Stephens

This is the best adventure/travel book written in this young century.

It's a robust, rugged, insightful, humorous, raunchy, wise, thrilling, intensely readable saga of how my favorite travel buddy, Albert Podell, overcame tremendous odds and hardships to achieve an almost-impossible dream of visiting every country on earth.

This book has it all—adventures, disasters, survival, victories, wit, wisdom, intriguing facts, fascinating figures, perceptive observations, graphic descriptions, history, geography, culture, politics, revolution, war, intrigue, spies, sin, sex, snakes, and sharks, all conveyed in a smooth, engaging, page-turning style that makes you feel that you are right there beside Al as he gets into one jam after another. And out.

*Around the World in 50 Years* memorializes, and takes us along on, a unique human achievement. To my knowledge, there is no other book by, or about, anyone, living or dead, who achieved this remarkable feat of perseverance, resourcefulness, and quiet courage.

It is not a travel guide, yet there is much that Al did from which a traveler could take guidance. Nor is it a book of traditional explorations or corny claims; Al did not go to any place "where no man has ever gone before," but he went everywhere with a brave heart, clear eyes, and an inquiring mind that made astute observations and discerned remarkable relationships, all told in a bright, vigorous, and eminently enjoyable style.

Al's travels required 102 separate journeys that encompassed more than 50 years and close to a million arduous miles. He highlights the major troubles, accidents, wars, breakdowns, robberies, problems, hassles, dangers, detours, misunderstandings, nut cases, and whack jobs he needed to overcome to survive to 196 countries. It describes only those travels and events that were particularly adventurous or engrossing and only those countries that were exotic or far from the tourist track, like Nauru and Lesotho, Benin and Tuvalu, Palau and East Timor, Saudi Arabia and Guinea, North Korea and Somalia, Congo and Rwanda and Yemen.

This fact-packed book is loaded with fascinating encounters with voodoo sacrifice rituals, king tides, tiger sharks, fruit-bat pie, the Ghost Fleet of Truk Lagoon, Cuban counterintelligence agents, Havana hookers, killer hippos, Zambezi River rafting, Kalahari sandboarding, primitive bungee jumping, bizarre foods, the New Guinea Wigmen, camel caravans, the slave trade, lovable lemurs, swimming with penguins, Islamic politics, the drowning nation, the Lord's Resistance Army, how to greet a gorilla, hunting with nomads, Pure Blonde Naked Pale Ale, and much, much, much more, all recounted in a fresh, funny, and exuberantly rollicking manner.

Although primarily an adventure tale, it provides a special background for understanding today's world and its dangers, splendors, animosities, oddities, politics, problems, and people.

Al would be the first to admit that this is not a tale of exceptional heroism, because the many dangerous situations and hair-raising adventures in which he found himself did not spring from purposeful attempts to put himself in harm's way, but were simply the result of ordinary ill luck, inadvertence, misplaced trust, foolish notions of invincibility, or just the way the cookie crumbled. Nor is it a book of miracles, because Al paid a high price for his many misadventures in injuries, illnesses, expenses, and girlfriends who gave up waiting for him to finish.

It's a book about the dedication, persistence, and indomitable will of a guy who spent a good part of his life pursuing his goal on ancient Third World airplanes; leaky, overloaded foreign ferries; and broken-down, jam-packed bush taxis driven on rutted roads at 100 mph by wild kids who never passed a driving test. He unrolled his sleeping bag at border posts, campsites, roadsides, jungles, glaciers, airport floors, and in hostels, *dahk* bungalows, tents, trailers, trees, teepees, campers, cars, caravansaries, desert dugouts, and flea-bag motels; alternately sweating and freezing; dodging dengue-fever mosquitoes by day and malarial ones by night; lugging more than 130 pounds on some trips while trying to get by on others with a Speedo and sandals, en route to 203 countries (seven of which no longer exist) to reach the 196 officially recognized today.

It's a damn good read! One of the best of its kind since Marco Polo. We learn what this world is really like and come to understand how, by just showing up for the job, day after day; persevering in the face of myriad misadventures, year after year; and never giving up, decade after decade, you can achieve your impossible dream.

—Bangkok, Thailand
October 2014

Harold Stephens is the author of 24 books of travel and adventure. He was, with Albert Podell, the co-leader of the Trans World Record Expedition and coauthor on *Who Needs a Road?* which is still in print after almost 50 years, and about 40 pages of which are used or adapted in chapters 2 to 5 and 7 of this book.

# CHAPTER 1

## Between a Croc and a Hard Place

I was on a quest to visit every country on earth, but I was about to get stuck, between a croc and a hard place.

I had just reached the inner section of the Okavango Delta of Botswana, where one of Africa's mightiest rivers fans out into the sands of the Kalahari Desert. I'd taken a jouncing two-hour ride in an ancient Land Cruiser and a two-hour voyage through tall reeds and flowering lily pads in a *mokoro*, a pole-pushed dugout canoe with the shape (and, it sometimes seemed, the width) of a large banana. Then an hour's walk through the bush to where a guide promised I'd find many harmless photogenic herbivores.

I was kneeling down, doing what any inquisitive outdoor guy does: examining half a dozen differing piles of animal excrement. The medium-sized crap with the pointy end was clearly from a porcupine. The huge tan ones of barely digested grass, tree branches, and palm nuts could only be an elephant dump. The blackish globular clusters were wildebeest. The tiny pellets were springbok. The small balls were zebra. The golf-ball-sized globes that contained fur and tiny mouse bones were from either a serval or a caracal. And—*holy shit!*—those fresh piles of pancake-shaped dung looked much like the spoor of Cape buffalo, the meanest and most dangerous animal in Africa, and one I'd been assured was *not* in the vicinity. But the scatological evidence was compelling: The turds looked like no other animal spoor,

5

Here I am examining animal spoor in the inner reaches of the Okavango Delta. The spoor of every animal is different in shape, size, and texture and can provide the knowledgeable outdoorsman with valuable information as to what game is in the area, and whether there are any dangerous carnivores about.

and, much worse, they were warm, almost steaming, no more than half an hour old.

I decided to get right out of there, so I rose up and . . . froze. There, not more than 80 yards across the knee-high grass, were about 15 Cape buffalo looking intently and angrily in my direction. Since it doesn't take much to provoke a charge by these beasts, who live by the motto that the best defense is a good offense, attack at the first sight of a perceived enemy, and use their long horns with fatal accuracy, I was nervous. Very nervous.

I thought for a minute: *What would Indiana Jones do in such a situation?* The answer was obvious: climb a tree. Only problem was that the trees in the southern part of the Okavango Delta are few, fragile, and far between. It was about 50 yards from me to anything climbable. Even that was no safe haven, because these beasts will charge a tree repeatedly and knock it down to get at their prey. They're infamous for their persistence. Once they decide to get you, they've been known to wait at the base of a tree for a day or more until you become faint from dehydration and sleep deprivation and fall out.

I thought for another minute: *What would Crocodile Dundee have done in this situation?* The answer was obvious. I tried, as casually, apologetically, and unprovocatively as possible, to saunter away from the wild buffalo in a circular arc that would take me far downwind from them and back to the *mokoro.*

After ten minutes of shaky sauntering, my way was blocked by a large pond where a family of hippos was bathing near the far edge and a congregation of crocodiles was basking on the right bank. The male hippo spotted me and opened his mouth wide, in what resembled a yawn but was actually a warning to back off, and the crocs started to bestir themselves.

Since the Cape buffalo is the nastiest animal in Africa, and hippos annually kill more people (including tourists) than any other beast on the continent, and those beady-eyed reptiles are more aggressive than the American alligator, I was in a tight spot.

I thought for a minute: *What would my portly scoutmaster have done in this situation?* And the answer was obvious: have lunch and let the situation resolve itself. I dropped down into the tall grass, out of scent of the buffalo, which were upwind, and out of sight of the hippos and crocs, whose olfactory apparatus is less acute, then carefully checked my situation: I had a ham-and-cheese on rye with mustard, a leg of fried chicken, an apple, and a very upset stomach.

When I finished lunch, the hippos and the crocs were still staring at my last-known address. I thought: *What would my old traveling buddy, Harold Stephens, do in this situation?* And the answer was obvious: take a nap in the afternoon sun under the cloudless Botswanan winter sky. I was pretty sure the hippos would not waddle a hundred yards from their pool to hunt me down; the crocs couldn't see me and should be sufficiently satiated from the impala, kudu, lechwe, and wildebeest that came to the pond for a drink that they wouldn't be hungry for a human hors d'oeuvre; and I knew that a Cape buffalo would not attack a dead person, a category I optimistically expanded to include a sleeping one. I also remembered reading—or did I?—that the buffalo had difficulty using its horns to kill creatures that lay flat on the ground. So maybe I'd be safe if I took a nap.

I awoke with a start about 30 minutes later after remembering another germane speck of buffalo arcana: If the Cape can't gore its grounded victim with its horns it will simply stomp him to death with his hooves. End of nap.

I peeped through the waist-high brown grass and was relieved to find the hippo family frolicking in the pond with no lingering interest in me, the crocs dozing on their crowded solarium, and no more buffalo in sight. I crept for the *mokoro* and home base, having suffered nothing more serious from this little outing than some dung-scented fingers.

Since you've just met me, and may be skeptical about this tale, and others to come, or wonder if I'm exaggerating, let me hasten to assure you that, given my extensive experience enhancing "true adventure" stories when I edited the magazines *Argosy, blue,* and *Modern Man,* if I'd decided to fabricate the story, it would have been *much* more exciting. Like this:

> The Cape buffalo snorted and charged directly at me. I ran to one of the few trees in the delta and clambered up just in time, his scalpel-sharp horn missing my leg by an inch. The beast relentlessly hammered the slender tree until it toppled, propelling me into the pond, where I bobbed up to see four crocs torpedoing right at me. I dove under the nearest one and swam onto his scaly back. I dug my fingers into his eye sockets and held on, steering him toward shore. The male hippo began to bear down on me, his deadly jaws wide open, capable of bisecting my body with one bite. On the shore, a pride of lions had gathered to be in on the kill. As my fate seemed sealed, a bull elephant lumbered into the pond for a drink. I seized his trunk and was hoisted to safety.

I was later assured by two Botswanan game wardens that I was safer with 15 Cape buffalo staring at me than just one. They explained that since a Cape will almost always charge when it feels threatened, there's less likelihood of one member of a grazing herd charging, because they each feel secure when chowing down with their buddies. The warden insisted that the real danger comes from encountering a solitary buck who, lacking the comfort and safety he feels in a gang, will charge to protect himself.

That assurance may be all well and good in theory, but since it would only take one angry iconoclast to wreck my day, and the risk of there being such a one among a mob of 15 is higher, I'd still prefer to be confronted with just one. Or, better yet, none.

At this point you might well be wondering: *What's a guy like you doing in a place like this?*

So let me take it from the top . . .

# CHAPTER 2

## A Late Start

It all began with Jack Kerouac's *On the Road*. I devoured it in one long day at the end of the 1959 winter semester at the University of Chicago, where I was the graduate fellow in international relations. Early the next morning I blasted out of academia and those gloomy Gothic towers and hit the asphalt, joyfully thumbing my way south and west on old Route 66, the Mother Road, through Towanda, Tulsa, Tucumcari, Gallup, Kingman, and across the Mojave Desert to the City of the Angels, then up the breathtaking coast road to bond with the Beats in San Francisco, yearning for more travel.

Three years later, already 25, I finally made it to my first foreign country, although it wasn't that foreign: It was only Canada.

My parents traveled little, never venturing farther from Brooklyn than Boston (once every four years to visit my father's siblings) because we were poor (my mother a secretary, my father a waiter in a succession of near-bankrupt kosher delicatessens where he never earned more than 70 dollars in a week) and because they found no delight in traveling. When they were quite young, they had each separately made the long and arduous train journey from their impoverished, pogrom-plagued villages in the hostile heart of Byelorussia to the teeming ports of western Europe, where they were jammed into the steerage compartments of dirty, overcrowded ships for a storm-tossed twelve-day crossing to the fateful examination at Ellis Island. That was, for them, enough traveling to last a lifetime. All my father ever wanted after that was "a roof that doesn't leak, enough food on the table, and a warm bed—with your mother in it." Their unwillingness to travel made me all the more eager for it.

I was at Fort Drum, near Watertown, New York, a sergeant in the Army Reserve on summer tour of duty, training my squad on the 155mm atomic cannon, a mean machine capable of hurling a nuclear shell more than 22 miles—about the distance to the Canadian border, although we never aimed it that way. At the end of our two weeks of live-fire exercises (without nuclear warheads), six of us crammed into the corporal's old car and headed across the St. Lawrence River for the nearest big city, which was Ottawa—Canada's capital—a neat, staid, pleasant, government town.

Canada looked to me a lot like the U.S., just a bit cleaner and quieter, with clearer skies and greener grass, and populated then only with white folks, all of whom walked slower, talked slower, and were more friendly and courteous than the Noo Yawkers among whom I grew up, but little likely to inspire anyone to imagine that foreign travel could be a fabulous joyride.

My next foreign foray came a year later, when I was picture-story editor of *Argosy*. A movie producer junketed me to Madrid, at whose outskirts he'd erected a cardboard-and-plaster full-size replica of ancient Rome to film *Fall of the Roman Empire*.

A week's free trip to Madrid could whet anyone's appetite for travel, but what made mine insatiable was a full-day stopover in Paris on my flight home, my first of a dozen visits since. I dumped my bag at an inexpensive *pension* in the Boulevard de la Tour-Maubourg but never made it to back to bed. For the next 22 hours I devoured the City of Light on foot—the Louvre, Eiffel Tower, Les Invalides, the Tuileries, Place de la Concorde, Panthéon, Luxembourg Gardens, the Left Bank, the Right Bank, the American Express Bank (cash resupply), Montparnasse, the Sorbonne, Notre-Dame, evening with the artists in Montmartre, night with the ladies of the Folies Bergère in Pigalle, and a glorious morning watching the sun rise over the twinkling city from atop the hill in the basilica of Sacré-Cœur.

Ottawa had been my first, shy, fumbling kiss; Madrid was heavy petting; Paris was going all the way, true love. I was hooked on travel and eager for some serious sightseeing.

On the practical side, I had a great job, good health, an apartment on fashionable East 55th Street, was dating some of the hottest models and actresses in town (a legacy from my previous post as an editor at *Playboy*), had saved enough to start an investment portfolio, and had a hundred other valid reasons to stay put. But I'd been editing *Argosy* for four years and wanted to stop living vicariously. I'd sent writers and photographers on dozens of ventures, voyages, and expeditions—by dogsled across Greenland, to Cocos Island and to Bora Bora, searching for Inca gold in Peru, hunting for pirate treasure in the Caribbean, bicycling from Cairo to Cape Town, even giving the wild young Hunter Thompson his first assignment—and I wanted an adventure of my own.

In December of 1964 I teamed up with Harold Stephens, a travel/ adventure writer and ex-Marine, to try to break the record for the longest direct, nonrepetitive, land journey around the world. We aimed to accomplish this by shunning the old Paris-to-Peking route (then blocked by the Iron Curtain and the Bamboo Blinds), and taking a longer, more southerly course, across the deserts of North Africa, through the Middle East, along Marco Polo's route across Central Asia, through India and Southeast Asia to Singapore, then across the width of Indonesia and Australia, and back to New York from Panama.

There had been four previous transworld auto expeditions, but all had taken shorter routes. The Great Race of 1908 had sent the competitors from New York to Alaska, to Vladivostok, to Moscow, then across Europe to Paris. The Wanderwell Expedition of 1919–1925 had wandered well over the map, but its direct route had taken its Model T Ford from Spain through Italy, Greece, Turkey, on to India, Japan, and San Francisco. The 1955 Oxford and Cambridge Far East Expedition had driven a Series 1 Land Rover from London to Singapore via Austria, Yugoslavia, and Turkey, but had not circuited the world. The remarkable 1956 solo drive of Group Captain Peter Townsend was poignantly recounted in *Earth, My Friend*. He pushed a Land Rover over a similar course but did go all the way around, partly as a healing process after Britain's royal family broke up his romance with Princess Margaret Rose and refused to permit her to marry him because he was divorced, something a royal just didn't do in those staid days before Di and Charles and Camilla.

Those previous globe-girdling expeditions had—after deducting for side trips, backtracking, indirect routing, and city tours—traversed 16,000 to 18,000 goal-oriented, nonrepetitive miles. By driving closer to the Equator, where the earth's circumference is greatest, and by filling in some oceanic gaps with drives across Indonesia and Australia and up from Panama, our goal-oriented, nonrepetitive mileage would exceed the others by at least 6,000, thereby establishing a clear and unbeatable record for the longest latitudinal land traverse of the globe. I optimistically named us the Trans World Record Expedition.

I wasn't wealthy, nor was Steve—only his mother can call him Harold—so we needed sponsors to provide the equipment and cash for what we envisioned as an eight-month jaunt. Within six weeks, calling on contacts I'd made editing magazines, we had 30 big backers, including Toyota, Dow, Du-Pont, Union Carbide, Firestone Tire, American Cyanamid, Thermos, Hat Corporation, Thom McAn shoes, Sea & Ski, the Bourbon Institute, SC Johnson, and Manischewitz, which wanted a photo of us sharing their matzos with Arab camel drivers in front of the Great Pyramid in Egypt.

We had sponsors for almost everything we needed, with a couple of manageable exceptions. I couldn't get a petrol partner because no oil company had service stations in every nation on our route. And the toilet tissue manufacturers turned us down because I could not contrive an acceptable method of photographing their product being used in a variety of exotic locations.

Several corporations, declining official sponsorship, nevertheless donated their products: Upjohn, figuring that we wouldn't be eating well, gave us three thousand vitamin pills; Johnson & Johnson sent a first-aid pouch and a snakebite kit with a note expressing the hope that we didn't have to use either; Allied Chemical showed both its charity and pessimism by providing a set of

Harold Stephens and me (with hat), the co-leaders of the Trans World Record Expedition, seated atop our Toyota Land Cruiser FJ40 at a press conference in Paris explaining our proposed record-setting land route around the globe. This was ten days into what would turn out to be an arduous 581-day journey. *French Government Tourist Agency*

inflatable splints; and Travelers Insurance, after rejecting us for a liability policy, sent us six of their trademark red umbrellas. Between the corporate givings and misgivings, we were well-equipped, fully bankrolled, and ready to hit the road.

On March 24, 1965, we watched from the deck of the *Queen Elizabeth* as our Land Cruiser and a half ton of supplies were hoisted aboard, bound for France. I was on my way to 26 new countries and a world of adventures.

# CHAPTER 3

## The Land of a Thousand Horrors

We off-loaded our Toyota 4×4 in Cherbourg and rendezvoused there with three men we had added to the expedition: Willy Mettler, a photographer from Switzerland; Woodrow Keck, a newspaper reporter from the Midwest; and Manu Bolar, a journalist from Spain. Sadly, none of them lasted until the end of the journey: Manu and Woodrow would give up and go home because of the delays and diseases that plagued the journey, and Willy would be captured and killed by the Vietcong in the Parrot's Beak of Cambodia. But our start, through France, Andorra, Spain, and Morocco, was bright with promise and few serious problems.

We did get stuck in an April snowstorm in the Pyrenees of Andorra and unknowingly pitched our emergency camp atop a smugglers' cache. We sustained several weeks of delay getting our air-freighted supplies through customs in Cadiz; smashed the undercarriage of our camper-trailer on Spain's rough secondary roads; and were trapped for two days in the Spanish blockade protesting the 250-year-long British occupation of Gibraltar. But these were minor inconveniences compared to what was to come in the months ahead.

On the plus side, in southern Spain we picked up both Steve's old Jeep and a small trailer to haul supplies, and three comely, adventurous, vacationing New Zealand nurses—Liz, Barbara, and Mira—who agreed to accompany us into North Africa.

We crossed Morocco without incident and entered Algeria late one night, where we decided to camp at the first clear spot. The border area was a mess of armed soldiers, concrete tank traps, and barbed wire, but a little past it we found an empty, hard-packed field, pulled in to it, pitched our camper and tent about 40 yards from the road, and were asleep in minutes.

"*Attention! Attention!*" Someone was shouting at us in French through a megaphone. It was early morning and I rubbed the sleep out of my eyes.

"*Arrêtez! Arrêtez!!*" The command came from an Algerian Army officer up on the road who continued to shout at us in French.

Willy blanched: "He says we shouldn't move. We're in the middle of a minefield!"

"Minefield? I'd hoped they'd gotten rid of those by now," I said.

"Got rid of what?" asked Woodrow, just waking up.

"The land mines. I edited a story about them at *Argosy*." More than seven million mines had been laid throughout Algeria, mostly by the rebels to blow up French troops and equipment during their war for independence, some to prevent an attack from Morocco. After the war nobody remembered exactly where they'd put a lot of them. They'd managed to dig up about half, but of the three million left, a few were apparently somewhere behind, around, or in front of us.

"What does he say we should do?" Steve asked Willy, who was translating.

After several shouted exchanges, Willy explained: "He says we should stay here. He has no mine detector. He says in four or five days the mine expert is due back in this part of the country. He also says we're a bunch of stupid fools to ignore all the warnings."

Down the road a sign with a skull and crossbones winked at us in the morning sun.

A four-day delay would be intolerable and unsafe with eight people eating, sleeping, walking, and answering calls of nature in a confined space surrounded by underground ordnance.

The safest way to get out was the way we'd driven in, but it was impossible to discern our tire tracks on the hardpack. Steve tried a tactic he'd picked up in the Marines. He took one of our arrows (from yet another sponsor) and to it tied a long piece of string, tied the string to a length of strong cord, and attached the cord to the winch cable on our car. He uncased one of our hunting bows (same sponsor) and shot the arrow as far as the road, where the officer hauled in, successively, the string, the cord, and the winch cable, until he had enough cable to work with.

Following Steve's shouted instructions, the officer found a sizable boulder, about 80 pounds. With the help of several nomads who'd stopped to see the *harib* get blown up, he rolled it to the road and wrapped the end of the cable around it.

When Steve started the engine to activate the winch, the rest of us took shelter beneath the camper, while he stayed in the Land Cruiser, his foot on the pedals, hauling in the improvised mine sweeper. The big boulder came tumbling and dragging along the ground, certain to detonate any mine in its path. With a solid *clink,* the boulder hit the bumper; the path was clear.

But was it really? The boulder had swept a trail wide enough for a pedestrian, but not wide enough for the car and camper. One at a time, seven of us walked to the road along the boulder's narrow pathway, with me last in line, pulling the winch wire, which, on reaching the road, I hooked around another boulder that Steve hauled in along a path parallel to the first.

It was halfway home when it detonated a mine. The world erupted. I was deafened by the blast. Rock and dirt exploded skyward and settled over our cars. But that was all: Our group was unharmed, the vehicles were operational, the path was clear, and we were back on the road.

Two days later, I was leading in the Toyota and Steve was following in his Jeep, when a blue Citroën passed him, doing at least 80 miles an hour on the narrow road. It swerved in behind me just in time to avoid hitting an oncoming car. At the outskirts of a village, the Citroën zoomed past me and, without warning, abruptly cut perpendicularly in front of me, risking a collision. I yanked the wheel violently left and crushed the brakes to bring the Toyota and camper to a slithering stop inches from the crazy Citroën.

The nurses and I tore out of the Cruiser, raging at the Citroën, who responded in French with a string of curses. Our normally phlegmatic Manu came up with a barrage that culminated in a pledge to defecate on the man's mother's genitalia to which the Citroën retorted, "May a pig die on the grave of your grandmother!"

The villagers rushed to the road, a crowd of about 40, to whom it was obvious, from the position of the cars, that the Citroën was recklessly at fault. Yet all of them took his side, as if they were afraid not to, even those who had seen him force me off the road.

A woman ran out of the house into whose courtyard the Citroën had been turning, waving a broomstick, screaming in French, "Go away! Go away, foreigners! Always foreigners. Always making trouble. Leave my husband alone!"

But I wasn't backing off: "Let me see your license," I demanded.

The Citroën's mouth fell open in shock, but he didn't budge.

"I said show me your license," I shouted, moving in on him.

"There, that is my license," he shot back in French, flashing a card from his pocket.

"This isn't a driver's license, and you know it," I yelled, after I caught a glimpse of an ID card that read MINISTRY OF PUBLIC WORKS at the top. "All this probably says is you dig sewers or haul shit away. It's a very fitting card for you, I'm sure, but I want your driver's license. I'll see to it you never drive again." I walked behind his car and wrote down the plate number.

That did it! The Citroën flew into a sputtering rage. He ran at me. I pulled back to punch him. Willy kicked him in the leg. The crowd started to move in. Steve jumped in to break up the fight. We couldn't understand why the Citroën hadn't just made a polite apology to get rid of us, but he was in no mood to apologize now, and we couldn't take on the whole village.

Two uniformed policemen broke up our squabble. They were somewhat embarrassed, but obviously on the Citroën's side. From the one who spoke English, the truth began to emerge: The Citroën was an important chap, the police commissioner of the entire district. (The card he'd flashed me didn't authorize him to dig sewers, but to arrest people, a job he'd won by being a fierce guerrilla leader in the war against the French colonials.) He was a notoriously reckless leadfoot whose wild driving was diplomatically ignored in deference to his position. We, however, had caused a *contretemps* by calling him out on it. The only way he could regain his stature and his village's respect was for us to admit that we were wrong and make peace.

And so we did.

The police built a roaring bonfire in the commissioner's courtyard, over which the nurses boiled soup and heated tins of meat. The commissioner contributed a five-gallon jug of wine. We were all friends now, *en rapport*, and the commissioner was happy. He showed us a postcard of Manhattan that a nephew had sent, and asked if we had ever been there. He told us how he'd blown up a train with *plastique* during the revolution, and that he'd killed at least 15 French settlers. He pulled out his gun and fired three shots into the night for emphasis. He drank until the wine ran down his cheeks. He chased Barbara around the campfire, trying in vain to pat her outstanding butt, as we wondered how to limit our camaraderie without giving offense. He sang bawdy French songs and roared with laughter when we played him back the tape recording.

Then things took a turn for the worse: He made a request we had to somehow refuse.

"I wish," he said, "I wish to buy that girl from you." He pointed to Barbara, blonde, full-figured, and glowing. I didn't blame him a bit for wanting her, but we had to get out of this predicament without pissing him off, because a man who'd killed 15 *pieds-noirs* wasn't going to think twice about shooting us dead if he felt he had been insulted by an American.

"How much will you pay for her?" I asked, emulating an ancient Arab custom in which wives were purchased.

"How much do you wish?" he countered, also following the custom, and I could see we were in for some hard haggling. And I could see that Barbara had stopped glowing.

I asked him what he thought a fair price, and he offered 1,500 U.S. dollars, cash or gold.

"Well, that's a good start," I answered. "But only for an average woman. It's not enough for her. Barbara here is exceptional." Exceptionally pale at the moment, I noticed.

"How much do you want?"

"Well, we just couldn't part with her for less than three thousand dollars.

She's no ordinary woman. Shining hair, nursing skills, nice disposition, and . . ."

"And lots of meat," the commissioner smirked. "All right, I give you two thousand. It's too much for a woman, but since you're my good friend, I'll give it to you."

"I'm sorry, but we just couldn't take less than three thousand, even from a good friend like you. We turned down twenty-seven hundred for her in Marrakesh from the Sultan's half-brother. We have to send part of the money to her mother."

"You do not bargain, Monsieur."

"Three thousand dollars is a bargain for a beauty like Barbara."

"As you wish. All right. I take her."

We were astonished! My ruse had failed. I couldn't conceive of anybody paying three thousand dollars for a woman outside of divorce court, but here it was. Barbara looked about ready to faint, when I recovered with, "But there's one thing I forgot to mention, dear friend. You see, we'd planned to sell these women as a group. They all go together. And because you are our friend, you can have the other two at a big discount, only two thousand dollars each, seven thousand dollars for all three."

"No, I do not want the other two. They are too skinny. Look," he said, pinching Liz, who screamed. "No meat. All bones. Like a sick camel. I could not even get two hundred dollars for her from the nomads. I only want the big one."

"But, you see, we have to sell them together. The one you prefer is the prize of the flock. You have excellent taste. You can understand why we need her to help us sell these other two miserable ones. Nobody will buy these scrawny chickens otherwise. Come on, special for you, as our friend, only seven thousand for all three."

We all held our breath while he thought it over.

"No," he said finally. "No deal."

And so, with a collective sigh of relief, our group drove on to Algiers, the Kiwis sitting in the back of the Land Cruiser singing, at the top of their lungs, "Máori Battalion March to Victory."

Algiers buzzed with activity, none of it conducive to a pleasant visit. Under

President Ben Bella it had become a center of anti-American propaganda and policies. We'd picked up its radio programs denouncing Americans as "imperialists, exploiters, fascists, and colonialists." Ben Bella had opened Algiers to international revolutionary groups. Its streets teemed with young rebels from the Mozambique Liberation Front and the Popular Movement for the Liberation of Angola. The city was plastered with signs and billboards extolling sacrifice, praising Socialism, saluting the Soviets, thanking Red China, and damning America.

Behind the flags and slogans, we detected unrest and discontent. High prices, low wages, half-empty stomachs, and disillusionment were rife. As were guns and barbed wire. Ben Bella's palace was surrounded by concrete tank traps and stout walls manned by half a hundred troops brandishing Russian machine guns.

We searched for the attractive campsites of the tourist brochure, but those sites were also victims of the war for independence that had despoiled the coast around Algiers with barbed wire, minefields, and watchtowers. We were forced to drive 15 miles to find a clear beach, where we set up our camper and rushed for the Mediterranean, eager to wash off the sand and sweat of a week of driving.

Steve plunged in first—and screamed for us to stop. The water was alive with leeches—wriggling, slimy, segmented worms as long as my foot—thousands of hungry black bloodsuckers. We ran out immediately, but Steve was in too far. By the time he made it back to shore there were two hot dog–sized wrigglers clinging to his legs and another, big as a sausage, sucking blood from his back. I pulled them off and cleansed his wounds. We retreated to the camper, utterly dejected.

Later that night, we sat around our dismal campsite getting ready for the next long stretch, to Cairo. Steve was studying maps, I was selecting photos for the sponsors, Woodrow was adding up his expenses, and the nurses were packing their knapsacks. Miles across the bay, the lights of Algiers beamed steady in the clear air, but everywhere else around us was absolute darkness, broken only by the glow of our hissing gas lanterns.

Suddenly Woodrow jumped up, screaming and holding his neck. Something had bitten him hard, and blood was oozing from the wound. But what? What kind of creature could slash a person's neck on a North African beach without being seen?

As I bandaged Woodrow's wound, I heard a faint warning buzz about ten yards away, like a rattlesnake, but lower in pitch. I turned toward the sound and saw a blur of black leap from the beach at my head. It caromed off the gas lantern and vanished. It was terrifying. We'd later be confronted by elephants in heat and tarantulas in our trousers, but we had no idea what demonic creature was attacking us now, and there's nothing more frightening than the unknown.

We waited, tense and sweating: two minutes, five, ten. Then another black buzz jumped at us. It grazed Steve on the chest and he swatted it to the beach and pinned it with his boot. It was one of the most hideous creatures I've ever seen, more a monster than any child of Nature. It was about five inches across, dark chocolate brown, with prominent front pincers and several sets of smaller side legs. It had the general shape of a crab, the hairy appearance of a spider, and some sort of rear wings that enabled it to fly or spring up to five feet high and 20 feet forward. And it died hard: Steve smashed the one at his foot ten times with an entrenching tool before it was finally stilled.

Our flashlights exposed a seething army of these things crawling toward us, but not before one of them sprung at me and nipped my hand. They were attracted to light, so we extinguished our lanterns and sat in the dark until we drowsed into nightmares of minefields and leeches and flying monsters.

The next morning brought no relief, for with it came mobs of unwashed, unruly kids, all curious to see the foreigners who were living on the beach, and all with a touch of larceny in their little hearts. What with two cars and trailers loaded with gear, we were thankful, when we took inventory that evening, that we'd lost only a can opener and a stack of paper plates.

We also lost the nurses that day, though not to looters: They were due back at their hospitals in London. We were sad as we watched their steamer sail for Marseilles. Ours was hardly a trip for the frail, and those Kiwis had borne up splendidly. Where others would have complained about the sun, the sand, the bugs, the food, and the flying crabs, Barbara, Mira, and Liz seldom lost their high spirits or good humor, a credit to their country and their calling.

Sometime during that night, as we slept, our camp had an uninvited visitor who cut the tarp on the small storage trailer and stole a suitcase loaded with winter clothing, mountain-climbing gear, and spare photographic equipment. We reported the theft to the police, who turned it over to the army, which was less interested in catching the thieves than in learning what a bunch of foreigners were doing camped on a beach with ropes and crampons and telephoto lenses. We were released only after hours of interrogation.

Given the aggressive wildlife, the thieving visitors, and the antagonistic political atmosphere, none of us wanted to remain in Algiers, but we had to stay: Cracks in the camper needed welding and the Jeep's generator had burned out and required rewiring. We had difficulty finding someone competent to do this work because almost every skilled auto mechanic and machinist had either fled back to France or been killed during the war, which had claimed 130,000 lives and exiled a million. After hours of searching, we found a welding shop for the camper and a technician who rewired our generator—and warned us that a revolution was imminent.

Though we doubted the thieves would return, we knew it was possible. So as not to be caught unaware, we stuck forked twigs in the sand in a circle around the cars and storage trailer, then ran a piece of string through them to a can half-filled with small stones balanced on a twig in a hole under the camper beside which Steve and I unrolled our sleeping bags. If anybody approached our equipment, they'd trip the string and rattle the can enough to wake us. In theory.

It was black and cramped under the camper, and I was sure the biting monsters would find us, but we managed to fall asleep. Hours later I heard something, but it wasn't the can rattling: It was someone unzipping the windows of the Land Cruiser. Steve was also awake, and handed me our .38 revolver. We slipped out from under the camper and got into position.

Steve flicked on our big flashlight. It caught three mean-looking men, their arms full of our supplies. I shouted at them to drop the stuff.

One of them did, but all three ran into the dark. We gave chase. I warned them to stop or I'd shoot. But they kept running. I fired twice into the air, but they kept going with our gear. I then fired *at* them, trying to hit their legs, though it was difficult to see in the moonless dark. On the third shot, I heard a groan and thought I saw someone fall. We rushed to the spot and found, next to a flying crab, Steve's safari hat, our binoculars, and some of our clothing. Our flashlight showed three sets of tracks moving up the beach, the one in the middle dragging, and here and there a spot of what looked like blood.

Had I killed somebody? Or just wounded him? How badly? Would he be back with a gang to get us? If he died, would his family or friends report us to the police?

We couldn't go to the police ourselves: They were already suspicious and unfriendly and not likely to treat kindly an American who'd shot an Algerian, whatever the provocation. Moreover, we'd averred at the border that we carried no firearms, knowing that if we declared our gun they'd confiscate it. The possession of that undeclared pistol alone could put us in jail, and that was the last place we wanted to be with an impending coup. We decided to clear out then and there.

If the burglar died or reported us, we assumed the police would look for us along the coastal highway east to Tunis, the best and most commonly traveled way out of the country, but one on which we knew Algerian troops had been stationed because of Ben Bella's dispute with neighboring Tunisia. We decided to avoid it by heading south, into the Sahara, where we were reasonably sure nobody would be looking for us. But we were not reasonably sure how to get through it.

When we'd inquired about traveling through the Sahara at gas stations the day before, nobody knew if it was currently negotiable, or what shape the roads were in, or even if there were roads. Our map indicated only thin unpaved tracks, ominous gray veins designated as *"terrible,"* and only one of which led into Tunisia. It was noted as subject to frequent closure by sandstorms, which meant we'd be forced to circle back through 800 miles of desert and mountains to link up with the World War II road through northern Algeria, by which time we'd be out of gas and the uprising we'd been warned about could be underway.

We broke camp and were on the move before dawn. Sunrise found us climbing through the Atlas Mountains, the natural barrier that protects the flourishing Mediterranean strip of North Africa from the encroachment of the great sea of sand, heading south toward the Sahara, into what the Arabs call "the land of a thousand horrors," the world's hottest and largest sand desert, 9.4 million square miles, larger than the continental U.S., stretching from the Red Sea to the Atlantic.

Hollywood had taught me to think of the Sahara as an immense waste of worthless, endless sand dunes, unbearably hot by day and freezing cold at night, without rainfall or water, except on a few oases, which I visualized as inviting blue ponds surrounded by beautiful gardens in the midst of an eternal desert whose life was unchanged and unchanging. These misconceptions were dispelled within two days after I met her: The only aspect of my Sahara vision that proved to be valid was "immense."

The flowing Panavision dunes of the movies comprise only 15 percent of the Sahara, concentrated in two or three areas. Most of the Sahara that we saw was an arid steppe, a low hard-packed plateau of gravel, sand, rocks, and some scrub grass. The rest is remarkably varied: It has massive mountains, high plateaus, volcanic formations, dried river beds, shadowy valleys, depressed salt basins, wind-eroded hills, and sparse plain. And it was far from worthless: Oil, gas, coal, iron, copper, gold, tin, tungsten, and manganese had recently been found there and were being exploited.

We did not find the daytime desert unbearably hot. Though the temperature went over 90 before noon and kept climbing, the heat was by no means intolerable, because the air was so devoid of moisture and in such constant motion that our perspiration evaporated instantly, keeping us cool and dry. We did require salt pills and a constant intake of water, and we had to avoid heavy foods, but as long as we stuck to this regimen, the Sahara was not unpleasant. It did cool quickly once the sun went down. With a cloudless sky overhead, the sand rapidly lost its heat, and there were no large bodies of water near enough to moderate the temperature shift, but it never dropped below 45 degrees.

We also learned that the Sahara had ample water, if you knew where to look, and received rain during winter, with some parts getting four inches—hardly enough to sustain agriculture, but sufficient to enable dormant seeds to germinate, dotting the desert with patches of green and bursts of bloom. The Sahara has no conventional lakes or rivers; They couldn't survive because the hot dry air can evaporate surface water to a depth of 13 feet in a year.

But below the surface there's another world. Fed by millennia of runoff from the Atlas Mountains and underground streams trapped in layers of cretaceous mantle rock, the realm beneath the sand is awash with sufficient water for centuries, *if* not tapped and drawn down profligately. Some aquifers rose to the surface centuries ago, as springs and pools, to create the oases, but most of the waters lay unknown and unused until around 1950, when geologists discovered and brought them forth. Along our route south, the water table was so close to the surface that we found functioning wells whose water was less than 50 feet down. Though we were never sure of the rules and customs, the wells seemed to be open to any thirsty traveler, with a pulley and a goatskin container or bucket ready and waiting, never any fences or NO TRESPASSING signs.

Because we all drank heartily—every other hour draining our personal quart-size thermos bottles and the pair of two-gallon jugs we shared—we found it necessary to stop every 30 miles or so to fill up, yet never lacked for a waiting well. Farther south, in the heart of the desert, the wells were fewer and deeper, but adequate for us. Surveys made a few years earlier had concluded that all the wells, springs, and irrigation ditches in the entire Sahara were consuming its water at one fourth the rate it flowed in. But that balance has been upset in recent years, and lives will be endangered if conservation does not become a priority.

Even more at odds with my idealized view of the Sahara were the oases, which I'd envisioned as photogenic pools surrounded by luxurious gardens. From the distance they seemed to live up to my belief. Through the clear desert air we could see the brilliant green tops of the palm trees. But as we drew closer the vision faded. Little was green at eye level: only brown tree trunks and brownish-red mud and rocks, and ugly houses with barbed wire around struggling gardens.

At the oases, water was highly prized and closely guarded. It ran from heavily fenced-in springs, along dirty canals that bordered the streets, into portions of private land dammed with rocks and rotting boards and protected by rusting wire. The houses were of weathered mud or yellowish clay, a few touched up with whitewash. Everything wore a brown coat of dust or sand from the encroaching desert and the ceaseless wind.

The bleakness was little relieved by the gardens, often a tangle of weeds or rodent-gnawed vegetables, inefficiently small after being passed on for generations, divided among brothers, split and split again, until they were no more than three feet by five, even the largest seldom more than 60 square feet.

Many younger inhabitants refuse to accept this way of life as the will of Allah. In contact with visiting Europeans, hearing about the wonders of modern science and industry, able to catch a truck ride and leave the desert in a few days, hundreds of young men had been heading for the coastal cities to find a better life, leaving the old people behind to tend the dying gardens and crumbling houses.

The other upholders of the old way of life, the nomads, were also undergoing a major transformation and may become people of the past, because the mid-century arrival of the truck diminished the size and importance of their caravan trade, as did the depletion of the desert gold deposits, the mining of cheap salt in Europe, and the decline of the ostrich-feather trade. The French colonizers struck two additional blows when they abolished the lucrative slave trade and the feudal dues paid to the nomads by the oasis dwellers. The nomads then switched to stockbreeding as a source of income, but the decline of the caravans decreased the market for camels, and droughts devastated their sheep herds.

The powerful nomad tribes were beginning to break up. Many were abandoning their obsolescent traditions, settling in oases, buying some date palms and cereal seeds, venturing into the formerly shunned occupation of agriculture—rooted peasants rather than proud, free wanderers. They'd been compelled to join the revolution that we saw coming to the Sahara, which was just beginning to be drilled by oil rigs, crossed by improved roads, bisected by pipelines, straddled by air strips, carved by mines, and sucked by gushing water pumps. This would bring drastic, and not always desirable, changes to the Sahara in the decades ahead, and I felt fortunate that I first saw her while she was still awesome and proud and not yet conquered.

After driving four days, we reached easternmost Tébessa Province. We were far enough south of the Aurès Mountains to make a run for Tunisia, hoping we could get through, despite the lack of reliable recent road maps. Those provided by the national tourist ministries were frequently misleading, generally glossy and colorful and filled with the thick reds and blues of well-paved roads more for artistic effect than cartographic accuracy, often indicating superhighways where camel trails could barely be discerned.

It was impossible to learn much about distant road conditions from the locals, few of whom had ever been more than 50 miles from their mud doorsteps. Some were fatalistic and untraveled, and told us that our road ended just beyond their oasis and that we could not move farther without a camel. Others were eager to please and reluctant to give offense, invariably telling us to continue in the direction we were heading, lest it be thought they were calling attention to our error. By far the most common, however, were those who didn't understand a word of what we were asking.

We turned northeast at El Oued, the easternmost of Algeria's large oasis towns, set amid dunes over 400 feet high whose lines differed from every angle but were always graceful. They were as picturesque as the Panavision version, and we found ourselves watching expectantly for a dashing warrior in a turban and flowing white robe to come charging over one of the dunes waving a scimitar, his powerful white Arabian stallion raising a plume of golden sand. But the only warriors who came were voracious flies.

As an homage to the Great Desert, then in its last days of untamed glory, we stopped our vehicles, and Manu and Steve and I raced to the tops of these golden hills, tumbling and sliding down, laughing and playing, making tracks where there were no tracks, thrilled by their vast unsullied magnificence.

But the minute we rested, the flies set upon us, vicious, biting bugs, twice as large as America's largest horsefly. Their presence amid these barren dunes, miles from any visible food or breeding spots, miles from any camels—to them a traveling amusement park and lunch wagon combined—was a puzzle to us, as surprising as the flying crabs. Where did they come from? What did they eat when we weren't around? How did they survive in the middle of nowhere? From the relentlessness of their attacks, we must have been the first food they'd seen in months. Fortunately, they departed when the sun set, but they were back by daybreak, an irritating alarm clock with no snooze button.

Their absence after dusk permits the Sahara traveler to relax and enjoy its sunset, one of nature's most dramatic spectacles. Because clouds rarely form above the desert, and moisture seldom enters its air to diffuse or refract, the sun descends as a blazing, hard-edged, crimson orb. In but a few minutes the dunes lose their dazzling glare and turn to soft colors, their lines muted, ever more graceful, as long shadows of purple, like pools of cool water, replace the bright harshness of day. The night comes quickly, and its stars are startling in their number and stunning in their brilliance. There is no sound for a hundred miles save the murmur of the cooling sands, no human save you, and I found myself wishing that the Sahara, however it may change, would never lose this magic.

The road from El Oued toward Tunisia was neither as bad as we'd feared nor as good as we'd hoped. It was asphalt in sections, but badly potholed, and clogged with camels who refused to get out of our way. It was covered with sand for long stretches, making the going slow, slippery, and confusing. Loose-blown sand is a deadly enemy of the Sahara traveler. Rocks can puncture tires, potholes can crack springs, and mud will mire you down, but nothing is as vicious as the Sahara sand, which at one and the same time blinds your vision, obliterates your route, batters your equipment, and assaults you personally.

The isolated Tunisian border post didn't open until 8:00 a.m., so we explored around it and, to our delight, found a wide pipe gushing pure, cold water into a substantial concrete basin in which the cavalry's camels were cavorting. We realized then that we hadn't had a shower since the casbah in Algiers. The Sahara is so dry, and our sweat evaporated so quickly, that we could get by for several *weeks* without bathing, but there are limits, especially for those accustomed to daily dunks.

With a roar and a rush, the five of us ran toward the pool, yelling loudly. The frightened camels dashed out, all except for an ugly albino veteran I had to slap hard on the rump. For half an hour, Steve and I bathed in the pool and stood under the gushing pipe, letting the water soak into every dehydrated pore of our bodies, while Willy took our photo, the same photo featured in *The New York Times* four months later—surely the first (and perhaps the last?) the *Times* printed of a full-frontal naked man—when we were reported lost in a deadly cholera epidemic in Afghanistan.

The pool was heaven until the camels regrouped and, led by the albino avenger, aggressively returned to reassert their rights. It was our turn to retreat. Besides, the border was about to open, and we were eager to get across.

Once through, we followed the dirt track toward the east and, as the sun came hotter into the sky, we began to feel the effects of dehydration. Our eyes burned and our lips cracked. We found no wells in this part of the desert, not a tree anywhere, not even a boulder to give shade.

Suddenly, as we peaked a slight rise, we saw a glorious sight in the distance: a rare desert lake! We gunned the engines, turned off the track, and raced the vehicles toward the water's edge. We soon left the soft sand of the desert and reached the hard-crusted surface that marked the periphery of the lake. But the water itself, that refreshing, beckoning water, was still distant, still farther than we'd thought. The faster we drove, the faster the water receded toward the horizon . . . until we gradually came to realize we'd been fooled. It was a mirage, a *fata morgana*, a classic deception of those shimmering sands, but a deception of such magnitude and perfection that we were all stunned.

The ground was packed sand and salt deposits interlaced with a network of the tiniest fissures, clearly a dried lake bed. The map confirmed it: Chott el Djerid, the largest salt pan in the Sahara, half as wide as Tunisia itself, half as long as Lake Erie, 70 feet below sea level, occupying an area as large as Connecticut, absolutely waterless and barren at this time of year. We forgot our thirst just thinking of this marvel, and chuckling over how we, supposedly old desert hands by then, had been so deceived.

We opted to rely on our compass and continue across the roadless lake bed a while, as it was a relief not having to dodge rocks and potholes and soft sand, and a thrill to be driving where, as far as we could tell, no vehicle had ever rolled before, leaving white tracks on the virgin soil. (Twelve years later I saw this odd place again, in a movie theater, but there it was called planet Tatooine, and plodding across its crusty sands were Luke Skywalker, C-3PO, R2-D2, and a holographic Princess Leia.)

After we crossed into Libya, we resumed our run on the old asphalt coastal road to the still-standing ruins of the third-century Roman city of Sabratha, where all was as silent as the desert night, lifeless as the desert day, and sea wind and weather were threatening to reduce to limestone dust what had once been part of the glory of Rome. I walked in wonder through the temples of Liber Pater, Isis, and Serapis, past a Christian basilica dating from

At the start of a sandstorm, Steve scouts for a route across Tunisia's 160-mile long Chott el Djerid, the largest salt pan in the Sahara. It can be crossed by boat in winter, but completely dries up in the summer, when the temperature reaches 120 degrees. Driving is dangerous because the salt crust is not firm.

the time of Emperor Justinian, and on the mosaic floors of the baths overlooking the sea.

I couldn't help thinking that this was once a bustling city in a mighty empire, a thriving city in a civilization that ruled most of the then-known world for over 400 years, a civilization that brought engineers and aqueducts and teachers and libraries to the most distant corners of the darkness, an empire relatively more powerful in its time than my own country in its, an empire whose enemies were just heathens on horseback and nomads on camels, yet an empire of which only these ruins remained.

Our host in Libya was Mohammed Soussi, the owner of a fledgling Toyota operation headquartered in Benghazi, and we came to know him well during our week in his company, while his men serviced our vehicles and repaired the camper undercarriage. On our last night, he hosted a farewell dinner for us, and after his other guests had gone, we sat on a terrace overlooking the city and talked. When the conversation turned to religion, he gave me an insight into his, declaiming:

"Islam gives meaning to my whole life. I could not live without it. It tells me everything I need to know and every way how to act. It is the greatest religion, the only true religion. Your religions are a fairy tale with miracles and sons of God and Trinities. With Islam there is only one God and He is all powerful. Mohammed is the one true prophet of God, and His writings are the only way that the divine will can be learned. The Koran is the final revelation. We need look no further and we need accept no other. The Koran tells us all we need to know about how to conduct our lives and how to submit to the will of God.

"I never worry. I never drink alcohol. I do not covet young girls, or boys, and I will make my marriage with the help of my father. I never think of suicide and I never think of taking drugs. I am not, like so many in the West, troubled by doubts and fears and neuroses. I know that Allah watches over everything we do, and that if we do everything as He has caused to be written in the Koran, we shall have our reward. I am serene and at peace with myself and the world. I am delighted with the sunrise, because it is the work of God, and with the sunset, because that is also His doing. And when I say my prayers and praise Him, I am sure that He hears them. Does yours?"

Because of the time spent mending the camper-trailer, we could make only a short stop at Leptis Magna, much as I'd have preferred to stay a week. Far more extensive and glorious than Sabratha, Leptis had been a showplace of the Roman Empire, birthplace of the powerful Emperor Septimius Severus, a handsome city of colonnaded avenues, amphitheaters, meeting halls, fountains, baths, basilicas, forums, libraries, arches, and some 40 major buildings. Unlike Sabratha, which had been built from local limestone, Leptis was fashioned from splendid multicolored marble brought from Greece, Italy, and Asia Minor, and its noble stone still stood gleaming as it had before the birth of Christ.

After leaving Leptis, we saw nothing for miles save the tiniest villages and the dullest desert. The road we followed was *La Strada Imperiale*, built in the 1930s by the Italian fascists. It still bore the scars of WW II, when it had been chewed up by tanks, blasted by dive bombers, blown apart by land mines, and cratered by artillery shells. The holes were strategically spaced and impossible to avoid. Whoever first suggested that "if nothing goes right, go left," never tried to negotiate this road.

The road's condition gave rise to some local humor:

Q. *What do you do when you come to a pothole?*

A. *Honk, in case somebody is in it.*

The roadside was strewn with the carcasses of giant truck tires that had been torn to shreds by the potholes and the desert heat. Many of the demolished tires were three feet in diameter and laced with metal mesh, so dense that two of us couldn't lift one, yet the road had shattered them. The only thing in the road's favor was that it was straight, arrowing across the desert, often running 30 to 40 miles without a turn or bend.

The desert sapped our energy and desiccated our bodies. Then the *ghibli* began, the dread Saharan wind that is the scourge of Libya. We'd been warned about the *ghibli*, but the reality went beyond description and further than imagination. It was a blow of pure heat like the discharge of a blast furnace. Inside the cars, which had no AC, the thermometers zoomed over 120 degrees. Whether we drove fast or slow, there was no getting away from the desert blowtorch. It blistered our eyes, cracked the insides of our noses, and parched our throats. Our temperatures soared, our pulses raced up to 130 beats a minute. Any exertion was exhausting: It was an effort to breathe, a struggle to move, a torment to drive. We were being baked alive, but could not escape the searing wind until it died of its own accord two hours later.

The *ghibli* is so much the bane of Libya that it's mainly to blame for the desert that covers 98 percent of it. Irrigation and fertilizers can make the sands bloom, but they can't beat the *ghibli*. Flourishing fields have been wiped out in a day, farmers ruined in hours. Only the hardiest olive trees and date palms survive. Because of the *ghibli*, Libya couldn't be considered a developing nation: "She's as developed as she's ever going to be," one old-timer opined, "as long as she has the *ghibli*. Once that wind hits, there's nothing left to develop."

Half the Libyans were still nomads, and we saw more of them as we left the desert floor and slowly climbed toward the hills of the Jabal Al Akhdar, where scrawny goats, sheep, and camels hungrily chewed tufts of grass and stubble into something digestible. The sun beat down without mercy, and there was no shade, not a bush or a tree anywhere. I felt sorry for the animals, and for the people who had never sheltered under a tree, lain in a flower-filled meadow, or basked in a cool brook. I thought of my parents' courageous migrations from their shtetls that had enabled me to be born in the most prosperous of lands, while these less fortunate people had been born in the most wretched. What if we, like them, had been born never to know a full belly, a day without fear of illness and uncertainty, a carefree love, a rewarding life? I had believed that people could be masters of their fates, that with ambition and perseverance they could rise and achieve, but I realized then that it was not true for all, and that for many—indeed, perhaps for *most* of humanity's billions—there were no grand opportunities, no high hopes, no worry-free days, no comforts but an early grave.

I soon felt sorry for us. We suffered another major breakdown of the camper-trailer (which we belatedly realized was unsuited for these rough roads), and labored all day to remove the axle. By nightfall our food and water were gone, except for the box of matzos, which I insisted we had an obligation to save for our photo op at the pyramids. We'd been traveling light on rations because of the exorbitant prices in Benghazi, planning to stock up in Egypt, and we'd drunk our water cans dry in a couple of hours from our exertions. Only one car passed all day. They had no water to spare.

We were preparing to settle down for a parched and hungry night when a military 4×4 pulled up beside us, and out jumped a trim Libyan army lieutenant who offered us his canteen. No genie leaping out of a lamp could have materialized at a better time.

The lieutenant, who told us to call him Ihab, was an instructor at a remote camp near the Egyptian border, about 50 miles east, where he taught guerrilla warfare, counterinsurgency tactics, demolition, traps, and sabotage to a company of commandos. He'd been to Benghazi on leave to visit his wife and was returning to his camp when he saw us.

I asked if he had any food. He thought for a moment, then pointed south. "We will get food from the nomads. They are passing through here on their way to summer pasture in the hills. I visited their encampment a few days ago."

"But aren't the nomads dangerous?" Woodrow asked. "Don't they beat up strangers and rob them?"

"Only the nomads with the five-sided tents. Even I stay away from them. But these are different. There will be no trouble if I am with you."

"You mean they're afraid of the army?" I asked.

"Not at all. We have no control over them. When we got our independence, the king promised the nomads they could come and go as they pleased, and we let them keep all their guns. They have no passports. They cross the borders as they wish. Our country is trying to persuade them to settle down and become farmers, but it will take years. It is difficult to build a nation when half its people are never in the same place from one month to the next. But they are too proud to be told what to do. It was their great-great-ancestors who destroyed the towns along the coast after the Romans left, and it was their sheep and camels, a thousand years ago, that pastured on the farms and ate all the grasses and pulled down the forests and caused this desert.

"Our legends tell us that once a man could walk all the way from Tripoli to Tangier in the shade of trees and gardens. But these nomads destroyed them all. They want to stay with their old ways. Every year more of them die. When there is no rain and no grass, you see everywhere the bones of their baby sheep and goats. The herds get smaller every year. Many of the families have only enough left to keep alive."

"Then how will they be able to help us?" Manu asked.

"The Bedouins here do well. They are near Cyrene and the hills, where there is always some rain and grass. Their goats and sheep survive."

"Then why don't more Bedouins come here?"

"It is forbidden. It would be war. Each tribe grazes where it has grazed for a thousand years. Each tribe has a boundary. If they find another tribe on their grazing land, they kill them."

"That doesn't sound like a very charitable attitude," Woodrow remarked.

"The Bedouins are not known for their charity."

"Then what makes you think they'll give us food?" Steve asked.

"You will give them a present, of course. Some clothing is always good, or jewelry. Also bring your rifles: We must show the nomads you are armed so they won't come back and rob you when you sleep."

"The only extra clothes we have are shoes, and we don't have rifles, just bows and arrows," I explained.

"That will do. The nomads wear shoes. And they will respect you as warriors if you bring bows and arrows, for their fathers used them before the British gave them guns in the war."

Steve and I left the others to guard the trailer. We drove four miles due south into the desert before Ihab stopped us: "We will walk the rest of the way," he said, "so that we don't disturb their animals."

I saw black tents outlined against the blackness of the desert night. What seemed like open space between the tents was crisscrossed with guy ropes, and by the time we'd stumbled our way through them, the whole camp was aware of our presence. Sheep and goats shied away, chickens and children scurried in front of us, and tethered camels snorted beside the large hide tents. The night air was fragrant with the scent of tea and baking bread.

Ihab led the way to the sharif's tent, at whose threshold we laid our bows to show we came in peace, and bowed to the smiling old man who bade us enter. We left our shoes outside, except for the pair we brought to barter. After a round of Arabic courtesies and formalities, the lieutenant explained the purpose of our visit, pointing to our gift. The sharif pointed to our bows on the threshold, whereupon they went into a long palaver before seeming to reach an agreement.

I inspected the surprisingly comfortable tent. It was about 40 feet in diameter and 15 feet high, with an earthen floor covered by thick carpets atop straw mats. The peak, which had wide holes at the seams, where air and light could enter, wasn't rainproof, but in a land where it sometimes doesn't rain for a year, that was not a major concern. As we'd entered, someone had drawn a curtain across the rear sections of the tent, which were the women's quarters and the kitchen. When strangers arrive, the women are hidden so as not to see or be seen.

The most remarkable aspect of the tent was its treasures: Stacked against half the length of the wall to a height of three feet were dozens of neatly folded carpets, each exquisitely woven, each worth a fortune. The chief proudly spread them before us. I saw something protruding from one of the rugs that looked like a rifle butt. The chief caught my gaze and pulled out an ancient

Italian rifle wrapped in rags. He pointed up to the center post, which was crisscrossed with cords from which hung other rifles. I detected the front sight of a rifle peeking out from under the chief's cushion. Four or five chests stood beside the stacked rugs, each a sturdy trunk studded with decorative nail heads. I could only imagine what was in them.

The sharif opened a smaller chest to pull out a box, inside of which I glimpsed a sparkle and shine and heard the clinking of coins. From the box he withdrew four small glasses with ornate rims. One of his wives entered from behind the curtain, bringing an old British army canteen filled with steaming water. She only partly hid her face from us, too curious to hide completely. She was close to 16, dressed in a scarlet skirt and white blouse, with gold bracelets on her slim wrists and ankles. She was full of life and energy, and I found her very attractive except for some bluish tattoo marks on her chin and between her eyes. It was hard to hide my admiration from her husband— and my envy of him. I found something overwhelmingly compelling about this old man and his nomadic life. This was the other side of that existential coin, a life with no bonds and no borders, no bosses and no time clocks, no meetings and no conference calls. It was moving with the sun, blowing with the wind, making passionate love in a great airy tent on a cooling desert beneath a canopy of brilliant stars.

The chief performed an elaborate ritual of pouring the tea back and forth from several feet above the glass, with obvious love for his labors. When he finally considered the brew suitable for serving, it was as sweet as honey, thick as liqueur, and hot as fire. He drank his without cooling it, and Ihab bid us to do the same. It scorched the lips, melted the teeth, and warmed the soul. The chief pressed another glass on us, then another. Refusal was not an option.

When the tea was finished, the chief clapped his hands. Two of his other wives came from behind the curtain, laden with food, which they placed at our feet: a big porcelain pitcher of thick goat's milk, a pile of flat brown bread, and a metal bowl holding several dozen small eggs.

"That's a good haul for a pair of shoes," I told the lieutenant when we were clear of the camp. "You're a great bargainer."

After a minute of silence, Ihab confessed: "I'm afraid I had to promise him more than the shoes . . ."

"What?"

The nomads, he explained, wanted us to help them hunt a gazelle. They didn't like to kill their sheep or goats at that time of the year, but they wanted meat. They couldn't hunt the gazelles on foot: The game had grown wary and wouldn't let them get that close. Nor could they hunt from camels, because the gazelles were too fast. So the chief had told Ihab they wanted to hunt from our 4×4.

The lieutenant added: "You can't refuse, or the nomads will be angry. I have already told them you were both great hunters in America. The chief expects you back as soon as you give the food to your men. But don't worry; I'll go with you. I would let them use my Land Rover, but the top doesn't come off, and the chief wants to be able to shoot from the car. Besides, the army already warned me . . . uh . . . here, have some milk."

We went back to the road with food for Manu, Willy, and Woodrow; un-snapped the canvas top from the Land Cruiser; removed the supplies; and left the others to guard the gear and the trailers. When we returned to the en-campment, the nomads happily jumped up and down. In a twinkling, nine of them jammed into the car's now-open rear compartment, all standing upright, all chortling and joking and spitting. They smelled as if they'd had raw garlic for dinner and their last bath a year ago. They were all ready for action, their guns bristling in every direction. Our vehicle resembled a red porcupine.

They had a specimen of almost every firearm made in the century, and the chief toted a shiny new Magnum Express that could easily dispatch an ele-phant. One elderly nomad, whose long beard and red tunic reminded me of Grumpy, the Disney dwarf, came running up with an ancient blunderbuss that looked as if it had been last fired during the war —of 1812. Finding no room in back, he scooted over me and wedged himself behind the front seat, his powder horn swinging against my neck as we headed farther into the desert.

Steve drove, I scouted from the passenger side, and Ihab sat between us, pointing the way through a haze of cigar smoke.

When I complained to him that I didn't think it was ethical to shoot an animal from a moving car, all I got for my moral concerns was a lecture about the imperative of survival and the laws of the desert, that the wildlife belonged to the nomads, and that Americans couldn't possibly understand because they were all fat and well-fed.

I was about to reply that our nomad pals had far from empty bellies, and probably enough treasure stashed away to buy a controlling interest in IBM, when Ihab turned out the headlights. They could be seen for 15 to 20 miles in the clear desert air, he explained, and would spook any game around. He might as well have blindfolded us; the thin slice of fading moon gave so little light that Steve had to drive more by touch than by sight, and seemed to be touching every ditch, rock, mound, bump, and hole west of Egypt. He slowed to 15 miles an hour, but the results were still devastating. He was cinched in tight with his safety belt, but seemed to be steering with his stomach and shifting with his knees, while Grumpy was swaying back and forth over my head, spilling gunpowder down my back. The car groaned as if breaking apart, and I wondered if this were a technique the lieutenant taught in his demolition course.

After a shaken-up eternity, we spotted distant gazelles silhouetted against the night sky. Steve reluctantly increased speed toward them, our lights still out, wishing he'd installed radar on our bumper instead of a winch. When the nomads opened fire, it was as if a small volcano had erupted. Then Grumpy discharged his blunderbuss, sending smoke and fumes and pellets all over the place. It was Vesuvius.

The nomads urged us onward, but with the bouncing of the car in the dark, I don't know how they hoped to hit anything edible. Half their shots went winging off in the direction of Uranus, and some peppered the dirt in front of us. I couldn't see a thing through smoke and smell, but was certain the gazelles were a lot safer than I.

Later, as we drove back toward our trailer, I asked Ihab if the sharif was badly disappointed about not bagging a gazelle.

"I don't think so," he smiled. "He's always wanted a ride in an automobile. And—oh, yes—he asked if you might have another pair of shoes. A little smaller."

All the next day we toiled in the scorching sun, nailing and boarding the camper floor back together, pounding the buckled aluminum sides into place, straightening the struts underneath. The following morning Steve drove the axle and one of our spare spindles to a welding shop in Tobruk. It was late afternoon before the work was finished and we were ready to roll. We'd lost two full days, and the undercarriage still had three bad cracks that we'd have to weld in Cairo, but at least we were getting back on the road.

Just as we were leaving, Grumpy came trotting over to our camp on a camel. The chief had sent him: Did we happen to have any shoe polish? Brown?

# CHAPTER 4

## Weighed Down in Egypt's Land

As we neared the Egyptian border town of Sollum, the sun was directly behind us and setting, a large crimson wafer quickly consumed by the immense appetite of the Sahara. We figured our timing was perfect, as dusk was usually the best time to reach a border post. If we arrived any later, the border might be closed for the night; if we arrived much earlier, the guards had time to waste, and they'd often waste ours in the process; if we arrived at dusk, when the guards were eager to finish duty, they usually wouldn't bother with a thorough search of our equipment. A thorough search was the last thing we wanted since our prohibited items included an illegal revolver, hundreds of undeclared dollars, and a half case of bourbon. I was particularly worried because Egypt required visitors to prove that they were *not* Jewish, and I could not do that.

We crested a bald, round mountain, and Egypt spread out before us, four distinct strips dwindling into the dimming twilight. To the distant left, and stretching over the horizon, the darkened Mediterranean broke black and white on the beach; to its right, the coastal strip, perhaps a mile wide, containing the beach, the border town of Sollum, and the thin trail of asphalt stretching east toward Alexandria; farther right, the escarpment of rugged, barren hills, a geological arrow aiming east-southeast; last, and barely visible, was inland Egypt, mile after mile of rock-studded sand, devoid of life and hope.

We coasted down the winding road to the base of the mountain, where a guard waved us off the road and toward the passport office. The big room was dim and filled with thick cigar smoke. It was furnished with splintered wooden desks, cracked leather armchairs, two pictures of President Gamal Abdel Nasser, two pictures of the Aswan Dam construction, and four army officers. (In most developed nations, passport control is handled by a specialized civilian department; in Egypt, as in most Arab countries, the military controlled the frontiers.) The officers were in their undershirts, their fat arms and faces sweating in the airless room. They were suspicious and arrogant. And in no hurry to get home.

After they'd learned that three of us were Americans, they ignored us for an hour and smoked their Cuban cigars. Then the interrogation commenced: Where had we been? Why had we come to the United Arab Republic? (This was, at the time, the formal name for the nominal union of Syria and Egypt.) Where would we be staying each night? How much money did we have with us? Were we planning to take pictures of the Palestinian refugees? What kind of work did we do? Where were our parents born? Were we connected with the American government in any way? Why did we have a big trailer with us? (Why indeed?) Had we ever visited Egypt before? Had we ever been to Israel? Were we planning to go there?

I became annoyed, but knew the officers were just waiting for one of us to lose his temper. When we'd gotten our visas weeks before, we'd filled out all the forms and answered all the relevant questions. Our passports were in perfect order, but the officers were determined to continue their game.

"You, what work do you do?" they asked me.

"I'm an art director for advertisements," I answered, using the cover story we'd contrived for those countries that barred foreign journalists, to credibly explain why we had so much film and such professional cameras.

Then they asked our religions. We each replied with a different Christian denomination, all true except for mine. I'd rehearsed this many times, even learned some Protestant prayers and religious theory, but my lip nevertheless trembled as I answered, and sweat bathed my forehead. The officer looked at me closely. Across North Africa, my prominent nose, dark eyes, and olive skin were oft mistaken for Arabic, whereupon I usually nodded modestly, congratulated the interlocutor on his perceptiveness, and pretended that my dear old dad had been born in such-and-such Arab country, usually picking one that was on a friendly footing with the one we were in. But it wasn't going to be so easy this time.

Egypt drew no distinction between Israelis and Jews, and we'd been warned that it required visitors to carry letters from their home churches attesting that they were members in good standing. I'd assumed I'd easily obtain such a letter from some priest or minister who wanted to strike a mild blow against religious discrimination, but they had all refused.

When the soldier asked me if I possessed such a letter, Steve, to distract him, started edging toward the door, purposely acting suspiciously.

"You!" the soldier shouted at Steve. "Come here. Show me your letter."

Steve showed it to him.

"Where are you going?" he asked Steve.

"First to Alexandria, then to Cairo, and across into Jordan," he answered.

"Jordan? How to Jordan?"

Steve told him we planned to drive from Cairo across the Suez Canal, then through the Sinai Peninsula.

"It is forbidden to go into the Sinai. No one is allowed. It is a war zone. Do not forget that we are at war with your ally Israel. Next year! You come again next year and then you can drive to Jordan. Next year there will be no more Israel."

Finally, and begrudgingly, the officer stamped our passports, and we were free to move on—20 yards to the Customs Office.

We'd been warned that Egyptian Customs was tough, but we were not prepared for what awaited us. In a blazingly bright room, four clerks behind a wide counter were assiduously searching the luggage and persons of a dozen Arab travelers and workers. They dumped the contents of trunks and suitcases on the floor, untied knots, opened boxes, poked through tins of tea and cookies, pulled off nailed covers, probed for false bottoms, checked all labels, searched through pockets and trouser legs and shoes.

In a small room to the right, a teller was exchanging foreign currencies for Egyptian pounds at the highly inflated official rate. Although ten American dollars fetched eight or nine Egyptian pounds on the free market in New York and Beirut, and close to that on the black market inside Egypt, the government was offering only four and a half pounds, and imposing severe penalties, including imprisonment, on anyone caught entering or leaving with more money than they'd declared. We'd planned to double our Egyptian money by exchanging our concealed dollars on the black market, but we also risked more than doubling our stay in Egypt—behind bars.

In front of the customs house, in the driveway where we'd parked our vehicles and trailers, two officers with flashlights were searching through the car ahead of us. They checked the undersides, looked beneath the floor mats, felt behind the seats, emptied the trunk, probed in the gas tank with a rod, and searched under the hood. In a state where foreign goods were scarce and the currency weak, smuggling was immensely profitable.

For 20 minutes we waited our turn. Almost everyone ahead of us had trouble: Half of them had goods confiscated and half had to pay import duties. These were all for minor offenses, like bringing in a can of fruit packed in Morocco or having a new blanket not made in Egypt. What would happen to us if their search uncovered our gun, our bourbon, and our undeclared greenbacks? It was a hot night, and we sweated profusely.

Fortunately for us, it had been a busy night at the customs post. It was late, we were last in line, and the tired guard did not search us thoroughly. I assumed he was just reluctant to go plowing through two loaded cars and trailers, but his conversation convinced me that he presumed Americans were so rich they'd never smuggle anything. He handed us a set of temporary Egyptian plates and closed the office.

Steve resolved to find a better hiding place for our pistol, quickly change our undeclared dollars, and take a hit for the team by drinking all our bourbon. I shook a bit and breathed deeply; you need a certain kind of nerveless constitution to be a smuggler, and I didn't have it.

Morning dawned clear, bright, and dry, and the sun came up warm against a blue-white and cloudless sky. The Mediterranean winked at us with friendly blue wavelets. Steve and I plunged in, and even Manu shrugged off his morning torpor and followed. The warm, foaming sea embraced us, washing off the dirt and sweat of days, soothing us, carrying us from the land, taking us into another world. From the roof of the cloudless ceiling of sky to the clear depths of the sea bottom, it was a world of beauty and contentment. We were at one and at peace with nature, three bobbing specks in the friendly caress of an eternal sea.

Before moving on, we visited the British WW II cemetery just past Sollum, a large, flat, sandy rectangle filled with several thousand simple headstones, shaded here and there by a tree or a flowering bush, the result of diligent care. Beyond the walls were no trees or flowers, just the dead sands. The gravekeeper clarified that the Anglo-Egyptian War Monuments Commission maintained the cemetery, one of a dozen that dotted the North African desert from Tripoli to Tobruk to the grand entombment at El Alamein. They held the remains of 35,000 Commonwealth soldiers who had died fighting to tie the tail of the Desert Fox when Field Marshal Erwin Rommel had been sweeping across Africa toward Suez, attempting to link up with the Japanese somewhere in India and conquer the world. The turning of the tide would come at El Alamein; the stemming of the tide had been here, at Sollum.

We walked among the neat rows of identical gravestones, all shining white and pure in the afternoon sun. Interred here were drivers and troopers, flight engineers and artillerymen, privates and sergeants, Canadians and South Africans, all brought from distant lands to perish on this uncaring killing ground. We read the inscriptions.

*Tell England, Ye who pass this way, I died for her and rest here content.*

*We will always remember you when the rest of the world forgets*
——MUM AND SISTER

*If love could have saved, you would never have died.*

The desert wind blew mournfully down the hedge of barren hills and across the graves as it swept to meet the sea. The eternal Mediterranean played a funeral sonata on the keyboard of the shore. The sun sank lower over the wasteland. *Every soil is a brave man's country.*

Our heads bowed, our eyes filled with tears, we walked in silence toward the gate. I looked at the last tombstones and thought of those who cherished these men but would never see their distant resting place. *In alien earth he lies, not for him the last, long slumber under friendly skies.*

We left the cemetery and stood gazing with misty eyes at the barren hills, the encroaching sands, the fruitless earth. The sun was on the far side of the mountain now, well along on its nightly journey into the Sahara. The wind picked up the somber lament of Taps as we headed east toward Alexandria. *He gave the greatest gift of all, his own unfinished life.*

By the next morning, the road had turned into a jagged torture track of loose white rocks against the whiteness of the desert. At one particularly treacherous spot, a crew of some 60 *fellaheen* wearing white robes and turbans, their faces covered with dust, appeared like apparitions—bent to their labors, kneeling on the harsh, hot roadbed. They struggled without aid of tractor, grader, or drill, attacking the reluctant rock with hand and muscle and primitive tools, chopping it with chisels, hitting it with hammers, carting boulders away on their backs, straining and sweating in the heat, descendants of the pyramid builders, still slaving after four thousand years.

Nine miles east of El Alamein the road swung close to the sea. We stopped and plunged into the beckoning pale water, washing off the hot dust of the deserts of Egypt and the cold dust of the cemeteries of the world. Then it was on to Alexandria, the Pearl of the Mediterranean.

There is no other city in the world like Alex, and the world can be thankful for that. It's a Coney Island full of fun-loving crooks, a carnival of affable criminals, a rowdy reunion of ex-cons. No metaphor can totally capture the carefree carnality and casual criminal spirit of the city, but here is what happened when we met the picaresque denizens of Alex and learned, the hard way, that the Pearl was only paste.

As we drove in through its outskirts, Alex was smoky and congested, with steel mills and cement plants in the midst of residential sections. Collapsing tenements stood beside caves dug into the hills, and people lived in both. It was a mess of overhead wires, trolley tracks, pushcart vendors, drying wash, muddy streets, belching smokestacks, blowing sand, littered alleys, unrelenting noise, and thousands of street urchins.

The kids swooped upon us as soon as we reached the edge of town. In seconds they jumped on the flat top of the camper, climbed onto the canvas roofs of the cars, hopped on the running boards, crawled across the hoods, and tried to wriggle their skinny arms into any opening, begging for *baksheesh*, or taking what they could. As soon as we chased them off, they came charging back, heaving pieces of sheep dung, shouting and laughing when we flinched.

As we neared the center of Alex, our assailants were older, their weapons were verbal, and their interests went beyond bouncing up and down on the camper.

"Pssst, you want nice girl? Virgin girl?" asked one strabismic pimp as he trotted alongside the Cruiser.

"Pssst, you want bad girl? Experienced girl?" asked his twin, who was trotting along the other side of the car. I drove faster, but not before a man wearing a *galabeya* leaped onto the running board and breathed a blast of garlic in my face: "You want change money? Good rate: Five pounds for ten dollar. Best price in Alex. How much you change?"

When I slowed down to push off the money changer, two of his competitors leaped onto the running board and clung to the door as I shifted into second, screaming their prices into my ear, trying to outbid one another, but offering no bargains. Meanwhile two rogues elbowed each other for possession of the other running board, one of them offering to sell us whatever we might want, and the other offering to buy whatever we might want to sell. Willy introduced them to each other and shoved them off.

When we stopped at a corner for cross traffic, a score of shouting Alexandrians besieged us, waving bottles of whiskey, photos of naked women, cigarette cartons, nylon stockings, Egyptian money, packets of hashish, all screaming their prices. Everybody knew that five foreigners had just arrived in two red 4×4s pulling two loaded trailers, and everybody was eager to sink his teeth into us before we learned what Alex was all about.

We decided to disassociate ourselves from the cars and trailers, at least until dark, when they'd be less conspicuous and we could look for a campsite without half the town at our heels and the other half in our pockets. We parked along the 26th of July Avenue, the most splendid thoroughfare in Alex, a wide boulevard that curved in a sweeping crescent from the sea. We walked over to an attractive outdoor restaurant where we hoped we could a) get a good dinner, b) shake off the entourage of pimps and peddlers, c) keep an eye on the cars so that nothing was stolen, and d) enjoy the sunset over the Mediterranean. We were partly successful: We saw the sunset.

The hawkers did not give up easily, and when our waiter chased them away, new ones took their places. We eventually succumbed to their entreaties, as they'd known we would. Willy bought a dozen colored handkerchiefs for the bargain price of 30 cents, and his nose turned green from the first one he used. Woodrow bought a wristwatch for four dollars after carefully checking what turned out to be the demonstration model, which the peddler then palmed, so all Woodrow got was the face and the back of a watch encasing a lump of dirt. Manu bought a bathing suit from a man lugging four suitcases of clothing. It was a size 36, as promised, but with a strangling size-24 jock inside. Steve bought a pack of Chesterfields at a high price, but still a bargain considering what American cigarettes usually cost abroad. He lit one and choked as the peddler disappeared while another one clarified that they were "Egyptian Chesterfields."

All this was going on while we were trying to eat. The peddlers were all around our table with their bags and boxes of merchandise, waving silk underpants in our faces and dangling brass bracelets in our soup, which, I admit, improved its taste, for the food was wretched beyond belief, and that's damn faint praise coming from someone who'd had only one full meal in the preceding five days. The soup was indigestible, the salad unchewable, the bread unbreakable, the meat uncuttable—and the bill unbelievable. We were charged 50 percent above the already high prices on the menu because, the waiter explained, it was an indoor menu and we had eaten outdoors. We were also charged extra for the bread, extra for the butter, and extra for the sugar and salt. Extra for the tablecloth. And extra for a couple of flowers one of the peddlers had filched from the vase on our table. To this were added fees and taxes, which, the manager told us with a straight face, were for such essentials as the waiter's old-age pension, repainting the kitchen, improving Egypt's balance of payments, and widening the Suez Canal.

We now fully grasped how pervasive the con game was in Alex. But it could have been worse: At least the restaurant had been a convenient spot for watching our cars.

As we crossed toward them, we noticed that the Jeep was *leaning* at us. We ran around to its far side and discovered five kids at work. Three of them had the passenger side jacked up and were removing its tires, a fourth was siphoning gas out of the tank, and a fifth was trying to jimmy the latch on the camper door. They were so brazen they didn't even try to escape, barely batting an eye when we grabbed them. The leader, a tough of 15, claimed they worked for a garage and assumed we were the car that had called for assistance. When I asked him how that justified siphoning off our gas, he replied that it was dangerous to work on a car with gas in the tank. We found a policeman, but the gang leader and the cop were old friends, and in the end we felt fortunate that we weren't compelled to pay for the "work" the kids had done.

We were just getting the tires back on when a leering man sidled up to Steve with a collection of pornographic pictures. When Steve turned these down, the man pulled a dozen vials of "aphrodisiac" out of his pocket, purportedly Spanish fly, absinthe, sperm-whale lotion, pulverized shark fin, and pepper extract. Steve told him he didn't need any.

"Okay. No need aphro. Muneer understand. You stud man. Then must need this." He winked and withdrew from his other pocket an assortment of condoms in various sizes, colors, and enhancements. Steve pushed him away and told him to try me.

Just then Willy came back, clutching a pile of Egyptian pounds he'd gotten from a money changer who was offering a decent rate, seven pounds for ten dollars, 35 percent better than the government rate. Willy pointed out a fat guy in an oversized overcoat standing next to a tree a few yards away. The man smiled a gleam of gold teeth. He spread his arms and opened his coat to show us packets of money held in place with safety pins: Egyptian pounds,

U.S. dollars, Swiss francs, French francs, British pounds, lire, pesetas, marks, dirham. . . .

Woodrow rushed over to him, waving a ten-dollar bill.

"What did you get?" Willy asked when he'd returned.

"Seven pounds. I gave him a ten and he gave me—hey, there's only six pounds here! Hey, mister, you only gave me six pounds."

"Yes, certainly," the money changer shouted. "Stamps. It's for stamps. One pound for black-market stamps."

"Oh. I didn't know about those. Black-market stamps. Well, uh, I mean, uh. . . ."

By then the money changer had vanished.

"You know, guys," I said, "this can be a great place if you've got the right attitude. What a wild bunch of likable crooks. It's my kind of town. I have to come back here someday."

Two men approached and wanted to know if we had any jewelry or foreign perfume to sell.

I sold them five bottles of our sponsor's OFF! insect repellent and unloaded that "watch" Woodrow had purchased.

Manu returned with a bottle of whiskey, shouting that he'd gotten a good price on Cutty Sark.

"Cutty Sark, my butt. That's colored water," I told him after I examined it.

"How can it be colored water? The seal's intact."

"Sure, and so is the press where they printed it."

I took the bottle from him, slipped it into our case of bourbon in the Cruiser, and waited. Within ten minutes a peddler came along hawking "Chevas Regale" [sic] for one Egyptian pound.

"Come off it, man," I told him. "You can't sell us any of that colored-water junk. We only drink the real stuff. See, we have a full case of real whiskey we just smuggled in today."

"*Real* whiskey?" he exclaimed.

"Sure thing, man. Here, have a sip." I poured him a straight shot of Wild Turkey.

The peddler drank, sighed, and smiled. "You want to sell some?"

"Sure, I'll let you have this bottle for eight pounds."

"No, too much."

"Okay, you can have a sealed bottle of Cutty Sark for only three pounds."

As we drove away, I chuckled that Alex was definitely one of a kind, and the kind of which one was enough.

We weren't quite sure where to go. Our plan was to camp outside of town, away from the crooks, and to come back the next morning to visit Pompey's Pillar, the Little Sphinx, and the Catacombs of Kam el Shuqafa. But it wasn't easy to find a place outside of town because we'd entered the delta of the Nile. Gone was the empty desert where we could open our camper and pitch our tents anywhere. Every bit of land here was either under cultivation or under water. It was here that the Nile, as it neared the sea, spread out into a triangle a hundred miles on a side, a lush green wetness that provided food and clothing and work and hope for most of Egypt's 30 million people. Only 50,000 hardy (or harebrained) souls attempted to live in the other, inhospitable, 97 percent of the country; the rest depended on the Nile, around which there was no space left for a campground.

After blundering down mud lanes and floundering through streams in the dark, we reluctantly settled for sleeping on the wide shoulder of a dirt road beside a stand of date palms abutting a cotton field. The mosquitoes, the first we'd encountered in Africa, were fierce and noisy, and the air smelled of manure, but at least Alex's crooks and con men were unlikely to find us.

The police found us instead. Just as we had the camper set up and were about to turn in, three policemen popped out of the field and indicated they wanted us to move. They spoke no English, but kept pointing around and saying *"klefti"* and drew their fingers across their throats accompanied by a *sscccchhhttt* sound, giving us to understand that cutthroats abounded who would slit us as we slept. At that point, we'd have been willing to believe anything anyone told us about Alex, so we broke camp and let a cop climb into each car to show us to a safer spot. For half an hour, we drove along roads a few inches above the waterline, crept over creaky bridges, and skidded down muddy lanes until we reached a spot not much different or far removed from the one we'd left.

We thanked the boys in blue for their help, and for being the first honest people we'd met in Alex. They were like friends in an enemy camp, and we missed them when they left.

We also missed a flashlight, a light meter, a wrench, half a seat belt, and the dashboard ashtray.

Early the next morning, one of the policemen was back, banging on the camper door. He gestured that he wanted us to give him a toothbrush, something he'd evidently forgotten to swipe the night before. We were so flabbergasted we gave him one.

We left Alex and cut through the delta toward Cairo on a new, paved expressway. The traffic was fast and heavy. The desert was gone, drowned by the river. Irrigated fields, stands of trees, mosques, homes, factories, and restaurants lined the road. It was a wholly different Egypt, mechanized and modern.

Cairo went by in a rush, a jumble of impressions, eight days of work and sightseeing and confusion. I remember isolated things: three days spent getting visas for Syria, Iraq, Lebanon, India, and Pakistan; crowded streets; repeatedly getting lost on the wrong side of the river; mosques and monuments; the Cairo Museum, where the world's most vital collection of archaeological objects was stuck in a dark tomb of a building, stacked like flour sacks in a warehouse; Woodrow sick with dysentery, and Willy and Manu with mild cases of Cairo colon; the Continental Hotel, a relic of Old World elegance, with cavernous, thick-carpeted halls and spacious rooms, where we slept between sheets for the first time since Benghazi, only the second time in 77 days.

I remember our toiling all week to get the cars and equipment in shape for the long, hot haul across the deserts of the Middle East; answering several dozen letters from friends and sponsors who, not hearing from us since Spain, had given us up for lazy or lost; and the meals at Rex, a wonderful bistro near the hotel where you could get a delicious bowl of spaghetti with salad and bread for ten cents. But most of all, when I think back to our days in Cairo, I remember the stunning women, the totalitarian atmosphere, and one very special camel driver.

Cairo was a paradise of women, bronzed, graceful, alluring—and unattainable. They were the sultriest in the Moslem world, having shed the veil and adopted such Western fashions as short skirts, high heels, and low neck-lines. On our first day I developed a stiff neck from watching them walk by. As good Moslem women, they did not fraternize with foreigners, not even a foreigner like me who can pass for an Arab when he tries. And believe me, I was trying.

But I thought I might overcome this problem and hit the jackpot with Ifti-tani, our beautiful chambermaid at the Continental. She was everything plus: bewitching and desirable, with flashing blue eyes, shiny black hair that fell to her shoulders, flawless olive skin, and a body that would make even the Sphinx cry out in envy. We were all captivated by her, but Iftitani didn't speak a word of English. Yet I was so sure that she was attracted to me that, when she came to straighten my room on our third day in the hotel, I invited her to dinner. Using pantomime, I pointed to her, then to myself, and then to my mouth as if I were eating. So what did Iftitani do? She called room service for me.

I decided to try a direct approach. After she had dusted my room, I pointed to myself, then to my bed, lifted up the thin blanket, smoothed the sheet, then pointed to Iftitani, then back to the bed. On my third attempt, she understood. And nodded her approval! I'd been worried that she might be angry with my bold approach, but she smiled.

Then she turned to leave the room. I rushed after her and pointed to the bed. Iftitani nodded reassuringly and pointed to my watch, then walked over to the wall calendar and pointed—and thus, without a spoken word, we lovers agreed to consummate our relationship at two o'clock the next afternoon.

I was deliriously happy the entire day, but the rest of my expedition were unsportingly, albeit secretly, jealous and rather depressed by my good fortune. The next forenoon, they all left early for lunch at Rex, not out of any sense of discretion, but from an inability to bear to see this romance unfold.

At two o'clock Iftitani, wearing her tight blue uniform, entered my room and closed the door behind her. I could barely contain myself. She went right to the bed and pulled back the blanket. She wasn't wasting any time, and I was fine with that, so I started hurriedly pulling off my clothing.

Which is when Iftitani screamed and ran out.

I was utterly puzzled and totally frustrated because I'd been sure she liked and desired me. When the others returned they commiserated with me, but hypocritically, wallowing happily in schadenfreude.

Later that afternoon, the irate hotel manager came up to complain about my behavior. It seems that our innocent Iftitani had thought I'd just wanted my sheets changed.

From our misunderstanding, I learned valuable lessons that helped me through years of foreign travel: If you speak a different language than the other, make sure—unmistakably sure—you and the other person are in agreement. Be sensitive when you're in a position of power, as a hotel guest is with an employee. Never assume that a member of a foreign culture will readily undertake an act that is proscribed in her society. And avoid presuming that just because a person is poor or working class, they'll do anything you want for money—even if you're the head of the IMF.

It was hard to move around Cairo without encountering the indicia of a police state: army camps, ordnance depots, and communications installations ringed the city. All bridges and many factories displayed signs banning photography. When we picked up our mail at the American Express office, most of it had been opened by the government censors, and we later learned that the letters we'd sent home had also been opened and then resealed with the censor's stamp. When we'd checked in at the Continental, our passports had been confiscated and held for several days while the secret police checked us out. When our film came back from the processing lab, the photos showing the poverty of Egypt had mysteriously vanished. When we made large purchases, the merchants demanded proof that we'd acquired our Egyptian pounds at the official rate, and signs warning of penalties for changing money on the black market were omnipresent. The newspapers and radio carried the official government line, and we saw no evidence of freedom of the press or speech. When the Algerians overthrew Ben Bella, Nasser's main ally, a shock ran through Egypt's hierarchy, which deployed troops discreetly—but not *too* discreetly—around Cairo to discourage the spread of anti-regime revolutions. (Those revolutions occurred anyway—but not until the Arab Spring, 46 long, harsh years later.)

But you can't dislike Egypt when it has people like Lamyi—Lamyi Ibrahim Ghoneim—the world's greatest, most charming, most charismatic, most cinematic camel driver, as he himself would confirm.

Steve and I drove to the pyramids late one afternoon to scout locations for sponsor photos we'd committed to take. As we looked around, a chubby, grinning, sixtyish Arab in a bright-green *galabeya* bounded by on a camel, shouting at us, "Howdy, kids. Dig me, baby. It's colossal. Twenty-three skidoo and away we go. Wowie!" He thrice circled us, then trotted back exclaiming, "Wasn't that the most, man? Isn't this camel the living end? Dandy, just dandy. May I present myself? I'm Lamyi, and this is Canada Dry." He pronounced it like the soda pop and handed Steve a multiply misspelled business card:

> CANDA DRAY
> camel for hire
> Poprietor: Pyramids Post, Giza
> LAMYI IBRAHIM GHONEIM Giza, Egypt.

We were still wary after being misled by the touts in Alex, but Lamyi won us over as he enumerated his credentials in what he thought was the latest hip Hollywood lingo. "I've been making the tourist scene here for forty years. My daddy-o taught me the trade. No other cat in the sport savvies it the way I do, kid. Whenever any bigwig pays a visit, the govmen't has me show him around on Canada Dry. He's the most, gentle as a lamb, comfy as a couch. Go ahead, you want to sit on him? Why, the last king and queen of Sweden said Canada Dry was super colossal. See, here's a snap of the queen on him. He's getting old, but he's the best in the business, kiddo. Prime Minister Churchill rode him. All the European princesses and counts who come out here ask for him. Even your President Roosevelt said he was the smartest-looking camel out here. And you know those tourist posters, the ones with the pyramids and the camel? Well, baby, that's us. Everybody takes our picture. I'm very photogenic. Even Cecil B. DeMille said so; I was his favorite of all the camel drivers. Oh, certainly I know CB, and all those other producers, too. I made a lot of pictures with old CB, *Ten Command-*

*ments* and dandy stuff like that. I've been in 30 movies, kid, 30. Now how can I oblige you?"

Lamyi obliged by meeting us the next morning, with his brother, two camels, three dogs, and a basketful of props and costumes to shoot photos for our sponsors. He arranged the scene, checked the sun's angle, adjusted clothing, posed himself for each picture, and, drawing on his extensive film career, instructed Willy and me how to take the photos. He was producer, director, press agent, and star all in one.

And he was magnificent. He gleefully smeared himself with Sea & Ski suntan oil, exchanged his turban for a Dobbs straw cowboy hat, modeled an Arrow shirt, poured a quart of sponsor's oil into our Toyota, and poured into himself a cup of the Bourbon Institute's best, which, he assured me, with a wink, doubtless had medicinal value and hence didn't conflict with his Islamic beliefs. He modeled a pair of Thom McAn desert boots, sprayed Canada Dry with OFF! insect repellent, lit a cigarette with our parabolic

In the desert beside the great pyramids in Giza, Egypt, I fulfilled two sponsor assignments by sharing a box of Manischewitz matzos and a bottle of bourbon with three Arab camel drivers, including Lamyi Ibrahim Ghoneim (right). *Willy Mettler*

sunray lighter, posed on the threshold of our Thermos Poptent, and smilingly chomped his way through half a box of Manischewitz matzos.

After the photo session—which Lamyi said was "such a dandy delight" he wouldn't accept our payment—he brought us to his home for tea and cake. The walls were covered with photos of famous people atop Canada Dry and travel posters on which Lamyi's smiling face gleamed against the backdrop of the pyramids. He proudly showed us letters from his clients (while we used the opportunity to discreetly slip his fee behind the cushions on his couch) and read favorite passages from them, discussed his life and the future of his disabled son, expressed his heartfelt hope for peace on earth among men of good will, and beseeched us to write him.

Tears filled his eyes, and ours, when we parted. We'll always remember you, Lamyi Ibrahim Ghoneim. I hope your son thrived, your tribe increased, your days were long and happy, you ascended serenely to Paradise, and may Allah forever hold you gently in the hollow of his hand.

It was time to get back on the road. The vehicles had been serviced, the letters answered, the sponsor pix shot and shipped, the supplies laid in, the crew rested and healed. Ahead lay the Middle Eastern deserts, now blistering in the heat of summer. It was good-bye to Lamyi and to the glorious women of Cairo, good-bye to the sparkling Mediterranean and the colorful con men of Alex, good-bye to spaghetti at Rex, to the cool hotel rooms, to innocent Iftitani, good-bye to North Africa.

We headed eastward from Cairo, planning to skirt the Arabian Desert on the north, bridge the Suez Canal, and then cut across the Sinai Peninsula to Jordan. Despite being warned that our route was forbidden and fortified, we were going to give it a go.

Less than halfway to the Canal, the narrow road was blocked by Egyptian tanks and soldiers. No amount of protests about freedom of travel did us any good. We could not cross the Suez and we could not cross the Sinai. Those doors to the Middle East were firmly shut. We were forced to retrace our route and return to Cairo, where we again petitioned the authorities for permission to drive to Jordan, and where our request was again rejected. "Next year," the guard had said, "next year, when there is no more Israel."

They told us that the only way to continue our journey was to take a ship across the Mediterranean to Beirut, Lebanon.

And where could we find such a ship?

Why, in Alex, of course!

# CHAPTER 5

## Into the Teeth of the Tiger

Five months later, after hard, hot crossings of Lebanon, Jordan, Syria, Iraq, Iran, and Afghanistan, I was hauling the camper down through the Khyber Pass into the Indian subcontinent. About 30 miles before Peshawar, the monsoon rains, of which we'd had a hint the night before, struck with all their fury. The afternoon turned dark as night. Lightning tore through the heavens. Down and down the rain drummed relentlessly. In 30 minutes the road was awash; in an hour the water was so high it threatened to flood the engine.

Even without the rain, the road was deadly. It was typical of the roads throughout Pakistan and India, a narrow asphalt one-laner with a four-inch drop onto the mud or rock shoulders on either side. They were poorly maintained remnants of the British Raj, built in the days before heavy auto traffic, so narrow that two cars could not pass abreast, forcing one of them to put a wheel onto the dangerous shoulder. We'd been warned that the local truckers willfully smashed into oncoming cars rather than slow down or move to the side, but we didn't believe it. Believe it! Western courtesy plays no role when a punctured tire or a broken spring can mean economic disaster for a trucker's family. It had become a law of survival for the trucker to hold the road, using every manner of highway bullying, from honking horns to blinking lights, to make the oncoming driver turn chicken and take to the ditch.

We had just cleared the Pass, and were a few miles beyond Jamrud Fort, which guards its eastern approach, when the spindle that held the camper's right wheel sheared off. We skidded 30 yards before I could get the bucking camper under control and stop. We were in a bind, on the narrow approach to a bridge over a river. We couldn't move with a wheel missing, yet we couldn't rightly block the bridge. We had to manually drag the camper off the road onto the shoulder, though that was only three feet wide with a 30-foot drop-off. The rear of the camper was dug into the mud shoulder; the front end jutted out over space. We used everything we could—jacks, rocks, boulders, tent poles, gas cans—to prop it up and prevent it from sliding down the steep embankment.

For most of the afternoon we labored underneath the precariously situated camper to unbolt and remove the axle, a delicate operation where any mistake could crush us or send the camper hurtling into the river. When we finally had the axle off, we loaded it into the Land Cruiser and I headed for Peshawar to find a welding shop, leaving the others to guard the crippled camper. It was evening by the time the spindle was welded into place in Peshawar, and the monsoons intensified as I headed back.

I'd gone only halfway when I was halted at a roadblock manned by four Pakistani soldiers who told me the rivers had jumped their banks and were flooding the road ahead. No cars were being allowed through. After I explained that I *had* to get back to the camper before it was washed away, the guards reluctantly agreed to let me pass. By the time I was a mile beyond the roadblock, it was completely dark and impossible to see in the driving rain. The road was covered with two feet of rushing, muddy water. I feared I might drive off the road and go completely under, so I enlisted help from a soggy local hitchhiker, who agreed to walk in front and scout a path. I gave him a flashlight and attached a lifeline from his waist to the car bumper. In this way, with the scout half walking and half swimming, I made it to the camper, which was close to toppling down the embankment.

We installed new supports, but these were undermined as fast as we could get them into place. It was nearly midnight when the downpour abated and we could brace the camper with jacks and gas cans. But it was too dark, and much too dangerous, to crawl under the camper to bolt the repaired axle into place, so we pitched the Poptents below to wait until morning.

Several hours later I was awakened by muffled noises above and stuck my head out of the tent. Two trucks were parked on the road. They must be curious passersby, I thought, and was about to go back to sleep, when I heard someone knocking a gas can from under the trailer. I grabbed the flashlight and zipped open the tent. My light caught three men pulling the jacks from under the trailer. We grabbed entrenching tools and started up the rocky embankment, but it was hard going barefoot. By the time we reached the road the bandits were in their trucks and driving off—with all our gas cans, both jacks, and some tools. And the camper was slowly sliding down toward the now-flooded river bed.

What kind of people would so violate the customary rules of survival as to pillage a disabled vehicle and steal the equipment we needed to repair it? The lawless tribesmen who inhabit the rugged border region between Afghanistan and Pakistan, that's who. Those independent, rifle-toting toughs who recognize no nation, no law, and no loyalty but to their clan. The same tribe of insolent hombres who, decades later, gave shelter and assistance to Osama Bin Laden.


After crossing Pakistan and India and visiting Nepal (where we sold Steve's old Jeep), we were so far behind schedule that East Pakistan was submerged by the monsoon, which sunk our plan to tow the camper across it. Manu, Willy, and Woodrow took a ship with the camper from Calcutta to Bangkok, where we agreed to rendezvous, while Steve and I headed the Cruiser toward the border between India and East Pakistan, hoping to get through before the threatened war began.

We were taken under Indian military escort to a bridge over a tributary of the Ganges that separated India from East Pakistan. Two Indian customs officers carefully checked our papers, reluctantly stamped our passports, and watched us suspiciously as we crossed the long, untrafficked bridge between the two countries.

In the car I mused that "If the Indians think we're Pakistani spies . . ."

Steve finished my thought: ". . . the Pakis are going to think we're Indian spies."

And that was exactly what they did think: We were greeted with the command to take every item out of the car for inspection.

We foresaw difficulty: Our pistol was in Steve's overnight bag, and the irascible officers were looking for some way to bust our chops. It was showtime.

"Every bag?" I asked the officer, holding one up. "This one, too?"

"Every one!"

I put the bag I was holding down and grabbed two more. "How about these?"

"Yes, those, too."

The officers stepped up and began searching through the bags as I pulled them out of the car. As they did, I'd open up others and helpfully dump clothing and supplies all over the bags they had started to search. In a few minutes I'd addled them. As the officers took a bag out of one door I'd surreptitiously slide it back in the other. I picked up an aerosol can of foaming mosquito repellent and insisted the officers let me squirt some on their arms for protection. Then I went for the backrest massage machine. I plugged it into the cigarette-lighter socket and invited the officer in charge to sit inside the Cruiser and try it. He was reluctant but, after much prodding, agreed, and I turned the vibrator on. In seconds the officer was purring contentedly, his eyes half-closed, like a housecat having his belly rubbed. Then the junior officer wanted to have his turn. Then the sergeant. When they resumed checking the bags they had no idea which they had searched and which they had not. In the end, they overlooked the gun bag and returned our passports. We breathed a tremulous sigh and drove on.

The country northeast of Calcutta and well into East Pakistan is a vast alluvial plain where, during the monsoon, jute grows in endless waves in the flooded fields. Every now and then a wide-rooted tree or thick cluster of bamboo broke the flat contour of the land. Along the elevated roads, built atop high embankments of hardened mud, slow-moving oxcarts or elephants hauled freshly cut bamboo and dried jute. The villages looked as they had throughout India: mud houses with pounded earth out front, where withered women stuffed twigs and leaves beneath blackened pots on mud hearths to heat their tea water.

Ferry boats and river steamers were the main means of transportation during the monsoon season. To reach Dacca, the capital, we had to take four of them. We drove into Dacca a little past noon on the second day. It was not an attractive or impressive city, with little to see and less to do. The U.S. State Department Personnel Office classified it as a hardship post.

We located the Government Tourist Bureau, from which we hoped to get a letter of introduction to facilitate our trip across the country. The deputy director was cordial and listened with keen interest about our travels, but when we explained our plan to drive to Chittagong in the southeast part of his country and from there on to Burma, he declared: "Gentlemen, I doubt if you can do it."

"We realize it's difficult," Steve admitted. "We know Burma has been closed to foreigners for years. All we want to do is give it a try."

The director paused before speaking: "I don't believe you understand. Haven't you heard the latest news? The hostility from India has caused a crisis. The Indians have bombed Lahore. There is no telling what will happen next. You had better register immediately with the police."

We promptly drove to police headquarters. In the Foreigner's Registration Office we found half a dozen officers huddled around an old radio. They interrupted their excited conversation only long enough to ink our names in the registration book, the only entries, I noticed, in many days. The officer adjusting the radio dials anxiously glanced at a clock on the opposite wall. The president of Pakistan, Field Marshal Mohammad Ayub Khan, was to address the nation in five minutes. All heads leaned toward the radio as the slow but truculent voice of their president announced that Pakistan was at war with the treacherous Moslem-hating Indians who'd been armed by a devious America.

We left the office to find crowds gathering in the street. Newsboys screamed the headlines: "LAHORE BOMBED. EMERGENCY DECLARED." A squadron of Pakistani jets roared overhead. We drove to a gas station to fill our tank and spare cans. Fifty cars and trucks were ahead of us, hoping to buy gas before it was rationed. As we waited in line the station manager came over to complain about the military aid America had given India.

"We helped arm India so she could defend herself against China," Steve explained.

"India used you. We warned it was a trick so India could get your guns to use against us."

"But look at your own army," I replied. "Every gun, tank, and plane you have is from the U.S., while India has British planes and German rifles and only a few American weapons. Every one of your pilots and officers has been trained by America."

He could not see our point. We had betrayed Pakistan, and that settled it.

A trucker rushed up to us, waving a fist, yelling, "Americans help India. You are no longer our friends. Yet even though the Indians have your guns, we will crush them anyway."

"But you're outnumbered four to one by five hundred million Indians whose soldiers may well be crossing your borders now," I said.

"We are not worried. Indians are moral cowards. We are Moslems. We have moral courage. This is key. We will win. We will crush them."

We gassed up and headed for the first of the three ferries we'd have to take to reach Chittagong to exit the war zone. At the ferry landing, ten miles east of Dacca, we handed our papers to the guard who, without looking at them, handed them back, shaking his head. "No ferry," he said.

"But we must take the ferry."

"There are no ferries," he repeated. "The government has taken them all into service. You might try the steamer in Narayanganj."

We rushed to Narayanganj and through its narrow streets to the water-front, where we saw a steamer loading cargo. We ran to the top of the gang-plank, where the mate said that if we wanted to book passage we'd have to go to the shipping office. We copied down the address and, after a half hour's search, found it.

"Sorry," a clerk said, "but the *Harappa* is not leaving Narayanganj."

"But she's loading now. We saw it."

"Maybe so, but we have just received orders from the commanding general of the port that no ships are to leave until orders come from the high com-mand in Dacca. You should return to Dacca and find yourself a hotel and wait. Even if you did get authorization to board, and even if we did get autho-rization to sail, you couldn't pass beyond Chandipur. The military has the road blocked."

We took his advice and drove to the American Consulate in Dacca to register. After checking our passports a guard led us to an agitated foreign service officer who was on the telephone: "All Americans are to report to the Consulate . . . No, we'll try to keep you posted . . . No, we have no official word . . . No, all communications have been cut."

When the officer hung up we introduced ourselves and explained that we'd just driven into the country. He was startled. He asked us to wait, rose quickly, and ducked into an office. In a moment he was back. "Mr. Bowling, the consul general, would like to see you," he said.

Bowling sat behind an impressive but cluttered desk flanked by the flags of the U.S. and the State Department. Three foreign service officers were poring over the newspapers on the coffee table as a secretary took notes. They were dressed in sports clothes, and I remembered it was Labor Day back home.

"You've picked a highly unlikely time to be driving through East Pakistan," the consul began. "And my assistant tells me you're journalists. I don't think the Paks will be too pleased when they find out—you'd be the only foreign reporters here."

"But we didn't come here to write about the war."

"Tell that to them! I advise you to keep out of sight and out of trouble until this whole thing has ended. I wish you luck." We were dismissed.

Next morning, under the headline: CHITTAGONG BOMBED, I read: "Indian Air Force planes launched unprovoked, cowardly attacks on civilian targets in Karachi, Chittagong . . ."

I scanned the next column, headlined RESPONSE FROM EAST PAKISTAN: "President Ayub's call to his countrymen to crush the Indian aggression on our sacred territory met with an immediate, spontaneous response from East Pakistan. The 60,000,000 people of the province now stand as one man behind Ayub to protect the sovereignty and sanctity of every inch of our soil. . . ."

The government's propaganda machine was trying to stir up the East Pakistanis, and for good reason: All the face-to-face fighting was in the other half of Pakistan, near Kashmir, 1,500 miles away and separated by Indian territory. Ayub's regime needed the support of East Pakistan to furnish soldiers and equipment and to put pressure on India's back, so he was involving them through the press and radio. But the aroused people of East Pakistan saw no invading troops, no one to release their wrath upon—except those who aroused suspicion. And who better than foreigners?

It became unsafe for foreigners to walk the streets. Several Americans were dragged from their cars and beaten. The media warned the populace to watch for suspicious-looking people and report them. The military exhorted the citizens to arm themselves and to shoot enemy guerrillas on sight—a directive that had to be modified when several Pakistani pilots were shot by their own people after bailing out of their disabled planes.

Most menacing was the appeal to the students: They were encouraged to become vigilantes, enforcers of the emergency defense laws. When a curfew was placed on Dacca they patrolled the streets hunting for violators, and during air-raid blackouts they combed the residential sections searching for glimmers of light, beating on fences and doors with sticks as a warning.

Steve and I were in a particularly uncomfortable position: We did not have diplomatic immunity or any cognizable function in Dacca, as the other Americans did. We had no friends there. Nor did we have a plausible excuse for being there. Who'd believe we were driving around the world through the middle of a war? It also looked as if we'd no longer even have a place to stay: Our hotel workers were casting increasingly suspicious looks at us. We expected our door to come crashing down any night and vigilantes to drag us into the street. We had no way to escape. Nor could we communicate with the outside world: All postal, telephone, and cable services had been terminated. We headed to the U.S. Information Agency (USIA) to ascertain if there was some way to send word to the Expedition members who were waiting for us in Bangkok.

When we reached the USIA, the staffers were boarding up the windows. We learned that the university students were on their way to protest America's aid to India and might attempt to sack the library. We weren't in East Pakistan to cover the war, but we could at least get photographs. I dashed across the street and into a four-story office building whose balconies offered a perfect vantage point for taking pictures. I raced up the concrete stairs and knelt down on the third-floor balcony, concealed from the street, while Steve hid

The day after the 1965 war began between India and Pakistan, the irate citizens of Dacca, capital of East Pakistan (now Bangladesh), staged an angry march on the United States Information Agency, claiming America was providing arms to the Indians. I came within seconds of being lynched.

himself in a parked bus. I soon heard the shouts of the marchers coming down Topkhana Road, and screwed a telephoto lens on my camera.

Suddenly, two soldiers came up behind me and dragged me inside, into a large room whose door read: CIVIL DEFENSE HEADQUARTERS AND OFFICE OF THE COMMISSIONER OF DACCA.

They held me down in a chair as four officers fired questions at me. A mob of agitated civil defense employees surrounded me. One pulled the film out of my camera. He snarled "Indian spy!" as he spat at me.

"Kill the Indian spy," another worker shouted.

"Death to the enemy," screamed another.

"Hang him! Hang him! Hang him!" the angry crowd chanted.

A porter came in with a thick rope, threw it over a rafter, and started fashioning a noose.

"Hang him! Hang Him! Hang him!" the room rocked with the chant.

"STOP!" I cried out. "I'm not an Indian spy; I'm an American magazine editor."

"Then why are you prowling around our Civil Defense Headquarters?"

"I have a very bad case of diarrhea. I caught some bad bug in filthy India. I just arrived in Dacca and was looking for a toilet. It's an emergency."

"Hang the spy! He's lying. Hang the liar! Hang him!"

With nothing to lose, I wrestled free, pulled down my pants with one swift motion, and explosively shat a greasy bright-yellow barrage all over the floor, making it graphically clear, even to the most vehement of the lynch mob, that I was not faking a stomach disorder. (I'd been afflicted with increasingly loose bowels and painful cramps for more than a week, but hadn't gone to a doctor, hoping the problem would cease. Instead, it had grown steadily worse.)

Still, all I had proven was that I could crap on cue. Thus, I was not only a spy, but a spy with the world's most disgusting party trick.

Just then Steve, who'd seen me being dragged off the balcony, pushed his way into the room and shouted, "What are you doing to my friend?"

They all turned to Steve.

"This Indian spy is your friend?"

"He's no spy. He's the editor of a big American magazine. And I write articles for it."

"It's forbidden to take pictures here," the ranking officer replied. "Show me your identification."

"We are reporting on the unity and impressive morale of the people of East Pakistan in the face of the Indian aggression," Steve told him, handing over his passport. "We are not spies."

The arbiter studied it carefully, then walked across the room and made a phone call. When he hung up, he turned to us: "We shall see."

Half an hour later, in walked the American Vice Consul, who'd been summoned to vouch for our identity. "I thought the consul general told you two to stay out of trouble," he said, as I removed the rope from my neck.

Although no noose was good news, Dacca was succumbing to hysteria. Hindus and Moslems, even old friends, were beginning to fight, raising fears that communal riots, like those of 1947 that claimed nearly a million lives, might reoccur. An emergency edict required all vehicles to have their headlights blackened with paint or covered with tape, which turned night driving into a demolition derby. Some took it upon themselves to camouflage their cars with tree branches and leaves, counterproductively making those vehicles all the more conspicuous, masses of green moving through a brown city. Even more ridiculous were the gas station owners who covered their pumps with foliage. When we stopped at one such station to get the daily gallon ration, I prepared to photograph the jungle-covered pumps, but the attendant yelled for the police, compelling us to drive away with neither photo nor gas. The government issued an edict proclaiming it a crime to carry a camera; anyone doing so was presumed to be spying. Two days later we discovered we were being followed; wherever we drove, a white Renault kept close behind us. When we returned to our hotel room we saw that our bags had been searched.

We needed to find a safer place to stay. A minister we'd met on the ferry had given us the address of his missionary friends in Dacca, so we went to see if they knew anyone who could put us up. We drove out to Dhanmondi, the section where the foreign community lived—the suburb the Pakistanis call the "Golden Ghetto"—and located their house. They weren't home. Their *chaukidar* (servant) looked at us suspiciously and told us we'd have to come back later.

As we climbed into our Cruiser, the air-raid sirens howled. The quiet residential street filled with noise and commotion. Residents ducked from their houses to scan the skies for enemy planes, while pedestrians caught outside ran for cover. The *chaukidar* impatiently gestured for us to hurry and leave so he could lock the gates behind us. But by now vigilante bands were running down the streets, chasing foreigners to cover, shouting and banging on the fences with clubs and sticks. Overriding the protests of the *chaukidar,* Steve drove our Cruiser into the yard behind the house, where it couldn't be seen from the street. I slammed the gates shut just as the mob reached them. We ran into the house, followed by the *chaukidar.* Having little choice but to give us shelter, he led us into a small pantry adjoining the kitchen, lifted a trapdoor, and pointed down into a cellar. We descended a dark stairway and he closed the door above us.

When the all-clear sounded, the *chaukidar* opened the trapdoor and led us into the house. The missionaries returned an hour later, listened with understanding as we told them why we needed to find a safe place to stay, and put us in touch with Bill Maillefert, the acting chief information officer at USIA, who knew as much about what was going on in Dacca as any American there.

We spent the next day at his home in Dhanmondi, discussing the war in general and our problems in particular. By the time we left, Bill had arranged for us to move in with Mike Schneider, an audio-visual specialist at USIA, who lived alone in a large house nearby.

We had plenty of company there: Mike's house had become the nightly gathering place for other unfortunate foreigners, mostly Americans, who'd been caught in the hostilities. We met a missionary, a USAID engineer, six Peace Corps volunteers who'd been ordered to Dacca from rural areas, and others who popped in and out with the latest rumors and directives.

On our second day at Mike's house we saw a directive from Consul General Bowling:

NOTICE TO AMERICANS IN EAST PAKISTAN

East Pakistan has become an area of hostilities. The Consul General
has therefore determined to evacuate all Americans in the near future,

using aircraft chartered by the U.S. Government, if they can be brought into Dacca. We hope to have aircraft in Dacca on Saturday. All Americans should report to the American Consulate General for processing as soon as it is convenient. They should bring their passports or other proof of U.S. citizenship.

We filled out the forms, wondered what would happen, and waited. A few started packing and closing their houses. But Saturday came and went, as did Sunday. And Monday. And Tuesday. There were no planes, no evacuation; only more directives and rumors.

When we weren't discussing the rumors, we listened to the shortwave set, perhaps the biggest rumormonger of all. First, we'd tune in to Radio Pakistan and hear that: "The brave Pakistani armies are advancing and inflicting heavy blows upon the aggressor in all sectors. Our brave *jawans* have destroyed 63 American-made Indian tanks in the Sialkot-Jammu section in the last 24 hours. Our gallant airmen shot down 21 enemy planes in today's action. We have lost only one aircraft." We'd then pick up All-India Radio to be told that: "The Indian Army is advancing. In a fierce battle in the Waggha-Attari section, we've smashed 56 enemy tanks while losing only two of our own. Indian jets brought down 42 Pakistani planes today, with no losses."

By the eighth day of the fighting, our running tabulations of the tanks and planes allegedly destroyed by both sides exceeded the combined losses of the Allied Forces in WW II.

Bowling had no guarantee that any evacuation could be arranged; his request had been met with three days of stony silence from the government. They then told him that no planes were available for charter inside Pakistan because they'd all been turned over to the military. When he explained he intended to bring in U.S. Air Force transports, the Pakistanis refused approval, claiming they couldn't risk having American planes land in Dacca as long as the airfield was being bombed by India. When Bowling pointed out that there really hadn't been any such bombing, they said that, in any case, the airport was reserved for Pakistani aircraft.

When word that the Americans were trying to evacuate reached the citizens of Dacca, it caused an outraged uproar. The government helped it along, channeling the people's frustration about their inability to quickly defeat the Indians into an outburst against America. Thousands marched through Dacca to the USIA and the American Consulate, protesting our aid to India and our "refusal to help Pakistan in her hour of trial." The locals threw rocks through windows and beat up Westerners. They severed all social relationships with Americans, even close friends. No American could walk or drive through town without fear of being attacked. The son of President Khan called Americans "warmongers with the Bible in one hand and Stengun in another preaching their weird doctrines to unreceptive audiences," and suggested that a mass uprising could prevent our departure.

Two days later it appeared that the Pakistanis might give the green light, for they presented Consul Bowling with a long list of items—gold, jewelry, cameras, radios, Pakistani money—that were declared war contraband and could not be taken out in an evacuation. This gave heart to the American community because it was the first sign that the Pakistanis were genuinely considering the evacuation proposal.

The hopes aroused by the directive were quickly dashed the next night by new rumors that ran through the foreign community. Steve was sorting our equipment at Mike's house, and I was concealing our film inside the linings of our suitcases, when a British consular friend of Mike's came rushing in. (No foreigners communicated anything important by phone anymore because the lines were tapped by the secret police.) He reported that the Pakistanis had decided to forbid the evacuation and hold the Americans hostage to prevent the Indians from attacking Dacca.

The next morning there were still no evacuation planes, but there were still more rumors: "The Pakis might allow Bowling to get the women and children out, but all men will have to remain behind."

The following morning, a USIA staffer came running in, waving a consular envelope of the kind with which we'd by now become familiar. "The latest directive," he shouted. "The latest directive on the evacuation." Mike tore it open and read it out loud to all assembled:

NOTICE TO AMERICANS IN EAST PAKISTAN

Subject: Operation Icarus

1. Due to the delay in obtaining official evacuation transportation, the following preparations should be made:

   a. Beeswax—this material should be collected by all persons and stored in an air-conditioned room. Beeswax will be delivered by Jeep to official homes. Private citizens must appear in person.

   b. Feathers—this will be distributed according to the length of each individual's arms, and will not exceed . . .

# CHAPTER 6

## Changing Goals

After two weeks of captivity, we were evacuated by a U.S. Air Force C-130 and flown to Bangkok, where Steve was hospitalized with hepatitis and I was treated for my intestinal issue, a virulent case of *Giardia*. I then flew to Japan to confer with Toyota, which was aghast that the Pakistanis wanted to paint their Land Cruiser khaki and draft it into their army. Steve cabled our camper-trailer sponsor in Wisconsin, whose CEO was a close friend of his influential congressman, Mel Laird, who headed the Defense Subcommittee of the House Appropriations Committee. Caught between the pressure from Tokyo and Washington, the Pakistanis caved and let us return to recover our vehicle and get back on the road.

By the time we did, Manu had given up and returned to Spain, Willy left to photograph the war in Vietnam, incorrectly believing that his Swiss passport guaranteed his safe passage, and Woodrow was off hawking multivitamins in remote Thai villages.

After another year of traversing the rest of the globe in relatively peaceful fashion, and with almost 42,000 miles on our odometer, Steve and I crossed the U.S. border at Laredo, to be welcomed by cheering customs agents, the press, and a totally transformed nation. Our formerly staid and complacent homeland had become, during the 19 months we'd been away, an alert, alive, aware, moving, modern, mind-expanded, turned on, tuned in, lit up,

After the Expedition concluded, I returned to my playboy ways, dating actresses and models and tooling around town in my homemade wooden sports car powered by a 1947 Chrysler 6-cylinder in-line Spitfire. For the next 30 years my ramblings around the world were desultory and sporadic.

teeny-bopper Go-Go Land. No Marco Polo returning home from 30 years abroad could have been as astonished by the changes as we were. We headed to New York—and a record of 22,252 nonrepetitive miles—on the new interstate highway system, as our homeland zoomed by in a flash of Mustangs, miniskirts, mods and rockers, go-go girls, Beatles and Rolling Stones, Head Start and head shops and Heaven to be home.

During the ensuing seven years I completed writing *Who Needs a Road?* with Steve, appeared on a dozen TV shows, got married, got divorced, became one of the Mad Men and rose to VP of an ad agency, spent three years as a good-government lobbyist, then entered NYU School of Law to get a degree so I could—depending on my mood that day—either get rich or save the world. I was working so hard and taking so few vacations, that I'd visited just 51 countries by 1982, up to a mere 63 by 1990, and 83 by the turn of the century, averaging only one and a half nations a year, all in a casual and desultory fashion, plus 49 U.S. states. (Sorry, North Dakota.)

But I was not aware of these numbers at the time; I kept no tab because I had no such goal. My goal was totally different: Ever since the final days of the Expedition, I longed to be the first person to ever travel by land completely around our world in a *longitudinal* direction. My plan was to drive from New York to the tip of South America, then somehow manage to motor across Antarctica, drive north from the Cape of Good Hope through the length of Africa, on to the northern edge of Europe, fly over the Arctic (which was not land, and therefore did not have to be driven across) to the northernmost shore of Alaska, and conclude with an easy run back to the Big Apple.

I'd carefully studied the route, noted the most favorable departure date, prepared a detailed budget that I was sure my previous sponsors would cover, written about this dream in both the hardcover and paperback editions of *Who Needs a Road?* and even begun to assemble a crew. For more than 30 years *that* was my dream, my ambition, and my obsession.

But I was thwarted by two big problems, and eventually defeated by one of them.

First, the way was not clear. The Western Hemisphere route was blocked by wars and sustained guerrilla fighting in Colombia, Guatemala, Nicaragua, and El Salvador. Europe presented the barrier of the Iron Curtain. Africa was aflame with wars or revolutions in Algeria, Angola, Chad, Congo, Democratic Republic of Congo (DRC), Ethiopia, Eritrea, Mozambique, Namibia, Nigeria, Somalia, Sudan, Rhodesia, Zaire, Uganda, Liberia, Ivory Coast, Sierra Leone, Burundi, and Rwanda that blocked any route through. (Sir Ranulph Fiennes did, from 1979 to 1982, successfully lead a longitudinal expedition around the world, and wrote an excellent book about it, *To the Ends of the Earth*, but he avoided the war zones by taking ship much of the way.) The land route would have to wait at least until most of the conflicts were resolved, which did not happen until well into the Millennium.

But it was the crossing of Antarctica by automobile that proved insurmountable. My dreams die hard, but I did finally conclude—and I hope one of you will one day prove me wrong—that such a crossing could not be achieved. I read. I researched. I tested. I studied. And I consulted experts. But I could not conceive a reasonably secure way of traversing Antarctica's many wide glacial crevasses and barrier mountains by car, or of keeping the vehicle intact in Antarctica's subzero temperatures. When I tested 4×4s in northern Canada in the dead of winter, the tires froze and shattered and the engine had to run continuously to keep the battery charged, the parts from disintegrating, and the essential fluids liquid—a feat not easily accomplished on a barren continent where there are no filling stations.

I created gas-consumption tables, worked out plans to parachute in fuel caches every ten miles across the Antarctic snowcap, estimated likely daily mileage to determine if the transpolar journey could be completed during the five-month window offered by the southern summer, but I eventually gave up. (Well, maybe I didn't completely *give up*, but it was, and remains, a dream deferred.)

The idea of going to *every* country sort of sneaked in to occupy that recently vacated spot in my mind and heart where lodged the quixotic hope of doing something glorious and original, an adventure no one had ever achieved, of not going gently into that good night, of going out with a bang rather than a whimper.

When I gave travel lectures, attendees asked how many countries I'd seen, but I had no list. As the Millennium dawned I finally totaled them: 83. I was dimly aware that there were between 190 and 200 countries, which meant I was equally dimly aware that I'd visited less than half.

I knew I preferred visiting new countries to revisiting those I'd seen, an attitude doubtless derived from the predilection I exhibited at age seven, when I started collecting postage stamps. I refused to specialize in any country or area, as my friends did. No, I wanted a perforated piece of paper from *every* stamp-issuing entity on earth, obscure places like Oltre Giuba, Rio de Oro, Two Sicilies, Bechuanaland Protectorate, Nejd, and Hejaz.

Above my teenage bed hung a 1920s poster from the Hamburg-American shipping line: *Mein Feld Ist die Welt* (My Field Is the World). This proclivity persisted through Cornell, where I studied foreign affairs, into the University of Chicago, where I was awarded the graduate fellowship of the Committee on International Relations.

It was like much other stuff in my life: I sought to try it all out, suck it all up, and grab all the gusto I could, including eventually having six different, and immensely enjoyable, careers—editor, writer, advertising executive, good-government lobbyist, lawyer, and theatrical producer.

Shortly after the year 2000 I thought it would be fun—little did I know!—to see how many countries I could visit. And off I went, whenever my law-practice clients and worthy opponents permitted.

By the end of 2003 I was up to 112. *That* was when I realized that it could be possible, and surely a compelling challenge, in the remaining ten to 20 years that the actuarial tables allotted me, to visit *every* country, that such a feat was doable, and that *I* could do it.

I researched to ascertain how many people had legitimately visited every country, but could find no such category, from Guinness to Wikipedia; nor could I find any book or article written by, or about, anyone who had gone all the way. I studied what constituted a country and looked over the horizon for incipient newbies. And somewhere along this vague way, I decided—yes, really, truly, and finally *decided*—that I *would* go to every country.

# CHAPTER 7

## Making a Splash

South and Central America are so vast, beauteous, diverse, and fascinating, but their roads were so poor, their river travel so slow, and their political crises so frequent, that it took me nine separate trips to visit all their 20 continental nations. I here recount some of the highlights that took place on, in, through, or under their lakes, rivers, and seas.

### TURNING TURTLE

During the homeward-bound leg of our Expedition, Steve and I had serendipitously pitched our camper by the estuary of the San Juan River on the Pacific Coast of Nicaragua on a dazzling night of the full August moon.

It was nearly midnight when, hearing noises, we exited our camper and found ourselves amid an *arribadas,* more than a thousand immense green turtles crawling out of the ocean to spawn, laboring up the slope to the dry part of the beach. They stopped about a hundred yards above the high-tide line, some near our camper. They scooped out holes more than a foot deep with their flippers into which, panting from the strain of digging and the pangs of labor, they deposited their eggs—one, two, three at a time . . . 60 . . . 80 . . . sometimes 100 in a clutch.

Steve and I lay on our bellies behind the holes, entranced, watching this marvel of nature, this miracle of creation.

Although exhausted from their labors, the turtles assiduously filled in these nests and leveled the surface to conceal them, then struggled through the soft sand, gasping and groaning in an almost human way, back to the breakers, back to the depths, never to see their young born—never to know that their young would never be born.

Because a hundred boys from the nearby town had been waiting on the beach that night for the annual return of the turtles. When they sighted a turtle emerging from the ocean, one or two of the boys peeled off to stealthily follow her to where she dug her hole, and dig one just behind her, a few inches away and several feet down, then tunnel through to her nest and catch the white, soft-shelled eggs as she laid them. The mother turtles, struggling with single-minded determination to perpetuate their species, never suspected the fate of their eggs as greedy fingers snatched them a handsbreadth away from the painful openings of their cloacae.

I was so upset that I ran up and down the beach all night lecturing the boys, in my incomprehensible Spanglish, on the principles of conservation and fair play, imploring them to leave half, or at least a third, of the eggs in the ground so there could be turtles and eggs for future generations.

But none of them listened. They were all too busy counting the eggs into sacks of a hundred, to be sold at the market in the morning. A few hungry boys were piercing the eggs on the spot with small twigs and sucking the yolks down as they were, raw and still warm from the womb.

A boy who had "borrowed" our flashlight returned it toward morning with thanks and a dozen of the eggs he'd gathered, the size of ping-pong balls, light and rubbery to the touch. As soon as he left, I took them and went down to the empty nests, where Steve and I gently buried these fragile seeds of life and hoped against hope that they would survive and endure.

## MISTAKEN IDENTITY IN LAKE NICARAGUA

The morning after we had reburied the eggs, we drove to Lake Nicaragua, at 99 miles long the largest lake in Central America, 19th largest on earth. It's a gloomy body, dominated by several volcanoes along its shore and by two perpetually cloud-shrouded peaks that rise 7,000 feet from an island at its center.

On the Nicaraguan beach where hundreds of endangered 400-pound green sea turtles had laid their eggs during the full moon the night before, Steve redeposits a batch into one of the nests that had been pillaged by the locals, who shortsightedly took every egg they could find.

In the sweltering heat of an August midafternoon we reached the lake's northwest coast and drove through the charming city of Granada, one of the first Spanish settlements in the New World, a carefully preserved town with centuries-old churches and gracious, balconied, colonial-style homes. Its only contemporary architectural feature was an impressionist piscine monument at the town traffic circle that looked out of place amid all that mellowed antiquity. We drove down to the deserted lake shore where, since we'd gotten so little sleep the night before, we made an early camp.

Despite the uninviting water, which was slate gray and streaked by oil, and a shoreline rimmed with tin cans, plastic bags, cartons, straw, rotting fruit, and some of the 32 tons of raw sewage flushed into the lake every day, Steve was so hot and sweaty that he plunged right in, then swam out about a quarter mile to get away from the garbage. I walked along the smelly, mushy shore and came across the bloated body of a cow, obviously dead for several days, rocking in the oily waves a few yards from the beach, with a gaping bite missing from its haunch.

As I was pondering Elsie's fate, I looked across the spooky lake and saw Steve swimming hell-bent toward the beach with—was it my imagination?— something black and sleek, like a large fin, protruding out of the water about ten yards behind him. At first I thought it was a shark, but I knew that could not be, because they live only in salt water, and this was a freshwater lake. Maybe a dolphin? But weren't they also saltwater citizens? Whatever it was swam away and Steve safely reached the beach.

Not until the next day did we realize how lucky he had been. We were told in Granada that the lake was infested with dangerous freshwater sharks, the only ones on the globe, the locals said, and that the monument we'd seen was intended to both celebrate them and warn visitors. We were informed that the lake, which is only a hundred feet above sea level, had been part of the ocean until a volcanic eruption sealed it off from the sea eons before, trapping millions of fish within it, most of which died as the lake, which bottomed out at about 90 feet, lost its salinity as the rains and streams poured in. But that one species of shark had managed to evolve, adapt, survive, and become the world's only finned freshwater man-eater. Fascinating!

And totally incorrect!

The sharks' actual provenance did not emerge until ten years later, when ichthyologists proved, through tagging, that those found in Lake Nicaragua bred only in salt water, which meant, by definition, that they were saltwater fish. Further research revealed that these were not a special species, but ordinary oceanic bull sharks that had swum 120 miles from the ocean, jumped the river rapids salmon-style, reached Lake Nicaragua in seven to eleven days, and lived there for as long as they desired by a process of osmoregulation. They had learned how to reduce the salinity of their blood more than 50 percent by absorbing gallons of fresh water and excreting 20 times more urine than when in salt water.

Aside from having swum in a lot of shark piss, Steve could have been in deep shit, because the bull shark is responsible for more attacks on humans than any other. They're temperamental, unpredictable, and aggressive—like Russian drivers—but nine to ten feet long, with powerful jaws, and will eat whatever mammals they can wrap their teeth around, from rats, dogs, and tree sloths, to antelope, cattle, and people. (In India, I'd watched their genetic cousins swim up the Ganges to eat the human corpses that bereaved families devoutly dumped into that sacred river.) Ichthyologists believe that bull sharks are the most dangerous to humans because, of the three main maneating species—great whites, tigers, and bulls—only the bulls habitually live in shallow water close to populated shorelines; the others live farther down and farther out.

The bulls were the apex predators of the lake. They're attacked only by tiger sharks and great whites but, since none of those lived in the lake, the bulls were able to thrive there. Until the Japanese came along in the 1980s and pretty much fished them out for their fins.

THE PEAK OF DEATH

If sweat and tears count as water, this harrowing incident belongs here, for it caused me to shed more of both than any other on our auto expedition.

The Inter-American Highway north from Panama City was bordered by thick tropical jungles and littered with the run-over carcasses of dozens of snakes, but it was paved and fast. Halfway up through Panama the cement ended and Steve and I entered its worst stretch, more than 200 miles of jolting corrugations, loose gravel, razor-sharp rocks, and spring-busting potholes, continuing through southern Costa Rica. Ahead loomed the highest mountain pass of our trip around the world, the 13,000-foot summit of *Cerro de la Muerte*, the notorious Peak of Death, a nerve-wracking rut of a crooked road with narrow curves bordered by steep cliffs, subject to dense fog, flash floods, and landslides.

We didn't make it.

A thousand yards below the pass, on a blind curve, we felt a sharp jolt and heard the shriek of tortured metal scraping on stone. Steve jerked the Cruiser to a halt and we leaped out to see our camper—20 yards behind us, its nose dug into the road, its A-frame still hitched to the Cruiser, snapped completely through at both joints.

It was our worst possible breakdown: Only a heavy-duty welding shop could fix it, and none existed on the Peak of Death. It made no sense bringing the A-frame to a welder unless we also brought the camper to which it had to be reattached, but it was not possible to bring the camper anywhere with its A-frame detached. We were stranded on a treacherous mountain road, on a blind curve, with trucks charging down, no shoulder on which to pull off, far from the nearest city, on the fog-shrouded summit of the highest peak on the Costa Rican section of Inter-American Highway at the height of the rainy season.

We concluded that the only way to get our trailer back on the road was to build an entirely new A-frame. We established a protective barricade of warning boulders and reflectors along the road, pitched our Pop-tent in a clearing we macheted out of the adjacent jungle, chopped down two mature bamboo trees, and toiled for three days with crude tools, trimming and shaping and fitting and binding the tree trunks into place.

We hoped this bamboo frame had sufficient strength and flexibility to enable us to haul the camper to a welding shop in San José. If it broke anywhere on *Cerro de la Muerte*, the camper could roll out of control and be dashed on the rocks below. But we had no alternative. We headed toward San José at a speed reduced from the 15 mph we had been doing to an excruciating crawl of 5 mph, to avoid straining the timber.

We reached San José nine days after we had left Panama City, a mere 317 miles away. But at least we'd pioneered an indispensable technique for other world travelers who find themselves stuck in the wilds with a broken trailer frame—if, that is, any other travelers were stupid enough to try to drag an easily breakable camper-trailer around the world.

## IN PERIL ON THE PACUARE

The east-to-west-flowing rivers of Latin America offer some of the best and fastest white water anywhere. The Andes run up the far western side of the continent like a spine, hundreds of high peaks covered with snow or drenched by rain that inevitably flows down to the sea, which is not far away, making the descent steep and filling the streams with flash and foam.

I should have known better, but I decided during a visit to Costa Rica to run the Pacuare, a challenging stream on whose steep sides lived kingfishers, herons, toucans, tanagers, and lizards, and whose thickly vegetated side gorges were home to jaguars, ocelots, monkeys, and sloths. The Pacuare has some of the grandest white water in Central America, with rapids ranging up to Class V on the international scale of VI, based on gradient, constriction, and obstruction. Its Class III rapids feature high to irregular waves and narrow passages that often require complex maneuvering. The Class IV are long, difficult rapids in constricted passages that demand precise paddling in extremely turbulent waters. As for the Class V . . . we never made it that far.

All the signs said DON'T DO IT DUMMY: It had been raining for a week and the river was boiling; it was the day after Christmas and the regular rafting shops were closed, so I ended up with a guy who had a patched, outdated raft and a hangover; I had no strong team, only my friend Anna and her two pre-teen kids, which meant we were woefully underpowered for the Pacuare. I was experienced enough to know better, but too determined to go for it—a frequent failing throughout my misadventures.

I was paddling for all I was worth on the left side of the raft, with Anna's son behind me, Anna and her daughter on the other side, our befogged guide perfunctorily steering in the stern. We miraculously managed to make it through Crazy Rock, Double Drop, Chicken Drop, and Pin Ball, and were halfway down to the Caribbean, when the raft was sideswiped in the Devil's Armpit and got pushed far down on my side. Anna's son was flipped overboard and clear, safe in his life vest, but I was stuck fast and sucking up water.

I was on my back, arched over the side, with my head completely in the water and my feet tightly wedged under my butt and beneath the raft's gunwale, on which my full weight was pressing down. I could not get free. I flapped. I floundered. I tried to twist, to turn. But I could not get free. The flow of water over my chest and face was too powerful for me to rise up and pull myself back into the boat, and my agility was impaired by a cumbersome life vest. The water kept pouring into my nose and mouth.

In my many decades in the water—kayaking, canoeing, diving, rafting, even surfing at big breaks in Hawaii—I'd never been in a more perilous situation. Although my face was only a few inches underwater, I was drowning and was powerless to do anything about it. It was truly one of those Is-this-the-way-I-go? moments.

As I was about to pass out, Anna carefully crawled to my side of the raft, reached out, grabbed a strap on my life vest, and hauled me back in, coughing, sputtering, and expelling a liter of water.

I was too shaken up to even think of asking her for some mouth-to-mouth resuscitation—although I corrected that oversight the next day.

## TORN BETWEEN THREE FALLS

Within a small area in northeastern South America are three waterfalls: one is the world's most awesome, the second is the world's highest, and the third is its most magical.

The most awesome is Iguazu, my favorite spot on the planet.

I fell in love with Iguazu the moment I saw her, thundering between Brazil and Argentina, and have remained faithful ever since. She is incomparably stunning, thrilling, and enchanting.

I'd reached her from Rio de Janeiro after a long and enervating bus trip, expecting to stay half a day. I stayed three days, mesmerized. I saw her first from the rim, almost two miles wide, over which she seemed to suck into herself the entirety of the region's rainfall and hurl it 270 feet over the basalt cap of the Paraná Plateau in 275 different drops, between which only tiny tufts of clinging grass survived.

After soaking up that remarkable sight for several hours, I clambered down a long metal walkway that merged into stairs that descended to a small island in the river at the base of the falls, where water came crashing down on three sides, its vapor rising 500 feet. I just sat there on a solitary bench in the jungle, not another person in sight, and stared, eyes wide in wonder, mouth open in astonishment, ears filled with the relentless roar, basking in the gentle mist, hour upon hour. It's like no other place on earth. Small wonder that when Eleanor Roosevelt first saw Iguazu, she exclaimed, "Poor Niagara!"

You may not be aware of it, but you have also probably seen Iguazu—in many movies: *Moonraker, The Mission, Miami Vice, Mr. Magoo.* And those are just the Ms.

Don't settle for the film version. If you only come face-to-face with one great place before you kick the bucket, make it Iguazu. And don't be surprised if you find me there, relaxing at the base of the falls, in the shade of a tropical hardwood, surrounded by misted orchids and butterflies, looking up in blissful exaltation. I'm heading back as soon as I can.

Some 500 miles farther north, in Venezuela, towers Angel Falls, the planet's longest uninterrupted plunge of water. I'd always assumed this moniker derived from the conceit that its lofty heights were home to the heavenly hosts; it wasn't until I got there that I learned it was named after an aviator, Jimmie Angel, who, in the 1930s, crashed his small plane two miles away, survived the wreck, discovered the falls, spread the word to the world, and got himself immortalized.

The setting is spectacular: The Churun River pours over the flat-topped plateau of the Guiana Highlands of southwest Venezuela straight down the smooth escarpment of Devil's Mountain into some of the world's thickest jungle, 2,648 unbroken feet down, down, down.

Not many miles away murmur the magical, miniature waterfalls of Canaima. They form a sparkling tiara in an idyllic, isolated region near Venezuela's southeastern border with Brazil and Guyana, in Canaima National Park, the globe's sixth largest such preserve, the size of Maryland, a rugged, unspoiled, barely populated wilderness of towering rock plateaus called *tepuis* that rise hundreds of feet straight up from the jungle valley, yet look like midgets beside the mountains of the Roraima range, which terminate 3,000 to 9,000 feet higher. These are among the oldest rocks on our planet, formed in the Precambrian era, and now riddled and scarred by eons of erosion, with gullies, sinkholes, and gorges hundreds of feet deep.

What I found most enchanting about the diminutive group of falls, none more than 50 feet high, which the locals called Hacha, Wadaima, Ucaima, and Golondrina—is that I could safely go *behind* them. To another world.

I'd slink out of my hammock shamefully late every morning and, after a breakfast of the juiciest mangoes and sweetest bananas, splash through the knee-high waters of the Canaima Lagoon toward this irregular arc of shimmering showers, pick my way along a strip of rock to the edge of a falls, then rush through the thinner curtain of plunging spume at its side to enter an intimate, cave-like compartment scooped out behind the falling water. I'd stand there and hear nothing but the water's roar all about me. I could see no sky, no ground, no trees, nothing but a blue-white curtain of pure frothy water crashing down an arm's length away. Everything else was blocked out. I was alone in an enchanted realm where I could dream and drift and watch and wonder in devout adoration of nature's power and majesty.

## BAD TIMING IN BELIZE

It was, as have been so many disasters in my life, the fault of a beautiful woman, or—to put it more accurately and less chauvinistically—of my adolescent, but lifelong, obsession with beautiful women.

She was an Israeli, divorced, stunning, and sublimely sensual. I'd met her via one of the personal ads I'd answered in my wilder days. After dating for a month, we flew to Cancun and drove down the Coastal Highway to dive the reef off Belize. Or so we thought until we reached its border, where the guards refused to let her across because she had an Israeli passport with no Belizean visa, a visa that I, as a U.S. citizen, did not need.

I was confronted with a dilemma of deprivation: either leave my love at the border for several days, or skip the scuba. After much consternation and cogitation, chivalry triumphed—the more cynical would think sex—and I retreated with my lady to Cancun and the noisy scene at Señor Frog's.

I next had the opportunity to visit Belize four years later, again in the friendly company of an exquisite woman, this time a Russian, this time *with* a visa. And again I almost didn't make it. We left from Cancun, driving a rented VW Beetle. I'd promised to show her the ancient Maya sites along the way; therefore, after making the customary tourist stop at the walled city of Tulum, I cut west and south through the Yucatán jungles along the Campeche Triangle to wow her with Uxmal and other ancient temples at Quintana Roo, Kabah, and Xlapak—none yet discovered by Spell Checker.

The girl was a total free spirit, a ravishing 20-year-old red-haired wild child who loved to take off all her clothes in the jungles and among the ancient ruins. If other tourists were about, she didn't give a fig, or a fig leaf.

Strolling through a lush jungle with an enchantingly carefree hard-bodied young beauty gamboling about, totally naked and glistening with the moisture of rainy-season sprinkles, did *not* make me eager to head back to the car and resume driving. I might put the pedal to the metal, but not in any way that'd get me closer to Belize.

I'd not yet taken my vow to visit every nation, but I *did* want to dive Belize. Therefore, at great personal sacrifice, we staggered into Belize City ten days after we left Cancun, surely an anti-record for that distance. But I was guided by the old Cunard Line slogan: "Getting there is half the fun."

Unfortunately, we got there too late for the other half. While we'd been busy canoodling, and only cursorily noting the extensive rain, Belize had been hit by Hurricane Keith, which covered its reefs with sand. A direct hit by a hurricane was an uncommon event there. Most such storms form off the African coast at about the same latitude as Belize, then start heading west, and eventually veer north; Belize is consequently rarely hit, the previous big one being Hattie, way back in 1961.

I was disappointed. I had dived all over the warmer world—Cozumel, Crete, Grand Cayman, the Red Sea, the Indian Ocean, the Great Barrier Reef—and I'd been looking forward to this reef Darwin called "the most remarkable in the West Indies." It's part of the 560-mile-long Mesoamerican Barrier Reef, the planet's second largest such aggregation, and featured 35 species of soft coral, 70 hard coral, and more than 500 species of fish. But few were visible when we were there. We tried Ambergris Caye, Half Moon, Rendezvous, and the Great Blue Hole, but all we saw was Keith-stirred sand covering and smothering everything, a sad sight for someone who loves reefs.

### AFLOAT IN TITICACA

For an otherworldly experience, it's hard to top the islands of the Uros Indians that float in the heart of Lake Titicaca. Their inhabitants are unique among the world's people in that they *create* the land on which they build their houses. Only the Dutch, with their formidable dikes, and the Dubaians, with their sand-dredged islands shaped like gigantic palm trees, do anything similar, but where they used soil and sand, the Indians used weeds.

Lake Titicaca is the earth's highest commercially navigable lake and the largest lake in South America. (Maracaibo does not technically count as a lake because it's attached to the ocean.) Titicaca is a chilly 12,500 feet above sea level, has a maximum depth of 900 feet, and sits astride the boundary between Bolivia and Peru, on the northern end of the endorheic Altiplano basin. It is the sacred lake of the Incas, the legendary birthplace of the first Inca king, and the watery womb from whose depths emerged their god, Viracocha, to create the sun, the stars, the humans, and, you know, do the whole Genesis thing.

In a clever instance of one-upmanship, the Uros Indians claim to predate the Incas, insisting they lived on the lake when the earth was still unformed and darkness was upon the face of the waters. Hard to say who wins that one, yet the Incas, despite their mighty stone temples and mountaintop redoubts, have long since vanished, while the lowly Uros still survive, two thousand strong, on their humble life rafts, which vary from the size of a soccer pitch to the acreage of three large football fields.

The Uros, bundled up in layers of wool clothing (topped by felt fedoras for the ladies) to protect them from the ever-present cold, the harsh Altiplano wind that sweeps across the lake, and the damaging rays of the high-altitude sun, were extremely welcoming when I and my traveling companion—tall, blonde, blue-eyed, short-shorts-sporting Jamie—disembarked after our two-hour boat ride from Puno. Some of the Uros men were so taken with Jamie that, had she but asked, they would have built her an island of her own.

Walking on these islands was not like anything else on earth. It's akin to striding across a water bed, except that you don't usually get your feet wet on a water bed or risk plunging through to your knees into 50-degree wetness. It feels a bit like hiking atop the quaking sands in the Everglades or the Okefenokee, but with a lot more bounce and no gators.

The Uros constructed these 40 artificial islands in the shallow parts of Titicaca, using the abundant stands of *totura,* a cattail-type, hollow, buoyant reed with thick roots. They pull up extensive mats of *totura* and lay them atop the sturdy living reeds that serve as a foundation, then build their homes atop those mats, regularly replacing the trampled weeds with fresh layers. Their boats and homes are constructed from the same reeds, giving the low treeless topography a monochromatic straw-colored hue.

As a safety measure against a campfire conflagration, the Uros had imported a few medium-sized rocks from the mainland to serve as insulating platforms for their cook stoves. Very few such rocks. Because the Uros know that people who live in grass houses shouldn't stow stones.

## GOING DOWN THE AMAZON

My first trip down the Amazon was the most difficult because none of us had any idea what we were doing.

I'd made a deal with girlfriend Jamie to take her camping through the Peruvian Amazon if she'd brush up on her high school Spanish and handle the linguistics. It was a no-go from the get-go. She got us completely lost leaving the airport at Arequipa when she confused the direction *al frente* with *enfrente,* and it got worse from there. I got so frustrated that I yelled at her, which made her cry and refuse to try any more translating.

We eventually found our way to Iquitos, a bustling Amazon port more than 1,800 miles upriver from the Atlantic Ocean, which I'd picked as a good put-in point. I proceeded to search for, and attempt, in my pathetic pidgin Spanish, to arrange with someone who owned a safe boat with a powerful outboard to take us on a weeklong cruise downriver and back.

I finally found a skinny kid of about 20 ferrying a load of bananas to Iquitos from the far side of the river in a sturdy, canoe-shaped, square-sterned, shallow-draft craft some 30 feet long. We agreed to meet dockside the next morning and commence our seven-day adventure.

I was puzzled when he showed up for departure with only the clothes on his body, and when I had to insist that we stop at the riverside gas station and fill up an entire 50-gallon drum. But it was not until nightfall, when the kid began to hyperventilate and Jamie condescended to translate, that our misunderstanding was revealed: He thought that I had hired him to take us on seven *separate* one-day jaunts on the rivers around Iquitos instead of one long, continuous trip. Even worse, he was strictly a cross-river ferryman who had never sailed more than half a day downriver in his life, had no idea where he was, and had no map, no compass, and no sense of direction.

I did have all those, so I told him, through Jamie, to calm down, and assured him that I'd get him safely back to his home within a week, ten days tops, as long as he kept the engine running. I marked the 50-gallon drum to keep track of our gas consumption, gauged the strength and speed of the current, and reckoned we'd need two days to chug back upriver for every day we went down.

And so we continued down our planet's second longest river, a tea-colored torrent of silt and rotted vegetation in that rainy season, so wide that we often could not see either side, which can be 30 miles away during the wet season (less than six miles during the dry season). So much water flows down the Amazon, which drains most of the rain forests of South America, that its discharge is greater than that of the world's next seven largest rives combined! Twenty percent of all the fresh water entering all earth's oceans came from the Amazon in those benign days before the polar ice started melting.

I had a great time. But Captain Kid was scared for the whole trip, especially when I coaxed him out of the main river to explore some of the tributaries, and then some of their channels. He absolutely drew the line when I asked him to take us down a drainage ditch. Poor Jamie vacillated from fascination to fright.

We saw leaping Amazon river dolphins, and manatees in clear pools, and we exchanged friendly waves with the scores of boats coming upriver each day. I bartered for fruits and vegetables with the few farmers who were trying to eke out a living along the riverbank, giving them sewing kits, cigarettes, candles, matches, and salt I'd brought along for this purpose; cash did one little good so far from civilization. We also bartered for tasty fillets of fresh river tilapia; a bit of beef; gigantic, mud-colored, mud-tasting catfish;

and some monkey meat, all of which we roasted at night over driftwood fires laid in pits we'd dug in riverside sandbars. Jamie and I slept in my tent and one night on the wide porch of a hospitable local whose first floor was built on poles 20 feet above the flood-prone ground. We never lacked for a variety of fresh food, and the river provided all the water we needed once we'd popped in purification pills.

The seasonally flooded forest (called *várzea*) through which we sometimes drifted, and the capacious jungles behind it, contained one-third of all the species of creatures on earth. We awakened daily to a kaleidoscope of curious butterflies and an enchanting symphony of chirps, warbles, caws, grunts, whistles, tweets, hums, howls, and ardent early morning mating calls, nature's paean to the dawning day. I was in my element, happy as a coonhound off the leash and on the scent.

One afternoon, in a stream no more than chest height and relatively clear, I impulsively did something that might seem stupid. (Okay, it *was* stupid.) I jumped overboard to wash off a week's accumulation of sweat and grime, then grabbed the knotted rope that trailed behind the boat and let it carry me lazily along for an hour under a sheltering canopy of tropical trees.

Captain Kid freaked out and kept excitedly gesturing for me to get back in, but I was pretty sure I was safe. I doubted that any bull sharks wandered this far from the ocean, and I'd tested the stream for carnivorous piranha by dangling a piece of meat over the side. I had, however, forgotten about the anacondas that lurked by these streams. When I saw a 15-footer slither along the grassy bank toward me, I quickly pulled back into the canoe.

It was a wonderful trip, my kind of trip, and I've returned to the Amazon for many more.

PLAYING WITH PENGUINS

I never swam in colder water. But it was worth it.

Amy—Jamie's successor—and I had sailed from Guayaquil to visit the Galápagos Islands, an archipelago of volcanic peaks, made famous by Darwin, that straddles the Equator 600 miles west of Ecuador. They lie directly in the path of the frigid Humboldt Current, which lowers the ambient water temperature to 74 degrees, rather nippy for lengthy immersion. The Galápagos are 97.5 percent national parks, plus a protected marine reserve that was our goal. Most visitors come to see the giant tortoises, iguanas, and Darwin's famous finches, but we went to frolic with the seals and play with the penguins.

We had no room in our luggage for wet suits, but had squeezed in thin dive skins, although whatever insulation they provided against the cold waters was probably a placebo effect—and a barely perceptible one. We plodded backward into the crystalline waters in our flippers and masks, watched by a curious audience of waved (but not waving) albatross, great frigate birds, and a family of blue-footed boobys.

As soon as we submerged, the brilliantly multicolored crabs clinging to the underwater rocks scurried from us and a Galápagos green turtle furiously paddled away. The dark marine iguanas ignored us while chowing down on seaweed attached to partly submerged rocks, the only members of the genus *Amblyrhynchus* to sup at sea. But we did not lack for companions: A raft of penguins and a pod of seals came to cavort.

The Galápagos penguin is the only surviving tropical penguin, and they peacefully swam right beside and below us, as if we were regular members of their raft. (A pack of penguins at sea is a raft, on land a waddle, on their nests a rookery, and their newborns constitute a crèche.)

The Galápagos sea lions, famous for their curiosity, took the opposite tack from the birds and swam directly *at* us, fast-moving, living brown torpedoes, heading right into our face masks, veering away only at the last second, just as we were sure they'd collide with us. Were they trying to scare us? Play with us? Or adopt us?

I can't say whether our aquatic playmates enjoyed us as much as we enjoyed them, but their close camaraderie was like none I'd ever experienced in the wild. I profoundly felt at one with nature and its fauna, kindred spirits sharing a pleasant afternoon by the seaside, a warm, tender, primordial feeling of belonging together on our pale blue dot.

MEDICAL MILESTONE

All these watery immersions gave rise to a condition that, though bothersome, did enable me to advance medical science—by inventing a procedure for alleviating *tinea cruris*, an irritating fungal infection centered in the groin area and commonly called jock itch. It's distantly related to *tinea pedis*, which is also better known as athlete's foot. (But if you have some athlete's foot in your groin area, you're much too hardcore for this family-friendly book.)

Since this malady thrives in hot, moist climes, I reasoned that the obvious way to ameliorate it was to subject it to a chilling and drying effect. To this end, I traversed much of Central America buck naked, balanced on the running board of the Expedition's Land Cruiser, my right leg spread out wide, letting the cooling breeze caress the afflicted zone. (I'm not sure whether this technique would work for a woman as I lacked the proper test equipment.) I have no photographic proof of perfecting this efficacious technique because Steve was not able to simultaneously drive and take pictures—which *must* be the reason the U.S. Patent Office rejected my application to commercialize this technique. (If you want to try this at home, do so only at night, on unpopulated rural roads, and in regions where your outstretched leg is not likely to collide with an oxcart or a jackass.)

Don't have a running board on your car? No problem: Just undress and snuggle next to the AC on max. Be careful not to overdo it and cause frostbite. A frostbitten appendage is not a pleasant sight, nor easy to cure, as I unfortunately had occasion to research one cold and stormy evening in Chamonix after skiing Mont Blanc at a windchilly 40 below. I located an article in a medical journal whose physician/author advised against the old-fashioned method of hopping into a hot tub, warning that the sudden increase in temperature might damage the family jewels. The good fellow recommended gently slipping the frozen member into something soft, lubricious, and at body temperature—and keeping it there for about two hours.

A touch of *tinea cruris* was hardly the worst affliction acquired on my travels. I've dearly paid my dues: I tore a hamstring in a glacial crevasse during a rescue operation; broke two ribs after I slipped off a cliff and landed chest-first across a felled tree trunk; broke another rib in a freak accident in Casablanca; tore the rotator cuff in each arm in high-speed ski accidents; contracted a paralyzing case of Lyme disease from the bite of a deer tick; required rescue during a disabling bout of nitrogen narcosis when a malfunctioning depth gauge led me down to 160 feet when diving off Curaçao; almost lost my left arm in Canada when a drug-resistant strain of staph took up housekeeping in my elbow following a nasty bicycling fall; and contracted that virulent case of giardiasis in India that knocked 25 pounds off my weight in three weeks—and saved my life from the lynch mob.

I also sliced my kneecap to the bone when my motorcycle skidded in a sand drift at the bottom of a steep hill on Aruba, which presented me with yet another opportunity to advance medical science with a brilliant technique for cleaning and disinfecting a wound with chlorine when no first-aid kit is handy: I searched for the nearest unpopulated backyard and jumped into their swimming pool.

# CHAPTER 8

## "Just Call Me God"

In this chapter, I'll let God speak for himself. But first, a bit of background.

God was the fourth of 13 children born to a poor fisherman and his fishmonger wife in a tiny village on the coast of Togo. God grew up in Ghana, educated himself as best he could, and, after his parents died when he was 19, took many lowly jobs to provide food and shelter for Bernard, his youngest brother, and himself, until he advanced to become a tour guide.

I was not aware of any of this, nor was I a happy camper, when I first met him in November of 2003 in the steamy, crowded airport terminal in Cotonou, the seat of government in Benin. I was exhausted after 23 hours of traveling from New York, and I knew my luggage had missed the Air France flight when I changed planes in Paris, because the baggage handlers at Charles de Gaulle Airport had called one of their periodic wildcat strikes. Moreover, I had serious misgivings about taking a tour, something I rarely do and usually hate. I'll only purchase a tour if I'm totally ignorant of the language in a large country where few speak any language I can comprehend (e.g., Kazakhstan, Uzbekistan, and 1980s China), or if the country required me to book one to obtain a visa (e.g., North Korea and Bhutan). This tour was different: I'd been seduced by a promo piece promising an in-depth cultural tour of the "Golden Kingdoms"—Benin, Togo, and Ghana—with an emphasis on voodoo, funeral rites, and slavery, an irresistible trifecta of creepiness.

A smiling, sweating giant of about 40, dressed like a game warden, greeted me: "Welcome to Benin, Mr. Albert. I am your guide, Godfried Peters Agbezudor, owner of Continent Explorer. But you can just call me God."

We drove toward our hotel to catch a few hours of sleep before an early departure for a two-day drive to a voodoo sacrificial site 330 kilometers north of Cotonou in that Kansas-sized country of nine million. I asked God about voodoo and, as he waxed ecstatic, I extracted my microcassette recorder from my carry-on bag and turned it on:

"Voodoo is a very serious religion all across West Africa. It is the worship of the natural things around you, how to make peace with them, like the thunder, fire, the wind, and rain, even smallpox. My father was a voodoo priest, and the oracle chose me to be the next one. I am a reincarnate of my father's father's father. I got the voodoo religion when I was a boy, going with my grandfather and father from ceremony to ceremony. At 21, grandfather initiated me into the high priesthood. I was taught how to call unto my ancestors, how to sacrifice, how to call upon the spirit of the elders, to chat with them. When I speak to the elders they reply. But the reply comes back in the form of an oracle that is manipulated by shells. And this oracle is something that is done by a specialist who sits beside me whilst I perform my rites. My asking for it comes out from the village, from the family, from everyone around me who says: 'Why don't we ask this question?' "

I interrupted him, a touch rudely: "Why don't we ask the question whether my luggage is likely to arrive from Paris before we leave here tomorrow?"

"No, that is not a question for the elders," he replied without taking offense. "I have spoken with Air France, and it will arrive tomorrow night. I'll arrange for my brother to get it and drive after us, so you will have it within two days. We should not wait for it. We need to get to the pilgrimage site to arrive at an auspicious day for making the sacrifice."

Apostate that I am, I asked him if he was sure the strikers in Paris were not making a sacrifice of my luggage.

"We take sacrifice very seriously here," he replied, still smiling, still without the stern rebuke I deserved. "I sacrifice first to the almighty God,

Godfried Peters Agbezudor—"Just call me God."—owner of Continent Explorer in Ghana, exits the barber shop where we had just gotten the best one-dollar haircuts available in Lome, the capital of Togo.

because the voodoo religion teaches that there is one omnipotent God. And this God created man and the voodoos. The voodoos have supernatural powers that man cannot see, unless they reveal themselves. When we make sacrifices we pass it through them because they have easy access to the almighty God. When we need to send a message, we call on the spirits of the voodoos to take this message through our ancestors and then to our almighty God. The voodoo spirits are never wrong. They may not tell you exactly what to do. They may tell you to go ask this person because he is authorized to give that answer. You may find your answer, or you have to keep looking."

I had visions that I'd have to keep looking for my luggage for the next two weeks, a long time to hang in a hot, humid climate with one T-shirt, one Jockey, and a pair of bush pants.

God explained that he was going to sacrifice to thank the powers for helping him get his own tour company and the ability to earn far more than the average Beninese, a third of whom earned less than the poverty level of $1.25 a day in a land where the average GDP was below $1,300 a year—less than a quarter of what I was paying God for this one fourteen-day trip. (Benin is one of the 48 poorest states in the global economy, peoples so shockingly impoverished that *the combined annual GDPs of those 48 poorest nations is less than the combined net worth of the three richest men in America*! And that is not a typo.)

We pulled into the hotel parking lot and, as I exited the old Land Cruiser, I noticed, in the backseat, two trussed-up somnolent chickens.

"God, why do we have two chickens in the backseat?"

"For the first sacrifice."

"Why don't we just buy a couple of chickens when we get there?"

"Because the voodoo religion requires me to talk to them for three days."

"About what?"

"I am required to explain to them why I am going to kill them."

And so, for the next two days, as we drove north on a bouncy two-lane tarred road toward the Dankoli Pilgrimage Site, I sat in the car in my same sweated-through clothes and listened to my tour leader explain to the two doomed birds that he had to sacrifice them to thank the gods for rewarding him with his own touring company, of which—lucky me!—I was his first client.

We left the humid, marshy, coastal region of long lagoons connected to the sea, passed through a hundred-mile stretch of undulating plains dotted with forest remnants in a savannah mosaic of thorn scrub and big baobab trees, and, after two days, reached a low plateau of flat land bordered by deforested, rocky brown hills, while God continually talked to the chickens, and the chickens continually pooped all over the car.

"God," I asked, "is it really necessary to explain your motive to the chickens over and over?"

"Very necessary," he replied. "Sacrifice is not that you get an animal and just cut the throat and let the blood spill out. You first talk to the animal. You have to consistently explain the reason why you are going to sacrifice it. You have to keep talking to it until you are sure the animal has got the message, because the first splash of the blood from the animal carries the message that has been introduced to this animal for the past three days or more. And this blood is going to go through the object on which this animal has been sacrificed and goes out into the world that is unknown to you and I."

"Are these regular chickens, like from the butcher shop?"

"We do not get our chickens from any shop. Every family raises a few chickens. For sacrifice we get a chicken from our own family. Always a male, a rooster. Never brown. Black chickens when we want to invite the spirits of the dead to listen. For my sacrifice, white is the right color."

"But why a rooster?"

"To send a message you need the proper animal. It could be a chicken, a sheep, a cow, a horse. Or a dog, because dogs are security; they watch while the owner sleeps. It will be sacrificed to the guardian god of a village. And dogs are special when it comes to messages. They run faster than anything, and they carry the message because they are the first link with humans. Different situations require different animals. If you are having a disaster in your family, you need at least a male sheep. We sacrifice sheep to Shango, the god of thunder. He is the giver of law, like a judge who raps his stick to make noise to command attention. If you killed somebody, which is against the laws of voodoo if you did not kill for a good reason, and you have been punished by the gods, offering a chicken will not be enough ransom for your guilt. The gods will tell you what animal you should sacrifice for your sin to be washed away. It may start from a cow—from one to two or three."

"God, we have a crucial election coming up in my country and I don't want our president to be reelected. I was planning to donate, as I always do, several thousand dollars to my political party when I get home, but maybe I should, instead, get a goat, talk to it for three days, and cut its throat?"

Without realizing I was joking, he replied, "No, I am sure a goat is not enough to get rid of a president. You will have to promise the gods *at least* ten cows. But do not sacrifice all the cows in advance. Start with two cows. As the election gets closer, two more. Then, if that politician is defeated, you must quickly sacrifice the other six cows."

(Unfortunately, I never got around to killing those cows, instead wasting my money on my political party, and my dear country ended up with "four more years" of that president and its worst recession in 80 years.)

On our third evening Bernard reached our campsite with my luggage, for which he'd been compelled to pay a "commission" to the baggage clerk of $100. Petty corruption of this sort is rampant in Africa, and Benin was no exception. It was beset with corruption and the typical problems of many African states: insufficient electric power, a weak business climate, chronically high unemployment, low literacy, high infant mortality (203 deaths per 1,000 births), inadequate potable water, limited natural resources (only some limestone, marble, and timber), underdeveloped subsistence agriculture, few food-processing facilities, overreliance on one crop (cotton, which constituted 40 percent of its GDP, 80 percent of export earnings), low wages for women workers, child labor, forced labor, an unreliable land tenure system, a rudimentary commercial justice system, game poaching, deforestation, desertification, a large external debt, little tourism, and a woeful shortage of cash.

But Benin, the first in that continent of 54 states to ever make a peaceful transfer of power from a dictatorship to a democracy, had resolved to deal with these problems and give its citizens tangible benefits of their democracy, and it was making progress toward that goal.


As we were nearing northernmost Benin, I asked God why we had to drive so far to make a sacrifice.

"It is very, very necessary to go to specific points where sacrifices are done. You cannot just sit somewhere and say, I am sacrificing. In our societies we have various altars, and each sacrifice has a specific place to go," he answered.

The roosters woke us the next morning at the first hint of dawn. God fed them, and the condemned pair ate a hearty last meal while he again explained the necessity for their impending demise.

We drove a few miles and pulled over at an unmarked and unremarkable spot that only the initiated knew. We followed a well-worn path up a hummock, then down, then up to a capacious fly-covered mound of animal parts, feathers, bottles, handwritten notes, papers, and other sacrificial objects, invisible from the road.

"Do you know why we have two roosters?" God asked me.

"Backup?" I ventured. "In case one escapes?"

"Not exactly. There are two kinds of blood sacrifices. One when the animal is shared as a communion with everybody. You take a piece of the meat to eat. The second is a sacrifice that goes only to the gods. Nobody touches it, not even the feathers or the fur; it goes out whole onto the altar. I am going to make both kinds now because I want Continent Explorer to be successful. It is very important to me, my son, my family, our future."

He untied the legs of the first bird and held it at shoulder height. "For this bird," he said, "I will cut its throat and sprinkle its blood on the pile. After three minutes he will be dead. And we will keep him. And Bernard will cook him for our dinner tonight."

And so it was done.

"But this other one is only for the gods. We will not take it. We will leave it all for them. And I will sacrifice it in a different way. No knife for him. I will pull out his tongue. And the bird will bleed to death. Also in three minutes."

And so it was done.


In a remote Upper East region of Ghana, I had an unexpectedly provocative experience. We were in the Tongo Hills, ten miles southeast of the regional capital of Bolgatanga, hiking a thousand vertical feet to the Tengzug shrine, a cave at the top of the hill that contained the most revered oracle in the land. After an hour of sweaty scrambling up the bare gray rocks—relieved by the shade from hundreds of thin, twisted trees whose radiant whitish trunks grew from cracks in the boulders—we were about 30 minutes from the top. A guard stopped us, as he did the other pilgrims and tourists, and told them that if they wished to proceed farther, they had to remove all clothing and jewelry above the waist, the disrobing to show purity in the presence of the spirits, the abandonment of adornment so as not to compete with the gods.

I was fascinated by the reaction of the foreign females, teenage to elderly, many of whom, judging from those reactions, had never been to a nudist beach or ever gone skinny-dipping. I sat near the guard and observed the scene for half an hour in the company of several dozen native idlers who had lots of time on their hands and a little lust in their hearts. I watched as each woman wrestled with this Hobson's choice: *Do I, after all my planning, spending, driving, and climbing, abort my visit to the famous cave, or do I, for the first time in my life, strut topless before dozens of strange men?*

We drove south from the Tongo Hills and reached the torrid, muggy Ghanaian coast in three days, there to inspect a brutal remnant of man's inhumanity to man: Elmina Castle, the oldest surviving European building south of the Sahara, keystone of the Triangular Slave Trade.

When the Portuguese constructed Elmina in 1482—with the help of a young Italian sailor named Christopher Columbus, whose ship brought some of its building blocks from Lisbon—it served as a trading post, the first in Africa. After gold was discovered nearby, Elmina shipped, during the early 1500s, close to 24,000 ounces a year. As the precious metal petered out, the traders began buying slaves from neighboring African chiefs. Then, reaching farther, they bought slaves from the king of Dahomey (now Benin) on what they called the Slave Coast. Then, farther still, they purchased those captured by Arab slavers in Niger and Mali; and, finally, they bought from victorious warrior tribes all over West Africa those enemy captives that had not been killed.

Thus began the highly lucrative triangular trade, where enormous profits were made by the nation that controlled it—first the Portuguese, then the Dutch, finally the British.

When the slaves arrived in that New World they were bartered for the locally grown sugar, rice, coffee, tobacco, cotton, molasses, and rum. This produce was then shipped to Europe, to be exchanged for copper, textiles, glass, pots, guns, and ammunition that were, in turn, shipped to Elmina and the other forts to pay for yet more slaves, with a profit made on each leg. And on it went, for 300 years, until ten million had been torn from their families and villages.

According to Godfried, up to half of those captured died on their long forced marches—sometimes a thousand miles—to Elmina, to Cape Coast Castle, and to the other holding pens we visited. Another third are estimated to have perished inside those slave fortresses as a result of poor food, unsanitary conditions, and inadequate ventilation, while awaiting shipment to the New World.

The barred cells and the "Door of No Return," through which the slaves exited the prison to board the ships for the Middle Passage, were ineffably sad, but I found Elmina's most monstrous feature to be the Governor's Balcony, from which the fort's commander looked down on the assembled female slaves and chose the most desirable to be brought, through a secret passage, to his bedroom. Anyone who refused his advances was shackled to one of the large black cannon balls we saw, and left in the open sun of the courtyard without food or water until she died, a warning to other reluctant women. (Rebellious male slaves and captured pirates were also starved to death, but confined in a small room.)

If the chosen female acquiesced to the governor's amorous embraces, she entered a deadly game of reproductive roulette. If she did not become pregnant before the governor tired of her, she was shipped out as a slave. If she became obviously pregnant before the next slaver sailed, she was saved and thereafter treated as a wife of the governor, and her child was raised as his, with a full education in a special schoolroom. But if her pregnancy did not become apparent until she was at sea, then, to conceal the governor's tampering with the merchandise, she was tossed overboard.

God's brochure had promised human funerals, and he provided three. I was tempted to ask how he arranged them to coincide with our schedule but, after having seen what he'd done to the roosters, thought better of it.

The first funeral was for a poor rural fellow, the second for a wealthy family leader. God noted that those attending the first were all from the decedent's tribe, whereas mourners of many tribes came to pay respect at the funeral of the big shot.

I asked how he knew that.

"By the scarification on their faces. In most of Africa, members of the different tribes are scarred in their faces as children in different designs. Their faces are cut with a knife, and salt is rubbed into the cuts to prevent smooth healing. The Yoruba have three horizontal scars on each side of the cheek. The Bariba have four long scars on the women and three on the men, all running from their temples to the bottom of their faces. Fulani women have blue tattoos around the mouth, and so on." (I had previously wondered how, when African countries were torn by their frequent civil wars, postelection riots, genocides, ethnic cleansings, or tribal conflicts, the participants could identify those they sought to kill. Now I understood.)

"Before the white man came here we had no coffins or tombstones," God continued. "We were burying our dead in straw mats, beaten cloth, or bark of trees, in sacred forests. But we have adapted to some of your ways, so most of us now use coffins and cemeteries. But we do not accept your speed. Your funerals are maybe one hour long. That is no time to respect the dead. On voodoo ground we spend at least three days for our funerals to help the dead enter into the world of their ancestors."

Our third funeral, a festive affair on Ghana's Atlantic coast, was for a member of the Ga tribe and featured the corpse in a coffin shaped and painted like a lit cigarette. The deceased loved to smoke, and a Ga coffin is designed to represent a principal aspect of the life of its occupant and serve as his or her happy home in the afterlife.

God explained that this custom originated a century ago when the fishermen who lived in Teshi village had themselves buried in caskets shaped like the hulls of their boats, and brightly painted like tropical fish. Teshi now had five workshops trying to keep up with the demand.

I visited one workshop and observed that the caskets were not crude affairs, but carefully carved and meticulously painted in flamboyant colors—a shoe for a cobbler (complete with a high shine and laces), a beer bottle for a barfly (polished to look like glass, with a Heineken label), a Mercedes-Benz for a corrupt official; for others, a Coca-Cola bottle, a pineapple, bible, camera, bird, lobster, hammer, a favorite pet. I watched the carpenters and painters finishing one for a 90-year-old grandmother who had never left her village but had long enjoyed the fantasy she would fly one day. Her many sons and grandsons had ordered built for her this remarkable coffin, a miniature jumbo jet with bright lettering proclaiming GHANA AIRWAYS.

"My choice," God said, "is a coffin shaped like my Land Cruiser. You would probably want a naked young lady with blonde hair and blue eyes and big boobies to keep you company in the next world."

These coffins cost $600, a full year's wages for most of these people, but they prefer to go into debt rather than send their ancestors to the next world in a cheap casket. As God explained, "That is what you never forget about these funerals—the coffin of the deceased. So it must be right. And it must be what the dead person would want.

"It takes three weeks to make a coffin like this," God continued, "so the body is put in the morgue for that time and kept cold. But some people select their coffin when alive, so it will be ready for them when they die. It must be kept with the carpenter until the funeral; it is bad luck to bring it home if you are alive." he told me.

I'm willing to take that risk, buddy. I've got a perfect place in my apartment for mine.

We completed our rectangular three-country tour with a visit to Lomé, the sweltering capital of Togo, where God took me to the Goro voodoo shrine to see a two-hour "happening" that combined elements of a fundamentalist tent revival meeting, a magic show, a séance, and a hot 70s night at Studio 54. Then a visit to the Lomé Fetish Market, the first, and the largest, anywhere. It was located on an out-of-the-way street lined with a hundred long tables loaded with thousands of dead animals and hundreds of thousands of animal parts: hair, paws, ears, horns, heads, skulls, tails, claws, gizzards, gonads, pickled tongues, plus tens of thousands of man-made fetish objects.

God noted: "This used to be a very small market where animal parts were sold. In the voodoo religion we need animal parts as our sacrifices. People bring dead animal parts to this place. They also bring live animals. Until 15 years ago, this was the only voodoo market in the whole of West Africa. But today you can find small ones in villages and other neighboring countries. But that of Lomé became so very known and popular to African voodoo worshipers that they travel here to buy stuff for the realization of their religion."

I purchased a matched pair of male/female voodoo dolls festooned with pins, a dark-brown sacrificial dish adorned with two raised white lizards, and a small monkey skull, all of which, I confess, I shamelessly pressed into service to gain support from the literary spirits during my writing of this book to guide it to an enthusiastic and well regarded publisher.

But, let it be clear, that even when sorely tempted, I never pulled out a chicken's tongue.

# CHAPTER 9

## So, When Is a Country Not a Country?

After visiting the Golden Kingdoms I was up to 112 countries, but still not sure what officially constituted a country or precisely how many existed. I needed to know *exactly* what makes a country a country and understand when and why a patch of land was recognized as an independent state.

Although I'd studied international relations in both college and grad school, I'd never had any personal reason to focus on what constituted a country. I just thought that a country is, well, you know, a *country*. If you're an ordinary tourist you don't usually care if you're about to visit a country, a colony, a state, a dependency, territory, condominium, tridominium, collectivity, protectorate, principality, mandate, an autonomous self-governing region, a non-self-governing territory, a trusteeship, or an amusement park. All you usually care about is whether you'll need a visa and will the place accept credit cards.

But if you've set yourself the goal of going to every *country*, you need to ascertain the accepted criteria for what qualifies as a country. And that wasn't easy. Even as reliable a source as *The Economist* concluded, in an article titled "In Quite a State," that "Any attempt to find a clear definition of a country soon runs into a thicket of exceptions and anomalies." Yet I needed to know where the goalposts were. It wasn't sufficient to accept Frank Zappa's delightful criteria: "You can't be a real country unless you have a beer and an airline—it helps if you have some kind of a football team, or some nuclear weapons, but at the very least you need a beer."

A sense of proper protocol dictated that for a place to get on, and stay on, my list of countries visited, *it had to be a country when I visited it, and remain a country,* which was far easier decided than done. This self-imposed rule meant, for example, that although I'd visited Czechoslovakia in 1969, I had to return, because it had split apart in 1993, and visit both the new Czech Republic and the new state of Slovakia. It meant that since Marshal Josip Broz Tito died a year after my 1979 visit to the fractious conglomerate called Yugoslavia— which he had held together by his force of will and arms—I had to visit each of the seven independent countries into which it broke apart. And it meant that despite my dreary visit in 1985 to the USSR (the Union of Soviet Social- ist Republics), after the Berlin Wall fell in 1990 and Communism collapsed, and those republics were no longer united or Soviet, I had to go back and visit *all 15* of the newly separated states.

It also meant—and you thought this job was easy?—I had to strike seven states, including the USSR, South Vietnam, East Germany, and the United Arab Republic, off my checklist after they ceased to exist as political entities.

I also had to hasten to complete my quest before being inundated by a tsu- nami of new nations riding the waves of self-determination, ethnic national- ism, and independence lately breaking around the globe. This encompasses the potential breakup (or breakdown) of Belgium into two separate countries, of Great Britain losing Scotland and maybe Wales, and a host of wannabes waiting in the wings: Abkhazia, Apiya, Aruba, Basque Country, Bohemia, Bougainville, Catalonia, Cook Islands, Curaçao, Greenland, Guadeloupe, Kurdistan, Martinique, Northern Cyprus, North Mali, North Nigeria, East Libya, East Congo, South Ossetia, South Yemen (aka Aden), Nagorno- Karabakh, Palestine, Padania, Pitcairn Islands, Quebec, Dagestan, Chech- nya, Sardinia, Assam, Sikkim, Nagaland, Meghalaya, Manipur, Metoram, the Sahrawi Arab Democratic Republic (aka Spanish Sahara), Somaliland, Ruri- tania, Tibet, Transnistria, Upper Yafa, and perhaps parts of Syria and Iraq.

But I could probably ignore Kugelmugel, Snake Hill, Hutt River, and other offspring of the micro-secessionist movement, as well as Tannu Tuva and

Texas (the only state to enter the U.S. by treaty, a treaty that its politicians periodically claim recognized its right to secede, despite an 1868 decision of the U.S. Supreme Court construing it otherwise).

Anyway, here we are, some 600 words later, and we still don't know what is a country. But what can you expect when more than half of them have been created since 1960?

First, let's get rid of the glib and easy answers.

No specified geographical mass makes a piece of land a country. Nauru, half the size of Staten Island, is an acknowledged country, as is San Marino, the world's oldest surviving sovereign state and constitutional republic, weighing in at a mere 24 square miles. Nor does statehood require millions of inhabitants: The world recognizes Vatican City as a country, yet it has a population of less than a thousand, and Monaco has only 36,000.

A place is *not* a country just because you live there and it has a name. Hotmail lets you register your e-mail account from its list of 242 "countries/ territories," the U.S. Department of Homeland Security visa rules contain 251 choices for "country where you live," and our Census Bureau International Data Base predicts the future population of 228 "countries." These organizations are not using the term "country" precisely; for them it's shorthand for domicile, the place you hang your hat, and includes such non-countries as Guam, Gibraltar, Greenland, and the Gaza Strip.

A place is *not* a country just because it issues its own currency; Aruba, the Netherlands Antilles, the Falkland Islands, and the Isle of Jersey all mint their own money, but are not countries. Nor is a place *disqualified* from being a state just because its national currency is that of another nation: The countries of Ecuador, El Salvador, East Timor, Marshall Islands, Micronesia, Palau, and Panama all use the U.S. dollar as the coin of their realms, just as the nations of Nauru, Kiribati and Tuvalu use the Australian dollar.

Nor do postage stamps prove statehood: Some of the most artistic stamps in my collection are issued by non-nations like Anguilla, Bermuda, Curaçao, Guadalupe, Martinique, the Tokelau Islands, St. Helena, Sarawak, Wallis and Futuna, South Georgia, Cocos Islands, Pitcairn Islands, Nova Scotia, Newfoundland, and the French Antarctic Territory. One country, Andorra, does not issue any postage stamps; it delivers the local mail for free, while relying on neighboring Spain and France to forward its foreign mail.

Diplomatic relations alone do not confer statehood, as these actions serve as recognition of the *government*, not the nation. Russia, for example, has diplomatic relations with the Georgian breakaway provinces of Abkhazia and South Ossetia, but those are far from being countries. The U.S. has refused to have diplomatic relations with the *governments* of North Korea, Iran, and (until 2015) Cuba, but that does not contradict America's acceptance of them as countries.

Membership in the UN is *almost* a reliable guide, because an entity can only be a member if it's a true country. *But,* not every true country is a UN member. Both Taiwan and Vatican City are regarded as countries, but they're not UN members, the former because the People's Republic of China challenged its status, the latter because it never applied, believing it can conduct its diplomacy more effectively by having the Holy See admitted as an "observer" at the General Assembly. Then there's Kosovo, which, as this book went to print, 112 states had formally recognized as an independent country, but which hasn't been admitted to UN membership because of opposition from Serbia, which lays claim to it, and Russia, which supports Serbia and wields veto power.

For more than 80 years, the guiding document has been the 1933 Montevideo Convention, which sets forth the four criteria for statehood: a permanent population, a defined territory, a government, and capacity to enter into relations with the other states. (A fifth, implicit, requirement is that the entity must seek to be regarded and treated as a state.) These criteria would allow an entity like Taiwan to be accepted as a state, but it has been thwarted in its attempts to do so.

The Convention forbids the use of military force to obtain sovereignty, yet at least 40 now-recognized nations have resorted to military force to overthrow their colonial masters. The Convention also excludes puppet states, yet this ban proved ineffective when the Iron Curtain descended across Eastern Europe after WW II and all the puppets of the Soviet Union were treated as countries.

If we look to political philosophy, we are confronted by two contradictory systems. The declarative theory of statehood holds that the political existence of the state is independent of recognition by the other states, but the constitutive theory maintains that a state exists *only* insofar as it is recognized by other states. Everybody clear?

So where are we? Well, I'm counting, as true countries, the 193 members of the UN, plus Taiwan, Vatican City, and Kosovo: thus, 196. (The question of whether Kosovo is legally a country recently came before the International Court of Justice, which had a once-in-a-generation opportunity to clarify the broad question of statehood. But the Court punted and never responded to the basic issue, instead holding, on July 22, 2010, that "international law has no prohibition on a territory issuing a declaration of independence," which is nice to know, but hardly a responsive answer.)

Now that I've defined two of the three words in my plan to "visit every country," my lawyerly inclinations lead me to elucidate on the third: *visit*. Since there are no rules in this sport, no international body promulgating standards, a visit could theoretically range from a minute to a lifetime. I have spent from one day to one week in every nation's capital, except for Dushanbe, the capital of Tajikistan, and traveled across the country in at least one direction in about 90 percent of the nations, the notable exceptions being Argentina, Brazil, China, and Russia, which are just too big to completely cross in enough time to still have a legal practice and a rent-stabilized apartment to come home to. I only dipped a toe in the DRC, where a band of child soldiers was killing anyone who entered the contested zone in the east; Nigeria, when Boko Haram was not welcoming Westerners; Sudan, where the government strictly confined me to the area around Khartoum; and Tajikistan, where I was trapped on a tour that only spent one day there, out in the boonies.

Furthest short of my goal had been Equatorial Guinea (EG), a rich but nasty little dictatorship with one of the worst human rights records. When I was ready for it, in 2003, it was not ready for me. Its government was not allowing visitors because it was heated up and worried about the trial of 13 mercenaries who allegedly plotted to overthrow the government. Not to be thwarted by a little formality like the lack of a visa, I flew south over EG to

A Ugandan gracefully carries a pile of tree bark on her head. African women expertly transport loads approaching 90 pounds in this manner, from oranges to buckets of water. In my 15 trips to Africa, I never saw any one of them drop or spill anything. *Gorilla Highlands*

Libreville in Gabon, then endured a jolting eight-hour ride back north on a terribly rutted dirt road to a part of Gabon that shared a watery border with EG. I prevailed upon an unsuspecting fisherman who had a little dinghy with a 5 hp outboard to take me across to the opposite shore, where I quickly hopped out, ran around, kissed the Guinean ground, smeared a bit of it in my passport, leaped back in the dinghy, and got the hell out of there. That was the best I could do, but I vowed to return legally once it permitted visits. (And did so in 2014, from July 9 to 13.)

Since I am not one of those rich yacht-owning guys who compete with each other for their self-created title of "The World's Most Traveled Man," I confess that I have not visited every one of the 7,107 islands in the Philippine Archipelago, or all the 17,508 islands and islets constituting Indonesia, but I've made my share of risky voyages on their rickety interisland ferries you read about in the back pages of the *Times:* "Ship Sinks in Suva Sea, 400 Presumed Lost."

I usually cross a country by bus, car, minivan, or bush taxi, but I crossed a handful by train (Italy, Switzerland, Moldova, Byelorussia, Ukraine, Romania, and Greece), two by river steamer (Gabon and Germany), Norway via coastal steamer, the Gambia and the Amazonian parts of Peru and Ecuador by motorized canoe, half of Burma by motor scooter, and I rode completely around Jamaica by motorcycle and Nauru by bicycle. I've also crossed three small countries by foot (to wit, Vatican City, San Marino, and Liechtenstein), and parts of others by horse, camel, elephant, llama, and donkey.

So, now that we know where we are, let's get back on the road.

# CHAPTER 10

## Doing God's Work

When I reached 129 countries, after plucking much of the low-hanging fruit, I again joined forces with God. I had so enjoyed his company, his delight in travel, his easygoing nature, sense of humor, facility with French patois, and his efforts and ambition to make a better life for himself and his family, that I decided to take another trip with God on my side. But this trip was to be different: I'd be the guide and God the guest. I'd be doing God's work.

Since God was still growing his business and had no spare cash, I'd offered to pay for the trip, which he liked, and to take him to several West African countries he'd never seen, and thus expand his range, which he liked. I'd study the route and the means of transportation, which he liked, and I'd select the camps and hotels where we stayed, which God did *not* like at all after he realized that my standard for what constituted tolerable tourist habitation was much, much lower than his.

The time was February of 2006 and our itinerary was Senegal, the Gambia, Guinea-Bissau, and Guinea (Conakry).

It turned out, not surprisingly, to be typical TIA—This Is Africa— which means lots of wasted time, slow transit, poor roads, starchy food, battalions of bugs, problems exchanging money, power failures, paranoid patriots, widespread petty corruption, and ubiquitous poverty, but at least the guns of war and the flames of revolution were on hiatus. Whenever anything happens on this continent that, by our Western standards, is odd, counterproductive, ineffective, inefficient, frustrating, unreasonable, dumb, bizarre, incomprehensible, or plain-out weird, the old Africa hands and the expats just shrug their shoulders and, with quiet patience tinged with resignation, intone: "TIA." Even though the revenues, productivity, and prospects of many African countries had surged since I'd first visited, more than enough TIA remained to frustrate any traveler.

God and I rendezvoused in Dakar, the bustling capital of Senegal, and immediately learned we'd blundered into a misunderstanding. God had presumed that, since I was in charge of the trip, I'd researched and obtained what visas *he* needed, while I'd presumed that since he had his passport and lived in Africa, he'd attended to this. As a consequence, we wasted an entire day trying to ascertain if he required a visa to Guinea, repeatedly phoning its embassy, which never answered, then walking for two hours to find it, where we learned he did not need one.

I rented a small car in which we headed northeast, along Senegal's Atlantic coast. After two hours we stopped by the seaside to watch a group of ten young men in dirty shorts and torn shirts performing one of the hardest labors known—panning for gold in shoreline beach sands. Three of the men shoveled the heavy sand into a large screen that stood on rickety wooden legs about two feet above the gentle waves, to catch any sticks and rocks and garbage. The other men knelt beneath the screen to catch the sifted sand in pans of sheet metal, or plastic, even a black frying pan with a long handle. They were surely outlaw operators, for few people could afford the €2,300 fee that Senegal charged for a two-year "artisan exploitation authorization." But the men seemed neither worried about the police, whom they had likely bribed, nor about my camera, for which they proudly posed.

Senegal has gold deposits in the interior, where you'd need to process one ton of dirt and rock to get .08 of an ounce of gold, as a Canadian mining giant had just agreed to do. The guys on the beach were working over far poorer deposits, hundreds of miles from the mother lodes in the mountains. These sands harbored the most miniscule traces of gold dust, which had run a gauntlet of river panners on its tumbling ride to the ocean, and lucky if they averaged .01 of an ounce per ton, i.e., one grain of gold for every 3.2 million grains of crap.

Panning is the poor man's prospecting. It has the advantage of ease of movement, ready accessibility, and low equipment costs, but is attenuated by small throughput and backbreakingly arduous work. Each pan, about 16 inches across, with slanted sides two to three inches deep, can hold over 20 pounds of dense, water-saturated sand, which the men have to shake and swirl repeatedly in the water, as they expel, first, the lighter sands, then the heavier ones, then small pebbles, all the time kneading the contents to break up any clods and crush any clay, concentrating it all down to the heaviest, dark-black, metallic sands and—they can only hope—a fleck or two of gold.

It takes a strong, experienced panner at least six minutes to concentrate a pan, at most ten pans an hour, 90 in a long and utterly exhausting day. At that rate, one panner and his helper could process three cubic yards of sand a week, about six tons, and each could end up with .03 ounces of flakes, totaling 1.5 ounces at the end of a full year. Sounds futile? Well, this teaspoonful was worth $2500, which was more than double Senegal's GDP per person, and more than ten times that of nearby nations.

One of the men gave me a pan to try. I could barely lift it, much less shake, knead, and swish it while preventing any golden grains from swirling out.

God merely stood on the shore and watched, offering no help whatsoever. After all, he'd moved up life's ladder to become a licensed tour guide, a middle-class semiprofessional, almost a member of Ghanaian society. No more manual labor for him: Every day was his seventh day, and God rested, although he had, on some windy days during our first tour, been observed to help Bernard set up a tent, and he was always available to demonstrate his bartending skills to his thirsty clients come cocktail time. But it was unfair to fault his indolence: I reminded myself that this trip was to be God's vacation, God help me.

The next day I was in Lake Retba, northeast of Dakar, and up to my neck in brine, while a recumbent God snoozed in the shade of the car. The lake has a salt content of 40 percent, almost a pound of NaCl in every liter. Large amounts of salt had precipitated out and were caked in thick slippery deposits on the lake bottom, from which they were shoveled up by the men who lived in the industrious village bordering the lake.

The men had long ago exhausted all the near-shore deposits and were working about 50 yards from the lake's edge, with eight-foot-long shovels, standing in water over their shoulders, for six to seven hours a day, to lift the salt-bearing deposits up from the bottom and dump them into their adjacent rowboats. I tried to do it, but I couldn't get any leverage without bending over, and I could not bend, for the brine was already up to my chin. Moreover, my skin was sore from the saltiness because I was not protected, as were the village men, with a thick emollient of butter from the local shea trees.

Once these heavily muscled, broad-shouldered behemoths had filled a boat with salted muck, they pushed it to shore, where the village women took over, scooping the briny mush into wide plastic washbasins, too heavy for me to pick up, that they easily lifted onto their heads and dumped into separate conical piles about ten feet up the beach. After these piles had dried out for a day or two, the women, who toiled ten to 14 hours a day, raked and consolidated them into much larger piles, about three feet high, that they left to dry in the hot Senegalese sun for several weeks, after which they graded the dry product by coarseness and color, from nearly white to almost brown, and shoveled it into large plastic bags that held over a hundred pounds. The men loaded the bags onto trucks, to be sold in the city, where they fetched about $40 a ton—only two cents a pound—roughly one-third of the world price for pure, mined salt.

Their work was typical of the division of labor I observed between the genders throughout most of black Africa, where only three tasks are considered sufficiently macho for African men to perform: heavy lifting or pushing; driving taxis, trains, tanks, and trucks; and working with large animals—camels in caravans, horses that pulled carts, donkeys that bore burdens, and oxen that were driven in treadmill circles to run the threshing machines at harvest time. Everything else was women's work.

A woman's lot was not a comfortable one by Western standards. If you're a married female in rural Africa, your husband's principal contribution to the homestead will be to wake you up with the sunrise and send you to fetch water from wherever the local well is, then have you fire up a warm

In rural Africa, where cars are few and trucks are costly, farmers and villagers use bicycles, donkeys, wagons, and carts to transport huge loads of fruits, vegetables, and other commodities to the nearest market, where they are either sold to local consumers or consolidated for shipment to the cities. *Gorilla Highlands*

---

breakfast for him and the kids—and there will be *lots* of kids—then send you out to tend the fields for the rest of the day, with the youngest child wrapped to your back, while he assigns one of his sons to drive the livestock to the pasture field, then goes back to sleep and wakes up in the afternoon to spend the rest of his day hanging out with his buddies, getting sozzled on whatever fermented grog you've had the time to concoct for him after hoeing the weeds, harvesting the crops, washing clothes in the river, scavenging for firewood, and preparing dinner. On special occasions, such as planting time, your husband might deign to walk beside you with a stick, poking holes in the tilled soil, into which you deposit millet seeds you carry in a large gourd.

Our next state was *the* Gambia, as the country is properly called, the so-called tongue of Africa, a sliver of land averaging only 30 miles in width, surrounded by Senegal on three sides and by the Atlantic on the fourth, looking like a skinny snake burrowing into Senegal. It's the smallest nation in mainland

Africa, and one of the poorest, making its negligible livelihood from peanuts. Since 1994 it had been ruled with a heavy hand by an eccentric former wrestler and army colonel whose hobby was persecuting and executing his political opponents, and often his own ministers, creating a permanent atmosphere of paranoia.

The Gambia River bisects the country lengthwise and was the initial European trade route into the interior of Africa. It had quickly become one of the first main conduits for the slave trade, and its banks were harvested for strong black bodies for 400 years, The Gambia is now a pilgrimage destination for black Western tourists where, as one travel site put it, "The people of the Diaspora can come to rediscover and reaffirm their African heritage and unite with their ancestral family."

In Banjul, the sleepy capital of this nation of 1.7 million, I negotiated with the owner of a 20-foot motorized cargo canoe to take me and God (and the pretty waitress we'd met the night before at dinner) up the Gambia River for two days. We started the voyage by making the obligatory rounds of the relics of the bygone slave trade, with mine the only white visage among the tear-streaked faces of the 20 American citizens of African descent we saw confronting their family origins on this most somber tourist trail. Our boat motored past St. James Island, lying low in the center of the river and 20 miles upstream from its mouth, where the conquering colonials had built a fort, now a ruin, that gave them control of the river, and a slave house, now also a ruin, which gave them control of tens of thousands of lives. We next visited the village of Juffureh, on what has become known as Kunta Kinte Island, in honor of the man whom Alex Haley, in *Roots,* claimed to be his great-great-great-grandfather, and where he was sold into slavery in 1767.

It was, for me, a strange experience. I was intellectually outraged by the slave trade, and my sense of justice was awake and aware of its terrible inhumanity, but I was unable to make a real, deep, personal, *emotional* connection to its horrors, to the deaths, the chains, the shackles, the rapes, the whippings, the killing of newborn children, the families torn asunder. As I looked around, at the tearful African-American families returning to their tourist steamer with the heavy heritage of their history on their bent shoulders, I felt like an outsider, an interloper, an intruder who had boorishly blundered into the mourning pain of grieving relatives at the funeral of someone I had never met, or knew only in the most superficial way.

After our canoe left the heritage trail and continued upriver, we saw little life or livelihood, just mile after mile, hour after hour, of dense mangroves lining the edge of the dark river, with only a few villages visible in a hundred-mile stretch. I pondered, as we chugged past the deserted jungle, if the *absence* of anything worth seeing was, in itself, something worth seeing, if the Senegambia region will ever recover from the slave trade, which saw three million of its inhabitants—almost twice its present population—shipped away on the Voyage of No Return.

Back in Banjul, it was back into a bush taxi for a tiring ride to Bissau, the somnolent capital of Guinea-Bissau, an impoverished nation of 1.5 million, mostly farmers, who raised peanuts, palm kernels, cashews, and cotton, more recently managing to make its mark as a smuggling hub for drugs shipped in from Latin America en route to Europe. As was the norm in most of Africa, the driver refused to depart until the van was full, which required 13 more passengers and consumed three hours. I've often offered, when my minibus was within a person or two of being full, to pay the driver for the empty seats in exchange for an immediate departure, explaining that my time was more valuable to me than the five dollars or so they charged each person for a full-day's drive. But for reasons I've never understood, no driver ever accepted my offer, even after I pointed out that if they left with a van having a few empty seats, they had space to pick up passengers along the route and make even more money.

When these situations became acute, as in terminals where three or four minibuses were delaying departures for the same destination, all still half empty, all competing for passengers, all biding their time until full, all prepared to wait for hours, I eventually developed a successful stratagem: I'd innocently sidle up to a competing van, start a quiet conversation with some of their waiting passengers, then offer them a dollar or two to switch their patronage to my bus which, I assured them, would be the first to leave—and so it was.

From Bissau, we took another bush taxi for a journey across the country that was painfully slow because Guinea-Bissau's coastal strip was cut by ten or more rivers and streams, around which we had to detour, or across which we had to take a ferry. It took us two dusty, jolting days to reach the frontier of Guinea-Conakry.

To enter Guinea-Conakry we had to take a ship across a river deep in the jungle. The ferry was resting on the river's other side, 400 yards away, waiting for passengers heading toward us, which consumed three hours. She was a large old rust bucket, with room for about 20 cars and several hundred people on a flat metal deck, and was propelled by a score of sturdy passengers pulling a river-spanning cable that ran through a winch contraption on the deck. As she crept toward us, I started taking pictures, until the captain pointed at me and began screaming. I then remembered that many of these countries are supersensitive about the taking of photos, especially near their borders, some requiring a police permit, so I put my camera down.

This did nothing to quell the captain's anger; he continued to rage and rave even after his ship reached our bank. I panicked and hastily chose to play it safe by deleting the dozen photos I'd taken of the ship and the frontier, but, in my nervous state, I pressed the wrong button—which was not hard to do on my early-model digital—and erased *all* the pictures from the trip.

The captain kept ranting and threatening to turn me in to the police once we got to the town on his side of the river. Several passengers from my van told him I was a good guy, not an enemy agent filming the frontier to facilitate an incursion, and he should cut me some slack. To help my cause, I joined the 15 or so passengers hauling on the cable, and made a big show of grunting and straining, as we pulled the lumbering boat across for 20 minutes. To assure the captain's clemency I gave him two new Big Apple T-shirts as I disembarked, and swore to never commit such a heinous crime again.

After that it was God's turn to get in trouble.

Guinea-Conakry—one of three nations using the name "Guinea"—is one of the world's most corrupt, scoring a dismal 2.1 out of a possible 10 on the Transparency International Corruption Index, and ranked 168 out of 180 on the Corruption Perceptions Index. I was not as surprised or shocked by Guinea's illicit practices as God was, having suffered far worse when I'd crossed the CAR (Central African Republic), several years earlier.

In the CAR my minibus had been stopped at *twenty-nine separate check-*

*points* along the 250-mile stretch from its capital of Bangui to the border of Cameroon. At a typical checkpoint, a policeman or military officer sat, about 30 yards from the road, under a thatched shelter furnished with a table and a couple of chairs. The locals passed unmolested, but I, the only white guy in the bus, was directed to see the officer, who told me I could either pay him five dollars—sometimes ten—or stay there and go no farther.

Before I'd left home I had been warned about this corrupt practice, which was rampant in CAR since most of these officials and officers had received no pay from the moribund central government in more than six months, maybe a year, and had gone into business for themselves. No tourist's excuse worked: They refused to believe a foreigner who said he had no money, and they'd threaten to arrest him as a vagrant if he persisted. It was impossible to bluff them because they'd simply keep you off the bus and let you wilt in the sun until you paid. I'd therefore come prepared with dozens of new T-shirts I'd purchased in Times Square souvenir shops, where, at seven shirts for ten dollars, they served as a loss leader to lure in tourists.

At 27 of the 29 checkpoints I was able to get through with the "gift" of a ($1.42) shirt, after extolling its virtues and exaggerating its price by a factor of ten. One lean, mean captain, sporting an AK-47 and wearing highly polished combat boots that he kept arrogantly propped up on the table and in my face, was not so easily bought off. I was compelled, after a lengthy bargaining session during which my patient fellow passengers ate lunch, to add a half bottle of OFF! insect repellant and two AA batteries.

The most outrageous such indignity had occurred as I was about to leave the CAR. The captain of the border post refused to return my passport and let me exit until I gave him ten dollars cold cash—no T-shirts. His colleague, who ran the health station, was employed to check the yellow-fever cards of those *entering* CAR to ensure they'd been vaccinated against this disease and consequently could not pass the virus to mosquitoes in CAR after coming from infected countries. He had no proper business even looking at my yellow card now that I was *leaving* his country, but he insisted on seeing it, carefully scrutinized it for ten minutes, and then demanded five dollars for the services he'd rendered on my behalf. Unless, that is, I preferred to try to continue my journey without my yellow card.

I didn't like or condone the system, but I'd learned, the hard way, that it makes no sense to tell someone to go to hell unless you have the power to send him there. And that you don't flip the bird to a guy caressing an assault rifle.

As a result of my treatment in CAR and other corrupt countries I was well accustomed to the shakedown routine, but God was not, because it was not prevalent in the tourism-promoting states where he plied his trade. He also misguidedly assumed that because he carried a Ghanaian passport, and Ghana, like Guinea, was a member of ECOWAS (the 15-nation Economic Community of West African States), he should be exempt from any improper bribery, tipping, or service fees.

In view of my experience in CAR, I did not understand why none of the corrupt police manning the eight checkpoints between the Guinean border and the capital of Conakry asked me for a penny. They hit each of the other passengers, all Africans, for a buck or two, which those passengers fully expected and wearily paid.

But not God.

His refusal to comply began as soon as we entered Guinea, where the passport officer asked him for a small tip for stamping him in. God flipped out and berated his corruption. I paid the bribe, pushed God out of the office, and laid the facts of life on him, to which he replied, "When the soldiers were hustling me to give them a bribe so they stamp my passport I was fighting with them because I am fighting corruption back in Ghana."

Good sermon, God. Wrong church.

At each checkpoint, my usually mild-mannered friend demanded to see the officer in charge, at whom he ranted that the extraction of money by the police for doing their job was illegal, that such corruption was a sin and a crime, that he was a citizen of a friendly ECOWAS state, that he was a tour guide who could bring needed business to their country, that he was traveling with an American friend who was aghast at this type of corruption, that the police were an embarrassment to their profession and their country, that he'd rather walk than pay, that . . .

He definitely got their attention. His fee for passing the next police station rose to three dollars.

By the time the taxi was stopped at the fourth checkpoint, God was so outraged and outrageous he didn't even wait for the tip to be solicited, but charged out of the van waving his Ghanaian passport and telling all and sundry that he'd never been so badly treated in his life and would never return to this craphole of a country. *That* cost him four dollars.

By the sixth checkpoint, on the outskirts of Conakry, God was $22 poorer, and so vociferous that he was threatened with arrest, at which point I interceded, paid the tip for him, and told the police he was suffering from a hangover and sunstroke.

In retrospect, perhaps I should not have interfered. "God Arrested" would have made an intriguing title for this chapter. But I didn't want him wasting away in prison. I'd already hired him to guide me on a trip to Timbuktu in 2008.

# CHAPTER 11

## Travels in SPAM Land

My next journey got off to a bad start. I'd set aside two weeks in July 2007 to revisit Japan to provide a gentle warm-up for the ensuing seven weeks of primitive touring in New Guinea and eight other island nations of the western Pacific. No such luck. I got soaked with ten straight days of rain, was caught in the biggest super-typhoon to strike Japan since they began keeping records in 1951, plus two (small) tsunamis, and a 6.8 earthquake rumored to have resulted in some leaking nuclear reactors.

I left Japan on a roller-coaster of a flight through a tropical storm en route to Papua New Guinea (PNG), where I was long delayed by Air Niugini (ANG), whose planes chronically took off *after* they were supposed to have already *landed* at their destinations. Of my three flights with ANG, one was delayed seven hours and none less than three, and the mechanics were continually pulling parts out of one plane to fix another. I suppose this cannibalizing came naturally, but it did not inspire great confidence. Yet ANG had the only passenger planes in PNG.

Soon after I reached the interior I witnessed the only deadly sword fight (actually long machetes) I've seen off the silver screen. PNG was near the end of elections, and tempers flared when the vote counting dragged on for a week. In many provinces, the rival candidates came from tribes that had forever engaged in warfare against each other.

The election disputes escalated into roadblocks and burning tires on the only dirt track of a trail running through the Highlands, with a few head bashings if you came from the wrong tribe or clan, and the torching of some huts. Nevertheless, these folks had come a long way in 70 years, when these so-called Stone Age tribesmen, living in the deep, steep, almost inaccessible valleys of inner PNG, saw their first white man, their first piece of metal, even their first wheel.

They were all welcoming to me, and my worst annoyance was 30 British bird-watchers who invaded the lodge where I stayed in the Southern Highlands. These avian aficionados were straight out of a *Punch* cartoon, replete with every conceivable appurtenance from rubber boots and ultra-high-powered binoculars to birdsong recordings and laptops flashing their life lists and current sighting goals, which they knowledgeably and passionately discussed for hours.

They somehow persuaded me to join them the next morning at 5:00 a.m. to go trekking through the moist and misty jungle looking for birds of paradise eating their breakfast, of which we saw five species, which greatly excited all but yours truly, who was wishing he'd been able to eat *his* breakfast before embarking on this rash misadventure.

But it had its rewards: I am now the only one among my pals who has seen the rare King of Saxony bird of paradise in the wild, though I doubt if those pals will now treat me with the reverence and respect I have long and unavailingly told them I deserved.

To escape the incessant Brit bird chatter, I garnered a guide and traveled to the isolated Huli Wig School on the banks of a sacred stream in the Highland jungles. To the Huli and several other tribes, a huge mop of hair is essential for status and respect. You just can't—so to speak—get ahead without it. You can't even marry until you've grown it fully. The "it" is not a factory-made object, as we think of a wig, but a piled-up hat of hair that was cultivated into a wide, slightly squashed, tightly knit Afro. It grew atop the scalp of a living man, supported from underneath by a thin circular frame and string to hold its shape.

The growers spend at least two years in the wig school under the keen eye of the Wig Master, living a monastic life, unable to touch women or even be fed by them, just growing their hair, bonding with the brothers by preening one another's wigs for hours with long-tined picks, all sauntering down to the banks of the sacred stream several times a day to repeatedly fill their mouths with "magic water" that, for an hour, they expelled upward as a fine mist aimed to softly settle on the wig and keep it moist. Because the wig could easily get bent out of shape, the men sleep on their backs with their heads supported by a wood neck rest eight inches high, one of which they gave me in exchange for a bottle of OFF! and a T-shirt.

Their routines are occasionally interrupted by a tiff with a hostile tribe, usually over a stolen woman or a pig—I'm not sure which theft engenders more action—for which they grab their bows and arrows and rush, whooping, into the jungle, much to the consternation of the Wig Master, who scolds them if they've torn any hair while bounding through the bush.

A well-groomed four-year growth of healthy hair can fetch the equivalent of $6,000 after it's been shorn off the scalp of the grower and sold to someone too lazy or busy to grow his own, after which the grower begins to grow another, until he retires and grows one he keeps on his head. (I assume that if a purchased wig passes to several generations, it would eventually be considered an *hairloom*.)

After I reluctantly left the multiple fascinations of PNG and landed in Brisbane to change planes for the Solomon Islands, I had a tad of a tussle with the Australian Agricultural Quarantine Service when they sought to confiscate the necklace of a dog's skull and bones, which my PNG tribal pals gave me after we'd dined on the unfortunate canine. (My pals didn't think I rated a pig, which is their most highly prized form of currency—50 to 60 of them buy a bride with superlative attributes. And no, I never was able to clarify what those hallmarks were.)

It took me a while to satisfy the Aussies that neither my necklace nor my cassowary thigh-bone souvenirs were likely to cause an epidemic of hoof-and-mouth disease among their precious cattle. But I knew I'd have to return to Brissie ten days later to change planes again, and I doubted whether, given my past experience with these overly confiscatory characters, I'd find such a reasonable customs lady again. (When I'd visited Australia in 1981, they'd seized ten quarts of harmless packaged powdered milk from me, offering only the arrogant explanation that I could buy powdered milk there. On this trip they considered confiscating three pounds of packaged wasabi peas I'd brought from Japan until I convinced them that no insect could possibly survive the wasabi.)

As I crisscrossed the Pacific, each of the island-nations I visited was distinct but had, except for Tonga, a generally similar history: 1,000 to 3,000 years of simple, idyllic life until, starting some 200 years ago, being "discovered" by the whalers, traders, and European powers, who then infiltrated, invaded, subjugated, colonized, and renamed them, and introduced Western values and religions that shattered their cultures. The islanders were then hit with WW II, which devastated their homelands physically, wrecked others spiritually, subverted their traditional diets, and led to their deplorable current condition—sluggish, obese, and vegetating—in the hammock and on the dole. This enticed ambitious businesspeople to move in from India, Australia, and China to take over what little commerce there was. Tonga escaped this because it was the only one of these island-nations always ruled by indigenous governance and never colonized, which gave the Tongans a feeling of communal pride and power the others lacked.

Tuvalu was one of the most pathetic. Formerly the Ellice part of the Gilbert and Ellice Islands, it was ruled by Britain until after WW II. That war, counterintuitively, was regarded by the elderly Tuvaluans I talked with as the best days of their lives, because the Americans got there before the Japanese (who were derailed by the Battle of Midway) and converted the island into a major arsenal for the war, and port to 174 U.S. warships by 1944. The islanders benefited in many ways: compensation for the land taken to build the port, the airfield, and the radio tower; four to five years of wages, cigarettes, chocolate, soap, canned food, and kerosene; and a monetized way of life.

The future is gloomier. Tuvalu will be the first country to disappear under the waves of the rising ocean. (The slightly lower Maldives are sufficiently wealthy to build a seawall.) It's the world's fourth smallest nation at ten square miles, composed of three islands and six true atolls, eight of which are inhabited—hence its name, which means "eight standing together" in Tuvaluan. Each is only three to four feet above sea level, with one shrubby hummock on the island of Niulakita (which I climbed in six steps) the highest spot in the country, 15 feet above the ocean. It is widely agreed that if climatic warming continues, life for Tuvalu's 10,000 inhabitants will be untenable within 40 years and finished within 100.

Tuvalu may not even last 40 years above the waves because of its location and the adjacent topography. It offers no barriers to the breakers and is subject to the most devastating king tides, pushing the waves over many of these islands, none much wider than a football field. (A king tide is the highest of the highest of Pacific Ocean high tides, occurring when both the moon and sun are their closest to the earth, aligned in perigee and perihelion.)

The fear of flooding consumes the inhabitants, a watery sword constantly hanging over their heads. They asked me: "How are we to live? Where are we to go? Who will take us in?" Surely not Australia, which was already rejecting boat people. Not Japan, which strives to keep its population pure and homogenous. Not Indonesia, already overcrowded. Tuvalu's deputy prime minister asked, "Do we turn ourselves into fish and live under water?"

Think about it from their perspective: They believe that we—yes *we*—are inexorably inundating their country and slowly drowning their children and their children's children with our gas-guzzling cars, wasteful energy practices, and reluctance to conserve. As their prime minister somberly told the UN in 2003, "It is no difference to a slow and insidious form of terrorism against us." At the conclusion of an unresponsive international Climate Change Conference, Tuvalu's spokesman lamented being "offered thirty pieces of silver to betray our people and our future."

Tuvalu is too impoverished to help itself. It has no natural resources, little income, no potable water save whatever rain can be collected on roofs and stored in tanks, and no longer any agriculture since salt water has invaded the pits that the natives had for centuries dug into the sand and filled with compost so they could grow *pulaka*, a form of taro that was their dietary staple. All that these 10,000 ethnic Polynesians have left are a few scrawny chickens pecking along the almost-deserted single-lane road; a pig or two in a pen out back of a collapsing tin-roofed shack; sometimes a peeling old fishing dory; and a flower-filled burial ground in their front yards where they inter their ancestors, whom they dearly respect, but whose spirits they no longer worship after being converted to Christianity.

Tuvalu's only income is derived from remittances sent by workers who toil overseas, some international aid, and the sale of stamps and commercial fishing licenses. Nothing tempts more than a thousand tourists a year to visit this flat, plain, quiet community that has no lamb, beef, diet sodas, beauty parlors, theaters, cell phones, HBO, or reliable Internet.

Since I can endure only so much sadness and tranquility, I wanted, after three days on Funafuti, to go diving, but there was no dive shop in the nation—and for good reason, as I learned too late. I trudged back and forth along the main (and only) road down the center of the capital island searching on both sides for boat mooring places and finally found a 19-year-old who agreed, for $100, to borrow a boat and throw together some snorkeling stuff. I went back to the Vaiaku Lagi, the country's only hotel, and rounded up a group of receptive guests: two Kiwis, an Aussie, an Italian, and a shy, deaf Japanese woman named Midori who was an Olympic badminton player. She told us, through her sign-language interpreter, that, although she'd never gone snorkeling before, she was eager to try it because, in the silent world beneath the waves, she would be, for the first time in her life, equal to all the rest of us—no longer the child of a lesser god.

But it was not to be.

The next morning dawned bright and cloudless, and the boy I'd hired took us 40 minutes out to a flat, shallow reef, covered by six to 15 feet of water, near a steep drop-off. We backflipped into the clear water, but inexperienced Midori jumped and landed atop some spiny coral heads and cried for help. She had badly scraped her leg and was bleeding profusely. We gathered around her and gently lifted her into the motorboat, where the Aussie elevated her leg while I applied pressure with a handkerchief to staunch the bleeding.

When we were certain her bleeding had stopped and that she was not in shock, we gulped some air and went back down to explore. We'd only been under a few seconds when in zoomed a large, blunt-nosed monster with faint vertical stripes along its sides—the dreaded tiger shark, a voracious hunter with powerful jaws; sharp, highly serrated teeth; and a superb sense of smell that had undoubtedly enabled it to home in on Midori's blood.

I froze as the brute brushed past me, heading toward the back of the boat where Midori had been. The tiger is one of the three deadliest sharks to humans but, unlike the great white, which will often take a bite of an arm or leg and decide it doesn't like the taste, the tiger will usually devour its entire prey. Tigers generally live deeper but will venture onto small shallow reefs like the one we were on.

I held my breath for the longest I ever had, let myself slowly rise to the surface without making any motion to attract unwanted attention, gently rolled onto my back, and directly sculled my way to the boat and lunged in. According to our Italian companion, who stayed down the longest, the shark nosed around, as if searching for something, but, not finding it, headed back down to the deep drop.

When we were all in the boat, I berated the "captain," who was by now slightly conked on kava, for taking us into shark territory. He pulled up his T-shirt to show us a jagged, dark purple, partly healed wound in his chest, the size of a serving platter, where he said a tiger shark had taken this bite out of him a few months before *at this same spot*. He looked at us with little sympathy and shrugged: "What's the big deal? None of you was hurt."

The only unpleasant occurrence on the next leg was caused by a huge breadfruit—about the weight of three grapefruits—that dropped 40 feet from its tree and beaned me while I was exploring the ruins of an ancient civilization on the island of Nan Midol in the Pohnpei Group in Micronesia. Luckily, as my friends have frequently pointed out, I have a rather hard head, so it takes more than an errant breadfruit to do me in. (A coconut falling 100 feet might do the job, so I looked up frequently during the rest of this tropical island foray.)

While scubaing off Truk and Palau, where dive tourism accounts for nearly half of the local economy, I did see squids, sharks, and octopi, but they were not large and acted more frightened that I'd eat them than the other way around. I saw no sea snakes, which are aggressive and had almost gotten me on the Great Barrier Reef in 1981, and none of the pain-inflicting, paralyzing stonefish, scorpion fish, and lion fish I'd often encountered in the warm waters of the Red Sea and Indo-Pacific region.

The Truk Lagoon was fascinating from underwater, filled with haunting relics of WW II. It had been the forward anchorage of the Japanese Imperial

Combined Fleet, home to more than 20 warships, five airstrips, a seaplane base, torpedo boat station, submarine repair shop, and communications center, the Rising Sun's most formidable stronghold on a conquered island.

Until February 16, 1944.

That's when the Navy launched Operation Hailstone and battered Truk Lagoon for three days with dive bombers and torpedo planes from five fleet carriers. We sank 15 warships, 32 merchant vessels, and sent more than 250 enemy planes to the bottom, where they remain today, as the "Ghost Fleet of Truk Lagoon," almost all lying virtually intact and clearly visible in their shallow tombs after more than 60 years, with just a bit of seaweed and coral encrustation, all resting in peace in the largest ship graveyard under earth's oceans.

When I came upon the well-preserved remains of a Curtiss Helldiver, one of the 25 American planes shot down during the attack, resting level in less than ten feet of clear water, I swam slowly down, slid into the opened cockpit, and silently thanked the missing pilot, and the others of the Greatest Generation, for having rid the world of the Axis menace and preserved our liberty, as I teared up and my face mask misted over.

Three days later the Aussie quarantine service finally got me. When I flew back to Brisbane to change planes, I reentered Oz with the same PNG souvenirs I'd taken both in and out of Brissie three weeks before, but got a much tougher inspector. After a heated argument, he agreed to allow in my dog bones and boar tusks, but insisted that the ornaments strung *between* the bones were not beads, as I averred, but "dried seeds of a noxious weed" that could not enter. I offered to leave the ornaments in quarantine at the airport overnight, but he rejected that, disdainfully cut both necklaces apart, and chucked out the seeds—I mean beads.

I flew out the next day and established a new personal worst by touching down in seven airports in one 24-hour period. While I was in Japan, and despite my having a reservation, Air Nauru had decided to discontinue their flights from Honiara, capital of the Solomon Islands, to Majuro, capital of the Marshall Islands. To make it to the Marshalls, I now had to fly from Honiara back to Brissie, sleep in the transit lounge, fly to Cairns, change planes, fly to Guam, change planes, fly down to Truk, then to Ponepae, Kosrae, Kwajelein, and, finally, Majuro. This was like flying from New York to Boston via Miami, Atlanta, Dallas, Los Angeles, Cincinnati, Buffalo, and Montreal. But I had to do it: The Marshalls were a country.

I also set a personal worst record for most continuous days of rain—33! I spent much of Day 34 drying clothes to vanquish nascent mold.

On the island of Tongatapu, the largest in the Kingdom of Tonga, the challenge was to buy gas and food on a Sunday. Tonga is one of the world's most devoutly Christian nations; hence, all commerce ceases from Saturday midnight to Sunday midnight, and *nothing* is open except the emergency room at the hospital.

The natives were long ago converted and are now either Catholic, Free Wesleyan, Methodist, Mormon, or Church of Tonga. The converts turn out in droves to Thank the Lord for whatever they have, all wearing their spotless, bright Sunday best, all walking in smiling family groups to church, where they romp and stomp and sing and clap and have a grand old Godly time. One minister told me that some parishioners have apologized to him for the devouring of his great-great-grandfather by their great-great-grandfathers. Or was this his attempt at missionary humor?

I'd been looking forward to trying Tonga's famous fruit-bat pie and their flying fox fricassee, but I was warned that these little hairy buggers were off limits to tourists and reserved solely for the nation's king and the royal family. I did detect a loophole—and only a New York lawyer would argue this—in that the king, after a 40-year reign, had died some months before, and his successor would not be crowned until a year later. Therefore, since there was no king . . .

I decided not to push it and to wait for Palau, where the indigenes also savored these crunchy critters, but where anyone could eat them. I went to a bakery in Koror, the former capital, and found several fruit-bat pies for sale for $35. But they were not what I'd envisioned; I'd hoped for a tart-sized taste, not a ten-inch multimeal. And I'd assumed the bakers gutted and cleaned the bats and ground them all up like mincemeat. Instead, each pie contained ten to twelve whole bats: And I do mean *whole*! Complete! Entire! The Works: wings, heads, fur, feet, and all. And they were all facing *up*, laid out side-by-side inside the fringing reef of brown crust, with their fragile little wings spread and touching, their hair thickly coated with dark purple jelly, hirsute ears erect and slightly pinkish, their tiny pointed teeth shining—and all of them looking, pathetically and accusingly, *right at me.*

I suddenly remembered my vow to never eat an endangered species. Surely these little guys must be endangered, right? I sort of recall having read that in one of my environmental magazines. I decided that I'd better make sure before I indulged. Maybe on Guam, where there were more bats, and the shops might sell me a simple order of fried wings? To go. With a side of slaw.

I tried to make up for this culinary cop-out by eating the mangrove clams in Palau, the mud crabs in Tuvalu, sea cucumber jelly in the Marshalls, the giant coconut crabs in Vanuatu, and drinking the kava in Fiji.

The one thing I steadfastly refused to eat is what has become, thanks to our WW II GIs, the national dish of almost every island nation in the Pacific: SPAM. I never knew there were so many brands and varieties. By my tally, the average South Pacific supermarket devotes 20 percent of its shelf space to SPAM and its progeny, and some smaller shops push it up to 30 percent. The locals eat it for breakfast, creamed, on toast (similar to the chipped beef dish that, in the army, we called SOS and uniformly hated); then cold for lunch, straight out of the can, topped with pineapple or papaya; and in all sorts of disgusting heated variations for dinner.

The other big dish in all these nations—again, blame our GIs—was fried chicken with French fries, the combination of which was producing a Generation XL of Big Fat Mommas and Papas, weighing in at way over 300 pounds, and giving these people one of the world's highest rates of heart disease and diabetes. *Pacific Island nations occupy the seven top spots on the WHO global obesity rankings.*

The majority of the islanders I saw never exercised, but sat all day (except Sunday) gossiping, listening to pop radio, guzzling Foster's, and thinking about *maybe* mending that leaky roof or dead motorcycle next week. At least we can blame the Foster's on the Aussies.

We cannot blame the Aussies for the multiple cups of kava the denizens of these islands ingest every day, a slightly sedating, foul-smelling potion they imbibe with much devotion and ceremony. It tasted to me like the bottled coyote piss I used to spray around my vegetable garden to keep away the deer and rabbits, and it combines the worst effects of Novocain and Dramamine.

Kava is brewed by grinding, pounding, or chewing the root of the kava plant, and is alleged by Western forensics to cause severe liver damage, a malady seemingly unknown to the Pacific Islanders, many of whom couldn't get through a day without a kava infusion, and who often live to their 80s—provided they stay away from burgers, franks, fries, SPAM, candy, and the other junk food to which *we* introduced them.

My next port of call was the island-nation of Vanuatu, birthplace of bungee jumping. More than 30 years ago, when it was a dependency called the New Hebrides, a Kiwi tourist who observed their tower-jumping ritual—a test of manhood among the locals—decided to make it safer, with sturdy elastic bands tied to a firm tower, and imported it to New Zealand, from whence it spread to Australia and around the world. In Vanuatu, however, it has remained for centuries unchanged and unnerving. Where the Kiwi had merely observed, Big Al intended to participate.

I climbed up a rickety wooden tower, as tall as a five-story building, to a shaky platform where they affixed jungle vines to my legs, as a group below turned over the soil beneath the platform so my face wouldn't get *too* smashed up. As I fell, I would *theoretically* break or bend some of the saplings that supported the jump platform, which would *supposedly* slow my descent from deadly to merely dangerous. As I timorously peered down from the sickening height of 60 feet, I suddenly realized that Vanuatu might be short on trauma surgeons, and that a broken neck might negatively impact my global goal.

I don't know whether the advancing years have more increased my wisdom or my cowardice, but I chickened out of the jump.

I was still shaking off the tower terrors when I reached Samoa, where my objective was far less dangerous: to climb Mount Vaea to the burial vault of Robert Louis Stevenson, my favorite teller of adventure tales. It was little more than a sweaty hour up the jungle trail, but after having gained ten pounds on the unhealthy Pacific diet, and grown soft from sitting in so many airplanes on so many long flights, the hike up the hill was a hot, hard haul for me.

Stevenson, who died at 44 of a cerebral hemorrhage after a life battling TB, had early fallen in love with Samoa, wrote numerous articles and books there, and asked to be buried there. He was so treasured by Samoans for his powerful political polemics on their behalf, for his storytelling in their oral tradition, and for putting on paper the first fiction story ever written in the Samoan language, that 30 native chieftains journeyed to his deathbed, established an honorary watch guard to keep his spirit company through the night, then carried the body of their beloved Tusitala—the teller of tales—on their shoulders as they hacked a path through the jungle and brought him up the small mountain to his final resting-place overlooking the peaceful Pacific.

I wept as I read the moving epitaph that he wrote for his tomb:

> *Under the wide and starry sky,*
> *Dig the grave and let me lie,*
> *Glad did I live and gladly die,*
> *And I laid me down with a will.*
>
> *This be the verse you grave for me:*
> *Here he lies where he longed to be,*
> *Home is the sailor, home from the sea,*
> *And the hunter home from the hill.*

# CHAPTER 12

## Hanging Chad

After Samoa, I had still 49 more nations to visit before *I* was home from the hill. My initial plan was to go to Africa and knock ten nations off my To-Do list in one continuous, contiguous, 55-day sweep, between January and March 2008, first crossing the Saharan belt just south of the Maghreb, through some of the world's poorest and roughest countries, successively from Sudan through Chad, Niger, Burkina Faso, and Mali to Mauritania, where I'd reach the Atlantic Ocean, then swing south, following the bulge of West Africa, to three states I'd been forced to bypass on my previous forays to the region because two of them, Liberia and Sierra Leone, had been in the midst of ferocious civil wars, while the indigenes in the third, the Ivory Coast, had been fighting a war between north and south and also killing anyone who looked remotely French, which, I'd assumed, to them *I* could remotely look. (Although I might also be terminated by a reader who had to struggle through that sentence.) Finally, if the turmoil then roiling Nigeria subsided, I might try to pop in there.

I anticipated that the most prevalent potential problems would be fairly routine African stuff, the usual mélange of muggers, bandits, kidnappers, corrupt cops, jihadists, rogue soldiers, freelancing mercenaries, unreliable cross-border buses, broken-down bush taxis, Saharan sandstorms, the dust-laden winter wind called the *Harmattan*, unsanitary water, poor diet, and deadly diseases, from malaria to Ebola.

I was to begin in Khartoum, the storied capital of Sudan, to which, after three years of unsuccessfully applying for a visa, I had finally found a way in thanks to a guy I'll call Nikolas. I had given up on the standard procedures, because whenever I asked the Sudanese Embassy in D.C. about the status of my visa application, I received the same reply: "It is being considered in Khartoum." Frustrated after 30 months of this, I had contacted an old girlfriend who was an administrator at the UN, who referred me to a knowledgeable operative at the Arab League, who kindly put me in touch with "a man who can help you," who, after vetting me to make sure I was not CIA, Mossad, Mormon missionary, Salvation Army, or similar undesirables, and after extracting a good chunk of change, which, he explained, had to be of sufficient amount to cross several palms, put me in e-mail contact with Nikolas, a European national long resident in Khartoum, who'd "make all the arrangements."

I precisely followed the instructions I was given: I took a Tunisair flight from Tunis to Cairo, arriving at Terminal One, and there collected my luggage and walked to Terminal Two, where I went directly to the Kenya Air counter and asked, verbatim, for "the flight that leaves at five minutes to midnight," the code I'd been given for flight KQ0323 to Khartoum. After the Kenya Air agent finished looking through my passport and mentioned the absence of a visa to Sudan, I told her, as I'd been told to tell her, "It has all been arranged," and, as I'd been further instructed, gave her my most winning wink. She hesitated for the briefest bit, winked back, issued me a boarding pass, and wished me a good trip.

At 1:40 a.m. I landed in Khartoum, where I was greeted by my "contact," a shady, Oakley-shaded Arab in a black leather motorcycle jacket, who had my visa in one hand and an open palm in the other, the latter of which someone along the chain had apparently failed to grease sufficiently, or so he insisted.

After I'd rectified that alleged oversight with a Benjamin, I was whisked by an arranged taxi to the Hotel Metropole, a picaresque joint likely designed by Robert Ludlum and operated by John le Carré. The first thing I noticed was that half its exterior was missing, covered over with boards and sheetrock, as if a bomb had ripped through it. When I asked the proprietor, he told me, somewhat reluctantly, but also proudly, that, yes, a bomb *had* ripped through it a while back, when a jihadist decided to get rid of the filthy infidels who roomed there, but only succeeded in killing three of the native staff.

I was assured it was not likely to happen again because, "As you Americans say, lightning never strikes twice in the same place." I thought of the Twin Towers of the World Trade Center but said nothing.

The lobby and sitting area were filled, even at that late hour, with several suited Western businessmen and a dozen veteran foreign correspondents wielding laptops, the journalists dithering over whether to finish and file their copy with their editors in New York, London, and Paris that night, or to shack up with their colleagues and file the next morning.

As I was the only backpacking type bunking at the hotel—tourists in Khartoum are as rare as virgins in Vegas—it became quickly clear that I was under suspicion, and that I was not getting invited to the slumber party.

But, for once, I had more pressing priorities. By dawn's early light I had to hustle to the Police Central Registration to have my arrival rerecorded and a piece of green paper pasted in my passport, a process that cost me a few more quid. I received there a lecture that I should not, for my safety—it's amazing the thoughtful procedures dictatorships around the world had instituted to ensure my safety—travel outside of Khartoum or Omdurman, its sibling city directly across the Nile.

I then had to flash over to the Information & Promotion Administration of the General Administration of Tourism of the Ministry of Tourism and Wild Life [*sic*] to receive another costly piece of paper, this one topped with a sketch of a 1950s camera, that granted me permission to take 35mm still pictures around Khartoum, *provided* I did not film "military areas, bridges, train stations, broadcasting and public utilities, such as water, gas, petrol, and electricity works" or "slum areas, beggars, and other defaming subjects."

This severely limited my artistic scope because almost every street in Khartoum could pass for a slum, and the only people *not* dressed like beggars were uniformed soldiers brandishing serious-looking weapons and dark-suited, sun-glassed, regime insiders toting briefcases, who looked as if they harbored reasonable apprehensions that any photo of them could end up on an Interpol WANTED poster or a dossier at the International Criminal Court. Nevertheless, just to make sure I didn't do anything foolish, the permit required me, before I began filming, to alert "the local government inspector, the town clerk, and the executive officer of general authority."

Oh well, at least I was free to photograph the "Wild Life." Since I saw no examples of the four-legged variety during my sojourn, I interpreted this edict loosely and took 50 shots one evening of dozens of spotlessly white-robed Sufi devotees in trances of ecstatic religious fervor performing the whirling-dervish dance inside a wide circle of 500 observant observers.

While I'd turned my back on the non-African world for two weeks, it had established another country I had to visit! But before I could shoulder the added burden of going to Kosovo and whatever other newbie nations the Powers might recognize, I had to focus on Africa. Next up was Chad, to which I could venture by either air or land once I determined which one was the lesser evil.

Because Sudan and Chad were in the throes of an undeclared war, no airline flew directly between them. If I opted for air, I'd have to fly east from Khartoum to Addis Ababa, then back west, three quarters of the way across Africa, to Bamako in Mali, then back eastward to Niamey, the capital of Niger, and from Niamey to N'Djamena, the capital of Chad, taking four flights and two days (and paying full freight for each) for what should have been a two-hour hop. I had no other air route from Khartoum—unless I flew via Cairo to Paris. TIA. This is Africa.

I'd customarily preferred to travel by land because I can't learn much about a country from flying over it at 35,000 feet. It was 1,213 desert miles from Khartoum to N'Djamena, which I could probably have 4×4'd in less than a week. But my limited Sudanese visa did not permit that. Moreover, and far more problematic, much of the land I'd have to traverse was in the western Sudanese province of Darfur, then terrorized by several thousand nasty nuts on camelback called the Janjaweed, whose main motivation in life was to slaughter the inhabitants, a vocation at which they'd been quite successful, killing more than 300,000 in six years, while driving 600,000 from their homes into makeshift refugee camps near the border with Chad. (The Sudanese government, which was reliably rumored to be arming, supporting, and directing the Janjaweed, put the death toll at only 10,000 and blamed Chadian rebels.)

As I was deliberating over this dilemma, the Janjaweed struck three towns in a remote part of western Sudan, sending 12,000 more Darfurians fleeing to Chad and pushing Chad's president to blast Sudan for provoking the violence and declare that if this continued he was going to send 300,000 refugees back into Sudan.

The origins of the conflict were complicated. Forty percent of the inhabitants of Darfur are not Arabs, but mostly members of the Fur tribe (hence the name Dar*fur*), and the Sudanese rulers were notorious for disliking non-Arabs. A persistent drought had parched the Darfur region starting about ten years before, but the government in Khartoum had not responded with much concern or assistance, which angered the Darfurians, after which one thing led to another and the genocide began. The problem quickly spilled over into Chad, whose president was unwilling to openly assist the Darfurian rebels against powerful Sudan. Chadian rebels then formed a United Front for Democratic Change and, in 2003 and 2006, attacked N'Djamena International Airport until driven back by French troops posted there to protect the Chadian government.

These hostilities made me fairly certain the land route would not win an AAA recommendation, but I believed it could be accomplished. All I'd have to do was load a sturdy, wide-tired 4×4 with a hundred gallons of gas, cross the Nile at Omdurman, as permitted by my visa, take a compass bearing of 250 degrees WSW, slip past the Sudanese Army with my now-invalid visa, skirt the Janjaweed paramilitary camps, cross the scorched-earth region of Darfur, dodge through the highly congested area of the refugee camps, and then zip across the remaining 300 miles of inhospitable desert infested with rebel militias.

But, alas, I was no longer the overconfident kid who'd taken the Trans World Record Expedition through worse without worry. I opted for the four flights.

The first three went relatively smoothly, although, as just about the only white traveler on board, I was accosted at each airport by every tout, bum, beggar, mendicant, pimp, and tip-seeking baggage agent not otherwise occupied. On my fourth and final flight, as we approached N'Djamena toward midnight, the captain suddenly announced that, No, we were not landing there after all, but flying on to Addis in Ethiopia, because there was too much shooting and too many dead bodies on the runway for a safe landing.

On that fateful February night, 160 corpses and hundreds of wounded littered the airport and the land around it, and a thousand more rebels ran amok below us in pickup trucks firing heavy machine guns, assault rifles, and rocket-propelled grenades. Seems the rebels inside Chad had decided to give rebellion another go and try to oust the uncooperative government and take over the country.

So why did they attack the airport? If some gang were trying to take over Washington, D.C., it's hardly likely they'd concentrate their efforts on Dulles International. But in Chad, a successful military action required the capture of the airport, because that's where France had stationed its tanks and its 1,500 soldiers. (France had actively defended this former colony since 1978, when the Libyan dictator, Muammar Gaddafi, attempted to seize parts of northern Chad, and tried again in 1983 and 1986.) The supportive French troops bivouacked at the airport enabled the government, throughout the battle, to safely land, refuel, and reload its four helicopter gunships, which then went on to shoot the shit out of the rebels. At one point during the day, the rebels controlled half the capital. But a pickup truck is no match for a heavily armed helicopter, and within a few days the rebels had been beaten back into the desert and N'Djamena became relatively tranquil.

None of which did me any good.

By then I was back in Addis, from whence I'd begun this costly, time-consuming, and fruitless jaunt, and was there informed by Ethiopian Airlines that—"Sorry for the inconvenience, Mr. Albert"—they were not flying to N'Djamena until the president of Chad lifted his declaration of a state of emergency. But—"Not to worry, Mr. Albert—you'll receive a refund for the unused portion of the four-flight ticket." (A refund Mr. Albert received only after four years, and nine e-mails, and, the clincher, an irate invasion of their executive suite accompanied by a local journalist who threatened to expose them.)

Chad's president decreed that the state of emergency would remain in place for at least 15 days, which was more time than I could afford; therefore, I sadly concluded that Chad had to hang for some other year, and caught a plane four days later for the same circuitous route to Niamey in Niger.

A persistent drought and the search for work had driven people from all over Niger to Niamey, expanding it from 3,000 in 1930 to more than a million, but it was still a sleepy, laid-back place on the banks of the River Niger. All the streets in my part of town were of deep sand, which reduced noise and traffic speed, and the dusty sidewalks were lined with beggars, bums, basket cases, and poorly stocked vendors of Kleenex, flashlight batteries, and single cigarettes. The few stores of substance were run by Frenchmen.

After I'd visited both the Grande and the Petite Markets, there was not much left to see in Niamey. And since a group called Al-Qaeda in the Islamic Maghreb was starting to kidnap Westerners there, I hopped a bus for a ten-hour ride westward to rendezvous with God and Bernard. They'd driven their old wreck of a Land Cruiser, which now had over 500,000 km on it, up from Accra, where they lived, to Ouagadougou, where we met and provisioned for eleven days of camping. Ouagadougou is the capital of Burkina Faso, the world's third poorest country, number 175 on the UN Human Development Index of 177, where half of the population lives, if one can call it that, on less than one dollar a day, where only 13 percent are literate, and desertification is a continuing problem. What followed was an eventful week:

Tuesday: I got hit by a small truck when crossing a busy street. Nothing broken.

Wednesday: Massive riots erupted in Ouagadougou, protesting rising grain prices, which had *doubled* in one year, partly caused by America's diverting some of its corn crop from food and animal feed to the production of ethanol. The locals burned tires, smashed streetlights, looted shops—just like on the *Evening News*. We cut our shopping short and scooted out of town, heading toward Mali. The rough dirt track leading to Gorum-Gorum quickly broke the tube leading to our vehicle's brake fluid reservoir, forcing us to spend hours looking for a welder. I got into a dispute with the denizens of Gorum-Gorum, where many of the houses are famously decorated with black and white stripes. They demanded I give them money for taking pictures of their houses, but I make it a point to never pay for photos because it sets a precedent that ruins things for the tourists who follow and who will be harassed if they don't also pay.

Thursday: Out for a morning constitutional, I crossed paths with a deadly saw-scaled viper. Fortunately, it was not in an aggressive mood and made no threat display, but it can be one mean killing machine. We broke the Cruiser's hood reenforcer on another rough road and had to hunt up another welder.

Friday: We cracked parts of the front and rear bumpers, requiring more welding and more delay. The temperature, which had been a bearable 117 degrees, zoomed off my thermometer's scale at 122. That night, while we were camped in the desert a quarter mile behind a small village, bandits struck and made off with two 25-liter jerry cans stored on the luggage rack atop the Cruiser and filled with $200 worth of precious diesel. I presume this was the handiwork of the teenage miscreants who'd walked out from the village to "welcome" us as we were pitching our tents at sunset and to see what there was to be had once we slept. It took days to replace the fuel because the nearest refinery was hundreds of miles distant, and the petrol trucks now avoided the area because of riots.

Saturday: My most malodorous and shocking misadventure took place on the darkened streets of Bobo-Dioulasso (which had just sustained a destructive riot), where I fell into an open manhole filled with raw human sewage. I rushed back to my hotel room to clean off the crap. After a long shower I flipped the switch to turn on the ceiling fan and was almost knocked out by an electric shock from the combination of a defective switch and my bare feet on the wet tile floor.

All things considered, a fairly typical week in Africa.

The highlight was our visit to Djenné, long a seat of Islamic learning and culture, and the oldest known city in sub-Saharan Africa, a bustling trading center on the banks of the Niger that had for centuries prospered from this direct shipping connection to Timbuktu, which had access to salt and gold. Djenné's main square offered an exotic counterpoint of several hundred farmers and merchants hawking spices, vegetables, cloth, and brightly colored plastic pails, while white-capped, dark-bearded, fiery-eyed imams hawked the teachings of the Koran to attentive youths in a score of outdoor *madrassas*, all competing for airtime against an omnipresent cacophony of chants, flutes, boom boxes, and switch-pitch drums.

I jumped into the market scene with a handful of my ever-popular Times Square T-shirts, and had, within ten minutes, traded five for two Dogon carvings and a sizable plastic washtub filled with enough veggies, spices, and cooking oils to feed us for a week. But I turned down a host of unsolicited offers for my New York Mets baseball cap.

The square was dominated by the most famous building south of the pyramids, the Great Mosque of Djenné, a UNESCO world heritage site that was the largest mud building anywhere, the apotheosis of the Sudano-Sahelian architectural style, and the culmination of any kid's fantasy of the ultimate sand castle. The mosque's base is set nine feet above the ground, atop a platform 245 feet long on every side, far larger in area than two football fields. Its three rectangular minarets, facing east to Mecca, soared seven stories high into the clear desert sky.

The mosque is made of sunbaked bricks molded from mud mixed with rice husks, held together with a mud-based mortar and covered with a mud paste that gives it a smooth, sculpted look. The walls are two feet thick and adorned with a forest of conical pinnacles topped with real ostrich eggs symbolizing purity and fertility. Every spring Djenné holds a weeklong working festival during which the able-bodied pitch in to repair any damage caused by rain and by the repeated expansion and contraction of the mud resulting from the large shifts between day and night temperatures.

I was not allowed to enter the mosque. In 1998 *Vogue* had commissioned a notorious fashion shoot there, featuring scantily clad models, which so outraged the devout townsfolk that non-Muslims had been forbidden to enter ever since. But I was content to sit in the square and marvel at this magnificent mud masterpiece.

Although God appreciated the Great Mosque as a work of art and an ideal attraction for his tourists, he didn't like what it represented. "When Islam came into West Africa," he told me, "it was introduced in Timbuktu, which

The Great Mosque of Djenné in Mali near the Niger River was built in 1907. It is repaired during a festival each year, and is the largest mud-brick building in the world. The lively market beside it features vendors pushing fruits and plastic pails and imams pushing the Koran and who knows what else.

became one of the highest education centers, and then it spread, by the Niger River, down here to Djenné in the eighth century, forcing the Dogon tribe to flee to their present-day location in the escarpment. Now, Al-Qaeda is trying to dominate Mali, Niger, and parts of Burkina Faso, threatening my business."

We were aware that time was running short to visit Timbuktu. We knew that a vast area around it on three sides was controlled by the Tuareg, a tough and ruthless tribe that disdained the central government in Bamako, believing it discriminated against them because of their lighter skins. For many decades the Tuareg had engaged in sporadic robbery and revolt in the region, and subjected Godfried to the most harrowing incident of his career:

"I was taking a group of six Italians into the heart of the desert where salt is mined, to a town called Taoudenni, 660 kilometers north of Timbuktu, near where some of these rebels have bases. About halfway there we were stopped by a gang of these people. They shot out our tires and took away our food and most of our water. They didn't kill any of us, but they went through every single piece of luggage. They took away all the money I had for the trip, all the money belonging to the clients, every single thing they wanted to take away."

I asked him how he survived.

"It was very, very miraculous. It was just the beginning of cell phones. My boss was carrying a cell phone operated by solar energy. The bandits did not know what it was and discarded it. So when they were gone, my boss, who I was assisting to guide these people, used the phone, which took the rest of the afternoon to get into contact with the military base in Timbuktu. We spoke to this one precious person, who I will never forget in my life, who knew the desert very well. 'Tell me the color of the sand where you are,' he asked, and we told him the color, and he knew exactly where we were, because he was someone who had been initiated by his father to go on the salt trade, so he was walking camels across the Sahara for almost all his life. And they came up to rescue us. It took them three days to come up the 350 clicks in their Jeep. They saved our lives."

The Tuareg had since formed the National Movement for the Liberation of Azawad in the far northeast corner of Mali and were dedicated to wresting control of it from the central government. They had been infiltrated and influenced by radical Islamists, and the most zealous of them were leading a new movement called Ansar Dine (Defenders of the Faith), centered in the lawless lands near Mali's border with Algeria in the forbidding Adrar des Ifoghas mountains, and dedicated to turning northern Mali, including Timbuktu, into an Islamic nation under strict sharia law. Adding to this danger, both Al-Qaeda in the Islamic Maghreb and MUJAO (Movement for Oneness and Jihad in West Africa) were increasingly aggressive in that large lawless region. If we fell into their clutches, we'd be either ransom objects or dead meat.

After much consideration—and well aware of my tendency to let desire trump security—I decided to take the chance and attempt the run to Timbuktu. I'd wanted to visit that storied town for half of my life, and this might be my last opportunity. I reckoned the reward was worth the risk.

From Djenné it was a two-day drive, via Mopti, across the desert to Timbuktu, all tough going, where we were repeatedly forced to choose between the hard-packed track with its teeth-jarring corrugated ruts or sand so dry and soft we had to roll or push our vehicle up every incline steeper than five degrees. We saw only one other vehicle that trip, a white van carrying three dazzling Italian women in bathing suits—were they a mirage?—stuck in sand over its hubcaps. We winched them out, and I wished I could have wenched them in, but they were headed in the opposite direction. The main traffic we encountered were caravans of donkeys—50, 100, 200, or more—carrying salt southwest to the port of Mopti at the confluence of the Niger and Bani Rivers, or bringing food and household goods northeast to Timbuktu. (Camel caravans seldom ventured far south of Timbuktu because they succumbed to the tsetse fly, which cannot live in the drier regions to the north.)

It was so dry in the Saharan belt that I saw only one cloud in 33 days, and no mist, dew, or fog. So dry that many areas received less than four inches of rain a year, compared to more than 120 inches in West Africa. So dry in God's vehicle with no AC and the windows open to catch a breeze, that after I'd soaked my clothes with water to keep cool, the moisture evaporated in ten minutes. So drying that even though I drank more than 20 glasses of water each day, I could barely pee two teacups worth at night. So dry that my nasal drip caused by the pollution in Ouagadougou congealed like a Wyoming waterfall in winter. So drying that when I tried to spit, I had nothing to spit with.

I ended the drive with a desiccated nose that cracked when touched and excruciatingly irritated eyes from a thousand kilometers of desert dust. God's old car ended up in the shop for two days with a broken ball joint, a cranky crankcase, and a leaking radiator that needed extensive welding.

Timbuktu has long been the universal byword for adventure, escape, faraway places, the mysterious inaccessibility of the Sahara, the middle of nowhere, the end of the road. And it is still all that, although it's now a dusty and dreary skeleton of the resplendent city it had been in the 14th century, when it was the capital of the Mali Empire, controlling the entire northwest quadrant of Africa and spreading the worship of Islam throughout the region.

The map shows why Timbuktu is still regarded as the epitome of wilderness adventure: It's one of the most isolated places between the Arctic Circles, set in the brutally hot heart of the world's biggest desert. Head west from Timbuktu and you face a thousand miles of burning sand wastes before you reach the Atlantic Ocean. Go north and confront 1,200 miles of killing desert before you reach reliable water in the foothills of the Atlas Mountains. Venture east and the nearest habitation is Agazir, 900 miles away, and it's just an obsolescent camel-caravan crossroads, with another 1,500 miles of uninhabitable space before any towns. To the south lies the Niger River, the Strong Brown God, snaking for 1,500 miles before entering the Gulf of Guinea in a massive, marshy delta, the same river that thwarted the French and British imperialists for a hundred years with pestilential fevers and fierce riverine tribes.

When Steve and I had driven through the dehydrating deserts on our way around the world, we'd talked about our desert dreams. His was to drink an ice-cold beer in the middle of the Gobi. (And we had, for the past ten years, been talking of visiting Mongolia together, where he'd have the opportunity to quaff that brew.) My desert dream—also a *dessert* dream—had been to suck up an ice cream in Timbuktu. To help move this fantasy closer to a reality, I had, way back in 1988, bought and stored a foil-wrapped packet of freeze-dried ice cream. Shortly before I left on this trip, I'd dusted it off, ignored the expiration date, and put it in my duffel bag. The evening we reached Timbuktu, I dined splendidly atop a blanket spread on the cooling sands as the round red orb of the sun set over the Sahara, savoring the ice cream for which I'd waited more than 40 years.

While God and Bernard voted for the comforts of a hotel near the auto repair shop, I pitched my sleeping bag in an old caravanserai on the edge of town where there was a warm wind blowing the brilliant stars around a cloudless black sky.

I met a Tuareg caravan driver there who invited me to his tent for some tea and goat, and where, in broken French, we exchanged stories, during which I consumed at least four pungent glasses of Tuareg tea laced with fermented camel milk. He told me how, like his father and grandfather before him, he ran his caravan of 120 camels, which plied the ancient route from the salt mines 700 km to the north. And I told him—to his astonishment—about subways, snowball fights, ice-skating, apartment buildings, elevators, skyscrapers, and—Allah forgive me—bikinis.

I felt at ease with the caravan driver, but not with other Muslims I met when I wandered the sandy streets of Timbuktu alone. For more than 30 years I had been comfortable with Arabs and greatly enjoyed their company. On several visits to Morocco I'd shared friendly meals with them in the casbahs and souks. On vacations in Israel I'd spent much time in East Jerusalem, where I had a favorite Arab barber. But on my last visit there, the faces were hostile, and three angry teens had thrown rocks at me. I sensed that attitudes and actions were changing, that the Arabs were no longer as friendly and welcoming. I was even becoming a little afraid of them. This feeling had been negligible, even after February 1998, when the leaders of various jihadi groups promulgated a fatwa titled, "Declaration of the World Islamic Front for Jihad Against the Jews and the Crusaders." I didn't take it seriously—until September 11, 2001.

After I put 9/11 in context with the bombings of the Marine barracks in Lebanon in 1983, of the Khobar Tower apartments in Saudi Arabia in 1996, the U.S. embassies in Nairobi and Tanzania in 1998, and of the *USS Cole* off Yemen in 2000, I began to perceive that ordinary Americans visiting Islamic lands might become targets. Yet I personally encountered no animosity based on my nationality until around 2005.

Most of the 1998 fatwa castigated the U.S., but the operative section that increasingly worried me as I traveled in Muslim countries and took note of increasing acts of Islamic terrorism, was this edict: "By God's leave, we call on every Muslim who believes in God and hopes for reward to obey God's command to kill the Americans and plunder their possessions wherever he finds them and whenever he can." Furthermore, before this trip I had scanned the *hadiths*, which elaborate the Koran and the utterances of the Prophet, and was shaken to find many exhorting the faithful to armed militancy. Those dictates didn't leave any wiggle room, yet I had six more Islamic nations to visit.

It's difficult for most Westerners to comprehend the dominant role religion holds in the lives of devout Muslims. I had a surprisingly frank conversation with two thirtyish Muslim high school teachers in Timbuktu, men who appeared modern and reasonable, wherein they told me, without equivocating, that their duty to jihad would continue until all of us infidels either adopted the Muslim faith or were forced to submit to Muslim rule.

Delighted as I was that I'd finally made it to Timbuktu, I doubted if I'd ever return.

Two years later, a fierce group of radical jihadis and Tuareg swept into Timbuktu, ousted the elected government, took control of the town and all northern Mali, imposed a brutal form of Islamic law, and turned it into a magnet for international terrorists—Afghans, Pakistanis, Nigerians, Ansar Dine, Al-Qaeda in the Islamic Maghreb. They destroyed three UNESCO World Heritage Sites revered by the townspeople, replaced the gentle style of personal worship practiced by the locals with a severe and repressive version of sharia law, stoned a couple to death for adultery, beat and imprisoned those who disagreed with them, sent hundreds of thousands of refugees fleeing, and vowed to end all Western influence and visits. French commandos eventually drove them north into the mountains, where they are still alive, dangerous, and determined.

When the repairs to our vehicle were finished, we headed south-southwest, from whence we'd come, after a day of which we would turn east toward Bandiagara and the Dogon Country, about 600 kilometers distant. After an hour of intense shaking on the washboard track, which had been worn down several feet to the unforgiving rock and hard-packed earth by generations of users, God, who'd had his fill of welding shops, instructed Bernard to drive on the softer desert but stay parallel to the sunken track.

Easier said than done. The sands were so dry and loose they offered little purchase, especially when we had to climb the numerous 20- and 30-foot dunes. After we'd gotten stuck three or four times, and had to dig, drag, and push our way out, Bernard avoided the dunes. Whenever he approached one, he'd veer around it, but invariably to the left, I noticed, southeasterly. Soon we'd lost sight of the track.

I have an excellent sense of direction, and after an hour of dodging dunes, I was sure we were heading southeast and getting way off course and far from the road, but God disagreed. I'd stored my compass in Bamako with most of my gear, making it hard to prove my hunch. We ran into a sandstorm, through which Bernard continued to drive, albeit slowly. The storm intensified and it blocked out the sun for an hour, adding more disorientation. Soon after the air cleared, we reached a track that showed clear signs of having been used by trucks and cars. God was sure it was the track we wanted, and chided me for my lack of faith in his sense of direction, but I was positive it was the wrong track. I looked at my map of Mali and concluded that it was a track toward Ansongo, a small town near the border with Niger and several hundred miles east of where we needed to be. I told this to God and complained that he carried no compass or GPS in this landscape without landmarks.

"I agree that it is very easy to get lost in the Sahara," he replied, "but only if your brain bearings are not working properly. We need no compasses. We go by the wind and, by night, we drive by the moonlight. GPS is something new in the world. It didn't use to exist when I was starting to guide. It is still new to Africa. I do not have a GPS because I do not think it is necessary. Getting lost sometimes in the Sahara is part of the fun as an explorer. It makes you discover new lands and more interesting places. A compass could be helpful, but I don't think it is also necessary. We don't use a compass. We don't use a GPS. We just travel as we feel."

I, for one, was feeling very unhappy. I *knew* that if we were indeed headed toward Ansongo, we could well be stranded there for a week if it had no gas, which was not my idea of "fun as an explorer."

When we stopped for a bathroom break, I took off my watch, laid it flat on the sand, and, with the help of a straight twig and the bright sun, used it as a compass. You align the hour hand with the shadow of the upright twig, and true south will then coincide with a point halfway between the hour hand and the twelve o'clock position on the dial. This technique confirmed we were heading southeast, but God was too proud to yield to a client's sense of direction or my makeshift azimuth indicator.

After half an hour we came to a well under a stand of palm trees where a score of people were encamped and watering their herd, the only people we'd seen in four hours. They spoke not a word of English, or French, or any of the many other languages God knew, but when I carefully repeated the world "Bamako" to them five or six times, they appeared to recognize it, and nodded. Although we were not planning to go all the way to Bamako, it lay in the general direction in which we needed to go, and I felt that, since it was the capital of their nation, they might know where it was. By gestures and a quizzical look I did my best to convey that we wanted to head toward: "Bamako? Bamako! *Bamako!*" They finally understood and pointed us in the correct direction—far to the right, more than 100 degrees west of the way we'd been heading.

God finally gave in and drove west-southwest. It took us two anxious hours before we reached the sunken track we sought and knew we were correctly headed toward Bandiagara.

Since then, God has let me guide him on four other trips—one over the Brooklyn Bridge and three along the sidewalks of New York, where he has a girlfriend whom he visits each year when it is the rainy season in West Africa.

In Bandiagara we had to wait 24 hours for a sandstorm to abate, then left for the all-day drive to the Bandiagara Escarpment to spend three days camping among the Dogons, one of the few ethnic groups to have retained their ancient customs and avoided conquest, thanks to their formidable mountain redoubts.

I'd been fascinated by them for 30 years, ever since I'd bought an elongated Dogon sculpture of what I thought was a dachshund but turned out to be their fanciful vision of a horse. I felt some trepidation, however, as we approached their redoubt because I wasn't sure the Dogons and I were compatible: They equate a woman's vagina to an ant hole and her clitoris to a termite mound, and I'd never thought about them that way. Nor did I want to.

The 400,000 Dogons inhabit the central plateau of Mali, south of the big bend in the Niger, in a region bisected by the Bandiagara Escarpment, a sandstone cliff 1,600 feet high and a hundred miles long. They fled there from other parts of Mali a thousand years ago, after they refused to forsake their ancestor worship and animist beliefs for those of Islam, and took up defensible positions along the cliff and within its caves. Under Islamic law, they were classified as *ar al-harib*, fit for slavery. The Arab slave traders had murdered the men they caught and shipped their women and children off to servitude in the burgeoning cities of West Africa.

They are not an aggressive people. They strive for peaceful tribal harmony, which they warmly display at periodic ceremonies where the women praise the men, the men thank the women, the children express reverence for the elders, and the elders acknowledge the contributions of the young.

They first lived here as subsistence farmers, channeling rivulets of rainwater that flowed to the base of the escarpment to grow pearl millet, rice, sorghum, tobacco, peanuts, and vegetables. They later fashioned an ingenious irrigation system and now make good money raising a substantial cash crop of sweet onions that are in demand throughout West Africa. As we drove through the otherwise monochromatic, khaki-colored topography toward the escarpment, we passed field after field of these onions, incongruously dark green, lush and cool.

The Dogons believe in female genital mutilation. FGM is widely performed through Africa, primarily as a tactic by male-dominated societies to deprive women of sexual pleasure, believing this will keep them faithful. The Dogons, however, employ FGM for an entirely different and, to them, totally fair and helpful reason. They believe that when their god created the universe, He was inexperienced and made some mistakes, leaving men with a useless feminine part, the foreskin, and women with an unnecessary masculine part, the clitoris. The Dogons, men and women alike, seek to correct these "errors" and enable each sex to assume its proper identity through circumcision, making men more masculine and women more feminine, by eliminating those "superfluous" parts—sort of equal-opportunity mutilation. They conduct the ceremony with great care and pride in a special circumcision cave using the sharp and sterilized instruments of the village blacksmith, after which they watch over the circumcised youths until all danger of infection has passed.

Far from being sexist, the Dogons accord women more esteem and equality than most African societies. A Dogon woman is not regarded as a servant or chattel, but as an independent person who comes and goes as she wishes. She is not required to share her husband with another wife, leaves her home whenever she wants, and is economically self-sufficient. She has her personal granary, where she keeps her clothes, grooming supplies, jewelry, food, and any money she earns from farming, basketmaking, or selling sculptures.

So how should our supposedly enlightened Western civilization confront the Dogon practice of FGM? Should we accept and respect it or try to impose our values on them? Are we right? Are they wrong? Who are we to judge?

We returned to Bamako and bade each other a fond farewell. Bernard gave me his XL Oakland Raiders T-shirt (which can be dangerous to wear on Jets turf), and I reciprocated with a Big Apple tee bearing the picture of a bright yellow taxi, which he treasures. God flew to Casablanca to meet his New York girlfriend and Bernard took a three-day bus trip back to Ghana. I was now a week behind schedule because of the breakdowns, so I flew to Mauritania instead of going by land as I'd planned. We left the battered Cruiser in a workshop in Bamako, waiting to receive a replacement radiator, although I think what it really needed to receive was Extreme Unction.

I chipped in for the repairs, but the decline of the dollar was a shocker. Its value had eroded 25 percent since I'd traveled the past summer, and merchants throughout Africa now shunned it. On previous trips, my dollars were always in demand. People had desired the dollar, saved it for a droughty day, and much preferred it to any other currency. Now they didn't want it, and it was almost embarrassing for me to ask them to take it. Its slide had been so precipitous and continuous that the money changers were afraid to hold it even one day, lest their profit on the exchange evaporate. It was a humbling experience for one who'd always felt proud and powerful dispensing green-backs.

I was not looking forward to the part of West Africa south of Mauritania. I take no pleasure in visiting once peaceful and prosperous nations destroyed by stupid wars. I'd delayed these visits for more than five years, waiting for most of the killing to stop in Liberia, Sierra Leone, Ivory Coast, and Nigeria. I was heartened when, a few days before my departure from New York, the Ivory Coast announced it was peaceful enough to start delivering the five million pieces of mail that had accumulated during its civil war. But I'd need a lot more good news to make me look forward to this slog.

Each of these states was sure to be, in its own way, distressing and depressing because of their recent civil wars and internal disputes. Most Africans had received, and therefore expected, little from life, but the citizens of three of these states had been well on their way to having it all before they blew it, and they therefore felt the loss ever more deeply. How humiliating to have been the shining success of the continent and to have pissed it away. How ironic to call such a country "developing" when it was sliding backward. I frankly admit that I was only going there to check them off the list, and I wanted to get through them as quickly as possible.

But I was thwarted right from the get-go. The flight schedules along my route were a shambles because the civil wars had so severely disrupted air traffic that they'd bankrupted many African airlines. Others had fallen victim to government corruption: The ruling elite in many of these countries treated the airlines as their personal toys, often commandeering them on short notice to fly their families somewhere, bouncing the paying passengers, eventually forcing them out of business. My plan to fly directly from Nouakchott, the capital of Mauritania, to Freetown, the capital of Sierra Leone, just a few hundred miles down the coast, proved impossible. I was compelled to fly from Mauritania to Dakar in Senegal, from Dakar to Abidjan in Ivory Coast, from Abidjan to Accra, the capital of Ghana, and, at long last, to a dilapidated airport in Sierra Leone, from which I had to take a five-hour journey by bus and ferry to reach Freetown because so many roads and bridges had been demolished, consuming two days for what should have been a two-hour jaunt.

Sierra Leone, with its abundance of gold and diamonds, had been a flourishing economy before it erupted into a ferocious civil war from 1991 to 2002. It was now one of the ten poorest on earth. It had been set back decades, with a crumbling infrastructure and dire poverty. I saw Freetown's dusty streets filled with the armless and legless victims of its recent fratricide, so numerous that the amputees held daily soccer games on homemade crutches, a pathetic poor man's Paralympics. I did not stay long.

The Ivory Coast had been, in the 1980s, widely hailed as an economic miracle and a model of West African stability. It began to destabilize in the late 90s, with the decline in cocoa prices and mounting foreign debt. It crumbled on Christmas Day of 1999, when the military staged a coup over unpaid wages, poor living conditions, and government corruption. And it collapsed into chaos in 2004 when machete-wielding mobs of thousands attacked French homes and military bases. By the time I felt it safe to visit, I saw only a decayed hulk, drab and lifeless, of peeling paint, crumbling concrete, buildings whose walls had been sprayed by machine guns, high inflation, high unemployment, the irreplaceable loss of the French expats who had run the economy, and few prospects. I did not stay long.

Liberia had been ruled for more than 150 years by former American slave families who constituted less than 5 percent of the population and treated the indigenous folks like dirt, but who nevertheless managed to create, until the 1970s, a profitable economy based on rubber and other natural resources. It was now an economy where the only ones doing well were those who sold barbed wire or supplied armed guards. Razor wire and broken bottles embedded in cement bristled atop every wall. Hundreds of UN soldiers with blue armbands protected the government buildings, most of which had been burned or ransacked. Security personnel in army boots and carrying nightsticks were stationed outside most shops. Yet, thanks to the paternalistic attitude and financial assistance the U.S. has long maintained toward Liberia (which the Liberians reciprocated with a strong and genuine love for America), I witnessed the hope for a better tomorrow there, with dozens of rebuilding projects dotting Monrovia, many sponsored by USAID. But tomorrow is not today, so I did not stay long.

My rapid exits from Liberia and Sierra Leone were partly due to my inability to communicate. Although English was the official language of both, they spoke it in a rapid, high-pitched patois with Creole overtones that rendered them less comprehensible to me than Uzbeks.

According to news I'd picked up from the backpacker brigade—often the most reliable source of travel tips—the Nigerians had not killed a visitor for at least three days, so I decided to give it a shot—and hope it didn't give me one. I'd vacillated about whether to visit Nigeria on this trip out of concern about the risky security situation; the continuing conflict between its predominantly Muslim north and Christian south; the religious uproar over the staging of its Miss World contest; the anger over the inequitable distribution of its large oil income, most of which was lining the pockets of the governing class; and a widespread belief that this once-leading light of African economies was going to hell in a handbasket. But—again that tug-of-war between safety and desire—if I was able to get there on this swing, that would vastly simplify my future travel plans, because I'd then have visited every country in the northern third of Africa except Chad and every country on its west coast as far south as Angola.

I flew into Lagos, the largest city in Africa, home to an estimated 21 million, and the only high-rise, glass-sheathed, Western-type city on this trip, and one of only three such on the continent. It combined the sweltering summer climate of Houston with the architectural ambience of Detroit, the exorbitant prices of Tokyo, and the hospitality of Turkmenistan. It had only two redeeming qualities: fast Internet with American-layout keyboards, and the best pepper-pot goat soup that side of the Caribbean.

Towering thunderheads had started massing above the coastline, leading to nightly bursts of precipitation portending the start of the rainy season, of impassable roads and insect infestations. I did not stay long.

I'd had enough days of dirt, flies, open sewers, rotting fruit, and cold-water bucket baths; of kids with machine guns, kids with crutches, kids with missing arms or legs; the ubiquitous odors of unwashed bodies; of daylong drives down dusty, rattling roads in worn-out vans; bumbling bureaucrats; brownouts, blackouts, and blowouts; trying to converse in fractured French; unpasteurized dairy products; storekeepers so poor they lacked change for a single dollar; chronically late plane departures for invariably indirect itineraries; ultra-slow computers with unfamiliar French keyboards; food vendors who washed their dishes in the same bucket of dirty water all day; merchants who falsely promised to give you "a good price"; and dozens of daily confrontations with the poverty, suffering, deprivation, and misery of others. I'd had my fill of TIA.

After so many weeks on the road, I was tired and homesick. I missed New York, my girlfriend, my cozy apartment, my bicycle, *real* ice cream, chocolates, sushi, salmon, Diet Sprite, the gym, hot showers, smooth sheets, NPR, *The New York Times, The Atlantic,* even *The Economist,* the stock market, the theater, movies, laundromats, bright light bulbs, English, and the St. Patrick's Day Parade up Fifth Avenue, which I might still make if I got a move on. It was time to head home.

# CHAPTER 13

## "Do Not Kidnap Anyone Today!"

I was not adequately prepared for my customs inspection when I landed in Houston en route to Miami after visiting Colombia in early 2009. Because I was arriving from a cocaine-exporting country, I presumed I'd be subjected to close scrutiny, and since I knew from my past experience with numerous strip searches that I fit the standard drug-dealer/ terrorist profile to which the Department of Homeland Security was so rigidly and myopically attached, I'd diligently prepared for a thorough search. I'd made a list for customs of the eight places where I'd hidden cash from possible bandits, so the inspectors wouldn't conclude I was laundering money or violating currency regulations. I'd carefully packed my powdered milk next to my whole-grain cereal so my inspector got the message that not all white powder is narcotic. And I'd listed on my customs declaration the copal and the emeralds in matrix I was bringing back from Colombian mines, so they wouldn't think I was a jewel smuggler. I thought I'd covered every base.

What I'd failed to consider was that a meticulous customs agent, with some time on his hands at five a.m., would go through *every* item in my luggage, including all my travel literature and papers, where he found my itinerary, which clearly stated, with the relevant dates, that I planned to "fly to Miami, fly to Haiti, tour Haiti," and then—*uh-oh*—"visit Cuba for a week," followed by "fly to Jamaica." The Cuba trip was prohibited by U.S. law ab-

On the main route from the capital of Port-au-Prince to the big city of Cap-Haïtien, the road was clogged with water, rocks, landslides, and garbage months after a big storm had hit. Haiti is the poorest country in the Western hemisphere and one of the saddest anywhere.

sent special authorization, which I lacked. This incriminating notation required a half hour of fast and convincing talking—not my forte at five a.m.—before I was finally released, albeit with a stern warning and a disbelieving scowl from the agent, after I'd lamely explained that "Cuba" was my nickname for an old Haitian girlfriend with whom I planned to reconnect for a week.

Haiti was so awful that I quickly understood why the customs agent had been so incredulous when I told him I planned to spend more than a week there, girlfriend or not. To paraphrase General Phil Sheridan, if I owned both Haiti and Hell, I would try to rent out Haiti and live in Hell.

Haiti is regularly ravaged by floods, tropical storms, and hurricanes. The weather can be wretchedly hot or bone-chillingly wet and cold. The thin chalky soil was now so depleted I felt sorry for the forlorn weeds trying to eke out a living there, although a few areas still retained the rich earth that had once made Haiti desirable as a sugar-growing colony. More than 90 percent of the terrain was too steep for sustainable agriculture, and the desperate attempts of poor farmers to cultivate it almost invariably resulted in erosion and environmental degradation. The country couldn't grow enough food to feed its population of ten million. The trees had been felled for firewood ages ago, and Haiti had no other fuel resources. The one abundant natural resource was hydroelectric power from the swollen rivers rushing down the mountains, but that was itself a destructive demon.

Haiti ranked near the top of the world corruption index, and its past rulers absconded with hundreds of millions. It languished at the bottom of the hemisphere's Human Development Index, with half the population illiterate, few children receiving adequate schooling, much child slavery, open violence against women, and persistently high unemployment. More than 80 percent of Haitians lived below the poverty line of $2 a day, 54 percent in abject poverty, and the richest one percent owned 50 percent of the assets.

It was the poorest nation in the Western Hemisphere and seemed to me the least happy. The Haitians appeared down and dour, with no time or inclination for frivolity. I heard not one laugh in a week, not even a giggle, saw no kids at play, not one happy face, although I was told Haiti has a culture rich with proverbs, riddles, jokes, songs, and games.

As I entered the shabby capital of Port-au-Prince, all that was missing was Dante's sign: ABANDON ALL HOPE, YE WHO ENTER HERE. Instead, the local Chamber of Commerce had strung a big banner across the road exhorting the locals, in Creole, to HELP HAITI'S ECONOMY. DO NOT KIDNAP ANYONE TODAY!

Although seldom visited by American tourists, Haiti has had, I believe, a greater impact on our lives and history than any other noncontiguous country in our hemisphere:

- Haiti is on the island of Hispaniola, and *that* is where Columbus landed in 1492, opening up the New World.
- Inspired by the American and the French Revolutions, Haiti's slaves rebelled in 1791. In 1804 it became the second colony in the Western Hemisphere to cast off a subservient yoke and proclaim itself a republic, the world's first black-led republic, serving notice that democracy might have a broad future in the New World.

- Its slave unrest and independence movement impelled Napoleon to abandon his ambitious plan to use it as a base for expanding his empire in the Americas, and motivated him to sell France's extensive landholdings in North America to the fledgling United States—in what came to be known as the Louisiana Purchase—without which our country would have ended at the Mississippi River.
- The successful Haitian uprising so terrified Southern slaveholders in the U.S. that they instituted harsher punishments for disobedience, which, in turn, fanned the fires of abolitionism in the North. And we all know what that led to.
- In the 1980s Haiti was unfairly designated as one of the Four Hs then thought responsible for the AIDS epidemic along with homosexuals, heroin users, and hemophiliacs.
- Haiti supplied a large part of the population of central Brooklyn, the only place in the U.S. where I've found a proper goat stew.

Because Haiti had few safe hotels, I'd arranged, through a missionary friend who runs an outstanding charity there called Beyond Borders, to stay at the Methodist Church Guest House in Pétionville, high up the hill overlooking Port-au-Prince. About a dozen American lay missionaries with special skills passed through there every few days en route to assignments around Haiti, where they performed valuable volunteer service for two weeks, from running medical clinics to building schools to drilling water wells. Since many of them were female—friendly, generous, innocent Midwesterners—and since I was one of the rare nonmissionaries allowed to live in the Guest House, it was akin to giving the fox the key to the hen house. But even this ol' fox was never able to put it in the keyhole because the lovely ladies were down the hall in a room of six and I was sharing a room of eight bunk beds with seven highly vigilant and protective male missionaries.

I'd rented a car for ten days, planning to cross the island from end to end and side to side. My local contacts persuaded me that, because of the wretched roads, the language difficulties, and the theft of all traffic signs for use as firewood or shack building, I needed a native driver. They recommended a teenage orphan who'd been in their care and could use the income. I met him, liked him, and hired him. He just forgot to mention one thing: He didn't know how to operate a car.

He showed up for departure with a third man, a surly lout *he* had hired to drive, while he would translate and show me points of interest. I now had two extra mouths to feed and house, one a driver who did not know how to drive and the other a driver who drove like a jerk. I fired the lout after three days of dumb and dangerous driving, and I drove us to Cap-Haïtien while he sulked in the back and my guide desperately searched for points of interest to point out, of which there were none.

After we returned to Pétionville, I dumped the lout and drove the orphan over the interior mountains to Jacmel for its annual Carnival. We stayed for two days with an American college dropout who was teaching the local women to weave handbags and change purses from discarded black garbage bags, one of the few items in plentiful supply on the island.

We all went to Carnival in blackface, a common and inoffensive practice in Haiti. If you decide to do likewise, do not make the neophyte's mistake of using motor oil or shoe polish for the cover-up. The preferred formula is a combination of powdered charcoal, clerin (an alcoholic beverage), and sugar cane juice. The flies love it, so add some DEET.

The only tangible benefits I derived from my visit to Haiti are eight powerful paintings in traditional Haitian style with African overtones, and a bit of voodoo lore my good guide Godfried had somehow forgotten to impart to me: If you ever need to kill a voodoo priest, be sure to cut out his tongue and eyes so he cannot direct any retributive demons against you from the afterworld. How come you never told me about that, God?

I had had high hopes for what I thought might be an exotic, offbeat, and un-touristed destination, but it turned out to be the worst dung heap I'd been in, which covers a lot of territory. Unless you love seeing poverty and misery, or have a calling for missionary work, or want to stock up on excellent paintings at low prices, I can't think of any reason to visit Haiti. In fact, I can readily think of many reasons not to go. To list a few:

- The Creole they speak is difficult to understand.
- The roads are among the worst anywhere and make driving, even

in towns, a torture. (The only worse roads I've driven are in the
Gambia, CAR, northern Afghanistan, and a six hundred-mile
stretch in Iran in 1965 that has surely been paved by now.)

- People encroach on the roads everywhere, and the hundreds of
  what should be road*side* stands come so far onto the surviving bit
  of concrete as to make driving a horror.
- The natives were not readily approachable. Polite and friendly
  when you're introduced by someone they know and trust, they
  generally present to strangers a dour, apprehensive, unwelcoming
  visage. It's nothing personal; they're just so beaten down by the
  daily grind of trying to stay alive that they don't have the energy
  to be gregarious.
- The locals were vocally opposed to having their pictures taken;
  they'd sooner throw a rock at you than pose for a picture (and
  if there's anything Haiti has in abundance, it is rocks). Their
  attitude stems from some voodoo beliefs mixed with generations of
  having their dictators' secret police spying on them, and their
  belief—not unfounded—that opportunists use or sell photos of the
  disadvantaged for their own advantage.
- Aside from the fine views offered from mountain roads in the
  interior (which few would dare to drive) the island lacks physical
  beauty. Even its beaches are bland and unappealing.
- The food available to travelers had little variety and was almost
  always fried. There are few restaurants because the people are too
  poor to eat out.
- Because Haiti is not self-sufficient in much and has to import
  virtually everything, prices are inordinately high, especially if they
  know you're a tourist.
- The governing elite did nothing for the people; it only put money
  in its own pockets. Six months after two hurricanes hit the center
  of the island, streets in the cities still were blocked with piles of
  mud and debris, and many of the washed-out roads had not been
  repaired, forcing me to make lengthy, arduous, detours.
- There was not much to do. The only legal diversions I saw the

locals engaging in were wagering at Lotto, playing awful music at
ear-shattering levels, shaking their booties, and rooting for any
African or Latin American soccer team that was opposing France.
• Above all, the future here seemed—and may well be—hopeless.
The nation survives, but barely, on international handouts. No
large industries functioned there, no minable mineral resources
enriched the land, no agriculture flourished (some sugar cane, rice,
a few tropical fruits). Several million children were attending
school, to graduate to a job market suitable for maybe a thousand.
Decades of mistreatment by a succession of despotic, self-serving
rulers have left the populace dismayed, distrustful, and beaten
down.

It's hard to enjoy a holiday in a land so poor that parents sometimes give
away their children to wealthier people to provide them with a chance for a
better life, where the bodily organs of deceased disaster victims may be sold
to medical shops, and where newly orphaned kids have been abducted after
natural disasters and sold into slavery or sexual bondage.

To be fair to Haiti, I admit I may have what sociologists call a "roadside
bias." Their theory is that some aspects of living get better the farther one
goes from the asphalt, that the more isolated residents are generally kinder,
more hospitable, helpful, and unassuming. This may be true, but many important services diminish the farther you get from the roads, including access
to good health care, education, entertainment, and food variety. Any way you
look at it, it's a sad, sad place.

And that was the situation a year before a 7.0 earthquake killed around
200,000 in 2010. Before the deadly cholera epidemic. Before the challenged
election. Before the return of dictator Baby Doc. And before Tropical Storm
Isaac and Hurricane Sandy hit.

The New York Times summed it up in November 2012: "They had little,
had endured much, and now need more."

Help by donating to CARE, UNICEF, Save the Children, or Beyond
Borders. But spare yourself the visit.

# CHAPTER 14

## Your Man in Havana

As I was waiting at Haiti's Toussaint Louverture Airport to board the aging Ilyushin airliner for my clandestine flight to Havana, the officials shepherded about 50 Haitians past me and onto the plane. They were mostly middle-aged and so gaunt and frail I wondered why they were flying. It was not until I was inescapably strapped in my seat among them that I found out they were heading to Cuba for medical treatment. For tuberculosis! (Ever try holding your breath for 90 minutes?)

I arrived in Santiago de Cuba misguidedly thinking I'd be welcomed as a Hero of the Revolution for defying the U.S. embargo and being one of the rare Americans to fly into Cuba without the official exemption granted by the U.S. to medical and missionary workers or attendees at a professional conference. Instead, I aroused their suspicions. They assumed I was CIA.

They asked my occupation, but doubted that I was "retired"; nor did they buy my story about trying to visit every country. They were skeptical of why I was carrying $4,000 cash, even after I explained I had six more Caribbean countries to visit. (They'd have been far more distrustful if they'd found the additional $4,000 hidden in my belt, boots, and a hollowed-out book.) My bulging 50-page passport led them to believe the Agency was sending me around the globe to foment trouble. And I'd walked off the plane carrying a copy of John le Carré's *The Spy Who Came in from the Cold*, which didn't help. But would a real spy have the *cojones* to do that?

They were on edge about the CIA. Recently declassified documents exposed that, from 1960 to 1961, shortly after John Kennedy became president, the CIA had conspired with the Chicago Mafia (which was angry at Fidel Castro for having closed down its lucrative Cuban gambling casinos) to have him assassinated.

A team of three uniformed and well-informed security agents questioned me for two hours. They studied each page of my passport, attempting to relate each entry or exit stamp to some contemporaneous anti-Communist or anti-Socialist world event: Did I have anything to do with the death of the authoritarian president of Turkmenistan? Was I involved in the referendum Hugo Chávez lost two years ago in Venezuela? What role did I play in the overthrow of the president of Fiji? Was it truly a coincidence I was in Khartoum the very day Chad attacked and almost captured it? Was I involved in the negotiations to renew U.S. rights to use the airbase in Kazakhstan? Why did antigovernment riots erupt the day I landed in Bangalore? Did I expect them to believe it was a mere coincidence that two days after I left the northeast of Sri Lanka, the government resumed its offensive against the Tamil Tiger freedom fighters? Didn't Latvia ask the Russian troops to leave shortly after I visited Riga? (They were bluffing on that one; my Latvian stamps were in a much older passport.) Hadn't the U.S. begun preparing Djibouti as a base from which to attack Saddam Hussein while I was there? Didn't Ethiopia and Eritrea resume their war shortly after I visited both countries?

I tried to explain, as politely as possible, that these were all really, *truly*, mere coincidences, and that if I had orchestrated even a quarter of the acts they suspected, I'd be the greatest agent provocateur in history. I repeatedly sought to convince them that, if I really were CIA, I'd have half a dozen passports at my disposal in various names, and there'd be no paper trail for them to scrutinize. All to no avail.

What ultimately persuaded them of my innocence was my response to their question about where I'd be staying in Havana. When I gave them the name of my backpacker's hostel and showed them the receipt for my reservation—made through an innocuous-sounding front in Toronto because the U.S. embargo did not allow Americans to use a credit card for any transaction in or with Cuba—they promptly stamped me in and allowed me to board the plane for Havana. They'd quickly concluded that no self-respecting CIA operative would ever stay at such a dump.

Havana was wonderful. The people were extremely warm and hospitable to the rare *gringo* they got to meet. (The city was packed with young tourists from Spain, France, Germany, Scandinavia, and South America.) Havana had a certain raffish charm, with a quarter of the guys selling cigars on the street and a quarter of the women selling themselves. In pleasant contrast to the horrible life-or-death atmosphere of Haiti, Havana was calm and relaxed, uncongested and peaceful. I saw none of the standard indicia of a repressive dictatorship or of a people unhappy with their government: no tanks guarding the presidential palace; no soldiers or cops with assault rifles on the corners; no ubiquitous photos of Our Dear Leader; no walls or billboards plastered with political slogans, save one tattered sign celebrating the 50th anniversary of the revolution. The people discussed politics openly, had high hopes for reasonable treatment from Barack Obama (who was just starting his first year as president), and showed no signs of being repressed or fearful.

I saw few cars on the streets. Most of the locals used the ultramodern buses or the tiny, brightly painted, three-wheeled putt-putts. But the cars I did see—the same cars they had before the revolution—were a glorious reminder of the Fabulous Fifties, ostentatious gas-guzzlers sporting tailfins, Dagmar bumpers, and a ton of chrome: Chevys, Fords, Plymouths, Dodges, Studebakers, Buicks, and Oldsmobiles, all lovingly cared for and repainted in brilliant colors, but mainly aquamarine. Here and there a few Soviet-era Ladas. Gone to the scrap heap were the magnificent cars of the 40s: the DeSotos and LaSalles, the Chrysler New Yorkers, and the big Caddies.

The food was plentiful and tasty. And familiar: My ex-wife was the daughter of an American engineer who'd worked on projects in Cuba in the 1950s, where she learned to cook delicious *piccadillo* and *ropa vieja*.

Columbus, after sailing along the coast of Cuba in 1492, exclaimed, "this is the fairest isle man has ever seen." But let's remember that Chris had limited experience with tropical isles in those flat-earth days, and that his opinion was expressed before eleven million hungry folks chopped the forests into

Because the Communist regime in Cuba forbids the ownership of valuable private property, there are few cars and no congestion on the island's roads. In rural areas, people and goods are often transported by home-made carts like these, and in the cities the few cars were lovingly preserved relics from the '50s.

plantations. The part of Cuba I crossed was mostly flat, with some hills and rolling terrain, pretty rivers, and three distant mountain ranges, some rising to 6,000 feet. I visited a lovely valley and a pretty good cave in the northwest. The jungles were gone, and though Cuba claimed to have 80 varieties of palms, the majority I saw were the misnamed royal palm, which looks like two telephone poles stuck end-to-end with a few leaves glued on top like a green toupee, its fruit only fit for pigs, the island's main source of meat.

The old colonial towns usually had a well-preserved central square, the Plaza Mayor, but the other parts looked as if they hadn't been refurbished since the Rough Riders charged up San Juan Hill in 1898.

Most of the land under cultivation was in cash crops, either tobacco or sugar, both of which were in trouble. Cuba lost its prized touch in rolling cigars when the old artisans jumped ship for Florida, and the sugar-based monoculture, which sustained it financially for two hundred years, had declined precipitously. After the triumph of Castro's revolution in 1959, sugar was able to prop up the economy because the Soviet Union, as a gesture of Socialist solidarity, agreed to buy all of it that Cuba grew at prices above the world market rate, and also barter some sugar for Russian oil priced below market. After the Berlin Wall fell in 1990, Mikhail Gorbachev cancelled that contract, and about 100 of Cuba's 160 sugar mills also fell, while many cane fields reverted to weeds.

The financial void had been filled, to some extent, by nickel mining and tourism, but the main hard-currency export was doctors, 40,000 of whom were working throughout South and Central America, with their paychecks going into the Cuban Treasury.

Everybody worked for the state in this Communist society. All the businesses I visited—banks, factories, tour agencies, farms, stores, cleaners, publishers, hotels, restaurants, and souvenir shops—were owned by the state. No meaningful private property was allowed, although those who owned land before the revolution were allowed to keep 80 hectares, and those who owned those wonderful old Buicks and Oldsmobiles were allowed to pass them on to their grandchildren. But Cubans could not sell their old cars or any of their land because Fidel had no tolerance for private property aside from inexpensive personal effects.

Although everyone was an employee of the state, the system was far less rigid than the one imposed throughout Red China from 1960 into the 1980s, where the state determined, early in one's life, what career one pursued and where one worked and lived. Once that had been decided, the hapless Chinese citizen was usually stuck with that role for life, or at least until a more enlightened leadership came to power with Mao's passing. To my eye it seemed that the Cuban form of Communism also worked better than that system in the USSR. The workers, waiters, and shop girls I encountered all genuinely tried to be helpful and give good service, even though they received nothing extra for it. In the old USSR, most of the people in those positions got their jollies by ignoring those they were supposed to assist or by treating us with open disdain.

The main economic problem with the Cuban system was that the government didn't pay the workers enough to live a comfortable life, even though nobody starved and all were guaranteed a high school education, unlimited free medical care, and a social safety net. Starting salaries in most positions were $12 a month, rising to $24 for more experienced or managerial workers. This low wage was the most vocal complaint of the Cubans with whom I spoke. They didn't mind being ruled by the Castro brothers, or not being able to have real elections, or not being allowed to march against City Hall, but they did mind trying to live in a workers' paradise on 40 cents a day. Everybody wanted to find a way to earn more money, even though everybody was supposed to be equal.

While I was there, the government was just starting to listen to them and to loosen up the system. In February 2008, after a full 50 years in charge of the Revolution, Fidel Castro had resigned, and his brother Raúl was promoted to president, bringing with him hope for liberalization, which, on my visit one year later, I could see was coming. Slowly.

The government had begun issuing licenses to individuals to rent out rooms in their apartments to tourists (with the government grabbing 65 percent), and had started allowing some folks to sell and serve food from their homes, but only through those windows opening onto the street. They could not yet convert the ground floor to a restaurant, but I felt it was sure to come.

The government was also not interfering with the young men who'd converted bicycles to pedicabs and earned unreported income ferrying people about. Prostitution and tipping from tourists had also become large sources of supplemental income, even though the police clamped down hard on the sex because selling one's body was officially incompatible with Communism, as it was deemed to tacitly express the participants' disapproval of the collectivist system. It was clearly a form of private enterprise—the most private of all—and an implicit statement that the government was not paying that person enough.

I was sad to leave Havana. It's one of the world's most livable cities and must have been spectacular during its glory days before, and for a decade after, WW II. It has superb weather in the Caribbean winter; bright, sunny days with cool ocean breezes from three directions; broad boulevards; little pollution; no traffic congestion; a score of sun-dappled, palm-treed parks with whispering fountains and plenty of comfortable benches; dozens of ornate old forts, palaces, and public buildings; convivial, well-educated residents; handsome, athletic-looking men and svelte, graceful women; and good food at reasonable prices, including some delicious pizzas for 30 cents a pie from home kitchens.

I had hoped the U.S. would abandon its embargo so others could enjoy Cuba, and was pleased when President Obama substantially relaxed the regulations on contacts. The embargo made little sense, other than as a Cold War vestige maintained to mollify an impassioned coterie of 1.2 million irredentist émigrés who regularly vote, primarily in Florida. It's been in effect since 1961, and Cuba had not collapsed, but had instead become the center of an anti-American Socialist coalition with Venezuela and Bolivia, supported by China. The embargo was counterproductive because it made Cuba more exotic and whetted the interest of Europeans and others to visit. It encouraged deception and hypocrisy, with visas easily obtained in Jamaica, flights taken from Haiti, and cases of Coke and Sprite winging in from the bottler in Mexico City. Does it make sense that this was the only country to which our government forbids us to travel?

The big news during my stay was that Fidel was alive! He made his first public appearance in many months, to greet the president of Chile, dispelling rumors he'd kicked the bucket. Nevertheless, Cuba is slowly moving away from his brand of rigid Communism and allowing, even encouraging, some forms of free enterprise, a trend that should continue as Fidel fades from the scene and other, less rigid and more liberal, leaders take over.

Cuba constitutes a remarkable paradox, a striking failure on human rights, but an outstanding success in human development, requiring the fair-minded monitor to give each its due.

As for human rights, there were virtually none. In almost every year of the last 45, more than 20,000 dissident Cubans had been imprisoned for political reasons, solely because of the way they think. Teachers and professors who did not espouse the party line were routinely purged. Homosexuals, religious practitioners, and other "undesirables" were sent to labor camps to be brutally "reeducated." The state controlled all radio, TV, and newspapers, and used them to purvey propaganda. Neighbors were organized to spy on neighbors through the Committees for the Defense of the Revolution. More than a million fled, mostly to the U.S. And though hard figures were hard to come by, it was widely accepted that between 15,000 and

17,000 people were executed by the regime, mostly in the formative years of the Revolution.

Against this bleak record of human wrongs, Cuba scores high on the Human Development Index (HDI), ironically attributable to the same authoritarian, state-controlled system. Its literacy rate was 99.8 percent, second highest of any state. Its infant mortality rate was among the lowest, and current life expectancy—which likely did not include the executed dissidents— was 78.3 years, 36th longest among mankind, on this largest and most populous island in the Caribbean. In 2006 Cuba was *the only nation* to satisfy the WWF definition of sustainable development, having reduced its ecological footprint to less than 1.8 hectares per capita. In 2010 it boasted an HDI over 800, third best in the Caribbean. And, most telling of all, Cuba's national baseball team regularly beat ours in international competition, winning nine straight World Cup championships in one stretch.

I don't imply that the ends justify the means, for the message is mixed in this "workers' paradise" just off our shores. It's like locking a person in prison for life, but providing him with first-rate tutors, outstanding medical care, and three square meals a day. You end up with a healthy, educated prisoner who lives a long, restricted, and incomplete life in a cell without walls called Cuba.

Several days after I left, Raúl Castro announced critical reforms that, without his saying so, moved Cuba away from total Communism. A month later, President Obama announced the U.S. was easing travel restrictions to Cuba and was introducing a "series of steps [to] be taken to reach out to the Cuban people to support their desire to enjoy basic human rights and to freely determine their country's future." By 2012 some 400,000 Cubans were self-employed—22 percent of the workforce—and Raúl Castro declared he wanted to move 40 percent of the country's output to the nonstate sector within five years.

I assure you, and my intrepid interrogators, that I had nothing to do with any of this. It was just another of those odd coincidences. Really.

# CHAPTER 15

## You Are What You Eat

I had few menu options on these journeys and little time to be picky about food. As a lifelong omnivore, I ate whatever was available—except endangered species, raw sea urchin, and tortured veal.

An essential part of the discovery and adventure (and sometimes the delight) of travel comes from sampling the unusual foods the locals eat, foods they've been eating for hundreds of years without noticeable harm. Dining on the indigenous fare also helped me better understand the local culture and economy and the way they lived.

In the course of my travels I've eaten: armadillo (in the hills of Grenada); zebra (Kenya); fish lips, fish eyes, fungus soup, duck's feet (all in China); kangaroo, ostrich, emu, and Moreton Bay bugs (Australia); fugu sushi (carefully prepared in Japan from poisonous puffer fish); guinea pig (Peru, Bolivia); snake (all over); spotted dick and blue-teat pie (England); horse (Mongolia, Kyrgyzstan, and CAR); possum pie, callaloo, dasheen, sapodillas, pawpaws, and cush-cush (various Caribbean islands); gnu, antelope, eland, gazelle, springbok, steenbok, klipspringer, kudu, nyala, and oryx (sub-Saharan and southern Africa); pigeon (France and Morocco); iguana (Central America); blood sausage (Colombia and Germany); smashed chicken infused with sugar and covered with ice cream (Turkey); crocodile (Africa and Australia); roasted duck gizzard, braised jellyfish, spicy soup of shredded intestines and organ meats boiled in blood, (all in China); pig's blood porridge, caramelized fish hatchlings, lotus root salad, steamed blood cockles, caramelized pork belly and Mekong rat (Vietnam); toasted leafcutter ants, oven-baked tarantulas, waxworm potato fritters, bees, beetles, crickets, worms, caterpillars, scorpions, wax moth larvae, and grubs (in many places, and not always intentionally); and just about every fruit and vegetable under the sun.

Among the more memorable culinary experiments was an anteater Steve and I found recently run over on a road in Panama. Not wanting to waste a good source of protein, we chopped it up, added salt and pepper, wished we had a box of Roadkill Helper, roasted it over a campfire, and it tasted . . . awful, like a burger marinated in formic acid.

And a platter of sea cucumber—a cold, black, warty little creature served as a gelatinous, forbidding-looking dark lump—which, once ingested, tasted like a mix of Jell-O, lard, and library paste.

Rats are, in contrast—and after you overcome any squeamish cultural bias—rather tasty, especially the big ones eaten in Africa, where they're called "grasscutters," an appealing appellation doubtless bestowed by the branding consultant who renamed the Patagonian toothfish as "Chilean sea bass" and the slimefish as "orange roughy." The locals skin the rodents, split them down the middle, spread them out flat, and roast or grill them. Each tastes exactly like what it ate. If it lived in a cane field, it tastes like sugar; if it lived in a pineapple patch, just Dole it out.

Unfortunately, the elephant dung beetle I ate in Kenya smelled exactly like what *it* ate, but I overcame this olfactory impediment with a liberal application of OFF! insect repellant under my nose. (Better to use perfume or aftershave if you try this experiment at home.) I felt guilty eating it because the dung beetle performs an invaluable service in disposing of animal waste, a dark and lowly job, but somebody has to do it. (On my short foray into Kruger National Park, one of my companions was a leading authority on dung beetles and gleefully rushed from one pile of hyena droppings to another with his magnifying glass. I tried to imagine his backstory, what childhood trauma impelled him to that career. After all, he could have been a proctologist.)

On one hungry morning near the Arctic Circle, I became an instant legend among the Inuit after I stopped at a riverside village while they were smoking a batch of just-caught *Oncorhynchus kisutch*. I purchased a live one, bit off its head, and ate the rest raw, savoring the freshest salmon sashimi possible, while the bemused villagers watched in horror.

Although I attempt to adhere to the know-what-it-is-you're-eating rule, that's not always possible, and led to an unsettling experience at a small eatery in Iran. After learning that the *plat du jour* was a meat-and-vegetable stew, and after carefully ascertaining how much they'd charge us for the stew, and how much for the use of their bowl, and the cutlery, and the tablecloth, and the napkin—we'd learned from the unexpected fees restaurants had hit us with from Alexandria to Baghdad—we ordered the stew and enjoyed a delectable dinner.

I wanted to know what meat we'd eaten so I could order it again, but since I spoke no Farsi, and my Arabic was pretty much limited to "IIow much?" "That's too much" "Where's the toilet?" and "Screw off!" I pointed to the empty bowl, contentedly rubbed my belly, blissfully closed my eyes, and spread my arms in the universal "What is it?" gesture, and suggested, with proper inflection, *"Moo, moo?"*

No, the waiter swiveled his head back and forth; it was not a cow.

I tried the *baa baa* of a sheep, the bleat of a goat, and the whinny of a horse, each to the same negative response, and had consequently exhausted my repertoire of farm-animal speech, except for the *oink* of a pig, which I was not about to insultingly suggest in that devoutly Muslim nation.

I again pointed into the bowl and gave the waiter a puzzled look and a questioning shrug.

In response to which came his reply: *"Bow-wow, bow-wow."*

(I need to learn to let sleeping dogs lie.)

In some situations you have no choice but to eat whatever is put in front of you, as when you're someone's guest in a land where refusal to partake is considered rude, and would cause your host to lose face. Steve and I were such guests of several Hong Kong dignitaries who'd been helpful to us. They took us to a gourmet restaurant in the colony's Wan Chai district, where we were seated around a circular table that had a grapefruit-sized hole in the center. Because of my strong convictions favoring conservation, I had much difficulty ingesting several of the courses, particularly a bird's nest soup and a jelly made of shark fins, but I had no way to decline without giving great offense.

Then came the killer: Near the conclusion of the meal, the stony-faced waiter brought out a live monkey in a basket. He deftly slipped the unsuspecting simian under the table and brought his head up through the hole in the center. Before I could comprehend what was happening, the waiter, with a hard, practiced swing of his cleaver, hit the little guy with a sharp blow to the middle of the forehead that broke through his skull, and, still with the same sweeping motion, flipped back the top of the animal's head to reveal its brain, gray and moist and pulsating inside.

With my hosts eagerly demonstrating the proper technique for scooping out pieces of the still-living brain with a demitasse spoon, and exhorting us to eat while it was still warm, and assuring me that no creature feels any pain when you consume its brain, I reluctantly dipped in.

That was not a dinner I'll ever forget. Or want to repeat.

At other times I've not been able to obtain a local delicacy. This happened on my first visit to rural Scotland, where I searched for some haggis, but was told it was served only on Bobby Burns' Eve. It also occurred in Dominica, where I'd been looking forward to the national dish of stewed "mountain chicken"—that branding consultant again?—but had to forgo it because an unknown disease had been ravaging the forest frog population.

I also failed on my quest to eat a mouse. I'd heard, at my campsite in Lilongwe, the capital of Malawi, that some rural folks ate whole mice charred on skewers. Although I am ever eager (within reason) to eat strange stuff, a mouse offered a unique experience. While I had previously ingested many crustaceans and aquatic entities in their entirety (e.g., clams, oysters, shrimp, baby octopi, snails, sardines, and fingerlings) and had consumed the main meaty parts of a few small animals, like rats and guinea pigs, I'd never devoured an entire mammal in one bite. The challenge of popping a whole mouse in my mouth—head, tail, feet, fur, guts, bones, heart, and all—was simultaneously exciting and intimidating, like my first—it was also my last—frightening dive off a six-meter board.

For starters, I needed to check out the cautionary tale I'd heard that these mice were dangerous to eat because they'd been killed with cyanide. I found this allegation to be false (probably started by the chicken farmers), and

learned that the mice were dug out of their holes in the fields by children trying to help balance the family budget.

It took a lot of asking around Lilongwe—I got the sense that mouse-
munching was frowned upon by the sophisticated city dwellers, and even
regarded as a disgusting relic of colonial poverty—until, on my last day
there, I tracked down a bearded old-timer at the main outdoor food market
who told me I could find the mice shish-kebabed at a stall way out in District
36; whereupon, he (for a $10 fee) and I took a minibus far out to the boonies
and, at about four p.m., found the sought-for shop—greasy but empty. We
searched around it and located the butcher/chef out back, cleaning up. I asked
if I could get some roasted mouse.

He gently scolded me: "We are all sold out for today. Come back tomorrow around noon. Your customs must be different from ours. We eat mice only
for lunch."

During my travels I've consumed a variety of mystery meats—grilled,
fried, or stewed—where the species was often unascertainable, as was the
precise nature of the body part, having been cut into tiny pieces before being
cooked. I'm sure I've chewed and swallowed countless meatish morsels, which,
when home, I'd never want to think about, much less eat, even if the Board of
Health would permit it. But on the road, I dutifully suck it all up, so far without obvious harm.

The only foreign staple I loathe is *injera*, the ubiquitous "bread" of Ethiopia
and Eritrea, a foul concoction of teff, barley, wheat, corn, and sorghum having the consistency of a kitchen sponge, the look of a lunar landscape, and
the taste of a week-old pancake gone sour. I don't think I could long survive
in Ethiopia, where it's famine one year and *injera* the next.

The meals I've had the most trouble getting down are the ones I cooked
myself, although these were, thankfully, quite few. Anything beyond scraping a
carrot exceeds my ability; I lack any culinary genes. I had the gas stove in my
apartment turned off when I moved in 40 years ago, and I've never regretted
it, nor have any of my visitors, who get taken out to a decent dinner.

Since I don't cook, and since I can munch only so many cans of sardines,
bags of nuts, or bunches of bananas when traveling, I usually seek a hot meal

I'll eat almost anything, but I wouldn't say I enjoyed a bowl of fermented mare's milk mixed with salted yak butter served to me at a Buddhist monastery high in the hills of Bhutan. Yet there was no way I was going to let the monks know how awful it tasted to me. *Claus Hirsch*

for dinner, generally at roadside stalls and street vendors rather than restaurants, counterintuitive as that may seem. Since sanitary conditions are a serious concern in poor countries, I don't want to take a chance at the restaurants, where I can't see what's going on in the kitchen. At the street-side stands, in contrast, all is in the open, and I can watch everything from the food prep through the dishwashing, if any. I usually carry chopsticks and plastic spoons and ask the vendors to put the food on a paper plate or a fresh banana leaf, so I don't have to worry whether someone with a deadly disease dined from the dish before me. When I have a choice, I select only stalls where the equipment looks clean and orderly, the food is covered, the flies are few, and the cook appears robust and healthy; I figure that if they've thrived on their own cooking, then the odds are in my favor. This approach has worked for me, and I have suffered not a single incidence of tourist trots, Tut's Tummy, Burma Belly, or Montezuma's revenge in my last 30 years abroad.

I regularly travel with a supply of cayenne pepper or chili powder, for both its taste and potential medical benefits. The active ingredient is capsaicin (8-methyl-$N$-vanillyl-6-nonenamide), which releases such intense heat in the body that some physicians believe it's the reason why dwellers in pepper-popular regions get far fewer colds and infectious diseases than expected. I have a great love of, and tolerance for, red pepper, winning several jalapeño-eating contests in Mexico, and usually covering a standard slice of pizza with three tablespoons of it. And I have not had a bad cold or flu since college.

When I do eat at a restaurant in the undeveloped world, I avoid the fancy ones catering to tourists, and head to the inexpensive little ones on the side streets, where the indigenes eat. Just don't let the names put you off. You can get a fine meal at The Bung Hole and Dirty Dicks and excellent ramen at the Phat Phuc Noodle Bar. If you find the fare at Virgin Tandoori too dry and unseasoned, you'll probably like what the Happy Crack puts out. And not to be overlooked are Hung Far Low, My Dung, and The Golden Stool. (These names are all legit; I lack the entrepreneurial vision to make them up.)

# CHAPTER 16

## Snow Beneath the Southern Cross

After visiting every state in the Western Hemisphere, I planned to finish the rest of the world in three big bites, each a year apart. The first chomp was the biggest, all 13 nations in southern Africa in 65 days between July and September of 2009.

But we all know what happens to the best laid plans.

It went wrong right from the start because I was unable to obtain a visa to Angola before leaving the States. Angola was notoriously stingy about granting visas to tourists, assuming that the only reason anyone visited their war-ravaged country was to steal diamonds. Angola's government was particularly hard on Americans because we'd backed their opponents in their long and bloody civil war. No one I knew had ever been granted a visa. The Angolans held my application for more than three months without taking action despite my exhortations that I needed to leave for Africa. Whenever I called their embassy for a status report, it was always the same, and always delivered in the same inscrutable monotone: "We are waiting to hear from Luanda." My only hope was to pursue my application when I was in an African nation in which Angola had an embassy, and the only such nation on my route was Mozambique.

This was my twelfth journey to Africa and presented the usual litany of pestilence and petty annoyances, all accentuated by prejudice and poverty:

bandits, pickpockets, muggers, con artists, and bag snatchers; corrupt officials who demand you pay them for doing what they are supposed to be paid
by their governments to do; dodgy border guards seeking shakedowns; some
race discrimination (with me a member of the minority); a couple of in-transit
nights sleeping on airport floors; the almost-constant threat of malaria, dengue, schistosomiasis, chikungunya, and a score of other unpleasant patho-
gens; platoons of snakes, spiders, and scorpions; squadrons of mosquitoes,
mites, midges, sand flies, and sand fleas; and battalions of bedbugs, hel-
minths, and skin-burrowing parasites. This was exacerbated by the hard-
scrabble situation of millions of Africans who had been crushingly impacted
by the burgeoning global financial crisis. Their economic losses, combined
with the jump in food prices, could mean the difference between life and
death. All compounded by linguistic difficulties (with two countries that
spoke Portuguese and at least five that palavered in an oddly accented French).
Then there were poor roads terrorized by recklessly driven, poorly maintained buses and vans; the brutally dry deserts in the Kalahari of Namibia;
impassable swamps in the Okavango Delta of Botswana, freezing nights in
the foothills of Lesotho; gangs of now-unemployed child soldiers in Angola,
Congo, and Mozambique; and, since I'd be camping out for half the trip, the
expected issues with lions, hyenas, crocs, hippos, and elephants (the last of
which, on a previous Kenya campout, disported a disconcerting proclivity
for taking nightmare-inducing nocturnal dumps on my tent).

Logistics are crucial on a trip of this length and variety of terrain. I toted
everything I'd need—except drink, dinners, and detergent—because they'd be
unavailable, or unreliable, or way overpriced in these countries. Since I didn't
want to drag a quarter ton of crap through 13 countries for two months, and
the African airlines permitted only 44 pounds, I organized a hub-and-spokes
itinerary whereby I'd store my luggage at a lodge in Johannesburg that was
gated and relatively safe in a city known for one of the world's highest crime
rates. From that base I'd fly to different quadrants in southern Africa, travel
through each by land for one to three weeks, and periodically wing back to Joburg for one quick night to replenish supplies and enjoy a hot shower.

As my route was far from doctors, I took a complete medical kit, from
hypodermic needles—the ones in African hospitals are often contaminated

with HIV—to six kinds of antibiotics and three antifungals. (Africa accounts for less than 1% of world drug sales, and offered few places that sold them.) Add a tent, eating utensils, binoculars, camera and peripherals, photocopies of guide books, eight paperback novels, water-purification pills, 70 packets of iced-tea mix, mountain gear, desert gear, rain gear, swamp gear, bush gear, game-tracking gear, snorkeling gear, etc., plus six 64-ounce plastic bottles packed with high-fiber, high-energy breakfast cereals, and I was lugging 130 pounds.

Money was another problem. Faced with few ATMs in the region, and no credit-card commerce out in the bush, I prepaid whatever I could before I left home and carried a hidden hoard of cash for the rest, each greenback selected in conformity with African monetary esoterica (e.g., they will not accept worn, torn, or crumpled bills, or bills with writing on them, or the older version of our $50 bill—the one with an ellipse around Ulysses S. Grant—and only the most recent, hard-to-counterfeit version of the $100 bill).

For accommodations, I planned to spend a couple of nights in my tent, followed by one in a downscale hotel to clean up, and occasionally visit a backpacker's hangout to obtain up-to-date info on which roads were open, which bridges washed out, which ferries still in business, and where the bandits and other bad guys were most active.

I got Hepatitis A and yellow-fever booster shots. Those vaccinations had once been considered valid for twelve years, but the international health authorities had recently dropped it to ten, which meant my official yellow-fever protection expired on the next-to-last day of my last segment, when I'd be en route from the Congo back to Joburg to reclaim my luggage and catch my flight to JFK. That one day should not have been sufficient to quarantine me, but I decided to be prudent and not provide some underpaid border guard with an easy excuse to put me in the pokey until I bought my way out.

On the first day of this trip, Murphy's Law kicked in and caused several setbacks: The Angolan Embassy held my application for so long that UPS was unable to deliver my passport back to me until three hours before I was scheduled to take off. The Transportation Safety Agency guards at JFK confiscated my lunch, a can of Chef Boyardee spaghetti and meatballs, insisting it was a liquid. A battery of violent thunderstorm cells delayed our takeoff for

100 minutes, causing my baggage to miss its connection in London. And on arriving in Joburg I learned that South Africa had just reported a swine flu epidemic in all of its nine provinces.

Most serious of all, my four-leaf clover was exfoliating. I kept it in the front of my plastic passport protector, and had taken it abroad for years for good luck and to mislead any anti-American terrorist kidnappers into thinking I was Irish. At South African immigration a pair of the leaves disengaged. How much luck could I expect from a two-leaf clover?

All in all, not an auspicious beginning for the easiest part of a hard trip.

Before leaving Tabo Airport, I bought several newspapers for the latest African news:

Nigeria—Four guards burned to death by rebels attacking an oil pipeline.

Mozambique  Ten tourists killed in bus crash caused by wild driver.

Kenya—Continuing difficulties starting investigation of post-election slaughter.

Malawi—AIDS orphans in high demand overseas.

Sudan—Attacks continue in Darfur region.

Mauritania—Muslim cleric denounces participation in Miss Universe competition.

Zimbabwe—Violent demonstrations disrupt drafting of power-sharing constitution.

Uganda—HIV infections reach new high, truckers blamed.

*Oh, Dear Africa!*

A clever headline in a Joburg tabloid captured my attention. The local prostitutes were petitioning for a raise in their rates to coincide with the influx of tourists expected the following year, when South Africa hosted the soccer World Cup, the biggest sporting event on the planet:

SEX WORKERS HOPING TO GET MORE BUCKS FOR THE BANG.

Next to it was a story about Bishop Tutu. That outspoken and highly quotable cleric had addressed a group of visiting missionaries and had concluded with: "In the beginning, we had the land and you had the Bible. And you said to us, Brothers, let us pray. So we bowed our heads and closed our eyes, and when we looked up, we had the Bible—and you had the land."

The large banner welcoming arrivals at the airport also made me smile:

WELCOME TO SOUTH AFRICA
HOME TO THE BIG FIVE,
AND THE OTHER BIG GAME

Because I'd been fortunate to see all of the Big Five previously, on this trip I'd try to spot the Little Five: the elephant shrew, the rhinoceros beetle, the buffalo weaver, the leopard tortoise, and the ant lion.

Two days later, I arrived by bus in Maseru on the happy occasion of the birthday of His Royal Highness of the Mountain Kingdom of Lesotho, a pleasant, land-locked, little, and little-known, country in the southeastern corner of Africa. It's the only nation where every bit of land is above 4,500 feet, and 80 percent of it is above 6,000 feet.

I'd purposely chosen to return to southern Africa in their winter because I find it far easier to travel with a bit of bracing coolness than the oppressive heat, rains, and humidity of African summers. I presumed Lesotho would be more than merely cool in view of its high elevation and far distance from the Equator, and so it was, with ice blocking the sidewalk gutters of Maseru as the temp fell below freezing by six p.m. and stayed down there till nine a.m.

I had no space for heavy winter clothing, nor need for it after those first five days, so I'd opted for the "layered" approach to staying warm. And layered I went around Lesotho, often wearing, at the same time, two sets of ski underwear, two T-shirts, and two sweatshirts. This drew hilarious laughter from a sweet young thing who'd picked me up in the supermarket and accompanied me back to my guesthouse—where she uncovered my wardrobe redundancy.

I quickly grew to appreciate why the national dress of Lesotho was a gigantic, thick, densely woven blanket made from the exceptionally warm wool of their high-altitude sheep and goats. The men wore one wrapped around their bodies; the women often wore two, one from the waist down as a skirt

and the other around their shoulders, with much additional clothing underneath. And they all wore ski-style wool hats.

On my first day out of Maseru, I miraculously managed to stay on a
horse through God Help Me Pass in the Central Mountain Range and was
able to survive the ride to happily celebrate both His Majesty's continued
good health—and mine. The horse whisperers had assured me they'd provide
me with a "gentle little pony," but the beast they produced was at least 14 hands
high, seemed to have a vision problem, definitely had an attitude problem,
and understood no English—or pretended not to.

The only thing that saved my butt was the Lesotho pommel, an arch-shaped
metal handle in the front of the saddle which the rider can, if necessary—and
it was quite necessary—cling to with both hands. It offered the further benefit that, unlike the pommel on a Western saddle, it does not bump, bang, and
batter your balls as you're pushed forward when trotting downhill; they safely
slide under it.

Lesotho is totally unlike the rest of Africa. Its far-from-low Lowlands are
reminiscent of the Big Sky Country of Montana, with wide flat plains and
valleys surrounded by mountains. Its middling elevations are akin to Arizona, with multicolored eroded buttes and sheer escarpments. And its highest elevations are a touch of Tibet: a cold, gray, treeless topography
surrounded by snow-covered peaks. It boasts the highest peak south of Kili-
manjaro and the highest low point (4,593 feet) of any country on the planet.

I loved camping out in the countryside on those clear, cloudless nights,
surrounded by snow-covered mountains close by, their steep whitened
slopes and icy summits shimmering in the starlight, hardly believing I was in
*Africa*, a wondrous Africa few travelers experience. I lay on my back on the
chilly ground beside my tent and looked up at brilliant Vega and Antares and
unfamiliar constellations I'd seen only in astronomy texts: Hercules and
Lyra, Sagittarius and Scorpius, Cygnus and Vulpecula and, off to the side,
Alpha Centauri and Beta Centauri pointing the way across light-years of
black sky to the Southern Cross. I was at peace with the universe and, as I
crawled back into my toasty sleeping bag, felt myself a most fortunate fellow.

Although spectacular, Lesotho is a pitifully poor land, populated by two
million, 40 percent of whom earn less than $1.25 a day. More than half the

In a scene atypical of Africa, the treeless mountains of Lesotho are covered with snow and ice in winter. It is the only state in the world entirely above 1,000 meters (3,300 feet), and its lowest point of 4,593 feet is the highest low point of any country.

populace is engaged in agriculture even though their country has little flat and fertile land suitable for farming. It has no commercial minerals save diamonds (including some real biggies, like the 601-carat Lesotho Brown and the 603-carat white Lesotho Promise); no big game to attract rich hunters; no forests, no ports, and no heavy industry, although it does have a big plant making Levi's jeans and exports more garments to the U.S. than any other state in sub-Saharan Africa.

For many years Lesotho earned foreign exchange from politically correct, socially concerned tourists who refused to visit South Africa during the period of apartheid and flocked instead to Lesotho's gambling casinos. But when South Africa's race laws were rescinded in 1991, and its black citizens were allowed to rule their land and elected Nelson Mandela president in 1994, most of the tourists reverted to its warmer weather, Western amenities, and varied amusements.

Lesotho was left with few tourists and only two, mostly deserted, casinos.

It survived on international aid, workers' remittances, garment making, Chinese projects (which come with tight strings attached), and, lately, the Lesotho Highlands Water Project, a multibillion-dollar-engineering marvel I visited that is financed by South Africa to capture, store, and transfer water to the part of South Africa where most of its mining and industrial activity takes place. When completed it will comprise five large dams to also furnish drinking water for the thirsty denizens of Joburg, about 200 miles downhill, and emergency drought relief for the Free State, while earning Lesotho royalties and satisfying all its electric needs.

Lesotho had proven to be such an ideal tourist destination, with spectacular scenery, good roads, virtually no crime, friendly people who mostly spoke some English; a salubrious climate, bright and cloudless winter days; and no malaria or other insect-borne diseases, that I was reluctant to leave.

I returned to Joburg to pick up some supplies and clean clothes, celebrate Nelson Mandela Day, and prepare to rendezvous with Anna, who was flying in for our visit to Namibia and Botswana.

I had a spare day and didn't want to hang around crime-ridden Joburg, which had 40 percent unemployment, so I took a quick round-trip down to Durban, one of my favorite cities, flying on South Africa's new, low-low-cost airline, Kulula, which was establishing a reputation as an offbeat company with a wicked South African sense of humor that tries to take the fear out of flying and replace it with fun. I got the message as soon as I walked onto the tarmac and saw the plane, painted bright chartreuse, with a vertical arrow in the middle next to the words THIS SIDE UP. Its companion aircraft, in the adjacent jetway, was designated as FLYING 101 and decorated with signs naming all the parts.

To cut costs and time, Kulula did not reserve seats; you just boarded and selected whichever you wanted. When several passengers on my flight took too long to do this, the attendant grabbed her mike: "Come on people, we're not picking out furniture here. Just find a seat and get in it!"

Then came the seat-belt announcement: "To operate your seat belt, insert the metal tab into the buckle and pull tight. It works just like every other seat belt. And if you don't know how to operate one, you probably shouldn't be out in public unsupervised." Which was immediately followed by: "In the event of a sudden loss of cabin pressure, masks will descend from the ceiling. Stop screaming, grab the mask, and pull it over your face. If you have a small child traveling with you, secure your mask before assisting with theirs. If you are traveling with more than one small child, pick your favorite." When the laughter had faded, she added, "If you need to smoke, the smoking section is on the wing; if you can light 'em, you can smoke 'em."

At this point, the stern voice of the copilot cut in: "Ladies and gentlemen, I apologize for that rudeness. Our airline has some of the best, friendliest, and most diplomatic flight attendants in the business. Unfortunately, none of them are on this flight. Nevertheless, I want you to know our company appreciates your money and hopes the next time you get the insane urge to go blasting through the air in a pressurized metal tube, you will think of Kulula Airways."

He then added: "The temperature in Durban is 20 degrees with some broken clouds. But do not worry; we will try to repair them before you arrive. I am now going to dim the cabin lights, both for your comfort and to improve the appearance of our flight attendants."

The flight attendant was able to get even once we reached our destination. After a bumpy landing, she announced: "Ladies and gentlemen, welcome to Durban. Please remain in your seats, with the seat belts fastened, while Captain Kangaroo taxis what's left of the airplane to the gate. Please take care when opening the overhead compartments because that landing sure as hell shifted everything."

As we exited the plane, I asked the head attendant if they always behaved like this. "Oh, yes, we believe flying should be fun, and so do our regulars. They even join in, like the little old lady who, as she was exiting the plane after a hard touchdown, asked the captain, 'Did we just land, or did we get shot down?'"

# CHAPTER 17

## A Poke in a Pig

On this leg of my quest I was doing something I'd never done in sub-Saharan Africa: I'd invited a woman from the States to join me. I believed Anna would not be in danger, because we were going to Namibia and Botswana, which were the safest in mainland Africa, with no wars or instability, and virtually no serious crime or communicable diseases.

The Namibians were so happy to have us visit that they gave us presents when we alighted at Windhoek's airport—brand-new anti-infection masks to help us avoid their burgeoning swine flu epidemic. These proved quite useful for driving Namibia's dusty gravel roads.

Anna has a true love of adventure, so we'd agreed that our first stop, after a five-hour drive from Windhoek on the Trans-Kalahari Highway, was Swakopmund, the self-proclaimed "Extreme Adventure Sports Capital of Africa," a sandy pilgrimage site for hundreds of international adrenaline junkies who thrive on sky diving, dune paragliding, dune parasailing, quad biking, sandboarding, and swimming with sharks—plus the really dangerous stuff. We were going to give them all a go, starting with a late afternoon of quad biking through the dunes.

After a few hours of tentative quadding, I had progressed, at least in theory, to the point where I foolishly believed I could venture the tricky maneuver of making a tight circle on the sloping face of a dune. This must be done at high speed to generate enough centripetal force to keep the bike adhered to the dune. I lost my nerve on the side of one steep dune and slowed down, which is the worst thing you can do because it allows centrifugal force and gravity to take over. I was thrown from the bike and landed hard on my crash helmet. Luckily, the half-ton vehicle did not come tumbling down on top of me. Anna smirked and did perfect little show-off circles around me.

The next day we tried sandboarding. We drove to a designated point in the desert where the board boys gave us each a helmet, a pair of gloves, elbow protectors, and a piece of polished, flexible Masonite board only one-eighth of an inch thick and just long enough for an average adult to lie down from shoulders to knees.

We climbed to the top of a 400-foot dune through the shifting sands, a task that became progressively more difficult as the sun beat down on the desert and loosened the footing by expanding the air space between the grains of sand, making this one of the most tiring—but hardly tiresome— sports I'd ever tried. Once atop the crest, you lie on your board, point it down-hill, lift up the front edge, hold your elbows high, have someone give you a push, and you zoom down the dune, reaching more than 30 miles an hour, before banging your belly on the inevitably bumpy bottom. It's a real rush. If you forget to hold up the front of the board, the leading edge digs in immediately and you flip over—hard.

Our last run was a radar-timed competition down a steep, scary dune. I went (almost) all out and was impressed with my 44 mph—until Anna zoomed by at 56. Some people just have no sense of moderation.

Back on the road, Anna, an excellent, if lead-footed, turnpike driver, was unfamiliar with African conditions, and despite my constant warnings to go slower, repeatedly bottomed out our VW the first day, rattled some bolts when she hit a big pothole the next day, and skidded badly the next on soft sand filling a dip in the road. No major damage done. But a real disaster was in the offing.

We camped in Etosha National Park in northwest Namibia, established in 1907 in what was then German Southwest Africa. For many decades it was the world's largest game reserve. It's basically a gigantic, flat salt pan—the natives call it the "Great White Place of Dry Water"—surrounded by woods and savannah grass and pocked with large water holes where multitudes of creatures, from giraffe to deer (and their predators) slurped up a sunset tipple.

As the park is home to four of the Big Five—elephants, lions, leopards, and rhinos—its regulations require you to always stay in your car. But that's not possible when nature makes an urgent call and the facilities are hours away; you just have to do your business where you are, quickly and cautiously, sacrificing the modesty of the bush for the less obstructed view offered by the road.

The animals were so abundant, and the dusty gravel roads so rough, that, for two days, we never drove faster than the posted limit of 40 km/hr. When we exited Etosha and reached the tar road, Anna, frustrated by those seemingly interminable days of slow driving, cranked it way up, as she was wont to do, to over 120 km/hr (75 mph). We were heading southeast toward the mineral-rich region of Tsumeb, with the faint winter sun setting at our backs, and diminishing visibility.

Suddenly—instantly—an immense wild pig emerged from the thick underbrush lining the road and ran directly across our path, about 50 feet in front of us, frantically followed by her five large piglets, with a big boar bringing up the rear. At our speed we needed at least 400 feet to stop our VW but, in the half second before impact, we had no time to do anything but scream.

The sow shrieked and just missed getting hit by our right tire. Our left front end smashed into the first of the hundred-pound piglets with a sickening thud. The collision broke the headlight housing on the VW, pushed in the turn light, ripped down half the front bumper, crumpled the left fender, and even—as Avis skeptically pointed out to me when I turned the car in several days later and told them somebody must have backed into it in a parking lot—inflicted a large dent in the steel frame. If we'd hit the mother sow or the boar, I'd be writing this from a hospital bed, or ghostwriting it from a mortuary. Half a second made that difference.

We had mortally injured the young pig, which was still alive and suffering in agony. I did not know what to do. Or, to be honest, I *did* know what to do, but lacked the courage to do it.

I'd been in a similar situation decades before, when one of my Cornell classmates was driving us by the shore of Lake Cayuga and hit a dog that darted out of the trees. That dog, like our poor pig, was fatally injured but alive. We had no gun with which to put him out of his misery. So I picked up a large, smooth rock, covered the suffering canine's eyes with my hand, and knocked him out. I then seized a jagged rock and administered a crushing coup de grâce through his skull to end his agony.

I contemplated getting out of our VW and giving a similar ministration to the stricken pig, but I didn't think his distraught and dangerous parents, who were hovering over his writhing body, would understand that I was acting as an angel of mercy in euthanizing their offspring. So we left the poor little guy to die a slow and painful death, and drove on to Tsumeb, in a sad and somber mood, with Anna weeping silently, and driving far slower than 120 clicks.

A week after leaving Etosha, and two days after the Cape buffalo caper described in the first chapter, Anna and I reached Livingstone in Zambia, just across the river from the town of Victoria Falls in Zimbabwe. I didn't want to revisit Zim and help finance the brutal Mugabe regime, so I'd chosen Zambia, which was democratic, peacefully multicultural, and ardently hospitable.

The next morning we stood in awe in the mist-soaked, rainbow-ringed park across from the brink of the falls, *Mosi-oa-Tunya*, "The Smoke That Thunders," the largest sheet of falling water on earth, 5,604 feet wide and 354 feet high, lofting a spray visible for 30 miles.

Later that day, with the Zambezi River raging through the gorge a thousand feet below, Anna, still depressed from killing the piglet, jumped off the Victoria Falls Bridge.

It was a bungee jump, the world's third highest. I took one look over the edge, almost lost my lunch, and decided not to follow her. I was also dissuaded by the concessionaire's somewhat gruesome and intimidating practice of writing the jumper's name and weight on his or her forearm in black indelible ink. They did this to ensure that every patron was affixed to the proper length and strength of cord, but from my pusillanimous perspective it looked too much like the numbers tattooed on the wrists of Holocaust prisoners in the Nazi extermination camps.

Noticing my obvious reluctance to jump, the pitchman suggested I might prefer their newest, and increasingly popular, thriller, the Giant

I almost drowned while rafting the Zambezi River Gorge, which contains some of the most powerful and ferocious white water on Earth, including the notorious rapids named Stairway to Heaven, the Devil's Toilet Bowl, Commercial Suicide, the Terminator, and Oblivion.

Swing, which, instead of plunging you directly down, where the G forces are so strong they can detach your retina, drops you halfway down the gorge from the center of the bridge while simultaneously swinging you out over the river in a frightening fast arc that almost, but not quite—unless you lied about your weight—smashes you into the sheer cliff face.

I told him it looked interesting, but that the line of waiting swingers was much too long for me.

The next day Anna went rafting through the tumultuous Zambezi Gorge. The first six rapids downstream from the bridge were not yet open to river runners because the water was too high and strong. These included the Devil's Toilet Bowl and my old nemesis, Stairway to Heaven, a 20-foot-high standing wave with a deep hole underneath, where I had, ten years before, spent a terrifying eternity of downtime flipped over and pulled under my raft into the swirling hole. Fearless Anna was still able to catch some wicked white water in the Muncher, Gnashing Jaws, Commercial Suicide, the Washing Machine, and the Overland Truck Eater, which left her exhilarated and fulfilled.

Anna left Livingstone the next day for her long flights home while I headed farther east on my crazy quest into Zambia, Malawi, and Mozambique.

# CHAPTER 18

## No Countries for Old Men

With many miles to cover and borders to cross after leaving Livingstone, most days now entailed a wake-up around 5:30 a.m., a rush to catch the 6:30 bus to the next main stop (only to be informed it would not leave until it was full, which was often 9:30), then an 8-to-12-hour ride in a rickety old vehicle designed for 50, reconfigured for 65, and crammed with close to one hundred. I would reach my destination around eight p.m., set up my tent in the dark, wake up the next morning to visit whatever brought me there, then pack up at dawn the following morning and shove off again. Day after day.

On one of these trips I heard that, the week before, a bus driver had stopped to have a few drinks while transporting 15 mental patients to an asylum near Lilongwe. When he returned to his bus, he found the patients had all escaped. Afraid he'd be fired for gross negligence, he drove to the nearest local bus stop and offered a free ride to the first 15 people to board. He then delivered them all to the mental hospital, advising the psychiatric staff that these patients were prone to wild fantasies and highly excitable. His deception wasn't discovered until three days later. (I still don't know if the tale was apocryphal—or ordinary TIA.)

As I headed east on my buses, circumstances changed markedly. The eastern half of mid-southern Africa was different from, and far tougher than, the western half. As a few examples:

- Per capita income in Botswana was $13,000; in Zambia, $1,400.
- No beggars in Namibia and Botswana (NB), many of them farther east.
- No bicycle riders on the roads in NB, lots of them in poorer Zambia and Malawi.
- A German-quality cleanliness in NB; dust, dirt, and grime to the east.
- Camping in Namibia usually meant sharing, with a few other tents, the lush, fence-enclosed back lawn of an industrious widow's home, with hot showers, kitchen privileges, cooking facilities, and sit-down, indoor, flush toilets. East of Livingstone, it was pit campfires and primitive latrines in crowded, dusty campsites.
- Although all these countries were experiencing a four-year drought, harming agriculture and livestock, its impact was far more severe in the east. NB, possessing great mineral wealth and a thriving tourist industry, was able to buy needed food, but the eastern states tottered on the brink of serious famine, relieved only by international aid agencies.
- The NB restaurants served German-style food, often with culled grilled game. Farther east, the grub at the roadside stalls was starchy, fried, and lacking in nutrients: cassava fritters, fried bread balls, rice, and dozens of dishes made of mashed-up corn ground into a powder and reconstituted into everything from bland pancakes to tasteless porridge.
- The temperature in NB had been in the 70s. It soared into the 90s after I'd crossed the Tropic of Capricorn.
- The rate of HIV infection rose from 20 percent in Namibia to well over 30 percent in the east. Life expectancy was reduced from 52 years in Namibia to 34–39 farther east.

These were no countries for old men. Or of them.

For the second time in my last three trips, I got hit by pickpockets. In the undeveloped world I wear pants or shorts with at least six pockets and try to distribute my valuable portable assets among them so no single picked pocket is a disaster. I knew the rear pockets were the most vulnerable and tempting, and I knew I was entering pickpocket paradise when I visited the fairgrounds in Lusaka to see the 89th Zambia Agricultural and Commercial Exhibition, so I headed directly for a men's room where I intended to shift my back pocket stuff to a safer location. But the bad guys beat me to it.

Two of them grabbed the large box I was carrying (filled with handicrafts I'd just bought at the Sunday Market down the road), pretending to help me carry it. While I remonstrated and tussled with them, their third colleague hit my right-rear pocket and made off with its contents: a plastic baggie containing a little cash ($20); a photocopy of my passport (30 cents); my ticket for the bus to Chipata the next morning ($6); and my last hundred sheets of soft, white, genuine U.S. toilet paper—*Priceless!*

Toilet paper is also the key to the system I use for comfort-ranking countries around the world. Unlike the rather esoteric econometric model utilized by the World Bank or the incomprehensible computer program employed by the International Monetary Fund, my Podell Potty Paper Rating (PPPR) System is simple, reliable, and easy to apply. It's based on the quality of toilet paper in that country's public restrooms and uses the following scale:

### COUNTRY'S WORLD COMFORT RANKING BASED ON TYPE TOILET TISSUE IN PUBLIC RESTROOMS

| 1 | Soft white |
| 2 | Hard white |
| 3 | Rough brown, green, or purple |
| 4 | Pieces of newspaper |
| 5 | Bucket of water (mostly in Asia) |
| 6 | No paper, no water. And no toilet seat. |
| 7 | No public toilets at all |

The PPPR System can also be applied to rating hotels: Just ignore those three or four stars the management has wishfully or misleadingly painted on the welcoming billboard, and head for the head to check the goods.

Moving ever eastward, I stayed at one rugged campsite (PPPR = 4) where I met a group of 16-year-olds from England who had just finished a ten-day backpack, carrying all their food, water, supplies, and tents, with no porters, across a dry, uninhabited, mountainous area in southern Malawi. (And I'd thought I did well if I backpacked for three days along the Escarpment Trail from Kaaterskill Falls to Windham.)

At my campsite in Lilongwe (PPPR = 2) I met four sturdy Irish lads who were bicycling from Cairo to Cape Town, frequently covering a hundred miles a day, even in mountainous terrain. (And I once believed I was doing well if I pedaled the level 25 miles from Westhampton Beach to Shinnecock Inlet and back before nightfall.)

At the Big Blue campsite on the shore of Lake Malawi (PPPR = 3) I met three brawny South Africans in the midst of a yearlong journey kayaking the length of the four largest African lakes and their riverine connections. (And I had been proud of myself if I managed to kayak from Riverhead out past the Peconic Bay Bridge and back before the tide changed.)

It's no continent for old men.

I took a break at Big Blue for four lazy days of much-needed R & R, tenting near the relaxed, almost Caribbeanesque, backpackers' town of Nkhata Bay on the western shore of Lake Malawi, the third largest on the continent, which 19th-century explorer David Livingstone called "the lake of stars." Unlike the Great Lakes, or New York State's Finger Lakes, or most U.S. lakes, which were formed by glacial gouging and scouring during the Ice Age 20,000 years ago, the three largest lakes of Africa were all formed more than a million years ago when tectonic plates tore Africa asunder, creating a longitudinal gash more than 2000 miles long. In this gash are the awesome Rift Valley in Kenya, the 3000-foot-deep gorge in Ethiopia that is the start of the Blue Nile, and Lakes Victoria, Tanganyika, and Malawi.

Lake Malawi contains the largest number of fish species of any freshwater body on the planet, including more than *one thousand* species of cichlids, which students of evolution regard as significant as Darwin's finches in the Galápagos.

Around Big Blue, I hobnobbed and bargained for carvings with the famed Malawi woodworkers; ate delicious whole local butterfish; hiked one of the few remaining rain forests in the country, where I managed to see (with the help of a nature guide) the elusive African broadbill, a species which, despite its prosaic name, is much sought by bird-watchers; kayaked along the lake's shoreline; tried repeatedly, but unsuccessfully, to clamber aboard one of the thin, tipsy, dugout canoes the natives use; scuba dived with Aqua Africa into an amazing variety of brightly colored freshwater fish, mostly cichlids, 95 percent of which are found nowhere else on earth; and slept ten hours a night to the sound of the waves lapping at the shore 15 feet below my tent perch.

I also spent the better part of two days chatting up and photographing a lovely British college student, and was sure I was making good progress. When she asked me to e-mail her a couple of the photos, I saw my opportunity. I confessed to not being very adept with a computer and slyly suggested I could deliver photo prints to her in London, in person, in six weeks, on my way home. And maybe I could take her to dinner after the delivery?

"No, don't bother," she said, smiling sweetly. "Just send them to me as an e-mail attachment. Perhaps you could ask one of your grandchildren to show you how."

Have I mentioned it was not a favorable environment for males of advanced age?

At the cramped Internet hut adjacent to Big Blue that housed six heavily trafficked open cubicles, I couldn't help but overhear the young man in the next booth skyping his mum back in England. It was, by his admission, his first call to her in three months and only his third since he left the English Midlands seven months before. Within ten minutes he told her the following: He had discovered his true calling, which was to become an artist of African scenery and wildlife, and had abandoned his previous career plan of becoming a photographer. He had sold all his photo equipment to buy expensive African hardwood frames for the paintings he'd exhibit in Berlin in the not-too-distant future (although he had yet to find a gallery). He thought he'd be home to see her in about three more years. He had a relationship with a girl in Mozambique but, not to worry, he no longer thinks he will marry her, although she might be preggers, but, again, not to worry, she doesn't mind keeping the baby because "it's the African way," and no big deal; and, Oh, yes, he might have contracted HIV, but the chances were slight, and, no, he hasn't had time yet to get an AIDS test, but he will get one within three months and will be sure to let Mum know the result. And give my love to Da. Bye.

\* \* \*

Two concerns persisted through my trek eastward: my need for a visa to Angola and my need for a root canal job on my lower-right bicuspid.

I'd exchanged gossip with the backpack brigade and found not a one who ever received an Angolan visa, although the Irish bicyclists were hopeful they'd succeed because "everybody loves Ireland." Even more discouraging, the woman who ran the camp in Lilongwe told me that in all her years of operation, she'd only had two guests who'd managed to snag visas to Angola, and that, if I managed to get one, dinner was her treat. She was depressingly confident she'd never have to make good on this offer.

As for the bicuspid, my dentist had tested it thoroughly a month before I left New York and advised a prophylactic root canal, but admitted, when I pressed him, that all his tappings and cold-air sprayings and X-rayings were inconclusive. I had not been in the mood for a *possibly* unnecessary root canal, so I opted for watchful waiting.

Sure enough, the little bugger started to ping and twitch about two weeks into this trip, and then caused a big abscess. Since there was no friggin' way I was going to submit to an endodontic procedure in Malawi, I dipped into my supply of Amoxicillin tablets three times a day for a week, which reduced the twinging, and I repeatedly stabbed the abscess with my hypodermic needle, which reduced the swelling, both of which made me somewhat hopeful I could drag this out until I returned home in another six weeks.

I left Nkhata Bay for the once-a-week, 25-hour voyage across Lake Malawi on the *Ilala*, a decrepit ship long overdue for the scrap heap that'd be familiar to anyone who read *Lord Jim*. It was an accident waiting to happen, with just two 22-person lifeboats, one life raft, and four life preservers—I counted them *very* carefully—for ten times as many passengers. It was one of those ancient rust buckets whose sinking, with hundreds drowned, flashed on the news for a few hours. But it was the only game in town if one needed to cross the lake. And this one needed to cross the lake.

Although I usually book passage in second class on Third World trains and boats so I can get to know the locals instead of the wealthy tourists, some sixth sense fortunately prevailed upon me *not* to use this occasion to assuage my colonial guilt, but to book a mattress on the first-class deck instead. Best decision I made this trip.

The second-class deck was hardly a deck, but an oppressively humid, fetid, unbearably hot corridor chockablock with bags, bundles, bawling babies, and about 400 sweating, half-naked, sharp-elbowed people compacted into a space for 50, with no seats, no lights, no toilets, no water, no AC, and no breeze. For 24 hours. (Third class was totally beyond belief, more a means of torture than a mode of travel.)

It was no ship for old landlubbers.

As the voyage drew to a close, I wanted to get off as quickly as possible. But that was not possible. Most of the villages where the *Ilala* discharged its passengers were too poor to build docks or jetties. You had to hand your luggage down from the upper deck into a wildly bobbing lifeboat, then climb 30 feet down a rickety ladder into the boat, which was loaded to within two inches of the gunwales, then endure the sea-sickening 15-minute ride to the beach, and then leap off, with all your luggage, into thigh-high water.

At the port of call right before mine, it had taken the *Ilala*, using this method, six and a half hours to discharge its passengers and its cargo of dried fish, bananas, galvanized roofing, motor oil, and complete homes of furniture, as a result of which we reached my discharge point, and my perilous plunge into the lifeboat, seven hours behind schedule and in the dead of night.

After I waded ashore, I saw no buses, minivans, or any other means of transport at the tiny border burg of Metangula, and I was assured I'd see none until morning at the earliest. After several hours of dickering, I prevailed upon the immigration officer, who was going off duty, to drive me and a Swiss couple two hours through the forests to Lichinga, the somnolent capital of Niassa Province in far northern Mozambique, which the locals accurately describe as *o fim do mundo*, the end of the world. It's the least populated province in Mozambique and one of the most sparsely settled in all Africa, comprising the lake, sheer cliffs, rocky escarpments, and inhospitable land. From the ship, I'd seen only four huts in the final five hours. In the car, we saw only six houses and two vehicles in a drive of 90 miles.

It was no country for anybody.

Women tending a tea plantation in Mozambique. In most of Africa, women do most of the work. The men limit their labors to three tasks: lifting heavy objects, driving trucks and other motorized equipment, and herding or working with large farm animals.

After another week, by then two days behind schedule, I made it to Maputo, the capital of Mozambique, a city so large and spread out that foot power had to yield to horsepower. I got about in worn-out old cabs and minibuses operated by kids who couldn't even pass the driving test in New Jersey. These cars had crumpled fenders, missing bumpers, threadbare tires, and shattered windscreens frequently festooned with decals assuring the passengers that THIS VEHICLE IS PROTECTED BY THE BLOOD OF JESUS, which failed to assure me as much as being in the good hands of Allstate, or if State Farm were there, or Nationwide were on my side.

After more than two centuries of being sold into slavery, followed by two more centuries of harsh and exploitative Portuguese rule, followed by the revolution that brought independence in 1974, followed by 15 years of internecine bloodshed between a Socialist government and rightist guerrillas, the people of Mozambique had, in 1992, finally embraced peace and laid to rest ZAPU and FRELIMO, RENAMO and SWAPO, UNIP and the MMD, abandoned their radical positions, and resumed the laid-back attitude and friendly Afro-Iberian-Brazilian style that'd made the place so popular with tourists in the 60s and early 70s. The only remaining public evidence of Mozambique's revolutionary vigor was the national flag—a shovel crossed by an assault rifle—and the names of Maputo's main avenues, which commemorated international Socialist soldiers and philosophers like Ho Chi Minh, Mao Tse Tung, Karl Marx, and Friedrich Engels, and the heroes of the African Battles for Independence: Kwame Nkrumah, Ahmed Sekou Toure, Robert Mugabe, and Julius Nyerere.

The last was the town's main drag, a wide hustling boulevard bordered by capacious restored Iberian-style mansions, painted in yellow, pink, and fuchsia pastels, behind concrete walls above which I could see wide, wraparound wrought-iron balconies and roofs brown with South American tile, below which operated hundreds of enterprising sidewalk vendors beside gardens of flame trees and palm fronds

I found no one in Mozambique who spoke fluent English, and only a few who were even comprehensible. Here, for example, is the word-for-word declaration from the back of my Mozambique Airlines ticket: "IT CASTRATES FOR EMISSION OF ELECTRONIC TICKET. I INFORM: If the passenger's trip understands a point of final destiny or of scale in a Country that not the one of the departure the Convention of Varsavia can be applicable." (Well, at least now you know which airline to take when you're ready to go to your point of final destiny.)

My main goal in Maputo was to get a visa to Angola. Since both Mozambique and Angola had suffered under the same Portuguese colonial masters, consequently spoke that same language, and had been the most radically leftist in Africa, there was a certain camaraderie between them, which was why Mozambique was one of the few nations in Africa in which Angola had established an embassy. That embassy was my only shot at the visa, but it was a Friday, and my flight back to Joburg—my point of final destiny—left the next day; I just had one chance.

As soon as I walked into the Angolan Embassy and said "visa," the official tried to get rid of me by declaring that I needed, as a prerequisite, a notarized letter from an Angolan citizen inviting me to visit. When I produced exactly such a letter from the Angolan agent of Emirates Airlines inviting me to come to Luanda to inspect the airport facilities, the consular officer was nonplussed, but recovered sufficiently to tell me his embassy did not grant visas to foreigners who were not residents in Mozambique, and that I should return to the U.S. and apply there. I told him, ever so politely, that this was a load of crap because every embassy was empowered to grant a visa to an applicant who personally presented himself at the embassy, regardless of where the applicant was domiciled, as long as his passport and application documents were in order—which was not universally true, but sounded reasonable to me, and came close to passing the red-face test.

After we danced around this mulberry bush for a while, he threw up his hands and told me it *might* help if I brought him a letter from the American Embassy in Maputo asking Angola to grant me a visa. When I sought to pin him down as to whether such a letter *guaranteed* me a visa, he was evasive. He eventually told me it depended on the mood of his ambassador, but he was sure I would *not* get a visa *without* such a letter.

So off I trotted to the U.S. Embassy, where a supercilious young deputy consul wasted time asking me why he should give me such a letter. He was exactly the type of bland careerist twit with whom our Foreign Service was overloaded. I told him, as sweetly as possible, he should give me such a letter because my damn tax dollars paid his friggin' salary, and the rent on the embassy, and because it should be no big deal for him.

He frostily replied that our embassy was there to determine whether to give visas to visit the U.S. to foreign applicants, not to help Americans obtain visas to Angola. I told him, a little less sweetly, that it was his damn job to assist U.S. nationals with any request that was legal and reasonable, as mine was. He was shamelessly more concerned with covering his butt by not performing any service out of the ordinary than with being compassionate or helpful. I thereupon took out my pen, asked him for his full name, and told him I'd report his attitude to my pals at the State Department (of which I actually have none), whereupon he haughtily said he'd see what he could do, and left the room.

A full hour later, he returned to show me the best he said he could do, a worthless, one-sentence letter simply stating I was a U.S. citizen who wanted to visit every country. He was not going to ask any favors of the damn Angolans and be indebted to them.

So I took his pathetic little letter and trotted back to the Angolan Embassy, where, without even reading it, they immediately complained that it was written on plain paper. I countered that it carried the rubber stamp of the U.S. deputy consul; they insisted I bring them a letter bearing the gold seal of the United States of America on official stationery.

So I went back to my embassy to get that gold-sealed stationery, which was not easy to extract from that unpleasant and unaccommodating twit.

And back with it I ran to the Angolan Embassy, where I was told, for the first time: So sorry, but the letter had to be in Portuguese, the official language of Angola. I told the official it was written in English, the official language of the good ole U.S. of A., but that only brought a shrug.

So back I ran to our embassy. I had started this process at 9:30 a.m., and it was now 2:20 p.m., and it was Friday, and our dedicated, hardworking envoys had cleared out and closed early for the weekend. I got no translation. And no visa.

Angola consequently became the hanging Chad of this journey. And I guess you could say that I had been Yanked around.


I left this part of Africa with a hopeful impression that these impoverished lands beneath the Southern Cross could finally look to a better future, that their citizens appeared genuinely pleased to be at peace and were eager to embark on a path to a safe and prospering life. Their terrifying memories and nightmares remained, as did the war-maimed bodies and the unexploded land mines. Brighter days were far in the future, and they faced a hard life immediately ahead, but they convinced me that they will persevere and prevail, and that no longer will these lands remain no countries for old men.

# CHAPTER 19

## Into the Indian Ocean

On the final six stops of my southern African peregrinations, I got dumped on from 60 feet up by a large indri, saw one of the world's only 80 golden bamboo lemurs in the wild, was arrested in the Congo, and had a quiet chat about American politics with three dead Malagasies.

The Comoros, my first stop, rated straight Ds: dirty, dull, dilapidated, deteriorating, and dismally depressing. And a dumpy PPPR of 4. My visit there even ended badly, but for that I had only myself to blame. My T-shirt boldly proclaiming I was BORN TO BE WILD was probably not the wisest choice of attire in which to enter the Comoros Airport security inspection area. They quickly took away my tiny nail clippers (which had passed unmolested through ten other airports), confiscated the ship-in-a-bottle souvenir I'd purchased in town the day before ("potential dangerous weapon"), scrutinized my Listerine bottle to determine if it exceeded the allowable volume (5 ml under, *whew*), and questioned me intently as to why I had pointy chopsticks in my bag (to avoid using their germ-laden cutlery, although I didn't say it).

In typical TIA fashion, the plane left the Comoros four hours late, causing me to miss my connection to Madagascar. The tardy airline treated me to a decent hotel and dinner. There, for the first time, I became the direct beneficiary of Islamic practices, the result of being seated next to three similarly delayed itinerant Muslim missionaries. The only dessert the hotel offered was a delicious rum-raisin ice cream, my first frosty treat in two months. The confection caused a heated debate among the imams, who concluded that even though it did not contain real alcohol, the rum-raisin flavor was a temptation to be avoided, the camel's nose in the tent of abstinence. The sole infidel at the table accordingly became the recipient of—and happily polished off—all four bowls of frozen bliss. Praise be to Allah!

I felt sorry my devout dinner companions had missed this treat, and I had even more sympathy for the challenges of their mission, as they explained it to me. Imagine the difficulty of arriving in some poor, remote, pagan village, a stranger in a strange land, proselytizing for a strange faith, and trying to persuade the villagers to forever abstain from any form of alcohol, drugs, dancing, pork, premarital sex, extramarital sex, recreational sex, Western TV shows, movies, revealing clothing, suggestive behavior, Danish cartoons, and lustful thoughts and deeds. All in exchange for a long shot at Paradise.

Before I embarked on this segment, the Malagasies—as the denizens of Madagascar prefer to be called—had turned on one another, killing more than a hundred as part of a political feud that had spread by spring to include general strikes of public employees, street and road barricades, gangs of hoodlums running amok, and growing anarchy. *The New York Times* lamented that, because of a heated dispute between the two men who each claimed to be its president, and the shooting and looting between their supporters, "Madagascar is now surely in the belly of the crocodile."

Since that didn't strike me as quite so dangerous as being in the teeth of the tiger or the jaws of the jackal, and since I'd just completed visits to the Seychelles (PPPR #2), Mauritius (PPPR #1), and Comoros, and didn't relish making a future flight back into the Indian Ocean solely to see this one unvisited country, I decided to go for it and hope the crocodile had a bellyful.

The country's current problems had begun as an electoral tussle between two "Big Men," egocentrics who hailed from different tribes and areas of the island, espoused divergent ideas about how their nation should be governed, had little liking or respect for one another, and gave only lip service to the rule of law and the democratic process. Such antagonistic African rivalries have frequently degenerated into the use of force, with each side taking to the streets to disrupt its opponent's political rallies and intimidate voters, precipitating elections marred by fraud and ballot stuffing, yielding disputed results, prompting the refusal to accept those results, giving rise to civil wars, culminating in the horror shows that had overwhelmed Kenya, Uganda, Rwanda, Angola, Liberia, Congo—and now threatened Madagascar.

As I flew over the globe's fourth largest island, I was disappointed, having envisioned a luxuriant emerald isle of dense forests. I saw instead a denuded topography of pale, poor, reddish earth, a land that had lost 90 percent of its native ecosystem as its ancient forests had been felled for furniture, firewood, and charcoal, and burned to clear ground for food. It was a land where scores of species had been exterminated since man arrived, including the pygmy hippo, the elephant bird (at 850 pounds the largest avian ever), and 19 species of lemur, among them the giant lemur, larger than a gorilla.

After 90 million years of separate evolution, Madagascar had become home to some of the most unusual—and now most endangered—wildlife and vegetation on our pale blue dot, including 70 varieties of lemurs, the planet's largest and smallest chameleons, and 120 bird species that breed nowhere else—*200,000* species in all, 80 percent of which have no other home on earth. The island had become a top concern of conservationists, but extensive damage has already been done, with the animals surviving only in national parks and reserves, while the locals continued to hunt, chop, charcoal, slash, and burn. (But before we get too shocked and self-righteous, let's put it in perspective and remember that America's original inhabitants exterminated the wooly mammoth and the saber-toothed tiger, and that our European settlers wiped out the passenger pigeon, decimated America's old-growth forests, its tall-grass prairies, the Everglades, the ivory billed woodpecker, and the grizzly, the bison, the mountain lion, and the wolf.)

After I landed and was able to inspect things more closely, neither the political nor the topographical landscape seemed quite so bleak.

The Malagasies had sobered up and realized that prosperity could not coexist with anarchy and violence and that tourists were not attracted to street warfare. By the time I arrived, the Malagasies were once again among the calmest and most gentle folks. And, to make sure they stayed that way, the striking gendarmes had returned to work and now had checkpoints all over the island, which was profoundly peaceful.

The tourists had yet to return. The industry was down more than 90 percent. I needed no reservation for hotels (where I was often the only guest), experienced no waits in any queues, no crowds in the national parks, and no trouble engaging English-speaking guides at a moment's notice. But it was sad to see their economy in shambles from the lack of visitors.

From the ground, the deforested land was surprisingly attractive, with multiple mountain chains and hundreds of wide, scenic valleys, every acre of which was under cultivation to feed its 18 million people. It resembled Asia, with flooded rice paddies glistening bright blue-green in the spring sun, the hillsides terraced and trimmed with sprouting carrots, lettuce, and cabbage.

The fruits and vegetables I savored were fresh and cheap: 25 cents bought me eight bananas, or six succulent tomatoes, or a pound of exotic fruit fresh from the forest. I dined contentedly on the tastiest tilapia, on zebu steak (which I'd never eaten), freshwater shrimp (which I had not known existed), and Chinese soup (in which floated a calf's knee and a dozen chicken innards I had not known were edible).

The zebu takes the place of cattle in southern Madagascar and gives the scenery an Asian cast with its huge horns, a fatty hump at the top of the neck, and long folds of flesh under the neck. Far more docile and obedient than cattle, zebu were everywhere, plowing the paddies and pulling heavily laden large-wheeled wooden carts along the roads. And they tasted fine, somewhat like buffalo, a bit chewier and less fatty than beef.

The soil in the valleys was loaded with kaolin (aka China clay), ideal for retaining water in the paddies and for making bricks. Every village I saw had a brickmaking yard on the edge of its farms, such farms usually having ten to a hundred paddies, each about the size of a basketball court or two, but with innumerable variations in shape to accommodate the topography. When the Malagasies added a new paddy, they scooped out the clay-rich muck, piled it up near the road, ran it through a one-brick press to squeeze out the water, let the bricks dry in the sun for a few weeks, then either carted the bricks to town to earn some cash or used them to build more houses, houses which will last a hundred years (except for their thatch roofs) and blend harmoniously with their concolorous environs.

The farmers then flood the paddy and often put in a school of small fish to eat the larvae laid there by mosquitoes and other pesky insects. The fish droppings drift down and fertilize the soil. The farmers later bring in a dozen domesticated ducks or geese to eat the fattened fish and add their own nutritious excrement to the mud, after which in go the young rice plants, one by one, each inserted by hand.

Half of humanity is dependent on rice, including many of the world's poorest and most vulnerable peoples. It is their staple food, providing more than one-fifth of *all* calories consumed around the globe, and is the only major cereal crop that can be grown in these hot and humid regions, which quickly wither wheat, oats, barley, soybeans, and rye.

But rice is under siege. Production surged in the 1960s, during the Green Revolution, as plant breeders increased its yield threefold to feed the expanding population in the nations where rice was the staff of life. But the yield per acre has not increased much since then, while the world's population has doubled and is heading for 9.6 billion by 2050, which will require another—and probably unattainable—doubling of rice productivity.

Climate change will also have a disproportionately negative impact on rice because rising temperatures will result in increased heat and drought and decreased available water. This, the agronomists at Cornell ominously predict, "will require people to rethink how rice has been grown for thousands of years," forcing the growers to abandon the system of flooded paddies that has controlled weeds since biblical times.

Most of us incorrectly assume that the omnipresent paddy water is required to hydrate the plants, but the real reason for the pools of water is to prevent *weeds* from taking root. Weeds are far more harmful to rice than to almost any other crop because the major weed in a rice field is a wild form of rice, a form sexually compatible with the crop being grown, resulting in an uncontrolled transfer of genes both ways, enabling the wild rice weed to withstand herbicides, and causing the modern, genetically modified rice to lose its high yield and head back toward where it was prior to the Green Revolution. As fresh water becomes scarcer, not only will those picturesque paddies be things of the past—but so may many millions of our poor brothers who depend on them.

Any global warming will harm tropical crops the most because those plants are already subjected to the maximum temperatures at which they can thrive.

On top of that, African agriculture had been hard hit with brown streak, a disease caused by mealy bugs, that had widely ravaged cassava plantations, and for which there was no cure yet. Because cassava (also known as manioc, tapioca, and yucca) is the third most important source of carbohydrates on the planet, and since millions of poor Africans rely on that starchy root for a majority of their calories, the prospect of widespread famine is frighteningly real. *Oh, Africa!*

Madagascar is most famous for its lemurs, 99 of 212 varieties of which have managed to survive, all in widely scattered national parks, and I was fortunate to see ten species in my ten days of driving 2,000 kilometers.

The prevailing theory as to why only Madagascar has lemurs is that, 100 million years ago, their prototypes evolved on the African continent and became inadvertent mariners when they were washed out to sea in storms. They floated across the 260-mile-wide Mozambique Channel to Madagascar 62 to 65 million years ago on lumps of vegetation while their less fortunate predators drowned en route. These accidental tourists speciated and filled unoccupied biological niches on Madagascar, thereby avoiding competition with other species for food or shelter and enabling the little guys to thrive.

The modern lemurs are indigenous and endemic to Madagascar and include varieties that are nocturnal, diurnal, crepuscular; or cathemeral, some of which estivate in the dry season—and I promise no more sentences like that. They range in size from the indri, which can top 25 pounds and has a haunting cry that carries for miles, to the tiny pygmy mouse lemur, which is the world's smallest primate and could hide in a teacup. They are all cute, cuddly, endearing, and lovable. (I was tempted to write a short poem about them, which would have been my first lemurick.)

The rarest is the golden bamboo lemur, not discovered until 1986. It lives only in the Ranomafana rain forest.

How does one get to see this singular little creature?

Looking for lemurs is not as simple as spotting squirrels in Central Park or pikas on Mount Whitney. First, I had to drive for two days to Ranomafana, then rise before the sun because the little critters are only active and eating from dawn to around nine a.m., then hire two guides to assist, one to search ahead for the lemurs and the other to drag me along through the forest. I hiked through mountainside woods for two hours; clambered up and down through dense, wet, cloying, slippery jungle; tripped on roots, vines, creepers, mud, and thorns; and plunged into dense thickets of giant bamboo, whose newest, most tender, cyanide-laced leaves the little guys like to chomp for breakfast.

The resolute searcher repeats this arduous process every day for an average of *three or four weeks* to stalk this elusive species that had avoided detection for hundreds of years. I was lucky and hit the jackpot on my first day, getting some pretty good photos of both the golden bamboo lemur and the almost-as-rare greater bamboo lemur. My hands and legs were covered with thorn scratches, I twisted my ankle, and I suffered the indignity of being shat on from high above by a large indri. All in all, a fair exchange.

Now, about talking to those dead folks . . .

The culture of Madagascar is replete with both voodoo, which came across from Africa, and ancestor worship, which came with the Malagasies' Asian forbears. These traits are combined in a remarkable ceremony called *Famadihana*, the turning of the bones.

After someone has been dead and buried about five or six years, by which time only bones and some sinews remain, the family exhumes the body, opens the coffin, lovingly washes the bones, tenderly anoints them with honey to preserve them, then dances with the bones to live music, puts them in a smaller, brightly colored coffin for reburial several days later, and parades them through the streets of whichever town the deceased resided in.

I witnessed this ceremony in a small village where the family had just disinterred Pop and the grandparents. The whole town celebrated. It was a joyous occasion, not in any way macabre or bizarre to them. They were having a fabulous party, making a gleeful noise, dancing in the streets, drinking and clapping, overjoyed to have their "dear old friends" back in town for a few days. The bones were then escorted by the celebrants to the family resi-

Villagers in southern Madagascar carry the coffin of a disinterred corpse during the ceremony known as "the turning of the bones," where the skeleton is cleaned, preserved with honey, and joyfully welcomed back to town like an old friend who had been away for about five years.

dence where, like dear old friends who'd been away for a long time, they were shown through the house, regaled with all the family gossip, informed about any of the chief changes that had occurred, had their advice sought about many of those changes, and were introduced to any new spouses and children.

As an honored foreign guest, I was invited to join the festivities and was particularly asked to explain to the departed—*uuuh,* I mean the dear old friends—the wonder of Barack Obama, the miracle of a black man—a very good, wise, and intelligent black man, they told me—the son of an African father, the husband of a woman who was the great-grandchild of slaves, being elected president of the mighty United States, an event that had struck Africa with amazement and stirred it deeply with joy and love and hope for America. And for itself.

As far as I could tell, the bones were pleased.

* * *

I flew back to Joburg to replenish supplies and complete this trip with a transit to the heart of darkness, the Congo and the DRC. I spent most of my time there dodging potholes and beggars, searching for something to eat, ferrying across the wide river between the two nations, bargaining for carvings (of which the Congos have some of the best in Africa), and losing much of what I wrote at the Internet café during the three or four daily blackouts and the ten or 20 short power interruptions.

When the power in my hotel went out, so did the overhead fan in my sweltering room, which meant I had to go out. Easier said than done. My half-star native hotel had no windows to illuminate its pitch-black hallway, and the porter put only one candle on the floor in the middle on the 150-foot-long hall. One candle.

There's not much to do in Kinshasa, and even less during a blackout (unless you're a mugger), but I found one benefit: I could get an inexpensive haircut. You see, half the dudes in town had their hair clipped down to the scalp and half were taking it a tad longer, in a new style they called "The Obama." Since both styles required the barber to use electric trimmers, he was effectively out of business during the blackouts, enabling me, as the only long-haired game in town, to negotiate for a scissors cut at half the price.

By this point I'd finished off 60 breakfast bars, 68 packets of iced-tea mix, 15 pounds of adult cereal, 49 Big Apple T-shirts, seven large paperbacks, 750 vitamin pills, three bottles each of water purification pills, mosquito repellent, and sunscreen, 20 compact Hyatt Hotel sewing kits (dispensed as gifts and tips), two pairs of worn-out jungle pants, one pound of matzos, six tins of sardines, eight gigabytes of camera flashcard memory—and twelve of the 13 countries I'd set out to see. And my tooth was twinging sharply. It was time to head home, so I decided to take a few farewell photos—and got arrested.

I had not been taking any photos in the Congos because I saw nothing photogenic, just grime and dilapidation. But I thought someone back home might like a look, so I walked out of my hotel and snapped two pictures of the food vendors across the street. This caused an immediate outburst of shouting, pointing, and fist waving from the locals, whereupon the omnipresent plainclothes police promptly pounced on me.

After a thorough check of my passport and documents, and a lengthy lec-

ture in heated French, they explained that the torn-up strip of worn tar front-
ing my hotel was one of the main roads leading from the Congo River into the
capital and that if the rebels (who had been contentedly raping and pillaging
many hundreds of miles to the east for the last couple of years) attacked from
the sea and came up the river to Kinshasa (which was about as likely as their
invading Coney Island) my photos could provide them with vital intelligence
on how to strike into the heart of the city. Which was just pure war-hysteria
bullshit. The only info the rebels could glean from my photos was where to
find the fly-besieged outdoor barbecue where I ate lunch, and *that* would wipe
them out quicker than any government weaponry.

After I rejected the response outlined above as too difficult for me to successfully translate into diplomatic French, I told the police that I was just a
simple-minded American tourist idiot who wanted a few snaps of this glori
ous place to show my buddies back home. I eventually got released on my
own recognizance.

The next day I learned why I'd been let off so easy in that normally repressive nation: The police had much bigger fish to fry, and size matters. The
morning headline proclaimed:

PENIS THEFT PANIC HITS THE CITY.

After more than 14 self-described victims complained, the Kinshasa police had arrested some dozen alleged "sorcerers," who were accused of having touched the victims to shrink their penises, often promising to restore the
equipment in exchange for cash. (No credit cards accepted.) The situation
was so inflammatory, with attempted lynchings reported, that the police also
detained the victims until the furor calmed down.

None of the Kinshasans congregated around the newsstand where I read
this had any doubt that these crimes had actually happened.

Hard as it may be for Westerners to understand, many West Africans either practice or believe in voodoo, black magic, and witchcraft, and a few
even commit ritual murders to obtain body parts and blood for occult practices.

An article in *Culture, Medicine and Psychiatry* on March 29, 2005, titled
"Understanding Genital-Shrinking Epidemics in West Africa," studied the
psychopathological aspects of these periodic panics—the researchers called it

mass psychogenic illness—in which people have been lynched or beaten to death after being accused of causing penises, breasts, and vaginas to shrink or disappear. The belief is called koro and is listed in the *Diagnostic and Statistical Manual of Mental Disorders*.

Preferring probative evidence to psychiatry, the Kinshasa chief of police informed Reuters that "I tell the victims that their penises are still there. When they tell me that it's become tiny or that they've become impotent, I tell them, 'How do you know if you haven't gone home and tried it?'"

I learned that penis thefts and shrinkings had also been recently reported in Cameroon, Ghana, Nigeria, Ivory Coast, Benin, Senegal, Sudan, and the Gambia.

So it looks like Big Al dodged another bullet. Or even worse, the loss of his gun.

Meanwhile, the rebels were still raping and robbing at leisure in the distant eastern jungles and have yet to make me an offer for my invaluable photographs.

# CHAPTER 20

## On the Whims of the Dragoons

With 21 nations left, I planned to knock off the ten most tranquil of them—Nauru, East Timor, Brunei, Bhutan, Burma, Mongolia, Kiribati, North Korea, and two newbies—between July and September 2010, saving for 2011 those I most feared might knock me off.

But after I'd purchased all 24 (nonrefundable) airline tickets and one (30-hour) ride on the Trans-Mongolian Express across the Gobi Desert, things started to unravel all along the route.

*Burma* (my preferred name for Myanmar) was beset by political unrest when the military regime used underhanded ways to prolong the house arrest of pro-democracy leader Aung San Suu Kyi before the promised elections. The elections *had* been scheduled for February 2010, so I'd blithely assumed that any demonstrations attendant upon it would be out of the way by the time I arrived. But in January the regime postponed the voting, and the rumor mill predicted a rescheduling for the numerologically auspicious date of October 10, the tenth day of the tenth month of the tenth (though technically the eleventh) year of the new century, which, lucky me, was right after I planned to arrive. Things were heating up and protesters were killed by the army a month before I was due to arrive there.

*North Korea* decided that the spring of 2010 was a good time to take some torpedo practice, sinking a South Korean Navy ship and raising tensions to the highest level in several decades. After catching two Americans who crossed its northern border without permission, North Korea tightened the entry requirements for U.S. citizens. They refused to grant a visa to any author or journalist—and would not disclose whether they considered me to be in either of those categories until I presented myself at their embassy in Beijing the day before my plane was scheduled to fly to Pyongyang.

*Mongolia* was beset by the second-worst drought in 60 years, which followed an exceptionally frigid winter, that one-two punch killing seven million head of livestock, the mainstay of the nation's diet and economy.

*China,* my gateway to Pyongyang and to Mongolia, and subsequently to Bangkok, was ticked off by President Obama's insistence that it raise both the value of its currency and its respect for human rights, and it retaliated with a policy change that denied U.S. nationals multiple-entry visas. Although I explained to their visa office why my itinerary required me to enter and leave China three times, and implored them to grant me a triple-entry stamp, they gave me only two entries.

*Thailand,* the airline hub through which I'd scheduled *twelve* flights, had suddenly erupted into violence between the red-shirted backers of the ousted prime minister and the trigger-happy soldiers who supported the replacement government. King Bhumibol Adulyadej, the revered 83-year-old monarch who'd held these fractious folks together for more than 60 years, was too ill to intercede, and might even have to vacate the throne for his inept son who was despised by the Thais on both sides.

*Nauru* was acting up, angry because the U.S. had charged that desperately impoverished island-nation with selling itself for Russian rubles when it became one of only four countries to recognize the breakaway Georgian provinces of South Ossetia and Abkhazia as independent nations.

*East Timor* was also problematic. An island-nation north of Australia, it was now almost cut off from the rest of the world. In the euphoria surrounding its birth, three airlines had rushed to provide air service, connecting its capital of Dili with, respectively, Singapore, Hong Kong, and Australia. But as East Timor's financial prospects dimmed, and neither trade nor tourists materialized, two airlines had flown away, and it was left with a thin, single-carrier lifeline from Australia.

Thailand has some of the most ornate and impressive temples in the world, with its architectural style totally different from its Buddhist neighbors in Burma and Bhutan. Here, at Wat Arun (the Temple of Dawn) on the west bank of the Chao Phraya River in Bangkok, a huge demon is the temple guardian.

Atop these concerns, I belatedly concluded that I needed to visit two extra countries to satisfy my criteria for visiting every state in today's world. One was Bangladesh (where I had come within a minute of being hanged as an Indian spy when its land had been called East Pakistan, which no longer existed). The other was the Socialist Republic of Vietnam (which was a different political entity than the South Vietnam I'd visited in 1965 as its war was heating up). Much as I wanted to skip the rerun and the distant replay, I felt that would be cheating. For the purposes of my quest, I had defined a country as a political entity as well as a geographical one. I therefore had to go back because I had never visited these newly created political entities. To squeeze them in, I had to add an extra week to my itinerary.

So much for the start of a simple summer sojourn intended to be spent peacefully picking off the easiest of the remaining nations.

Adding a pervasively sad undertone was the poor health of Steve, my dear buddy and old travel companion. Steve and I had agreed, back in 2007, to mesh our schedules for the summer of 2010 so we could reunite for our last hurrah together, one final, freewheeling, 4×4 trip, across the steppes and deserts of Mongolia to visit the haunts of Genghis Khan.

Steve was seriously injured in December 2009, when a tiger attacked the elephant on which he was riding in a remote part of Nepal. In the course of a long recuperation in a Bangkok hospital, Steve fainted several times for reasons unrelated to the attack, but which his Thai physicians were unable to ascertain. When he grew worse, he was emergency airlifted, feeble and incoherent, to the VA hospital in San Francisco, and was there diagnosed with widespread Stage IV lymphoma. Our final trip together was not to be.

As I made preparations, with a heavy heart, to start the Asia segment by late July, Steve was in intensive care, but he managed to send me a farewell e-mail: "Sorry to let you down, old pal. We would have had a great time on the trail of the Great Khan."

# CHAPTER 21

## Murphy Moves to TomorrowLand

Through that winter of 2010, I tried to maintain contact with Steve in the VA hospital, but the doctors had him so doped up to mitigate his pain that our conversations were frustratingly incoherent.

Knowing Steve as well as I did, I was sure this inveterate traveler and macho adventurer, then 84, would prefer to have died with his boots on rather than be painfully poked and probed by oncologists and subjected to all the debilitating side effects of chemotherapy in a likely losing battle. What grander, more glorious, more memorable, and more appropriate curtain call could a guy like Steve ask for than to be killed by a tiger that had pounced on the elephant he was riding while on the trail of a story in the Nepalese hinterlands! Now *that's* the way to go!

Was the tiger a cosmic cat that failed to fulfill its mission? Or did fate have more in store for Steve?

Steve had the strongest constitution of any guy I knew, and he was still alive when I got a call through to him just after the 4th of July. He was in obvious pain, his memory was shot, he'd developed an excruciating peripheral neuropathy, and he lapsed in and out of semiconsciousness, but, as we said our good-byes, he managed to mumble, "Al, buddy, you have to finish the world. Win this one for the Gipper. Come on, bring this baby home for me."

And that was what I promised to do.

\* \* \*

First on my list of ten was Kiribati, a midget nation comprised of one raised island and 32 atolls in the middle of the Pacific, hundreds of miles from anywhere, just on tomorrow's side of the International Date Line, where Today ends and Tomorrow has already begun. It had been on my schedule when I'd visited the Pacific in 2007, but I'd never reached it because, shortly before I was to arrive, the only airline flying the Kiribati-Nauru route ceased operation, filed for bankruptcy protection, and left me with a useless ticket and two missed countries.

That carrier, reincarnated as Our Airline, resumed service in 2009, providing me with a second chance to reach Nauru and continue on to East Timor. I would have to fly the once-a-week Monday Air Pacific from Fiji to Tarawa, the quiet capital of Kiribati, and visit for eight days—not because there was anywhere close to eight days' worth of stuff to see there, but because Our Airline only flew from Tarawa to Nauru once a week, on a Tuesday, leaving me with a choice between a hasty one-night stand in Kiribati or a boring eight. I chose the latter. If I encountered any delay leaving Kiribati, it would wreck the rest of my journey.

I became so tense about this scheduling that this ol' road warrior morphed into an old worrier. From spring into summer I was worrying about *everything*—flights, visas, the political situations, weight restrictions, supplies, logistics, accommodations, diseases, endurance. What the hell was going on with me? Why had I become such a worrywart?

I pulled back, took a hard look, and came up with a three-part explanation. First, I was totally dependent on one airplane, owned by an airline with an unreliable past, flying a route only once a week, to get me out of Kiribati on time to begin to catch 21 tight airline connections to 14 countries. Second, I had been sitting on the sidelines for a year and had lost my sea legs, my travel reflexes, my on-the-road confidence. I needed to get my groove back.

The third reason was the most pertinent, but the hardest for me to accept: I was getting older, well past the age when people traveled the way I did. At most of the abodes where I stayed, on most of the trains and buses I rode, in most of the countries I visited, I was decades older than the other voyagers.

Independent travel in the underdeveloped world was a young guy's game, requiring sturdy legs, strong arms, sharp eyes, loads of energy, a reliable memory, a high tolerance for problems and delays, and a phlegmatic demeanor, all of which I was losing.

Had I played the game too long? Should I join the blue-rinse brigade on those cushy cruise ships? Did I think I was Peter Pan? Was I the wise, seasoned, competent, world traveler I thought I was? Or just an aching, aging, crotchety wreck of an old fart foolishly following an impossible dream far beyond his ability to achieve it? Should I give it up? Or should I suck it up and make a strong final push to get the job done in the few fair years I might have ahead?

The answer came slowly, but inexorably: I would follow my impossible dream. And I would keep my promise to Steve.

With renewed spirit, I set out for the Pacific and Kiribati and what I hoped was the penultimate part of my great adventure.

If you wake up on Kiribati earlier than any of its 110,000 other inhabitants, you'd be the first person on earth to welcome the new day. Other than that, there's nothing special or spectacular about it.

In some ways the capital island of Tarawa was akin to Dune Road in the Hamptons. It's a 25-mile-long spit of sand no more than a few hundred yards wide and less than twelve feet high, with the ocean on one side, a ten-mile-wide lagoon on the other, and a two-lane road down the middle. Just make a few adjustments. Change the Hamptons sand to finely crushed coral; put a 22-mile-long reef a mile offshore on the ocean side; add six or seven serpentine twists and a couple of causeways of crushed coral and sand to connect several dozen separate islets; change the road to crumbled tarmac with open sewers and storm drains on either side instead of bike lanes; remove three zeroes from the value of the homes on each side; replace the carefully manicured gardens and hedges of the Hamptons with crabgrass, hibiscus, palm trees, breadfruit, and frangipani; scatter about 500 multicolored shipping containers along the road edge for use as stores, storage, and housing; throw in some lethargic, skinny mutts dozing in the sun, scampering chickens, and

There are few private cars and almost no traffic in the poor island-nation of Kiribati, even here on Tarawa, the capital island. The country is only a few feet above sea level and will sink beneath the waves of our warming planet before the end of the century.

pigs grunting in the shade; add a dilapidated hamlet of weather-worn, corrugated tin-roofed shacks about every four miles or so, plus five or six downscale lodges and handicrafts shops; and, wherever houses concentrated, a dark and dingy little stall selling dusty necessities at high prices; and, along the entire route and on all the beaches, strew every conceivable kind of refuse, wreckage, and rubbish, and you've got the picture—and an understanding of why only ten tourists alighted from the 737B that brought me there.

Another drawback is the absence of competitive banking. The nation has only one bank, resulting in monopolistic, obscene exchange rates. The guideline I use to determine if I'm getting a fair deal, even when I don't know the latest rate, it to compare the rate at which the bank is buying dollars to the rate at which it sells them. If the difference is around two or three percent, as it is in most big tourist cities, it's a fair shake, and the bank is making a fair profit. The ANZ Bank on Kiribati had a spread of 12 percent, plus a 3 percent commission. If I had given them 108 USD, they'd give me 100 AUD, and if I gave them back those same 100 AUD, they'd give me only 92 USD. I'd lose 18 percent of my money! To make matters worse, no place in Kiribati let me pay for anything with USD, so I was compelled to exchange at the bank.

Kiribati could be a paradise if it cleaned up its act physically and fiscally. It has miles of potentially exquisite beaches unspoiled by any high-rise developments, a splendid abundance of collectible seashells, safe swimming, excellent reef and big-game fishing, no harmful snakes or animals, almost no mosquitoes, a constant, refreshing breeze that dissipated the heat, no beggars, nobody going hungry, no serious crime, and some of the world's most gentle, kindly, hospitable inhabitants. You could buy a house for less than your annual rent in the States. And no matter how poor your sense of direction, with only one road, and water on each side of it, you'd always find your way home.

It was an ideal place to lose track of time and get away from it all. The four-page weekly newspaper featured only sports stories and an occasional political scandal. The TV—despite the huge dish antenna outside my room— carried only one channel, and it was slavishly devoted to rugby, following the sport with the sun, almost 24/7, across the British Commonwealth, from Fiji to New Zealand, across Australia, to South Africa, to England. The only break was a program called *Monday Night Raw,* which I hoped would be for adult entertainment, but was only wrestling.

Mary's Motel, where I stayed, had Internet access, but it took more than half an hour to log on because the national system could handle only a few users at a time.

Kiribati had none of the street corner repairmen who flourish in most of the Third World. I found no cobblers (because many of the indigenes went barefoot, and the others wore flip-flops they fixed with pieces of tape); no watch repairers (because the precise time in TomorrowLand was not vital, and you could get an inkling of the hour from the bright sun and shadows); no tailors or seamstresses (because it was cheaper to sew it at home); and nobody to repair or replace the cracked frame on my reading glasses (because there were no opticians, just a couple of shops that sold magnifying glasses).

Well aware how difficult it could be to buy essentials in a place like this, I'd packed three pair of glasses and a repair kit, but I sat on two pairs of them in three days, cracking their frames, while a baggage handler crushed the third, whereupon I found, to my dismay, that my Krazy Glue had dried up since Africa. I commenced a nationwide glue search, covering six mini-marts, four hardware stores, and three office supply shops, in the last of which I found three tubes of Super Glue, only one of which was still usable. I liberally applied it to bond glass and rim so I could keep reading my paperbacks rather than go bonkers from boredom.

Many of the indigenes were Micronesians who understood some English, and most of the teenagers spoke fair English they learned in high school, but they all preferred to speak their own i-Kiribati, one of the 450 Oceanic languages. Long gone from the Pacific was the pidgin adapted from the 1940s GIs, which was still widely spoken when I first visited the South Seas in 1981. I missed it because it had a distinctive charm and was fun to puzzle out—as long as the message wasn't urgent. Some of it was simple, "Hurry, chop chop, me kickee ass bilong you." Some was simplified, as when Apollo 14 landed two astronauts on the moon: "Tupela igo daun wokabout long mun." (Two fellas went down and walked along the moon.) Some was a touching transformation rather than a literal translation, as when the first line of "The Lord's Prayer" became: "Papa bilong yumi Istap Antap." (Father on top belongs to you and me.) And some, like the delightfully salient difference between women and men—"Bokis along missus"—I'll let you noodle over.

Kiribati became a country in 1979, after the British colony of the Gilbert and Ellice Islands peacefully divided. The mostly Micronesian Gilberts became Kiribati and the principally Polynesian Ellices became Tuvalu. Until 1985 Kiribati had only 16 mini-atolls, totaling less than 100 square miles, strung across the Equator, only one of which was more than a dozen feet above sea level. All but one were classic coral atoll lagoons set atop a submerged volcanic chain, just flat arcs of coral sand adorned with coconut palms. Over many hardworking generations, the islanders had been able to create pits of fertile humus in the barren sand by mulching organic material, and there grow bananas and taro, papaya and pandanus, melons and breadfruit, tomatoes and cucumbers. Periodic shortfalls of rain make agriculture difficult, and the intense heat makes it impossible to grow leafy salad stuff and most vegetables, which are imported from Australia on refrigerator ships. These narrow isles lack potable aquifers; every drinkable drop came from collected rainwater or desalinated seawater, or, if you were really rich, from bottles of imported FIJI Water.

Shortly before 1860, American missionaries arrived and persuaded the natives to stop their island-against-island wars and modify some of their harsher rules of behavior. The old practices permitted a husband who found his wife being unfaithful to bite off her nose, and punished a male philanderer by putting him in a canoe, in a strong offshore wind, without water, food, or even a paddle. I'm not sure if the doomed lover was allowed to take his inamorata's nose along as a memento. Or a snack.

Tarawa was the scene of one of the foremost battles in U.S. military history. At the start of WW II, the Japanese seized and fortified dozens of islands throughout the Pacific to form a ring of defenses around Japan. Tarawa was garrisoned by 5,000 crack Japanese troops and studded with more than 100 concrete machine-gun nests, 55 large artillery pieces, many Type 95 Ha-Go tanks, and underground blockhouses made of concrete and reinforced steel, their roofs curved in low arches to deflect shell impact and covered over with layers of logs and dirt to conceal and protect them. So essential did the Japanese High Command regard Tarawa that, after they captured Singapore, they relocated its British 8-inch coastal defense guns here to beat off a potential Allied invasion. The Japanese commander boasted that a million men could not take Tarawa in a century.

Then came November of 1943. American amphibious troops landed on the island and took it in four days, at a cost of 3,200 dead and wounded in some of the fiercest fighting in the Pacific Theater. After the drawn-out, see-saw battles for New Guinea and Guadalcanal, Tarawa was the first quick and decisive land victory for the U.S. in two years of Pacific warfare, our first such penetration of Japan's ring of defenses, our first overwhelming demonstration that the Japanese Army was not invincible. America confidently marched from Tarawa to victories at Kwajalein, Eniwetok, Saipan, the Marianas, Tinian, Guam, Peleliu, Leyte, Luzon, the Philippines, Iwo Jima, Okinawa, and the end of the WW II in Tokyo Bay 20 months later.

I visited the landing beaches on the tiny islet of Betio, now connected to the rest of Tarawa by a mile-long causeway recently built by a peaceful

Many cannons—this one on Tarawa—litter the coasts of several dozen islands in the Pacific where the Japanese had bases in World War II. The nearby jungles hold the rusted carcasses of tanks and artillery pieces and destroyed concrete pillboxes and machine-gun nests.

Japan. I saw that wild coconut and breadfruit trees were beginning to obscure the remains of the war: the armor plate scorched black by American flamethrowers; the rusting axles and motors of U.S. landing craft piled on the shore; the outsized, oxidized cannon barrels lying in the shallow waters; the grotesquely twisted shapes of the coastal guns blasted by U.S. battleships; the blockhouses and pillboxes, still intact more than sixty years after the bloodshed; and the Japanese military cemetery, bright with tokens of remembrance left by the loving families who visited.

A number of the smaller islands that now comprise Kiribati had been owned until recently by the U.S., pursuant to an obscure Act of Congress passed in August 1856, officially titled the "Guano Islands Act," but more commonly called the Bird-Poop Bill, which declared:

> Whenever any citizen of the United States discovers a deposit of
> guano on any island, rock, key, not within the lawful jurisdiction
> of any other government, and not occupied by the citizens of any

other government, and takes peaceable possession thereof, and occupies the same, such island, rock, or key may, at the discretion of the President, be considered as appertaining to the United States.

Hundreds of islands and islets around the globe were covered with various kinds of guano, often piled up to 150 feet high, and the U.S., pursuant to the Guano Islands Act, appropriated dozens of them on behalf of its far-flung citizen miners, including such larger places as Kingman Reef, Johnston Atoll, Palmyra Atoll, and Baker, Howland, Jarvis, and Midway Islands. This Bird-Poop Bill is still in our federal statute books today, as Title 48, U.S. Code, Sections 1411–1419.

Since this law is discretionary, it does not require that every such crappy island be annexed to the U.S. or retained in perpetuity. Accordingly, Congress, in 1985, as a gift to the new nation of Kiribati from the people of the United States, relinquished control of, and ceded to Kiribati, those guano islands within its domain. And that's the straight poop.

Although international news was hard to come by on Tarawa, I heard rumors that the U.S., in retaliation for North Korea's increasing militarism and threatening behavior, had barred visits there by American citizens. Since the Korean War armistice agreement had been signed back in 1953, I was too stunned to believe that my dear government had waited 55 years, for the very week that I flew off, to suddenly ban travel to Pyongyang. This seemed so improbable that I dismissed it as a fantasy and stuck with my itinerary.

Then Murphy's Law, which is grounded in the perceived perversity in the universe, took over: Whatever could go wrong did go wrong.

The only planes serving Kiribati were the Air Pacific flight that landed there on Tuesdays at three p.m.—i.e., the flight I took to get there—and left at four to return to Fiji, and the Monday flight on Our Airlines, which hopped via Nauru and the Solomon Islands to Brisbane in Oz. That was it. All those flights were fully booked for several weeks in advance. If I missed mine, I could be stranded on Tarawa for weeks, with no other way to get to where I needed to go—unless I were willing to risk hundreds of miles of ocean in an open boat. Aware of this situation, I had twice stopped in at the Our Airlines office in Bairiki—Kiribati's capital city—twice confirmed my reservation, and twice been told that all was in order.

On my last scheduled day on Tarawa, anxious to minimize any risk, I arrived at the airport three hours early for the four p.m. flight to Nauru and presented my ticket. After more than an hour of waiting, while officials mysteriously huddled over my passport, I was told that the computer flashed DO NOT BOARD when my name had been entered. They did not know why and were e-mailing their main office in Brisbane for an explanation. After a nerve-wracking delay that seemed interminable, Brisbane told them I lacked a visa for Australia and must not be allowed to board the plane, not even to fly as far as Nauru.

I explained that I did not intend to formally enter Australia, but was merely in transit through it to Dili in East Timor, and had planned to spend my time sleeping in the Brissie transit lounge, as I had done three years before, and had packed my foam camping mattress and blankets in my carry-on for that very purpose. The perplexed agent pulled out a dusty Australian Immigration Department rule book, and we went through it, page by page, while the other passengers prepared to board. Toward the end of the book, the small print informed us that even if a transit passenger was willing to be confined to the airport, if that passenger's layover in Australia exceeded seven hours, he needed a transit visa. My connecting flight from Brisbane was scheduled to depart *nine* hours after I arrived.

I freaked out and came about as close to fainting as I ever had. If I missed this flight, there was not another open one to Australia for weeks. Moreover, there was no room at the inn: Mary's Motel was full for the next two months because 36 U.S. military personnel were arriving on the next day's flight from Fiji with a new type of ground-penetrating radar, hoping to find the remains of several hundred U.S. servicemen who had died during the Tarawa landings but whose bodies had never been recovered. These graves-registration specialists had booked every room at Mary's, and the spillover had fully occupied the few other hotels and lodges on the island. I would have to sleep on the beach for a week, and longer if no seat opened up. I was SOL on all counts and close to panic mode.

My only hope of salvaging some of my itinerary was to get on the weekly Air Pacific plane back to Fiji the next afternoon and move onward from there, but I had no idea if any seats were available. I phoned Mary's, which sent their van back for me an hour later—Kiribati has no taxis—and we raced for the office of Air Pacific, about a third of the way down the island, where they told me that, yes, they had two open seats on the flight to Fiji the next day, the only available space for a month. I was saved!

But not! Because they also told me that Fijian regulations would not let them fly me to Fiji unless I held an ongoing ticket and companion visa. The only ongoing destination from Fiji that made any sense for my purposes was Australia, but I had no Aussie visa. It was now 4:28. We phoned the Australian High Commission (AHC) and they told us that it usually took three days for them to issue a visa. Figuring I might do better in person, I jumped into Mary's van and we raced another third of the way down the island to the AHC, arriving at 5:02, two minutes after closing time, but I looked so agitated and pathetic that they let me in. They gave me an application for a transit visa, told me to bring it in the next morning at eight a.m., and again cautioned me that it had to be approved in Australia, which rarely happened in less than three days. Since I had only six hours the next day in which to get the visa, and get the ticket, and get to the airport, the AHC suggested that I go on their Web site, where "those applications are processed more quickly."

I rushed back to Mary's, which was able to give me my old room for one more night, cranked up their balky Internet, went on the designated Aussie government Web site—and found that they did not issue transit visas over the Web. And there was no mention of quick service.

I was getting desperate. I ran through a mental map of the flights that departed from Fiji. The only other countries in the right direction for me were New Zealand and the Solomon Islands, but both required visas. A handful of islands were serviced from Fiji, but none had any connections onward to anywhere I needed to go, and most of them also required visas. I could fly back to the States without a visa, but that was ridiculous.

I located a flight from Fiji to Seoul departing in two days. This sounded doable because I knew Americans did not need a visa for South Korea. But when I checked more closely, I found that the only circumstance in which I did not need a visa to land in South Korea was if I had an ongoing flight from there to another country within 60 days (which required yet another visa).

Bingo! I had a valid visa for China! So I purchased flights on the Internet going from Fiji to Seoul and Seoul to Beijing. All I had to do was print the confirmations and show them to the folks at Air Pacific, and I could fly with them to Fiji the next day and get back on at least part of the trail.

It was 9:30 p.m. and I was exhausted from stress. Since Mary's reception desk closed at 10:00 p.m., I asked the late-shift receptionist to print out my ticket so I could get to sleep and try to forget this dreadful day. She activated the printer, which took an agonizingly long time to spit out the page. And when it emerged it was blank. The printer was out of ink! And this reception-ist had no clue where to find a replacement cartridge.

I dashed back to my room, grabbed my camera, and took two photos of the computer monitor showing my flight confirmations, but I doubted if any airport agent had been presented with such atypical evidence of a flight con-firmation or was sufficiently flexible to accept it.

No, I had to get the confirmation printed. I dragooned an accommodating NGO guy who was staying at Mary's, and he agreed to walk me over to his agency to see if they had a working printer. We had walked about 15 minutes to the center of Bairiki and were near his office—when the lights went out. All over the island. The second power failure since I arrived. The situation had become redonkulous.

We lingered for more than an hour, but no power came on; I'd have to wait until morning and hope the hotel printer had ink by then.

I spent a nervous and fitful night, sure that something would go wrong, as Murphy's Law was ascendant. I was trapped on an undeveloped island with none of the amenities we take for granted in the States—working printers, fast Internet, reliable electric power, taxis, rapid transit, dependable airline agents.

At 8:30 a.m. I was at Mary's reception desk, which still had no ink car-tridges. I called the agent at Air Pacific and she told me that my in-camera photo of my reservation to Seoul would not cut the mustard. I needed a printed copy of that ticket out of Fiji before Air Pacific would allow me to board their flight to Fiji. I raced to the office-supply store in town and, of course, they were out of the cartridge that fit Mary's printer. Then I ran to the only other outlet in town, where I found the right cartridge, and ran back to Mary's. It was now close to 11:00 a.m. We fired up the printer and it worked! Was Murphy finally giving me a break? I then went on Mary's computer to bring up the e-mailed confirms of my flights to Seoul and Beijing so I could print them. But Yahoo Mail was unreachable. I tried for an hour, but the computer couldn't connect. (I'd noted, when I first arrived at Mary's, that I could most easily— i.e., in less than 30 minutes—get onto Yahoo Mail at 9:00 or 10:00 p.m., but rarely before, because of insufficient capacity.)

I was frantic, and I'm sure my blood pressure was stratospheric. The receptionist told me that the Internet café in town had better connectivity, so I ran over there, but still could not connect with Yahoo Mail. It was now noon, the airport was almost an hour away, and the flight to Fiji closed for boarding at 3:00 p.m. I was close to a nervous breakdown.

As a Hail Mary pass, I phoned the Air Pacific agent, explained my plight, gave her the number of my Air Korea reservation, and asked her if she could track down my confirmation on her computer and print it out. She had never done anything like that before but agreed to try. In the hope—my only hope—that she would succeed, I rushed to get Mary's van to take me to her office and then to the airport. But good old Murphy was still doing double duty and had arranged that the van was being washed and cleaned—surely for the first time since Christmas—to pick up the arriving military personnel that afternoon.

I ran to the van and grabbed a sponge and soaped and hosed like mad to get us on the road. By 1:50 we were in the airline office and received good news: The agent had been able to find and print my Air Korea confirmations from Fiji. All I had to do was pay her for the Air Pacific ticket to Fiji and I could be on my way. I gave her my AmEx card, which required her to contact her head office in Australia for approval, which took a half hour. And we did *not* get approval! Barclays bank, which serviced my AmEx account, declined the charge—despite explicit instructions I had given them before I left New York that I would be using the card in Asia. (I later learned that Barclays had lost those instructions, and since this charge was coming in at 5:00 a.m. EST, when fraudsters try to slip by, the banks assumed someone had stolen my card, and therefore had put a block on it.)

It was now 2:20, leaving no time to send my Visa Card info to Australia for approval.

I offered to pay for the ticket in cash, but they would not take U.S. dollars—nobody does in Kiribati—so I got back in Mary's van—whose driver was beginning to lose patience with me despite the two fashionable New York T-shirts I had generously given him—and we raced to the ANZ bank—where the guard issued me a printed number indicating my position in the queue.

Twelve numbers were ahead of mine, all, it seemed, with lengthy business to transact. And all the tellers but one were out to lunch. (Murphy works in unpredictable ways, but was covering all the bases.) I located the woman who held the next number to be called, bargained with her, gave her five dollars to exchange her number with mine, and shot to the head of the queue.

By the time I got back to the Air Pacific office with the 764 Australian dollars, it was 3:00 p.m. By the time we got the airport it was 3:20 and the departure gate had closed.

*But* the workers recognized me—the bearded American who had almost fainted the day before when he was denied boarding—and were sympathetic. They let me in and vocally cheered me on as they rushed me through the item-by-item big-bag inspection (no X-ray machines in this outpost), the luggage weigh in, the ticket check, the departure tax payment, the immigration exit stamp, and the search of my carry-on bag. I raced aboard the plane three minutes and 30 seconds before it took off for Fiji. And collapsed.

I arrived in Beijing two days later, a sleep-deprived nervous wreck, five days off schedule, $6,000 poorer, 7,000 miles off course, and with no possible way to visit Nauru or East Timor on this trip. But at least I was no longer trapped on Tarawa. Big Al was back in the game.

# CHAPTER 22

## To the Land of the Great Leader

In keeping with their secretive nature, the North Koreans refused to provide any hint whether I'd be granted a visa. They'd required me to travel halfway around the world to Beijing, surrender my passport, and not learn until the day before my tour was scheduled to fly to Pyongyang whether I'd be permitted to go. I was concerned about the ban they'd imposed on writers and journalists, and worried that some of the 250 magazine articles I'd written might come to their attention, although the most politically sensitive and inflammatory had fortunately been written under a pen name.

The circumstances were not auspicious for a visit or a visa. During the week I waited in Beijing, North Korea made daily threats to protest the continuing exercises by the South Korean Navy close to the disputed zone between the countries. The North captured an ROK fishing boat that supposedly entered that zone and the North fired more than a hundred artillery shells near the disputed Northern Limit Line.

My buddy Dennis Doran, his son Andrew, and my friend Svitlana, who were joining me for the visit to North Korea, had flown in to Beijing from the U.S. the day before, bringing the supplies that were too heavy for me to lug around the Pacific. Our foursome walked over to the North Korean Embassy at 2:00 p.m., as instructed. It was straight out of a spy novel, a full-block complex of sinister-looking, small-windowed, sturdy buildings, their roofs bristling with large antennae and communications equipment, mostly hidden behind a high concrete wall topped by broken glass and barbed wire. The main entrance was guarded by a squad of unsmiling, heavily armed soldiers who refused to let us enter. Every other embassy gives applicants their visas in its consular section, but not the North Koreans. No foreigners were allowed inside the walls. The guards directed us to the street corner at the end of the block-long concrete barrier.

At the appointed time, a gaunt man in a threadbare suit emerged from the complex, looked about furtively, collected several hundred dollars cash from each of us, and returned our passports *with visas* and strict instructions to be at the airport early the following morning. We had made the cut! We had achieved what less than a thousand American civilians had in the 57 years since the cessation of open warfare on the Korean peninsula. We were on our way to the Hermit Kingdom, to the Land of the Great Leader.

When I'd arrived in Beijing I'd received an e-mail from the foreign agency through which I'd arranged this tour. It was not your typical cheery predeparture best wishes, but a decree, a strict set of rules and regulations that provided a chilling foretaste of what I'd encounter in the Hermit Kingdom.

I would not be allowed to travel or walk around by myself without a guide. I would not be allowed to bring a laptop, bring a cell phone, carry a camera having more than a 150mm lens, take any photographs without permission of my guides or of any type of military installation. My camera flashcard would be checked, and all unauthorized photos deleted, which, the e-mail made it clear, would earn me the displeasure of my guides. I would not be allowed to refer to the country as North Korea, but only as the DPRK (the Democratic People's Republic of Korea), and, if I had to mention it at all, I could only refer to the occupant of the other part of the peninsula as "the south," never the ROK. I was warned not to talk about history or politics or sensitive issues, because what I had been taught in my society might not conform to what my hosts knew to be the truth, and a respectful guest did not want to upset his hosts, right? . . .

I must never criticize the regime, or the DPRK, or Kim Il Sung, or Kim Jong Il. To the contrary, I would be required to pay my respects to Kim Il

Sung at the Grand Monument and when viewing his body at the Kumsusan Memorial Palace, where I would have to bow to him, and where I would have to wear a collared shirt and a tie.

I was prepared for most of this nonsense, but the requirement of a tie and a collared shirt caught me off guard, and I was unwilling to buy them to honor the dead dictator. I e-mailed Dennis before he left home, and he promised to bring an extra tie for me, although I doubted it would accessorize well with my tropical shirt. My other wardrobe worry arose from the promise I'd made to my pals in the Gotham City Land Cruiser group to wear their club's T-shirt, which features, in large letters, their slogan, GOT ROCKS? which, to the Koreans, looks like ROK, the name by which "the south" calls itself. A ROKy start, you might say. Or you might not.

The old Tupolev jet to Pyongyang had barely taken off before I was in much more serious trouble with the North Korean—oops, I mean the DPRK—authorities. Dear Dennis had, at the Beijing Airport, just before we took off, handed me a totally hideous, blue-and-purple striped tie from the early Eisenhower era that was not a sufficiently somber match with my red-green-and-white flowered Aloha shirt to placate my humorless hosts, even though I was technically compliant with their mausoleum dress code. But, far worse, Dennis had unthinkingly handed me a full-page article from a March issue of *The Wall Street Journal* to read on the plane. It was headlined NORTH KOREAN DICTATORSHIP TO COLLAPSE SOON, and featured a large photo at the top of Kim Il Sung, the DPRK's dearly departed Great Leader. I knew this article was too blatantly inflammatory to bring into the DPRK so, as soon as I sat down in the plane, I tore off the headline and the picture, folded them to conceal their content, and put them on the vacant middle seat next to mine, intending to dispose of them after the seat-belt sign went off.

I never got the chance. The guy at the window seat grabbed the papers in a paroxysm of rage, screaming at me. He was wearing a short-sleeved white shirt, a tie, and a large flag pin of the DPRK, the standard uniform for government functionaries, and the passport on his lap identified him as in the diplomatic service. He jabbed at the crease I'd made through the center of the Great Leader's face and did his best to uncrease it, while scolding at me in Korean as if I were a horrid barbarian imperialist. I then remembered one of the many rules of behavior in the DPRK: You never fold, crease, spindle, or mutilate a photo of the Great Leader. Never.

I apologized profusely, in my best stupid-heathen-idiot routine, tenderly retrieved the offending paper from him, smoothed out the crease as well as I could, and lovingly and respectfully tucked it into the pages of my book, while he nodded approvingly.

Later, 32,000 feet over the South China Sea, when the diplomat had fallen asleep, I made a quick trip to the toilet, where I put the Great Leader's photo to proper use.

I was not prepared for the modernity and wealth of Pyongyang. I'd expected a shabby, run-down town not much different than the capitals of many poor nations, so I was amazed to find instead a clean, modern, prosperous-looking, smoothly functioning, and livable city. It may be the world's largest Potemkin village, but it more than did its job of creating a favorable impression.

I saw thousands of trees bordering the streets, vast tracts of grassland, gardens, even vegetable farms, and was told that the city had more than 40 parks and the most green space per capita of any major city. The dozens of gleaming white 30-story apartment buildings I saw, home to the regime insiders, were unabashedly contemporary—cylindrical, curvilinear, or layered, most with terraces—each separated from its neighbor by a hundred yards of trees and carefully cultivated shrubs.

I was taken to three immense arches; more than ten impressively powerful monuments and commemorative towers, many over a hundred feet high; and saw at least 30 gigantic public buildings of shining marble and polished granite. Each subway station (300 feet down in case the West tries to nuke them) was spacious and attractive, with cheerful art and colored lights, and not a speck of trash anywhere.

And it was just as pristinely clean throughout the countryside that I was allowed to see. When we were driven two hours south of the capital and two hours north of it, all we saw along the new, treelined, eight-lane highway were tidy towns of neatly dressed people and peaceful cooperative farms, lushly green with ripening rice, corn, and beans. I knew that our hosts were not about to show us any poverty or shabbiness, and that their job was to make us disbelieve that this was a dictatorship in which famished citizens ate undigested corn kernels they dug out of cow manure and where more than half a million died of starvation in some years. We were never shown those skeletal people, or DPRK's A-bomb plants, or the factories where they made Rodong medium-range missiles for Iran, Syria, and Pakistan.

Only if we looked closely could we discern some implicit indications of poverty: Our bus drove for 30 minutes during which we did not see another car on the superhighway; half the people walked and the other half rode bikes, often two on a bike; every bit of land not used for buildings or green space in this 80 percent mountainous nation was given over to growing crops, as far up the hills as they could push it; everybody was quite thin; there were few streetlights, and other outdoor lights were kept low, except those illuminating the propaganda palaces; interior lights were frugally controlled by motion sensors, daylight sensors, and insert cards; in the hotel bowling alley, if I didn't roll my ball within a few seconds, the lights illuminating the pins went out; restaurants used miniature napkins and stainless steel chopsticks to conserve trees; and our guides wore the same clothes four or five days in a row without washing. Ironically, the harsh heel of their dictatorship has generated one of the smallest carbon footprints of any nation.

In six days I saw not a single dog or cat, because the people could not afford to feed them, or had eaten them long ago. In five hundred kilometers of travel through this meat-deprived land, I saw not one goat, sheep, or cow. In one residential park, I saw a man catch a squirrel, stomp it, cut off its tail, and proudly put it, still alive and quivering in its death throes, into his bag to eat for dinner, as he made clear from his joyful gesticulations. It was difficult to reconcile the gleaming apartment buildings with residents stomping squirrels for dinner, but such is the paradox of the DPRK.

The tour was heavy on anti-American propaganda and nationalism bordering on xenophobia. We were taken to, and proudly told in fervid detail about, the humble home where Kim Il Sung was born, and then shown his awesome, four-story mausoleum, fronted by a plaza of one million square feet, surrounded by a moat, and reached though a marble hallway 450 yards long that I was allowed to enter only after my shoes had been dusted, disinfected, and blown clean. We were driven to the Workers' Party monument, and the Martyrs' Cemetery, and the 150-room International Friendship Exhibition, a repository carved into Mount Myohyang for the 90,000 gifts the Great Leader had received from other nations (mostly expensive and ornate, with only one from the U.S., a Wilson basketball signed by Michael Jordan and presented by Secretary of State Madeleine Albright). We were taken on a long drive to the DMZ (the four-kilometer-wide and 240 km-long demilitarized zone between North and South Korea), to Panmunjom (where the armistice ending the fighting of the Korean War was negotiated and signed in 1953), and to the Concrete Fence (a wall 250 km long, built by the South from sea to sea across the peninsula, "to keep our nation forever divided," we were told, and behind which the puppets of the South were planning a new invasion since their earlier one had failed). The next day to the museums—the three Museums of the Revolution, and the War Museum (filled with U.S. planes, tanks, and guns captured in the Korean War during America's "cowardly retreat"), and the Art Museum (featuring portraits of the Great Leader performing various heroic functions). Finally to the Juche Tower (commemorating the Great Leader's Socialist/Confucian philosophy of government); the captured US "pirate-spy" ship *USS Pueblo*; and, everywhere—and I do mean everywhere—portraits, murals, paintings, posters, billboards, and signs exhorting the populace to struggle and strive, and depicting the Great Leader encouraging farmers to grow more grain, workers to produce more machines, miners to dig more coal and iron, soldiers to be prepared to fight their imperialist foe, and children to zealously guard and defend the future of the nation.

Even the meals were part of the propaganda effort. Either because the North Koreans believe that all imperialists have ravenous appetites, or because they wanted to demonstrate that the claims of food shortages and starvation in their country were false, they sought to stuff us, at every meal, with three to four times more food than any human could possibly ingest at one sitting. Each meal, including breakfast, featured soup, at least five kinds of vegetables, a fish dish, a beef dish, a chicken dish, a pork or duck dish, plus a variety of other treats, from spicy squid to bean curd casserole, glassy noodles to scrambled eggs, frankfurters to potato pancakes, and on and on. This imperialist gained ten pounds in six days.

Even the amazing Arirang Festival (aka the Mass Games) had a propaganda function, but it was, nevertheless, the greatest show on earth. It featured 100,000 students, soldiers, dancers, singers, acrobats, gymnasts, martial artists, and cutely costumed children, all performing together in absolute split-second unison. Twenty thousand students seated on the far side of the stadium, having practiced for three months, used colored flash cards as they are used nowhere else with such precision. In two seconds, a wave rolled perfectly from one end of the stadium to the other while, down on the stadium floor, thousands of brilliantly costumed dancers and gymnasts flawlessly moved as if one, and then instantly disappeared into the darkness. The true purpose of the Games, aside from impressing the crowds and bringing in lots of foreign currency, is to teach the North Korean people the power of the collective, to demonstrate how the discipline and surrender to the collective required by the Great Leader's form of Communism can produce extraordinary results. It's a performance where one small misstep or mistiming by even one performer could spoil the entire effect. Such mistakes are not tolerated in the land of the Great Leader—and there were no mistakes.

A disturbing aspect of the trip was that Dennis and I and the other American tourists were treated as carriers of an infectious disease—a disease called information—and skillfully prevented from having *any* contact with ordinary citizens, lest we contaminate them with our Western ideas and knowledge of the outside world.

North Korea is the most closed society on the planet, ranked 196 out of 196 by the annual *Freedom of the Press* survey. All access to information from or about the lands beyond its borders is rigidly controlled by the government—no Twitter, Facebook, or YouTube, only Bright Star, which links to official documents and censored news. Of its 25 million citizens, only a few thousand, all members of the hardcore elite, are allowed access to the Internet. TV sets only receive the government stations, which feature slanted news and patriotic propaganda. Personal radios are illegal, and the government jams international broadcasts just in case. Incoming travelers are searched for subversive literature and CDs, and their cell phones are confiscated for the duration of their visits. Private ownership of fax machines is prohibited. Copiers and printers are closely guarded to prevent the dissemination of unauthorized information. Six months before we arrived, a factory

I was taken to see an orphanage in North Korea, where the children had been taught to perform a song to charm visitors and prospective adoptive parents. But few people outside the party elite can afford to adopt an orphan in a land where hundreds of thousands starve.

worker was publicly executed by a firing squad because he'd spoken by phone to someone in South Korea about the price of rice.

The regime tightly controls information because they don't want their citizens to understand the benefits of democracy: to become aware how badly off they are and how poorly they live compared to much of the rest of humanity, to realize that their cousins in "the south" were not really rummaging through garbage dumps and eating rats for dinner, as they had been taught, and that the world regarded their revered leader as an unpredictable cross between a spoiled child and a dangerous nut case.

How did they prevent us from saying even a single word to an ordinary North Korean in a week? By constant isolation, assiduous observation, and attentive minding.

From the moment we went down to breakfast in the morning until we finished dinner, we were rarely out of sight of our two guides and their two blue-uniformed assistants. We were accompanied, closely, everywhere we went, even to public toilets. At the Arirang Festival, our group of 20 tourists were seated together, in a section set aside exclusively for foreigners. If any of us had to use the restroom, one of the minders went with us. As we were exiting the giant stadium, I lingered back, attempting to mingle with the crowd, hoping to chat with a local for a minute, but one of our minders was soon at my side, politely, but firmly, pointing out that "Our bus is that way."

When I was doing laps in the hotel pool one night, a group of four regime stalwarts and their families were granted special access. I tried my best to be friendly and chat with them, but they acted as if I wasn't there.

When my friend Svitlana needed to get some socks, the guides offered to purchase them for her. When she told them she preferred picking her own clothes, they put us in the tour bus, drove us to a special department store where only regime loyalists were allowed to shop, accompanied her to the hosiery counter, and supervised her purchase. She was not able to exchange a word with the salesgirl. And when she went to the pricey hotel spa for a massage, she was assigned a masseuse who spoke not a word of English.

Our Yanggakdo International Hotel—which accommodated only foreign tourists and diplomats—was built on a small, unpopulated island in the Taedong River, completely cut off from the city. It was brightly lit and carefully designed and groomed to prevent concealment, with a narrow access bridge that was policed and checkpointed 24/7. And every door leading out of the Yanggakdo was guarded.

On my fourth night I found a way out: On leaving the basement pool, I purposely took a wrong turn, innocently wandered down several deserted underground corridors, and came upon a small unlocked exit door way in the back of the hotel. I cautiously pushed it ajar and found it opened on a small, vacant parking lot. I stepped out. No one was there. I was free! I sauntered away from the hotel in the direction of the fog-shrouded bridge. I'd gone about 40 feet when a police officer materialized beside me and suggested that it might be dangerous to wander about so late at night. Much safer I should return to my room. *Now!*

The sole instance in which the ban on communication was lifted was when we were taken to a restaurant and allowed to personally inform the waitress whether we wanted "tea" or "beer." (Things do not go better with Coke in the Land of the Great Leader.)

As pervasive as the surveillance was the cult of personality, the near-deification of Kim Il Sung and his progeny, the only hereditary rulers to govern a Communist country. I don't profess to understand this adoration, because I was barred from asking the locals about it, but I got the impression that the majority of North Koreans actually did revere their Great Leader. Everywhere we went—to his birthplace, to his monuments, to the building displaying the presents he'd received, to his mausoleum—hundreds of DPRK citizens, wearing either their best clothes or their newest uniforms, were paying him homage, usually in groups of ten to 50 brought from their school or factory, all silent, solemn, a few even crying, all exuding sincerity, although I could not be sure.

The DPRK does not deny that Kim Il Sung died, but neither does it quite treat him as dead, more like immortal. It's not just his memory that lingers on: It is his essence. His birthday is the state's highest holiday; his words its Bible. He remains their "eternal president." His son, Kim Jong Il, was their General, but the post of president is eternally occupied by his father.

How I wish I could have gotten into their minds! As an outsider, I could not tell if they were befuddled or brainwashed, pretenders or true believers in the regime's rash promise that, in 2012, the 100th birthday of the Great Leader, their wretched, resource-poor land would at last become a "great and prosperous nation." The one thing I could clearly ascertain was that the thousands of stony-faced, somberly attired locals emerging from their visit to his sacred tomb to the martial strains of "The Song of General Kim Il Sung," who passed ten feet from me on a parallel people-mover inside the immense mausoleum, did not think that the tie Dennis had lent me worked well with my Hawaiian shirt.

It was equally easy to discern that Americans were not generally held in high regard inside the Hermit Kingdom, which perhaps explains why, aside from our paid-to-grin guides and greeters, we saw not one smile or friendly face all week. The attitude of the regime toward America was well summarized in a pamphlet they sold us, which begins by referring to 9/11 as "an attack on the nerve-center of the Evil Empire." The broad thesis of the pamphlet was that "In its very origins the U.S. was a state founded and expanded by means of terrorism, which has always gone hand-in-hand with the

U.S. policy. The U.S. emerged as a nation above the sea of blood of indigenous Indians and expanded ten-fold in westward wars of conquest . . ."

Our use of "terrorism" culminated in the way we allegedly mistreated the
North Koreans:

> shooting, suffocating by poisonous gas, hog-tying before drowning,
> burying alive, burning to death, throwing down into mine pits,
> tearing the body limb-from-limb using oxcarts, sawing off faces,
> hammering nails into the forehead, gouging out eyes, cutting off
> ears and noses, hacking off women's breasts, disemboweling preg-
> nant women, trampling fetuses, and driving pointed sticks into
> vital parts.

(I've been meaning to scrutinize the Pentagon budget to find out how
many of my taxpayer dollars they spent on those limb-sundering oxcarts.)

This visit was a fascinating peek at a totally bizarre and topsy-turvy
world, unlike any other on the planet, but it was a great relief to get out and
breathe free.

About a year after I left, Kim Jong Il died, and his regime passed into the
hands of his third son, Kim Jong Un. Hope that this Swiss-educated young
man might liberalize the dictatorship was quickly dashed by an announcement from the DRPK news agency that "To expect 'reform and opening' is
nothing but a foolish and silly dream, just like wanting the sun to rise in the
west."

# CHAPTER 23

## In the Steppes of Genghis Khan

When was the last time you gave some serious thought to Mongolia?

Don't feel ashamed; you are hardly alone. Modern Mongolia has no impact on our daily lives. Yet, for more than 200 years, Mongolia ruled most of the known world and established dozens of the institutions that have become essential parts of contemporary civilization.

Some of us remember, from a brief mention in some ancient-history lecture, that Genghis Khan—his name means "World Emperor"—and his sons, and their Golden Horde of hardy, ruthless warriors, swept out of the wilds of Mongolia on their sturdy ponies, and between the years 1150 and 1300 overwhelmed and conquered the lands we know today as China, northern India, Pakistan, Persia, Afghanistan, Kazakhstan, Uzbekistan, Iraq, Syria, Ukraine, the rest of Eastern Europe, and most of Russia, reached the gates of Vienna, Cairo, and Constantinople, and created the largest empire in history. Had the Mongol general, Prince Batu, not been called back home for consultations in 1242, he would have reached the Atlantic with his army, and we might today all be speaking Mongolian and eating horsemeat.

What we were not taught is that the Mongols, aside from rewriting the rules of warfare, also ushered in the modern age and some of its principal principles and practices. Genghis Khan consolidated many smaller states into large countries to create Russia, China, and India. He overthrew a feudal system built on aristocratic birth and privilege and replaced it with one based on individual merit and achievement. Although his warriors slaughtered the soldiers and leaders of the lands he conquered, he did not treat the vanquished inhabitants as slaves, but accepted them as valued citizens of his realm—as long as they paid their taxes. He vastly increased trade between nations, reduced tariffs, and established a rule of law applicable to all, even to the rulers. At a time when almost every nation adhered to just one religion, he enshrined religious freedom and tolerance (although his descendants converted to Islam and spread the Muslim faith). He abolished torture in his realm, invented diplomatic immunity, sought a universal alphabet, instituted the first inter-nation postal service, and eliminated bandits throughout his territories so that travel and trade could flourish.

This sparsely populated nation, a mere one million people then, with only 100,000 warriors, did far more than any other to shape the modern world. To unite their holdings, they built more bridges than any conqueror in history, and then passed, from one end of their empire of 12 million square miles to the other, from the heart of Europe to the shores of the Pacific and back, the knowledge of architecture, agriculture, metal casting, pottery, poetry, and literature that they had accumulated from all the lands they had conquered. They created and instituted paper currency, an accurate calendar, multinational maps, and free primary school education for every child.

Their empire fell apart after two centuries because of squabbling among the various grandsons and great-grandsons of Genghis. His heirs had intermarried with the Yuan Dynasty when they moved their capital to Beijing to more centrally control their empire. In 1368 the Yuan and the Ming Dynasty took over and pushed the Mongols back north. All they had left in the end was a relatively small land and a reputation for brutality and destruction. Their very name gave root to the pejoratives "mongrel" and "Mongoloid."

Mongolia was closed to travelers until recent times. In 1924 it became the second nation to install a Communist government and was thereafter, until Gorbachev and *glasnost,* tightly controlled by Russia. The Communists, who believed that religion was the opiate of the masses, campaigned to eliminate Mongolian Buddhist Lamaism (which had largely supplanted Shamanism when it arrived from Tibet in the 1600s). To achieve this goal, from 1937 onward the Soviets burned or blew up 767 temples and monasteries, murdered 30,000 monks and thousands of political dissidents and intellectuals, sent thousands more to Siberia, and took steps to eradicate Mongolian customs, culture, and national identity. It was only after the dissolution of the USSR that Mongolia began the long and painful process of rebuilding its culture and finally fully opened itself to tourists.

I was curious to see what these people were like 700 years after ruling the world and then being swept into the dustbin of history. Because theirs had always been a nomadic culture—save for a brief period, during the height of their powers, when they settled down and ruled first from an ornate city they built called Karakorum, and then from Beijing—a nomadic journey across the steppes seemed like the way to go. I had planned to do this with Steve, but he was gravely ill, so Dennis and Andrew Doran joined me.

Mongolia does not allow foreigners to rent cars; you have to hire one with a driver. The vehicle we ended up with was a 13-year-old Toyota Land Cruiser 80 that had been ridden hard and put away wet, sporting shocks that were shot, springs that barely functioned, seats whose padding had been compressed to the consistency of concrete by a decade of bouncing butts, windows that would not roll down, and a steering wheel on the wrong side of the car. The driver we ended up with was a stubborn jerk who lacked the most rudimentary knowledge of how to use a gearshift or a compass, had no sense of direction, and was generally a total asshole. Other than that both car and driver were fine.

The Mongolian transport infrastructure had not changed much since the days of Genghis Khan. There were only 600 miles of paved roads in a land twice the size of Texas, forcing us to bump, buck, and bang the Land Cruiser across rivers, streams, mudholes, and the timeless tan dirt trails traversing the vast seas of grass toward the low hills on the horizon that enclose the hundreds of picturesque valleys in the center of the country.

Here and there we'd see a few *gers,* round tents that Westerners incorrectly call "yurts," because that is what the Russians, who were trying to abolish

Mongolia, with its boundless steppes, high mountains, inhospitable desert, poor infrastructure, and small population, is (along with Dominica) the most unspoiled nation on earth. A typical nomad family lives in a portable *ger* heated by dried animal dung as they seasonally move their herds to greener pastures. But a huge new copper mine and the first paved road across the nation may soon change that way of life.

Mongol culture, called them, based on the Russian word *yurta*, which means hut. Not far from the *gers*, we'd see herds of livestock: 10 to 50 horses, or 50 to 300 cows and yaks, or 200 to 2000 sheep and goats, rarely comingled beyond that. Some changes had occurred over the centuries: Most *gers* now had a wood-burning iron stove in its center, one of every ten sported a satellite dish, and a good number had a 4×4 parked out back. And a few herders now ride motorcycles instead of horses to keep their herds on the move.

The population had risen, but only to 2.9 million, a third of whom lived in the capital of Ulan Bator (UB). A quarter were still nomadic shepherds, moving to greener pastures at least four times a year; another quarter were seminomadic, roving during the warmer months, settling into their base *ger* for the punishing winters. But their days as a peripatetic people may be numbered because of impending disruptions, both meteorological and mineralogical.

Climate change may cause such deadly winters and parched summers that itinerant animal husbandry will no longer be viable, while the recent development of the earth's largest copper mine in the south Gobi Desert, which will eventually account for 30 percent of Mongolia's GDP, will entice nomads to settle in mining and smelting jobs providing secure wages.

Of all 196 countries, Mongolia appeared to me the least spoiled (with the possible exception of Dominica), 80 percent untouched by man, like taking a time machine across centuries. The endless clear blue sky and lush wide valleys were similar to the Montana of 1840. I felt as if I were riding through an old Western, and expected to see the Lone Ranger galloping across the unbroken plains shouting a hearty "Hi-yo, Silver, away." With fewer than three million people in a land as large as Britain, France, and Germany *combined*—giving it the lowest population density of any country—and with 34 million head of livestock, it's a sublime pastoral experience, unlike any elsewhere. (Other parts of the country, while also mostly unspoiled, are topographically different, with the giant Gobi Desert in the southeast, forests and taiga in the north, and large, rocky mountain ranges in the far west, including at least 20 eternally snow-capped peaks.)

Because the Mongolians have been dependent on nature for their personal survival and the nation's advancement, they seek to live in harmony with the land and not defile the environment. When they moved a camp, I saw them even fill in the holes they'd dug for tent poles. They showed a reverence for nature that derived from shamanism, a spiritual practice whose believers seek to reach altered states of consciousness to interact with the spirit world and channel its transcendental energies to this world. Some of this will change as they shift into the modern era, burning wood in their stoves instead of dried cow patties, soon completing an east-to-west artery across the nation that will triple its miles of paved roads, ramping up the gargantuan Oyu Tolgoi copper mine, and increasingly moving from the wide open spaces to UB in search of the good life. But, for the time being, earth has no unsullied place like it.

Many Mongolians earn their livelihood from domesticated animals: 20 percent of its export income derives from them, and they produce 21 percent of the world's cashmere. But a drought the winter before I visited had turned seven million livestock into deadstock whose bleached bones littered the terrain.

The national diet has changed little over the centuries, with a dominant emphasis on meat and dairy. The Big Five here are cattle, sheep, goats, horses, and (less frequently) camels or reindeer, and the locals refer to themselves as "The People of the Five Snouts," all of which they boil, steam, roast, fry, grill, heat under pressure, or cook from the inside by filling the animal's stomach cavity with large hot rocks. They use this high-fat, high-protein regimen to stave off the cold in a climate where winter temperatures reach minus 40 degrees. The Mongolian vocabulary has no words for either "cholesterol" or "arteriosclerosis," and their fatty cuisine is so bland and boring on the Western palate—nomads have no time to grow herbs or spices—it makes Wales seem like a culinary center.

Vegetables are scarce for three reasons: The growing season is too short for most produce; nomads do not remain in one place long enough to till, plant, and harvest crops; and they do not like or respect vegetables because they view all green edibles as fodder fit only for animals. No fruits, either. In our 1,200-kilometer circuit, I saw only one vegetable garden, one field of wheat, and not a single fruit tree. It's no country for old vegetarians.

Since I like to eat strange stuff, I enjoyed a superb horse steak on my first night (although the locals tend to overcook their meat); tried the staple of fermented mare's milk at a monastery (yuk!); loved a bowl of fresh goat yogurt topped with tart wild currants served by a comely milkmaid at a parking lot beside a volcano; ate my first roach (no, it's just an indigenous freshwater fish); drank a pot of milk tea seasoned with salt and butter (an indiscretion not to be repeated); and savored a platter of fresh yak butter, cheese, and yogurt with a dairy family, although that was imprudent since none of it was pasteurized, and brucellosis (aka undulant fever) is common there.

For those who like less exotic fare, or some vegetables, UB has a host of "ethnic" restaurants, including Kenny Rogers Roasters, El Latina, the Detroit American Bar (what were they thinking?), Los Banditos, Planet Pizza, the Brau Haus, five eateries that begin with the name "Broadway," and The Original Irish Pub (which, to Dennis's consternation, didn't serve Guinness).

Those tourists wanting to dip a finger into the local food can dine at the fashionable "First Mongolian Restaurant Established 1602," but, alas, that's a fake, since it serves "Mongolian hot pot" and "Mongolian barbecue," neither of which is indigenous, having arrived in UB from Inner Mongolia, an autonomous region of China. Outside UB it's pretty much potluck.

My main gastronomic complaint was that Mongolians, who traditionally eat for survival rather than pleasure, have no familiarity with the concept of dessert, my rectification of which necessitated several nocturnal treks to a new UB supermarket for boxes of Choco Pies.

Although I survived the food, I almost didn't survive the UB traffic, which was the least pedestrian-friendly I'd ever encountered (until I got to Hanoi)—far worse than Paris, Tehran, or even Albania. The drivers ignore the yield signs, stop signs, pedestrian walkways, the rare red lights, and, when they can, the few traffic cops. They're more aggressive than a New York cabbie, zooming around corners at high speed from hiding places on tree-shrouded boulevards. I thought I was becoming paranoid because I believed that the cars heading my way speeded up whenever I tried to cross a street. But *Lonely Planet* confirmed it: The drivers are not actually aiming to hit you, but they are speeding up to warn you that they rule the road, you have no rights of way, and that you'd better be very careful, or very quick.

A word about the climate: Mongolia is blessed with 260 sunny days a year, and though I visited in its wet season, six of our eight days passed without a cloud. The sky was an intensely rich shade of blue, attributable to the country's average elevation of 5,000 feet. Mongolians call theirs "the land of the blue sky" and worship it in a shamanistic way, the most visible evidence of which are the thousands of deep blue *haday* (scarves) they insert in the hundreds of *ovoos* (stone cairns) or tie to the wood teepee constructions that dot the terrain.

Because Mongolia is far from any ocean that could exert a moderating effect on its temperature, and because the cloudless skies let the land cool quickly at night, it's common for the mercury to plunge more than 50 degrees from noon to midnight, with the consequence that on three August nights we needed to light the stoves in our *gers*.

I was able to visit four sublime monasteries: a large one in UB that had avoided destruction by converting to a museum, an expansive one that has been rebuilt in Karakorum using the stones from the ruins of the ancient capital's former palaces, and two that were hidden so high in the hills and so far off the beaten tracks they were overlooked by the Communists. Since Buddhism came to Mongolia from Tibet, the temples in the monasteries have a Tibetan look, from the bunting to the prayer wheels to the embroidered hangings to the brightly painted Buddhas. Mongolia once had 100,000 monks, and one monastery for every 2,000 inhabitants—to the credit of a wise Chinese diplomat who centuries ago concluded that, because his country had been ravaged so many times by Mongol armies, it would be wise for China to build temples there to turn the young men into peaceful monks rather than ferocious warriors.

When I'd reached Mongolia, I still lacked the visa I needed to return to China to reclaim my luggage and catch my flight to Bangkok. I was down to Plan D, after failing with:

Plan A. Before leaving New York, obtain the triple-entry visa I needed to land in Beijing on my flights from, respectively, the Pacific, North Korea, and Mongolia. But the Chinese consulate only gave me a double-entry visa;

Plan B. Secure the third visa in Beijing. After spending a full day to find the visa office and fill out the application, they informed me that, to process it, they needed ten working days, which I did not have, and required a Beijing bank account with $3,000 in it, which I also did not have.

Plan C. Acquire the visa at the Chinese Embassy in Pyongyang. Fuggedaboutit!

And so I tried Plan D. Get the visa from the Chinese Embassy in UB, which my Mongolian guide had, months before, assured me would work. But she'd forgotten that August was when hundreds of Mongolian students who attend college in China applied to renew their visas. Since the Chinese Embassy only granted 40 a day, this was problematic. We hired the guide's sister to save me a place outside the Chinese Embassy by getting there at 4:00 a.m. She somehow lost her place, and when I arrived at 8:00 a.m., 70 kids were ahead of her, none willing to defer to a tourist.

On to Plan E. I'd forgo the return to China and fly directly to Bangkok, while Dennis and Andrew, who'd been issued multiple-entry visas in New York before the policy changed, retrieved my big bag in Beijing and brought it when they met me in Bangkok. I purchased a ticket for a flight out of UB on Monday with MIAT, a notoriously unreliable airline whose initials, veteran travelers claim, stand for, "Maybe I'll Arrive Thursday."

I'd successfully gotten past check-in, weigh-in, immigration, and security at the Genghis Khan International Airport, and was urgently searching for a bathroom and beginning to believe that Murphy had finally cut me some slack, when an airport policewoman tapped me on the shoulder, shoved a copy of my boarding pass under my nose, and pointed downstairs.

I asked her, in my best Monglish, if she knew where the toilet was.

She barked, "Poowdle—Custum!"

I explained that when you gotta go, ya gotta go.

She countered that when Customs calls, *that* is where ya gotta go. So we went.

In the dreary basement baggage room, three customs officers were gathered around my duffel bag, which they gestured for me to open. They pointed to a white object nestled in worn T-shirts. It was the complete skull of a young horse that I'd found on the prairie, a casualty of the drought the previous winter.

I gesticulated that this was much ado about nothing, that I had not killed it, nor stolen it, and that I had washed it, and even toothbrushed it, so that it was sterile. But that didn't satisfy them. The troika held a loud, argumentative conference about whether my possession or exportation of the skull was illegal, immoral, inadvisable, or just stupid, as the clock ticked toward takeoff time and the call of nature remained unanswered.

I finally noodled it out: These guys believed I was trying to abscond with part of their national heritage, one of the precious dinosaur fossils strewn about the Gobi Desert, like those I'd seen in their national museum.

Given the language barrier, and my inability to draw, I tried a charade. I reached into my duffel bag for a blanket, folded it, got down on my hands and knees, put the blanket on my back as if it were a saddle, and then galloped around the room, hoping I emulated a horse, not a velociraptor, while doing my best to whinny and to suppress the urge to surge for the bathroom.

The customs guys either understood my message or decided that I was a dangerous wacko who should be deported as quickly as possible. They released me and put my bag on the conveyor belt for the Bangkok flight as I ran for the MEN's.

# CHAPTER 24

## On the Wings of the Dragon

Our visit to Bangkok began with a bang.

Andrew exited the air terminal in high dudgeon because customs agents had confiscated the three Russian military-surplus bayonets he'd purchased at a hilltop flea market in central Mongolia. To help him forget his loss, he asked that I take him for a Thai massage, one of life's most sybaritic experiences.

I drove him to one of the many large clubs in the lively red-light district of Patpong, where 60 lovely ladies, ages 18 to 28, were seated on a three-tiered stage, all provocatively dressed, each with a big numbered button on her dress for identification.

The main change over the years was that the women are no longer viewed through a one-way mirror that had enabled the patrons to inspect them without being seen. Now it's all open, and when the women see a client appraising them, they each attempt to establish eye contact and win his favor (and their rent money) with all manner of smiles, winks, nods, air-kisses, shakes, shimmies, cleavage drops, leg crossings, leg un-crossings, deep-inhalation chest enlargements, and pantomimed sex. All demurely done, of course.

Once you select the lady and pay the fee ($150 for two hours), she takes you upstairs to your own spotlessly clean, dimly lit, soundproofed suite that is half Turkish bath and half bedroom, where she gently undresses you, while gigglingly pretending to be impressed with the size of your equipment. She then joins and bathes you in a large deep tub before leading you to a comfortable, cushiony, heated plastic air mattress, where she turns you ass up and soaps you all over with buckets of warmed suds. She next climbs aboard your back and massages you with her powerful thighs, from toes to head, performing feats of contortionism with intense erotic energy. Then she turns you right side up, for an even more sensual massage. If your gun is still loaded after all this—most guys will have shot their full clip and any spare ammo belts by now—she takes you to the big, firm, freshly sheeted, perfume-scented bed and presses your trigger.

Most guys stagger out in 30 to 50 minutes. But not our Andrew. Since he had never been in a place like this, and had never before paid for sexual servicing, he did not know the worldwide unwritten rule of gentlemanly bordello behavior: You quit after you come. Orgasm and out. You scored; game over.

Andrew naïvely assumed that, since he had been quoted a price for two hours, he was entitled to continue to conjugate and copulate for the full 120 minutes, and so he did, with the result that I was kept waiting far longer than I ever anticipated until the loving couple came downstairs, and the lady had high hopes of packing her bags and moving to join our boy in Jersey City.

The future of these emporiums, which have long thrived in parts of Southeast Asia, is problematic. As the region prospered, affluent local patrons gravitated toward long-term relationships with concubines and mistresses. Meanwhile, sexual tourism has come under fire. And reformers contend that these pleasure palaces encourage sexual servitude and the exploitation of women, and demean them as little more than sex objects. The defenders of the system argue that these establishments offer the girls, who typically come from poor rural areas where they faced hard and hopeless lives of grinding poverty, the rare opportunity to earn good money in a safe environment and climb into the middle class, sometimes even marrying their clients. The proponents further maintain that a woman should be free to do what she wants with her body, including selling it or renting it out for the evening, as long as no compulsion or abuse is involved. I was torn twixt the yin and yang of the debate. I was a devout, equal-opportunity-believing, ERA-supporting, card-carrying liberal mysteriously trapped in the body and mind-set of a horndog.

On none of my previous trips to Thailand had I visited the infamous Bridge on the River Kwai that WW II Japanese prison commanders had forced Allied POWs to build as part of the Death Railway. To rectify this omission, Dennis, Andrew, and I took off at dawn from Bangkok in a rented car for the long drive west to Kanchanaburi.

I should have stayed with my memory of the movie, because the reality was disappointing.

In my recollection, the gorge was so wide and deep it required a towering timber trestle. But the film, I later learned, had been shot at Kitulgala in Sri Lanka. Kanchanaburi had no yawning gorge, and the unimpressive bridge was no more than 30 feet above the muddy, sluggish water, and was further robbed of any grandeur by a bright, blue-and-yellow, toy-like tourist train that crossed it every 15 minutes. Moreover, the original wooden bridge built by the captured servicemen had been destroyed by Allied bombs. What the tourist brochures were calling the "Bridge on the River Kwai" was a steel span the Japanese had captured in Java and shipped to Kanchanaburi, believing it more likely to survive bombing.

Notwithstanding this substitution, the adjacent area should have been treated as hallowed ground, sanctified by the 60,000 British and Dutch POWs and other slave laborers who died building the railroad that provided the Japanese with a vital supply line for their troops in Burma, who were trying to fight their way to India and bisect the British Empire. Instead, the bridge environs had become a blighted honky-tonk mishmash of shops selling junk jewelry, smuggled rubies, fake rubies, handbags, T-shirts, junk food, and tacky souvenirs. It might be tolerable if the tourist traps were set apart from the bridge and the exhibitions about it, yet they were contiguous and inextricably entwined. There's the combined "Art Gallery and War Museum," the conflated "Death Railroad Museum and Miss Thailand Directory," and, high above them all, the "Best View of Bridge and Toilet." It's a travesty. Watch the movie, but don't waste time visiting the scene of the crime.

The Bridge on the River Kwai in today's Thailand is not the tall wooden trestle built in 1942 with the blood of thousands of Allied POWs, but a steel span the Japanese captured elsewhere and installed at Kanchanaburi in 1944. The Death Railway has been replaced by a diminutive, brightly painted tourist train.

The fallen have fared a bit better. The Commonwealth War Graves Commission created and maintains a peaceful cemetery away from the tourist area, "in honoured remembrance of the fortitude and sacrifice of that valiant company who perished while building the railway from Thailand to Burma during their long captivity."

The headstones are small, white, and uniform, rising only an inch above the verdant carpet of grass, aligned in precise rows too long for me to see their end, with solitary trees providing some shade and emphasis, all surrounded by a mile-long, neatly manicured hedge and bordered by flowering plants, all immaculately maintained by a dozen groundskeepers. The plaque near the gate read: "I will make you a name and a praise among all people of the earth when I turn back your captivity before your eyes, saith the Lord."

The inscriptions on the headstones were sentimental, loving, and sorrowfully proud, like those I'd seen 40 years before at Sollum, relics of an era when those qualities informed and guided the Greatest Generation:

*For King and Country.*
*To live in the hearts of those we love is not to die.*
*He lay down his life that others might live free.*
*They gave their lives and all that living means, my sons.*

Heading to Brunei, we ran into massive monsoon thunderclouds and turbulence in the path of our A319 to the south, Sinabung volcano spewing ashes from Indonesia on our west, and a killer typhoon to our east that became the strongest to hit Korea in 15 years. We arrived in Brunei, shaken but safe, for several days of planned boredom and decompression in Asia's strictest Muslim country during the final week of Ramadan.

*The Brunei Times,* which I read in flight, carried an "Invitation for Expression of Interest" from the Ministry of Religious Affairs, for a position for which I was ideally qualified—"Consultancy on the research and handling of low morale activities in Brunei Darussalam." The scope of work included: "1. Definition of Morale. 2. Database of Low Morale Activities. 3. National Plan for Low Morale Activities Reduction."

Some might scoff, but this task offered a worthy challenge in a country where the heat and humidity are oppressive 24/7/365, alcohol is prohibited, pornography is forbidden, gambling is outlawed, amorous couples face fines and jail for hugging and kissing in public, and adulterous lovers can get hard prison time. You can't even hope to play footsie with your friends' wives because, at most large dinners, the men eat at one table while the women and children eat at another. No wonder morale was low!

The main forms of entertainment and excitement in boring Brunei were wandering through the scrubby jungle that covers 75 percent of the small country, chilling to the AC at the extravagant indoor malls, visiting the free amusement park on the north coast, or paying tribute at the grandiose Regalia Museum, which immortalizes the outfits, swords, and medals worn by His Majesty Paduka Seri Baginda Sultan Haji Hasanai Bolkiah Mv'izzaddin Waddaulah, Sultan and Yang Di-Pertuan Negara Brunei Darussalam since he became the 29th sultan in 1968. At some 600 years and counting, his is one of the world's oldest surviving monarchies, and the only absolute monarchy in

Asia, so absolute it tolerates no democracy, no opposition, and almost no political activity.

Although some superficial similarity can be perceived between Brunei and the oil-rich Gulf States in terms of size, wealth, population, religion, form of governance, reliance on guest workers, and high expenditures on opulent buildings, Brunei pales in comparison. It lacks the drive, the business virtuosity, the brilliant entrepreneurship, the world-class architecture, the cosmopolitan attitude, and the throbbing vitality of Dubai and Abu Dhabi.

What you get instead is a tranquil, law-abiding Familyland boasting one of the world's highest GDPs per person, thanks to its vast oil resources. It's a land where your health care is first-rate and free, your cities are spotless, your housing and other needs are subsidized, you pay no income tax, and you receive a guaranteed pension. The cooking, cleaning, and dirty jobs are done by Indian and Filipino guest workers, and your education—which stresses Malay culture, Islam, and monarchy—is free as far as you can go. Monarchical though it was, we saw no dissidents, heard no hotheaded revolutionaries, encountered no Arab Spring–type upheavals.

Yet even the Sultan was bored with the easy life in Brunei and allegedly indulged in a harem of 40 ever-changing gorgeous women from various nations, each paid about $10,000 a week, all of whom, to shield the Sultan from criticism, were imported by his younger brother, the playboy Prince Jefri. Several women who claimed to have been lured into the harem had sued the Sultan for making them sex slaves, but the courts had granted him sovereign immunity.

Prince Jefri owned 80 flashy autos and a luxurious yacht called *Tits*, that was accompanied by two yacht tenders, named *Nipple 1* and *Nipple 2*. If I'd taken the morale job, I would have consulted Jefri on how to liven things up. And add some class.

Dennis and Andrew headed home. It had been refreshing to have male company for once on these trips, and particularly men like Dennis, with his irrepressible Irish good humor, sanguine outlook, and impressive repertoire of droll stories, and fearless Andrew, ready for any adventure, except strange food. On the other hand, it had been a chore to constantly look for bars where

Dennis could get Schweppes Tonic Water and Bombay Gin—impossible in bone-dry Brunei—while searching for McDonald's and Pizza Huts to satisfy Andrew, and resisting his repeated requests to return to the club in Patpong, where the young superstud was likely now as welcome as a card counter in Vegas. I flew back to my hub in Thailand for a busy night of resupply and repacking before I sallied forth on the road to Mandalay.

*Tip to the CIA:* If you need to extract information from a captured terrorist, don't waste your time, and risk international opprobrium, with waterboarding. Just take him for a visit to the Burmese countryside during their hideously hot and humid summers and seat him in one of the unimaginably uncomfortable two-wheeled horse carts they use for carrying tourists over their bumpy dirt trails, and he'll soon confess to anything. They are hell on wheels. If he passes out from the ordeal, you can instantly jolt him awake him with just one cup of tar-thick Burmese tea (which I had to dilute 15:1 to bring it to the brink of drinkability). And when he's confessed and has no further value, you can finish him off with a dish of Burmese hot-and-spicy fried finger eels.

I'd delayed visiting Burma for more than 40 years to be politically correct, hoping that my boycott would bankrupt its tyrannical regime, which went by the marvelously sinister name of SLORC (the State Law and Order Restoration Council). With the passing decades, I realized that my position was more reflexive than reflective and, after giving it some serious study, concluded that my tourist dollars would not be propping up the despots, who made their millions by controlling the lucrative trade in rubies, minerals, timber, gas, and oil. I realized instead that tourism was one of the only vocations from which ordinary Burmese could make a few dollars to avoid the extreme poverty that afflicted the nation, which had the lowest per capita income (adjusted for purchasing power parity) of any country in Asia. Others might argue that if curbing tourism deprived the Burmese people of their dollars, they might grow so discontented that they'd rise up and overthrow the dictatorship, but that was unlikely with this docile populace. In the election of 1990, the people had given 80 percent of their votes to the opposition, yet when this was ignored and invalidated by the regime, the country remained tranquil.

Whether from political correctness or the economic recession, few travelers or their dollars were present in September 2010. On my flight that landed at the tourist mecca of Bagan, I was the sole sightseer to disembark. In my Bagan hotel I was one of only four guests, served by a staff of 30 to 40. Yet Bagan is the heart of Burmese tourism, an ancient religious city where a thousand thousand-year-old temples, monasteries, and dome-shaped stupas stud the region—the ones left after Kublai Khan demolished the other 12,000 in 1268. It's a stupa-endous place, deserving far more visitors.

Another reason for the absence of vacationers was that the regime (renamed SPDC in 1997) had scheduled elections for the following month, motivating travelers to stay away for fear that the voting might lead to violence. I didn't think it would. I assumed the process would be peaceful, and that the SPDC would count the ballots as it pleased—it had barred all international monitors—and render it a futile exercise, as it had done before, without active dissent. To curtail foreign activists and provocateurs in the run-up to the election, the despots had ceased granting visas-on arrival at the international airport. You had to apply at the Myanmar Embassy in your own country, which thwarted spontaneous wayfarers.

Workers in the travel industry told me they were hurting badly. At every place I visited, I was the only mark in sight, besieged by dozens of hawkers. It made for low prices, but it was sad to see so many nice people forced to scramble for so little.

Burma has for many centuries been shaped by two forces, Buddhism and the Irrawaddy River (transliterated as Ayeyarwady by the military government).

The Irrawaddy begins, as do most of the great Asian rivers, high in the glaciers of the Himalayas, more than 24,000 feet above, and 1,350 miles northwest of, the Andaman Sea, into which it flows. The Irrawaddy runs down Burma vertically before spreading into a gigantic, nine-pronged, nine-million-acre delta that is the lifeblood of the nation and the heart of its rice culture. For centuries it was, and remains today, the entryway to the country, navigable for almost a thousand miles. The river was actually the "road" popularized in Rudyard Kipling's 1892 verse, which highlights its aquatic components:

> On the road to Mandalay,
> Where the flyin'-fishes play,
> An' the dawn comes up like thunder outer China 'crost the Bay.

Burma is 80 percent rural, one of the least developed nations in Asia, a place that time forgot, a consequence of its isolation by the international community after the military took over in 1962, and especially so after SLORC gutted any real democracy in 1984. It had great economic promise, with commercial deposits of oil, gas, lead, silver, tin, tungsten, nickel, mercury, antimony, copper, cobalt, zinc, iron, gold, and rubies, but those proceeds went into the pockets of the Army, an army of more than 1.3 million in a country needing no army, a country long at peace with its neighbors (India, Thailand, and Bangladesh), and where even ever-acquisitive China is no military threat—because it just buys up whatever it wants. Most indigenes are poor, living on $1.50 a day.

It has the world's highest mortality from snakebites—harboring two especially nasty specimens in the aggressive Russell's viper and the Asiatic king cobra, which can grow to 18 feet—because the locals, being Buddhists, won't kill the snakes, or any of God's other creatures. The domestic animals I saw in the countryside were not pigs or cows being fattened for slaughter, but beasts of burden—oxen in the dry zones, water buffalo in the wet zones, elephants in the mountains—and a few goats raised for their milk and wool.

The type of Buddhism practiced in Burma preaches that there are three planes of existence: the sensuous world, the animal world, and the worlds of hells and purgatories. These are, of course, in addition to the 16 planes of the subtle material world. Governing a person's daily behavior are 37 Nats— demons and evil spirits combined with angels—who demand respect and (much like my ex-girlfriends) offerings of money, food, and flowers if one wants to live a peaceful and happy life. My favorites were Princess Golden Face, the

Little White Lady with the Mule, the Old Man by the Solitary Banyan, and the Lord of Five Elephants.

As I understand it—and I don't swear I do—the Nats take care of day-to-day events and problems while Buddha guides believers toward the afterlife and reincarnation. The Burmese try to do enough good deeds to ensure they do not come back as a dog, rat, frog, female, or other lower form of life. The position of Burmese women has somewhat improved in recent decades, but girls are still the first ones pulled out of school to help their families earn money. Eight out of ten of the souvenir and soda vendors I encountered were girls, some as young as ten, sadly finished forever with schooling and the chance for a satisfying life.

Theravada Buddhism means lesser, and it's more conservative and stricter than other versions, with fewer pathways to nirvana. You really have to toe the line to avoid coming back as a frog. The monks who follow it must abide by 227 rules! They eat one meal a day, which they must obtain by begging, and are allowed only eight possessions: three robes, a razor, needle with thread, medicine, an alms bowl, and a strainer (so they won't accidentally ingest any living thing when they drink).

From what I experienced, the Burmese profoundly believe in Buddhism and live it devotedly. They are the most unfailingly polite and docile folks I ever encountered, rarely take offense, seldom get angry, and conclude every interaction with a gentle bow and a smile, with their hands clasped before them. I may just be a jaded Westerner, but I felt many of them took hospitality to an uncomfortable extreme, where attentiveness crossed the line into hovering, appreciativeness became fawning, and the provision of services tended toward servility. This unfortunately made them ideal subjects for a totalitarian regime, which may explain why they'd suffered under one for 50 years.

Because Burma was so isolated, it was not until I reached Bangkok, en route to Bangladesh, that I caught up on the news, some of which did not bode well for the swift completion of my appointed rounds. Potential new nations were popping up over the horizon. The island of Bougainville announced its first move to end its association with New Guinea and become independent; Belgium was so beset by insoluble political problems, based on linguistic differences and cultural and economic incompatibility, it seemed ready to split into two new countries; and Scotland was contemplating a secession that would make Great Britain less great.

The airport in Dhaka, the capital of Bangladesh (formerly Dacca, the capital of East Pakistan) almost did me in, as airports had throughout this trip. I arrived at the terminal at 5:00 a.m. for my flight to Bhutan, so early that the *muezzin* was just calling the faithful to first prayer over the loudspeaker. I was so sleepy that I staggered into the men's room with my eyes half shut and failed to see the urinals against the far side wall. What I did see, right in front of me, was a tub-shaped tile enclosure about eight feet long with three spigots and a drain, which I drowsily assumed was a communal urinal, somewhat like the ones we had in the army at Fort Leonard Wood. So I did my thing.

Only as I was zipping up did I realize it was not a giant pissoir, but the ablution fountain in which devout Muslims performed *wudhu*—washing their arms, face, and feet before they pray. Luckily for me, Al Jazeera was not on the scene to record my transgression. With the Muslim world in a furor that week because an American preacher had threatened to burn the Koran, I think that Podell pissing on a semi-sacred font might have been inflammatory. And one near-lynching in Dakha—however it's spelled—was enough for a lifetime.


"On the Wings of the Dragon," is the slogan of the Royal Airline of Bhutan, whose flight into Paro is breathtaking, as the plane threads a needle between 16,000-foot cliffs and makes a last-minute 90-degree turn to land at a 7,300-foot-high airstrip in a narrow valley.

The Bhutanese believe their sublime alpine paradise is the original, and the only remaining, Shangri-la, and rigorously protect it by limiting visitation to "low volume, high value" tours. This Land of the Peaceful Thunder Dragon is a pristine kingdom bordered by 200 snowcapped peaks of the higher Himalayas, an idyll of thick forests and soaring mountains where gray langur monkeys cavort by the roadside while rushing rivers of foam, fed by towering waterfalls, irrigate divine valleys dotted with whitewashed farmhouses set amid rich fields of green lettuce, golden barley, and red buckwheat, all watched over by

16th-century castle-like monasteries, their prayer flags fluttering in the wind under a cloudless cerulean sky.

It is the last of the Himalayan Tantric Buddhist kingdoms, what with Tibet now part of China, and Sikkim and Ladakh having merged into India.

It has a homogeneous population of 800,000 sharing a common background and beliefs within a tradition of Tantric Buddhism that promises them peace, protection, and prosperity. It has an abundance of fruit and timber, and copious hydroelectric power, sold to India for foreign exchange. It is a land that has never known a conqueror, a country so isolated until recently that it has acquired few of the vices or shallow values of contemporary civilization. It's all governed by an enlightened constitutional monarch dedicated to the preservation of that peace, prosperity, and a healthy environment—and it's as close as one can get to heaven on earth.

The people were as polite, kindly, and welcoming as those of Burma, but much happier and far less servile because they practiced a more liberal form of Buddhism, had a per capita income 20 times higher, and were not living under a dictatorship, but a benevolent ruler.

I saw a large part of the country by driving 1,200 kilometers along some exhilarating (i.e., terrifying) mountain roads with passes close to 12,000 feet. I petted the national animal of Bhutan, the takin, an odd beast with the head of a goat, the nose of a moose, and the body of a cow, that reminded me of some of my worst blind dates. From a teenaged shepherdess who'd set up shop in a mountain pass I purchased a local staple, dried yak cheese, surely the hardest and most tasteless substance eaten by humans anywhere.

I successfully made a six-hour climb up to 10,000 feet and Taktsang Palphug, the Tiger's Nest, an amazing monastery set near the top of a powerful waterfall, incredibly carved into a granite cliff wall nearly 3,000 feet above the Paro Valley. The undertaking initially (C.E. 747) required the intercession of the gods, who propelled Padmasambhava—a sage guru known as the Second Buddha—up there on the back of a tiger, in the wrathful form of Guru Dorje Drolo, to subdue the evil spirits of the region. The vanquished demons were transformed into the protectors of the dharma, the monastery was built in 1692 around the cave in which Padmasambhava meditated for three years, and the Bhutanese have lived happily ever after. (I promised my aching knees—which were not living so happily—that if I ever tried this ascent again, I, too, would engage the services of a volitating tiger.)

The indisputable high point of this journey occurred when I got to see my old travel buddy, Steve, whom I—and his Thai doctors—had given up for a goner in the spring, after he was diagnosed with Stage IV lymphoma. But Steve's sturdy constitution, the constant attentions of his loving wife (who spent 27 straight days and nights by his bedside in the VA hospital), and six rounds of intense chemo there had beaten back the cancer, enabling Steve to return to his home in Bangkok four days before I arrived, and to meet me for a memorable Thai dinner spent reminiscing about friends and adventures past, but far from forgotten.

Aware that the Big C all-too-often returns, I privately resolved, on that joyous night, with renewed determination, to visit the last 14 countries and complete this pilgrimage while Steve, who first got me on the foreign road, was still around to celebrate with me.

I headed to Hanoi for four days before heading home.

It's hard for me to imagine how Hanoi would be any different if the U.S. had *won* the Vietnam War. The locals were guzzling Pepsi, shopping in stores named "Dapper Dan" and "Elle Fashion" and "American Apparel," wearing jeans and Western clothes, using English letters on all their signage, and blaring U.S. top-forty tunes from every radio. They were devoted practitioners of free enterprise and capitalism; somewhere along the way, Ho Chi Minh and General Vo Nguyén Gian Gap morphed into Donald Trump and Bill Gates.

I had been in South Vietnam in the fall of 1965, when the U.S. was about to enter the war against the Viet Cong in force, and I admit I was in favor of our intervention. I liked the people I'd met in the South and naïvely didn't want to see them crushed by the nasty Communists from the North. As I heard the artillery thumping at night in the distant outskirts of Saigon, I even thought of reenlisting in the Army, resuming command of my 155mm gun crew, and blasting the Cong. I was not aware then, or for many years—because our government had lied to us—that the people of all Vietnam preferred Ho Chi Minh—who had driven out the French colonialists and longed to forge a unified, modern nation—to Ngo Dinh Diem, whom the U.S. supported and kept in power, an authoritarian mandarin who yearned to retain the old feudal society despite his hypocritical speeches about the need for social justice.

After spending several days chatting with the residents of Hanoi— good, friendly, energetic, hardworking capitalists—I wondered what was I thinking back in 1965 and how we blundered into that senseless war . . .

I sat in the lobby of my little hotel, which was, surprisingly, decorated with Hollywood posters for *Apocalypse Now, Good Morning Vietnam, The Quiet American, Full Metal Jacket,* and *Hamburger Hill,* and I wondered . . .

I visited the Museum of the Vietnamese Revolution and the Museum of Vietnamese History, both of which convincingly demonstrated that the movement for Vietnamese nationalism began around 1853, many decades before Communism was even a light in Engels's eyes, and I wondered how smart guys like JFK and LBJ and Bob McNamara got it all so wrong . . .

I visited Hoa Lo Prison, the notorious "Hanoi Hilton," and saw the cells where U.S. fliers were chained and tortured for years after being shot down while bombing the North, and I wondered . . .

It became apparent to me, in sad retrospect, that our obsessive fixation on our Cold War containment policy against Russia and China prevented us from realizing that the nascent indigenous revolutions in French Indochina, in northern Malaysia, and in Indonesia were not part of a global Communist conspiracy, but more akin to our own American revolution, the forceful expression of the pent-up desires of long-colonized peoples to be free of abusive foreign control and be able to determine their own destinies. Many lives would have been saved, widespread destruction averted, and much poverty, disease, and deprivation alleviated, if we'd been more understanding about, more sensitive to, and more supportive of, those legitimate, nationalistic, anti-colonial aspirations, and listened to those officers in the State Department who were experts on the region, instead of branding them as "soft on Communism."

On my final morning in Hanoi, seated for breakfast across from the poster promoting *Hamburger Hill,* I was unexpectedly served by my waitress with a start-off bonus plate of shredded pineapple, which, through my glue-smeared glasses from Kiribati, looked like the scrambled eggs I'd ordered. I liberally doused the yellow mound with pepper and ketchup and didn't realize my error until the first, strange bite. To save face, I felt obliged to eat it all, while smiling at the bemused waitress as if this were the way I started every morning. Sixty-five consecutive days on the road had taken their toll. It was time for me to head home.

# CHAPTER 25

## A Tropical Depression

East Timor, the first of the four sovereign states created in the 21st century, has a history of sorrow. The island of Timor, whose eastern half it occupies, was first subjugated, enslaved, and divided by the Portuguese in 1769, while the Dutch moved in and took over the western half. The Portuguese refused to invest in East Timor and it became a backwater trading post. World War II brought a harsh occupation by the Japanese, during which 40,000 to 70,000 natives died. This was followed by a locally resisted reassertion of Portuguese colonial control, which Lisbon finally relinquished in 1974, after the Dutch half had become part of Indonesia.

East Timor declared its independence in 1975—and it lasted nine days. Indonesia, which is predominantly Muslim, invaded, occupied, and annexed East Timor, which is predominantly Catholic. The East Timorese rebelled and fought a bloody 20-year guerrilla war, during which 100,000 to 250,000 of them died and 300,000 were forcibly abducted to the western part of the island, while the world stood idly by, tsk-tsking but doing nothing. Finally, in August 1999, the UN sponsored and supervised a referendum in which the East Timorese voted, overwhelmingly, for independence. But that was not the end of their sad story.

The anti-independence forces, armed and aided by Indonesia, commenced a savage scorched-earth campaign of retribution, destroying homes, irrigation systems, schools, the water supply, and the entire electrical grid in the country, devastating the infrastructure and bringing ruin to the new nation. The guerrillas withdrew in April 2008, allowing East Timor, by the time I arrived, to have experienced three years of peace, its longest ever. So many people died during the past decades that only three percent of the population is older than 65! I was an ancient there.

Recovery will take decades. Among the one million people surviving, the death rate is close to the world's highest. Their life expectancy ranking is 155 of 195. Forty-two percent live below the poverty line. And the country ranks an abysmal 176 in purchasing power parity and 120 on the Human Development Index.

I saw little industry—just printing, soapmaking, and weaving—although oil and gas had recently been discovered in the Timor Sea and a pipeline had been built to Darwin, where the gas was cooled and liquefied for shipment. They grow some coffee, rice, corn, cassava, sweet potatoes, cabbage, mangoes, and bananas, but livestock is costly and scarce.

The signs of poverty were everywhere. I saw few private vehicles, most of them old, a third of them motorcycles. The people wore worn, old, drab clothes. The first pop-up ad I saw on their Internet was for repairing generators, and the next was for repairing pumps. The wharf area of Dili, the capital, was crammed with empty shipping containers stacked four-high, evidencing a glut of imports and a paucity of stuff to export. There were almost no new buildings. Vehicles from the UN and NGOs abounded, as those agencies endeavored to aid the struggling nation. Large businesses were rare, and they, and the hotels, and the travel agencies, and the dive shops, were owned, and usually operated, by Aussies, while the other shops and stores belonged to overseas Chinese, leaving little for the locals beyond sidewalk cigarette-and-candy stands, and fish markets where they hung the day's catch from trees bordering the corniche.

A few visionary dreamers tout the land as "the next Bali" because of its numerous beaches, calm waters, isolation, and laid-back nature, but it has a long way to go. The roads are poor and the vegetation is not as luxurious or charmingly "tropical" as in most of the South Seas, just dowdy. The beaches are narrow and often brown, covered with discarded plastic bottles and other garbage, bathed by a muddy sea filled with raw sewage, and abutting the noisy main road around the island. Almost nobody speaks English. The denizens are friendly, but shabby. The water is not safe to drink. Flies are everywhere. Dengue and malaria are common. It has a few good reefs, but no other tourist attractions, no breathtaking scenery, no impressive palaces or exotic temples, although I did bike to an unimposing statue of Jesus on a hill overlooking the ocean that they claim is the second largest of any. But I don't think Bali has to worry.

The daily downpours are so heavy that—no exaggeration—they completely drown out the sound on the TV, even at its loudest level, and when they get really intense, even block out the TV satellite feed and the Internet. They leave large puddles all over, which seldom have time to dry before the next deluge, making mosquitoes abundant and walking difficult. I did not see a patch of blue or a spot of sun in the five days I stayed because the La Niña effect was fully dominant, as it had been for more than a year, even during what was supposed to be the annual dry season.

Going from bad to worse, I arrived at long last on sleepy Nauru, a speck in the Pacific, 25 miles south of the Equator, little known and rarely visited, a sad story and a strange piece of work, the 185th nation on my quest.

At 26 square miles, it is the third smallest nation, larger only than Monaco (0.7 square miles) and Vatican City (0.2 square miles). With fewer than 10,000 inhabitants, Nauru is ahead of only Vatican City (population 850), the smallest internationally recognized independent state by both area and inhabitants.

Nauru was first settled about 3,000 years ago by Micronesian and Polynesian peoples who eked out a subsistence living on fish, pandanus, and coconuts. Germany conquered and annexed the island in 1888 after a ten-year guerrilla war that reduced the population to 900, most of whom were poorly treated by the conquerors.

In going for my goal, I've often had to visit some unappealing places, but Nauru is, literally, a shithole, having once been covered by some of the thickest guano deposits on earth. Guano is the untreated excrement of fish-eating seabirds, and it became extremely valuable as fertilizer after its discovery off the coast of Peru and its study, in 1802, by Alexander von Humboldt, who determined it was high in phosphorous and nitrogen and low in offensive odor. Its worldwide exploitation on a massive scale began in the 1840s and continued for more than a hundred years, until guano was partly replaced by synthetics. Although Peruvian guano is the finest (because it was deposited in one of the globe's driest climates, thereby preventing the erosion of its valuable nitrates), Nauru's guano was so rich and abundant it made the Nauruans, from 1967 to 1974, the wealthiest per capita cats of all mankind. But almost all those centuries of bird droppings have now been stripped and shipped away, and the funds they brought have disappeared.

Nauru's boom-to-bust saga began with a *doorstop*. In 1896, during his ship's brief call at the island, a cargo officer of the Pacific Island Company picked up a pretty rock he thought was a piece of mineralized wood. He planned to polish it and make some marbles for his children, but that got postponed and the rock got detoured to his office in Sydney, where it served as a doorstop. Two years later, a management official in the company's phosphate division was transferred to Sydney, saw the doorstop, had it tested— and found the world's highest-quality phosphate! That find brought several billion dollars into Nauru's treasury during the next century but, unfortunately, lured the population into dependence on this sugar teat, away from which it has been difficult to wean them.

From 1914 until 1968, Nauru had a bewildering procession of landlords and foster parents: Australia, Britain, New Zealand, the League of Nations, the Japanese (during WW II), who used the people as slave laborers, with only 800 surviving, and the UN.

A brighter day looked to be dawning in 1968, when Nauru became a free and independent nation. The funds earned from selling the phosphate were deposited in a royalties trust that, for several delirious decades, funded a welfare state that gave its citizens the second-highest GDP per person and the world's highest standard of living.

But nobody saved for a rainy day. When the last good phosphate reserves were exhausted in 2006, the nation had no other source of income. It was an environmental wasteland—an ugly, barren, strip-mined mess of innumerable coral pinnacles largely unfit for human habitation.

A crumbling tower and a ruined conveyor belt that once supplied the world with phosphate and made Nauru the richest per capita nation for several years are sad reminders of that once-flourishing industry now that the guano has run out. Ugly limestone pinnacles scar the country's interior where the guano was extracted. *Tony Wheeler*

The Nauru Phosphate Royalties Trust was 90 percent depleted as the result of large-scale siphoning of funds by Britain and Australia and stupid investments by the fund managers in Australian-rules football teams that lost and London musicals that flopped. Nauru's government changed hands 17 times in five years. The Nauru National Bank became insolvent. Unemployment officially topped 49 percent and was surely higher. Most of the inner island, from whence the guano was excavated, is pockmarked with unsightly holes ringed by limestone pinnacles up to 40 feet high. Rising seawaters are lapping at the thin strip of level ground around the island's perimeter, which stands only about five feet above mean high tide. And its poor citizens are left to try to live in a land that is all pooped out.

Nauru appealed to the International Court of Justice in 1993, seeking compensation for the damage done by a century of rapacious phosphate strip-mining by foreign companies. It reached settlements with Australia ($50 million paid over 20 years), New Zealand ($12 million), and Britain ($12 million). But the high cost of maintaining an international airline on which few flew, combined with the government's financial mismanagement, led to economic collapse in the late 1990s, and to virtual bankruptcy by the Millennium. Things got so bad by 2006 that the only commercial airplane servicing the island was repossessed by creditors, cutting the country off from civilization for four months—and leaving me, you may recall, in the middle of Micronesia with a worthless ticket and a wrecked schedule.

With their guano almost gone, the entrepreneurial Nauruans tried to make a living in myriad ways, most of questionable legality. The nation became a tax haven, where anyone with $25,000 could open his own bank, no questions asked. It next did what destitute damsels had been forced to do since time immemorial: It sold itself to the highest bidders. First to Russian criminals, who used its banking system to launder money. Then to Australian politicians, who wanted to get rid of the hot potatoes known as "the boat people"—those desperate, poor, unskilled, brown-skinned refugees and asylum seekers who braved the oceans to reach Oz to escape from war, oppression, dictatorship, or poverty in their homelands in Afghanistan, Iraq, Iran, Sri Lanka, and other sad places. The Aussies made an agreement with the Nauruans—the "Pacific Solution"—whereby these undesired immigrants were dumped on Nauru, which shortly thereafter closed its borders to prevent outsiders from monitoring the refugees' condition.

When international opprobrium shuttered these career paths, Nauru started selling its diplomatic soul. In 2002, after the People's Republic of China promised to give it more than $130 million in aid, Nauru withdrew its recognition of Taiwan. But two years later, it broke off relations with the PRC and again recognized Taiwan as the Republic of China. The Taiwanese were now struggling to farm the island and are producing most of its vegetables. Nauru received $50 million of "development aid" from Russia and, in exchange, became one of only four countries to recognize, as independent nations, the breakaway Georgian provinces of South Ossetia and Abkhazia. (I met the man, a young American fluent in languages, who handles most of these arrangements for Nauru's Foreign Office and, while he was unwilling to reveal any details about upcoming deals, he impressed me as someone who had a secure job with strong growth prospects.)

Even the U.S. allegedly got into the pay-for-play action, reportedly offering to modernize Nauru's infrastructure in exchange for curtailment of the island's lax banking laws that had allowed the financing of activities that were illegal in other countries. Under this secret deal, code-named "Operation Weasel," Nauru also allegedly agreed to establish an embassy in Beijing and there operate a spy-like "safe house" and courier services for the Americans. After the deal became embarrassingly public—pop goes the Weasel!—our government denied knowledge of it and refused to make the promised payments, prompting Nauru to sue us in an Australian court, whose initial judgments favored Nauru.

All in all, a sordid saga of the developed world's military, economic, and geopolitical imperialism, and its harmful results.

Nauru's new scheme, as explained to me by the nation's Director of Tourism and Economic Development, was to knock down the millions of leftover limestone pinnacles, grind them up, and sell that residue. The director floundered and fumfered when I asked him of what commercial use the crushed pinnacle pieces were, and whether anyone had done a marketing study or cost-effectiveness research on this proposal. He assured me the nation was not in financial straits and still had a positive balance of payments, but his irrepressibly boosterish personality made it hard to distinguish fact from hope. For example, he assured me that none of the younger people were leaving the island for better opportunities elsewhere and that its population had actually grown, to "about 20,000, maybe even 30,000." But when I asked the head of the government's Statistics Department, he put the population figure at a stagnant 9,080, and when I asked the woman who ran the Bureau of Immigration how many had immigrated *to* Nauru in the last three years, she looked at me as if I'd taken too much sun, and replied: "None. Not a single one. Why in the world would anyone want to live here?"

Questionable conduct was so widespread on Nauru that, until shortly before I visited, it was one of the toughest places on our big blue marble to which to obtain a visa. The authorities were sure you were either an investigator or a journalist—neither was welcome—but surely not a tourist, of which they had none. In a radical postmillennial policy change, Nauru began issuing visas and attempting to lure tourists, although the Director of Tourism assured me "we are just gearing up."

The country was now averaging 13 tourists a month, so if you really wanted to get away from it *all*, Nauru might be the place to go. Because only eight flights arrive per month, the odds are you'd only have to share the plane with 5/8 of another tourist. My flight had only one other tourist who alighted at Nauru (plus ten locals and four aid workers) and, judging from his dress and demeanor, he looked like the kind of seasoned traveler who was willing and able to go anywhere. When we both ended up at the same hotel (the island offers a choice of two), and started to talk, I learned he was Tony Wheeler, the man who founded Lonely Planet—my guide, my guru, my God, my gosh!

To be fair, Nauru is not without a certain forlorn charm for the tired tourist seeking tranquility. It has no nightlife or entertainments and almost no international phone service or Internet to distract you. The thin beaches are adorned with legions of unusual limestone pinnacles, the reef an easy swim for snorkelers, the first dive shop opened the month before I arrived, and fishing for tuna, bonito, and other big boys is among the best in the Pacific. The locals are relaxed, convivial, seemingly happy, and welcoming (except the Chinese, who tend to be dour and alienated). Almost all the locals speak excellent, unaccented English and are far easier to understand than the Aussies. There is no malaria, dengue, or other deadly bugs or dangerous wildlife. The tap water, which comes from the desalination plants, is safe to drink, and you can buy a delicious meal of 20 large pieces of fresh tuna sashimi on a giant plate of coconut rice for only four dollars, all washed down for a dollar with a Coke or a Fiji beer. Could *this* be "the next Bali"?

Since so few Nauruans can find work, they sit around and grow fat on a regimen of SPAM, fried chicken, and other fatty foods introduced by the GIs who liberated the island in WW II. The population is among the planet's heaviest, with 95 percent being overweight or obese. The portions in the local eateries are twice as large as anyone should eat. Most of the adults I saw were above 300 pounds. Their inter-island airline has configured a creative way to accommodate them: In the front 20 rows, the middle armrests do not lift up, as they do on most jetliners; instead they swivel sideways so that three seats abreast can be reconfigured to fit two fat folks.

A bonus of this visit was that I was able, for the first time in all my travels, to totally circumambulate an entire nation under my own power. (I had tried in San Marino, but it was too hilly and its border poorly delineated, and I had intended to circle Vatican City on my last visit, but that coincided with the investiture of Pope Benedict, which made it far too crowded.) I traded two worn T-shirts (NYU and Orlando) and one tired tank top (Cozumel) for the all-day loan of a thick-tired bike, on which, starting at 7:00 a.m. (to avoid the midday sun, which is brutal just 25 miles south of the Equator), I pedaled the perimeter of the country in four hours.

Content with my singular achievement, and ready for some R & R, I headed for Brisbane, but was there confronted with a discomforting realization.

I knew this was likely the last time I'd ever see Australia, that Oz was over, that I was done Down Under. I realized that, because of age and obligations, I would not be able to revisit this land I'd known and enjoyed for more than 30 years, one that had provided me with much love, beauty, excitement, friendships, and adventures. But I was not ready for the type of adventure it threw at me this time.

Brisbane is one of the world's most livable cities—sparkling, energetic, prosperous, and progressive. It boasts clean air and clean streets; wide sidewalks; inviting plazas; dozens of picturesque parks, gardens, and arbored walkways; and a superb pedestrian mall. It was the domain of handsome, flab-free, health-conscious young studs in bike shorts, and lithe lassies who were everything plus, wearing tiny cutoffs with black hiking boots or diaphanous sundresses with high heels. It's a cement South Sea paradise, 21st-century style.

First time I visited Brissie was 1981, heading hot up from the Gold Coast where I'd been practicing my Hawaiian big-board technique and Aussie slang on the local surfies—"G'day, mate. Heaps rad bra, eh?"—before dropping in on the Sunshine Coast for a bit more bronzing, then on to spectacular diving on the Great Barrier Reef. I was backpacking, bunking at Australian Youth Hostels (AYH), chowing down on kangaroo burgers and emu steaks, a wayfaring wanderer loving the beauties of Australia and blissfully enjoying carefree promiscuity in the back of long-distance buses with a series of sun-tanned Sheilas in those last sublime times before AIDS came along and spoiled all the fun. Oh, what a difference a day makes.

On this trip I'd shifted from the AYHs to the landmarked edifice across from the Central Train Station housing the backpacker's haven known throughout the international footloose set as X Base Brisbane, where I was the only guest over 28. It had been built a hundred years ago for the Salvation Army as a way station for homeless dipsomaniacal souls who pledged to shun Demon Rum in exchange for a tiny room, daily sermons, and three squares. It was now a popular venue for international hookups, but the women guests treated me as an interloper.

I tried, without success, to get my groove back in the basement's Down Under Bar, where much of the meeting and greeting took place. To assist the pre-mating process, the bar hosted a daily "Full On, Flat Out" nonstop, wild scene fueled by Pure Blonde Naked Pale Ale. It featured Minglah Monday, ("Beer 'n Babes"), Temptation Tuesday ("Beauties 'n Bikinis"), Wicked Wet Wednesday ("Wet T Contest"), Thumpin Thursday, Funky Friday, Sinful Saturday, and Seedy Sunday, all at cut-rate prices, but at high cost to one's liver, hearing, and sleep, which I willingly paid, but to no avail. If I'd been a narc, I could hardly have been less popular, or more the object of unwelcoming looks. I'd been shunted off to the realm of fantasy. Oh, yes, what a difference a day makes.

During the previous ten years, as I'd traveled through nations where STDs were rampant, I'd refrained from hunting quail, although it had once been my favorite sport. Now that I was back in safe territory and ready to resume the chase, I did a reality check and got the message—loud and clear—that it would be unseemly, unwelcome, and unsuccessful for me to try romancing any of the 20-something beauties who roused my interest.

I'd never been a lech or a sexual predator, even though it got depressingly lonely on these multi-month voyages. I'd previously relied on my appearance, charm, suitability, and *joie de vivre* to foster mutually pleasing liaisons on the road—where it was impossible to enter into serious relationships because I was never in one place for more than a few days. But all I could foster at the Down Under Bar was the eponymous Aussie lager. I no longer fit into the singles scene, and the harder I tried to talk and dress as the young guys did so naturally and effortlessly, the more awkward I became. This was a new kind of adventure for me, and not one I was prepared for or cared to continue.

Reality bit hard: I was no ageless Peter Pan, no timeless Indiana Jones. No longer Keats's Bold Lover, "for ever panting, and for ever young." I'd best get the hell out of Dodge and return to my mission.

But first I drowned my sorrow in a farewell feast with an old Brissie buddy at a restaurant whose French chef specialized in "Advanced Australian Fare," which no old drover would recognize. I ordered, and gluttonously consumed, the enormous "Native Platter" of barbecued crocodile, emu prosciutto, munchy muntries, glacé lilly pilly, dukkah, smoked glacé guandong—Spell Checker just gave up and went down in flames—lime glacé, tender greens covered with bunya nuts, seared rare kangaroo, a delicious confit of Tasmanian possum, home-baked whole-wheat damper dipped in macadamia oil, rosella chutney, anisata salmon gravlax, Moreton Bay bugs (*Thenus orientalis*), and, for dessert, at a nearby bakery, a heavenly lamington covered with coconut-crusted chocolate—all for less than the cost of a used car.

Farewell, Brissie. I'll dearly miss you and the fabulous times we've had. Good-bye, Oz. No, not my customary *au revoir*. Because, my dear old friend, I know I won't ever see you again.

# CHAPTER 26

## Second Thoughts

After visiting Kosovo and Portugal, and shifting into final preparations for the Nasty Nine, the news from those lands caused me to have serious second thoughts about the safety and sanity of continuing this quixotic quest.

Let's start with **Chad**. I thought the rebellion there was quiescent, but Amnesty International had just reported that both the rebels and the government forces were busily recruiting and abducting children to become soldiers, and few things frighten me more than a heavily armed, trigger-happy preteen. A few weeks earlier, the JEM rebel group accused the Chadian government of plotting with the Sudanese to begin a joint operation against them, and Agence France-Presse reported that both Chadian and Sudanese forces were on red alert because many Darfur rebels had left their hideouts in Libya and crossed the border. It was still a hanging Chad.

**Rwanda** had been relatively quiet after 1994's horrendous, hundred-day bloodbath in which a million Hutus and Tutsis were slaughtered, although recent elections had been tainted, and journalists and opposition politicians had been persecuted. My planned route was across the country, down to Kigali, into the Southern Province, skirting the DRC through the Nyungwe Forest, and across Rwanda's southwest border into **Burundi**. Then Australia's Department of Foreign Affairs issued this warning:

With murderous guerrillas, Islamic terrorists, rampant corruption, rigged elections, increasing poverty, disease, travel restrictions, at least one nonfunctioning government, and citizen discontent in the "Savage Seven" countries that I still needed to visit to complete my quest, I took time to consider the prospects, evaluate the odds, and decide if the game was worth the candle.

We advise you to exercise a high degree of caution in Rwanda because of the risk of rebel and criminal activity. Pay close attention to your personal security at all times . . . Grenade attacks have occurred in Kigali and Southern Province. We advise you to reconsider your need to travel to the areas bordering Burundi because of the high risk of conflict between government forces and rebels and banditry. These areas include the Nyungwe Forest. We strongly advise you not to travel to the areas bordering the Democratic Republic of the Congo . . . because of the volatile and unpredictable security situation in this region.

Uganda had appeared quiet, at least compared to five years before, when the Lord's Resistance Army (LRA) was on a bloody rampage. The LRA was now mostly active in the DRC, but President Obama announced that the

U.S. had dispatched the first of a group of military personnel to help the Ugandans fight the LRA. On October 14, 2011, he declared that:

> For more than two decades, the Lord's Resistance Army (LRA) has murdered, raped, and kidnapped tens of thousands of men, women, and children in central Africa. I have authorized . . . combat-equipped U.S. forces to deploy to provide assistance to regional forces that are working toward the removal of [LRA commander] Joseph Kony from the battlefield. During the next month, additional forces will deploy, including a second combat-equipped team . . .

I had arranged, six months earlier, to visit Uganda accompanied by James Stedronsky, a law school chum who was an outdoor enthusiast, so I'd have someone to cover my back, especially since I'd be camping out for most of the two weeks there, but Jim bailed out the day after the troop announcement, sending me this e-mail:

> I'm not traveling to Uganda as a US citizen while US special ops are chasing an outrageously dangerous group through the country. It's too dangerous, Al. You have no idea whether someone can make a buck selling you to some rebels. You need to seriously discuss this with some other people whose judgment you trust. It's blatantly reckless to travel alone under these circumstances. You need to discuss this with mature people who are very close to you and care about you. You know better than anyone that when traveling you have to continuously weigh risks and change plans. A US military intervention ranks with these. Don't decide this by yourself and don't insist on going "because this is what I do."

But, Jim, this *is* what I do.

The world's newest state, **South Sudan,** had become even more dangerous. It had been my hope, for the previous five years, that the achievement of independence in July 2011 would end the fighting between the South's animist population and the Muslim-dominated North. But the violence instead intensified along the disputed, mineral-rich border zone. Hundreds were killed and dozens of villages burned to the ground in the three months following independence.

In other parts of the new nation, more than 2,400 had been killed, 3,000 wounded, and 26,000 cattle stolen in fighting between the Murle and Lou Nuer communities. (Cattle rustling is a main source of insecurity in South Sudan, as cows represent wealth and social status, and are used as "blood money," and compensation, and payment of dowries.) The International Crisis Group noted that "Sticks and spears have historically been used to carry out rustling and the violent disputes it often causes. However, the proliferation of small arms changed the nature of this practice, making raiding far more deadly."

Then there was Yemen, to which the Arab Spring had come late, but ferociously, with an almost successful assassination of the autocratic president, followed by heavy-handed government retaliation, which was killing about ten protesters a day, while Al-Qaeda made the most of the disorganization and turbulence to consolidate its hold on South Yemen, countered by escalating attacks by American drones to pick off terrorist leaders. Admittedly not the best time to visit—unless you were an arms merchant.

Even well-developed Kenya, which had been calm after two of its largest tribes hacked each other up following an election two years earlier, and which I'd have to transit to enter Somalia and South Sudan, went ballistic a few weeks before I was scheduled to depart, and dispatched its army into neighboring Somalia to attack the terrorists of Al-Shabaab, who had kidnapped a French tourist and killed her. The fittingly named spokesman for Al-Shabaab, Sheikh Ali Mohamed Rage, vowed his group would attack Kenya with a vengeance in retaliation.

He would carry out this threat on March 12, 2012, when assailants hurled four grenades into the Nairobi bus station, killing at least six and injuring more than 50. Twenty other grenade/explosive attacks in Kenya killed 48 and injured more than 200 in 2012. On September 21, 2013, Al-Shabaab ter-rorists invaded an upscale shopping mall in Nairobi, killed six Kenyan sol-diers and 61 civilians, and broadcast that this was retribution for Kenya's military support of the Somalian government.

The worst was **Somalia**, often cited as the most dangerous country on earth. I knew Al-Shabaab had established a brutal reign in which they whipped women for showing their ankles, chopped off the hands of petty thieves, and beheaded those suspected of being disloyal. They had banned TV, music, gold teeth, and bras as offensive to Islam. But I didn't realize quite how dangerous it was until I received an e-mail from the manager of a hotel in Mogadishu to whom I'd inquired about their accommodations and how far it was to walk to the nearest restaurant. He replied:

Dear Al, I will try to guide you as best as I can on your planned trip. Mogadishu is unlike any place on earth. There is no such thing as "going for a walk." You cannot walk out of our compound whenever you want. You will be immediately spotted, and kidnapped within minutes. There are no taxis. You will need armed Somali security guards, who will take you in a convoy of Toyota Surfs with blacked-out windows should you need to move around, even 100 yards. Security guard escort service plus vehicle and driver is $350/day. Foreigners cannot move around (even with armed guards) anywhere in the city after sundown. We cannot offer a rate without meals be-cause you will starve! There are no restaurants you can go to out-side our compound. Either you eat at our place or you do not eat. For these reasons, coming here as a tourist is wildly expensive and not recommended. Our clients are journalists, diplomats, and UN staff, who have received hostile-environments training. Moving around the city, you may encounter small-arms fire, possible IEDs, grenade or RPG attacks. If you're still interested in visiting, please let me know.

And he was trying to *encourage* my visit.

* * *

When high risk is closely linked to the reasonable possibility of a high reward, as in the stock market or romance, I've often given it a go, with much success in the former, and only a few dozen disasters in the latter. But when it came to this travel game, the high-risk countries offered scant rewards. They were, more often than not, sad, sorry, lawless lands with few things worth seeing, unless you had a fetish for starving, homeless people; ruined infrastructure; wounded and malnourished children; and bullet-pocked buildings. When traveling in lawless lands and failed states, high risk comes with a high possibility of an untimely funeral—if, that is, your next of kin is fortunate enough to locate your body.

On my scoreboard, the reward was always the same: just one more country. Whether it's France or Somalia, Canada or a killing ground, it still only counted as one country, regardless of the risk involved. For that reason, I'd diligently sought to avoid the dangerous hot spots when they were inflamed, and visit them only after they'd cooled down. My overall venture may have been fraught with perils, but since I'd never been an adrenaline junkie, and was no longer the blissfully ignorant, foolishly invincible youth who naïvely set out on that drive around the world decades earlier, I did whatever I reasonably could to minimize the risk. I never consciously went in search of danger. When it confronted me, I'd tried to make the best of it and find a way out of it or around it. I was a living oxymoron—a cautious adventurer.

But I could no longer do that or be that. I was down to the nitty gritty of the Nasty Nine, none of which showed signs of becoming completely peaceful before I got carted off to the assisted-living facility or the booby bin. If I was going to go for the goal, now was the time. I'd dodged and ducked and avoided the big dangers as long as possible, but now I had to put up or shut up.

I could have stopped here, at 187 countries, and lived peacefully in my cozy, souvenir-filled apartment, enjoying my sweet girlfriend, my good pals, the spa at Chelsea Piers, my front-row ballet seats, my pile of must-read books, and enough savings to lead a comfortable life. Or I could continue the adventure and risk it all for an objective that to most probably seemed meaningless and inconsequential and whose origins and attraction I but vaguely understood.

After much consideration, I decided to go for it.

I arranged to leave on November 18, 2011, for Saudi Arabia and Yemen, then into Africa, and I hoped to be back in the States and up in Vermont before the end of ski season.

I never made it.

# CHAPTER 27

## My Meddle in the Muddle East

Despite my e-mailed entreaties to my friends asking that they not try to talk me out of my plans, only ten of them advised me to "Go For It!"—four adventurous types, three free spirits, two beneficiaries of my will, and one who asked to be added to it.

The legion of naysayers recommended I stay home and live a long and peaceful life. Some sent me brochures for attractive retirement communities. A friendly shrink offered me a free mental evaluation. My cousin Larry tried to lure me down to Vero Beach by promising to make me blueberry pancakes for breakfast. My insurance agent advised he was unable to get me that million-dollar term-life policy now that he knew where I intended to travel. And Professor John King, my forensic pathologist pal at Cornell, who usually autopsies pigs and sheep around the world that have died of mysterious diseases, thoughtfully volunteered to "help get what is left of you home."

I partly heeded their advice by beefing up protection. I hired two security experts and six guards with assault rifles and an armored car for Mogadishu, and I agreed to take Andrew Doran, who is a fearless martial-arts expert and crack shot, for the most dangerous parts of the trip—once I was sure they hosted no massage parlors to tempt him. I went to a rifle range to reattain the sharpshooter rating I'd earned in the army, and shot 245 out of a possible 250 points at medium range on a semiautomatic with basic slit sights! Not bad for a squinty dude who can barely see his shoes on an overcast day. I was ready for action.

I left for Saudi Arabia well prepared, thanks to literary agent Steve Ross, who treated me to a lunch of bagels and lox with a schmear, not easily obtained in Riyadh. I'd selected Saudi Arabia to begin this final segment as the safest of the Nasty Nine. But events on the ground invariably trump careful planning and showed it was naive of me to assume, with the Arab Spring in full bloom on its every side—in Egypt, Syria, Yemen, and Bahrain—that the Desert Kingdom could remain immune, especially given its large and restive minority population of Shiites encouraged by Iran to foment trouble within its main challenger for regional supremacy.

The day after I arrived, the police killed two protesters in Qatif in the heavily Shia Eastern Province, which I needed to drive through the following week to reach the causeway to Bahrain and my flight to Africa. Two days later, at the funeral of those protestors, unidentified assailants killed two police and wounded several bystanders, as others burned tires and set up roadblocks.

The next day the Saudi Interior Ministry (while scrupulously avoiding any mention of Sunni/Shia tensions) denounced the killings as "incited and dictated by foreign malicious plans using unknown criminal elements who have infiltrated among the citizens and are firing from residential areas and narrow streets." It warned that "Whoever deludes himself about violating order will be deterred strongly. Those who cross the line will be dealt with severely and with maximum force. We are a country targeted by many plots."

So much for my peaceful start. As a result of this violence, my group of seven acquired an armed escort for most of each day. Police checkpoints had been set up every forty miles along the main highways, and as soon as our van stopped at the first to present our travel authorization papers, a patrol car with flashing lights took up station either in front of or behind us and escorted us for most of the rest of the day, most closely when we visited desolate archaeological sites. Personally, I'd have felt safer without the flashing lights, which do little to deter determined terrorists, but instead alert them to a high-value target.

Our group proceeded unmolested, and the locals welcomed us. One of our group did break a couple of ribs while scrambling around, but we couldn't blame that on any foreign criminal elements. The same day, two relatives of our driver were killed, but that occurred in Syria, which was starting to heat up and break down.

Because it's difficult to be well informed about 196 nations, I didn't have a deep understanding of Saudi Arabia before I arrived there. I knew it possessed, pumped, and sold more oil than any nation, banned women from driving, and was an absolute monarchy whose official religion was an ultraconservative form of Islam called Wahhabism. And I knew it forbade females from wearing revealing or provocative clothing, and that its sharia courts imposed the death penalty for adultery.

I further knew, from personal experience, that it was a damn tough place for which to get a visa. I had tried, five years earlier, at both the Saudi Consulate in New York and the Saudi Embassy in Washington, but they just held my application for months and never gave me an answer. I then tried again, two years later, in Bahrain, and was again rebuffed. After I insisted on knowing the reason, an unusually candid consular officer took me aside and admitted, "Look, we have lots of oil money, so we don't need your few tourist dollars. We have two million Muslim pilgrims visiting every year to do the Haj or make Umrah, and they are no trouble. Some of our conservative citizens do not want non-Islamic Westerners coming and stirring up our people with liberal ideas. And we certainly do not need the bad publicity if you are hurt or killed in our country by some radical. All together, it just makes no sense for us to allow in tourists."

Unable to refute his logic, I decided to go around it. I attempted, the next day, to saunter across the causeway from Bahrain into the Saudi city of Dammam to see if I got a warmer reception there. I was brusquely turned back midway.

In September of 2010 several travel publications had reported that the Saudi Commission for Tourism and Antiquities had banned the issuance of any visas for tourists, except devout Muslims. Because I *had* to get in to complete my quest, I might have to "convert" to Islam for a while, read the Koran, study with a mullah, attend a mosque, and forget I was an oversexed Jewish atheist. Instead, I found a lead in *International Travel News* that enabled me to reach Saudi soil—albeit $9,000 poorer—dressed in desert gear and devoutly following an elderly archeologist/cultural anthropologist from the University of Texas who was the world's authority on the minute clay counters utilized in the Middle East some 7,000 years ago to keep financial accounts, which, she had posited in her two-volume opus, gave rise to the first writing. My role? Don't ask. Don't tell.

Because Saudi customs and etiquette are tightly structured and taken seriously, and their violation could give unintended offense, we had to learn the rules, among which, as set forth by our internal facilitator, were these:

> Don't discuss unpleasant topics in social situations.
>
> Accept the first cup of coffee as an acknowledgment of the host's hospitality (even if you don't drink it). But do not accept more than three cups.
>
> Eat and pass food and things only with the right hand.
>
> Handle food with the first three fingers of the right hand only.
>
> Don't let your fingers touch your mouth or tongue when eating from a communal dish.
>
> Leave a portion of the meal uneaten.
>
> Depart after the presentation of incense.
>
> Do not show too much admiration for a Saudi's possessions because he may feel obligated to offer you the item under consideration.
>
> Do not prematurely withdraw if a Saudi man holds your hand.
>
> Men and women should avoid physical contact in public.
>
> Do not beckon or point with the fingers.
>
> Do not photograph people, particularly women, without first asking permission.
>
> Do not expose the soles of your feet to Saudis or make idiomatic references to shoes.
>
> No alcohol, pork products, pornography, or religious books and artifacts not related to Islam are permitted in the country.
>
> Homosexual behavior and adultery are illegal and can carry the death penalty.
>
> Public criticism of the King, the royal family, or the government is not tolerated.

Saudis are very conscious of personal and family honor and can
easily be offended by any perceived insult to that honor.
Islam is the only legally and officially recognized religion.

In addition, we had to comply with the dress code for foreigners issued by the Society for the Encourage [*sic*] of Virtue and the Elimination of Vice, which decreed that men cannot wear any type of shorts, tight trousers, or fitted shirts (which left no wiggle room for a guy who'd gained 15 pounds in the past year).

You think all this is easy? Try sitting on a carpet in pinching pants with your bare feet tucked underneath you for two hours while fetching fried rice from a communal bowl with the first three fingers of the right hand and trying to ingest it without touching your mouth or tongue while simultaneously passing the pita bread to the guy next to you with the same right hand and desperately trying to get the pepper dish without pointing at it as you praise the weather for the tenth time while taking care not to praise the furniture and longing for the incense to be presented although you are eager (without giving offense, of course) to find out exactly who is killing whom and why in the Eastern Province, all this while still absorbing your first contact with Saudi culture—the bold caption atop the entry form distributed on the arriving flight: DEATH TO DRUG TRAFFICKERS.

Our experiences were more relaxed and pleasant than what we'd anticipated from the instructions.

Almost every male Saudi we encountered shook our (right) hand warmly (but not uncomfortably long) and told us "America is good." The police who enforced religious discipline ignored my belly-stretched T-shirts. When the call to prayer sounded, as it did five times a day, all businesses closed promptly—but not quite; in the open-air markets, you could usually find a shopkeeper in the back of one of the stalls who was keeping watch over his neighbors' stalls and willing to surreptitiously transact business. The netiquette in computer cafes was to lock the door until prayers were over, but let you stay and continue messaging. Traffic did not stop. And the few people who loitered on the street were not rounded up and forced to attend services. Although non-Muslims were forbidden to enter the holy cities of Mecca and Medina, our group's van took an unauthorized "shortcut" through the heart of Medina and didn't get stopped.

I got a pleasant surprise in Jeddah when we ran into a group of 14 teenage Saudi girls from a private school taking a tour with their teacher to study old buildings. Only three kept their faces covered; all the others were eager to chat, in excellent English, take photos of us, pose for photos with us, and generally behave like typical American teenagers. Nothing like this was repeated for the rest of the trip, and we never again had the opportunity to speak to a Saudi female. It was a fascinating glimpse behind the veil, and I wondered how these girls would fare in their strict society when the time came for them to marry and conform.

All in all, we had a great ten days visiting digs at Al-Ukhdood, Yathrib (Madinah), Al Via, Al Jout, Za'abal fortress, Hail, and the Zubaida Route, trotting around to look at (and try to interpret) rock carvings and inscriptions from 2,000 years ago, poking about in scores of tombs carved into sandstone cliffs in the desert behind elegant facades adorned with snakes and eagles and the five steps to Heaven, and picking over bleached bones around the ruins of ancient caravansaries. These last were situated along the routes by which spices and incense had made the land transit from Yemen to the Mediterranean, before Arab sailors learned how to put the seasonal monsoon winds to their advantage and sail up and down the narrow, coral-reef-fringed Red Sea, an innovation that wrecked the overland caravan trade around C.E. 75. We had fun, but were beyond hopeless when it came to semiotics and distinguishing among recondite inscriptions carved in Aramaic, Palmyrene, Nabatean, and early Arabic, as our professor gently noted.

During this time, the president of Yemen agreed to leave office (again), which mollified the protesters a mite, but the state still lacked a functioning government to issue visas, which put me in a dilemma. I always try to enter a country legally, with visas and passport stamps and all such folderol, and had only once departed from this procedure, in exigent circumstances, but I realized I could well be doddering or dead by the time Yemen resumed issuing visas. When our group reached the Saudi city of Najran on the edge of the Empty Quarter, to poke around the ruins of the ancient settlement of

Al-Ukhdood in Wadi Najran, only two uninhabited miles from the Yemeni border, the temptation proved overpowering.

I offered our guide $200 to take me up to the border, but he told me it was too risky because the Saudis were on the alert to prevent jihadis from slipping across from Yemen. He said the Saudi military had cleared a wide stretch of land on the border, had installed heat sensors, were erecting a fence (not yet completed), and had 4×4s with searchlights patrolling the area—all of which presented an irresistible challenge to me.

Aided by a visibility diminishing dust storm that night, and abetted by a local with an SUV who succumbed to my offer of $200, and with my absence from our motel covered for by two members of my group, we drove about two miles past the airport to a dark and deserted area, hung a hard right, and headed up the sandy slopes for several hours, until we crossed into an unguarded part of Yemen.


Yemen was like traveling back in time. I stayed in the Old City part of its capital, Sana'a, a UNESCO World Heritage site that is a maze of narrow, winding old alleys lined by the world's first skyscrapers, six to seven stories tall, built of large stone blocks many hundreds of years ago, originally illuminated inside through window holes covered with thin sheets of alabaster polished to transparency.

The people were remarkably friendly. The countryside was like Arizona on steroids: The mountains, which soar from 6,000 to 11,000 feet (the highest in the Middle East), were often topped with an enchanting ancient village reached by a breath-stoppingly serpentine road and surrounded by a high, thick wall, entered through a gate out of the Arabian nights. The food was varied and delicious, albeit too spicy for most Westerners. And there were more signs on the walls proclaiming—in an artistic combination of black, green, and red paint—DEATH TO AMERICA than I have ever seen. The full translation was even more disturbing: "God is great. Death to America! Death to Israel! Damn the Jews! Power to Islam."

I chanced upon a wedding at a remote village on a high plateau where most of the fierce-looking tribal guests had walked in from the hills for the

On a barren hill overlooking Wadi Bahr in Yemen, 15 km north of Sana'a, I provided a perch for a young falcon. The birds are carefully trained, highly prized, and heftily priced status symbols throughout the Middle East, where they are used for hunting small animals. *Debbie Ricci*

festivities dressed in their newest automatic rifles and rocket-propelled grenade launchers. They vied to have their photos taken with this rare Western visitor and insisted I hold their weapons as they entwined their arms over my shoulders. Lucky for me I'm from Poland.

My long background evaluating female bodies provided me with vital sociopolitical insight as to why Yemeni women average a svelte and inviting 115 pounds while Saudi women tip the scales over 210, why these lithe ladies glide by in shimmering black silk robes while the similarly attired Saudi women plod by like oxcarts whose wheels are out of line. I respectfully submit five reasons for this telling and informative difference, ones you will not find in any World Bank analysis.

1. The Yemen women stride about briskly, freely, independently on their own, comprising fully half of the pedestrian population. The Saudi women are rarely allowed to walk about, and on the rare occasions when they do, must keep a respectful three paces behind the hulking, slow-moving male relative who is chaperoning them.

2. Yemen is far poorer, and consequently has fewer cars, so walking is a way of life. In Saudi Arabia, as in the other wealthy Gulf states, foreign guest workers drive the overweight denizens almost everywhere in luxurious, air-conditioned cars, severely limiting exercise opportunities.

3. The Yemenis, being poorer, are more restricted in, and conscious of, food consumption, while the Saudis just pile it on.

4. Although times may be changing a little in Saudi Arabia, it is still a bastion of arranged marriages, where the parents pick the mates and the parties take whatever is offered. In Yemen, the teenagers are more independent, and often conduct lengthy courting interviews before marrying, interviews in which looking like an oxcart would not be advantageous—unless the prospective husband is primarily seeking someone capable of heavy hauling.

5. The climate of the most populated parts of Yemen, which are mountainous, is brisk and cool, encouraging aerobic walking,

while that of sea-level Saudi is so torpid and enervating that not
even mad dogs or Englishmen try it.

After several days in Sana'a, I grew weary—and somewhat wary—of
all the DEATH TO AMERICA signs, and all the pamphlets I was handed in-
forming me that "None has the right to be worshiped but Allah." I opted to
fly to a remote part of Yemen where there were no active jihadis—the island
of Socotra in the Indian Ocean, about 500 miles south of Aden. I can't say it
was a brilliant move, because I'd forgotten that Socotra was near that part of
the Somali coast where the pirates had their lairs. Thwarted by convoys of
European warships from snatching the easy maritime pickings as they had
done several years before, the pirates had turned to looting and kidnapping
in the surrounding land areas, including the three sister islands west of Socotra. So far they'd left Socotra alone, perhaps because none of its towns
appear to have been rebuilt since they were devastated in a war with Egypt
more than 50 years ago. It looks too poor for any self-respecting pirate to
waste his time.

If they did come, they'd meet little resistance because the populace is too
stoned to care, totally trashed around the clock. It's a long-standing part of
Yemeni culture to chew qat, the mildly narcotic leaves of an evergreen shrub
(*Catha edulis*) that is Yemen's biggest cash crop, fetching its farmers five times
more per acre than fruit. Surveys show that 70 to 80 percent of the male residents chew qat at least three times a week, for four to five hours a day, causing
qat cultivation to soar from 8,000 hectares in 1970 to 107,000 today, and sucking up 55 percent of the country's daily water consumption. A national average
of 20 percent of family income is spent on qat, with many families closer to 50
percent. The locals further deplete their budgets and health by smoking cigarettes while chewing qat and by washing down the sticky green mess with
two-liter bottles of Coke or Fanta.

Although I seldom put any raw foreign greens into my mouth without
peeling or disinfecting them, curiosity overcame caution and I chewed two
leaves of qat. They were so bitter I spit them out in less than a minute. I then
added some chewing gum as a sweetener, and that enabled me to chew four qát
leaves for five minutes, but to no effect. To get any sort of a buzz, you need to

wad up both cheeks with 50 to 60 leaves, which is why the island looks as if it's suffering from a severe mumps epidemic.

But Socotra is not without its charms and is hailed as the Galápagos of the Indian Ocean. Its plateaus are a UNESCO World Heritage site, a Global 200 Ecosystem, and the world's only home to the dragon's blood trees, stately arboreals shaped like upright umbrellas. They supposedly grew from the blood of a dragon who'd been gored in a titanic battle with an elephant, notwithstanding that evidence of the existence of either species has never been found on the island. For more than a thousand years the islanders have tapped the trees for their sap, which hardens into the dense crimson resin they call cinnabar. It became a staple of the ancient caravans, which traded it across Asia Minor for use as a paint pigment, medicine, stain for glass and Italian violins, wool dye, pottery glaze, ornament, cosmetic, breath freshener, and adhesive for false teeth. I bought home a baggie for those of my friends who needed some of these repairs.

I visited a cave big enough to hold my apartment building, snorkeled over four species of distinctive brown coral on the Diahann reef, and fed the world's cutest vultures— bright orange and yellow and almost cuddly—when they invaded my picnic at the bottom of Dacrah Canyon. They turned up their beaks at my offerings of tomatoes, cucumbers, and oranges, and only grudgingly ate an apple, but they loved my leftover pita bread.

Far as I could tell, the big daily event in the island's biggest town was the feeding of the goats. The five or six produce stores on the main drag closed around 4:00 p.m., and the grocers discarded the cardboard boxes they no longer needed. They tossed them into the middle of the street, where several dozen goats quickly descended on them, tore them apart with practiced skill, and chewed them up and chowed them down in a grand feast. Their clear favorites were the boxes labeled WASHINGTON STATE APPLES.

I may have established a new culinary trend on the island. When walking past the village fish shop—several big boards on the ground—I noticed the fishmonger hacking some prime albacore and bonito into chunks with a machete. I prevailed upon my hotel to buy a few pounds of that dark red tuna, then skin and bone it, wash it with bottled water, and then serve it to me raw with rice. It was delicious, some of the freshest sashimi I have ever had. The locals were terrified to eat any—"Raw fish? Are you crazy?"—but I persuaded a few of them to try a small piece, and soon they were all asking for more and marveling how they could really taste the fish flavor, while simultaneously economizing on cooking fuel, leaving more funds for *qat* consumption.

The problem was the condiments. As every sushi lover knows, the fish is merely a vehicle for ingesting the soy sauce and wasabi. I tried the hotel's "Sweet Soy Sauce," but it tasted like a melted Hershey bar. After sampling all that was in the hotel's cupboard, I found one sauce that was sufficiently salty. To get the vital wasabi bite I experimented with whatever I had on hand. I essayed some pulverized CIPRO from my medical kit, but it was too bitter, and also likely to raise a race of superbugs. I considered adding a schmear of SPF 50 sunscreen or some athlete's foot balm, but felt that neither of these would provide quite the piquant punch of the Asian radish. I settled for the Heinz mustard.

On my last night, ten Taiwanese tourists checked into the hotel, saw what I was eating, started shouting "Sushi, sushi," and demanded that they be served the same on the following evening. It might be the start of a food fad, but I'm sure it will not displace the *qat*.

I returned to Sana'a the same day that a German national was kidnapped by tribesmen from Yemen's Maghreb region, who hoped to exchange him for several of their brethren who were in prison for various antigovernment activities. As this was the ninth kidnapping of a foreign tourist from Sana'a in the year, I figured it was time for me to get out of Dodge.

I flew to Beirut the following day and drove through one of its suburbs about 30 minutes before a suicide bomber blew himself up on the same spot.

I was down to the Savage Seven.

# CHAPTER 28

## Guerrillas and Gorillas

Some days a guy just can't catch a break.

Gulf Air goofed on my flight to Ethiopia, stranding me for 33 hours in Bahrain, not normally a bad place to be stuck for a day—unless it happens to be a major Shia holiday and the Shia are angry because the ruling Sunnis had called in Saudi troops to crush a Shia-led rebellion.

When I strolled through the diplomatic quarter in the capital of Manama a minivan exploded behind me. When I retreated to my hotel, the pool was frigid and none of the gym equipment worked. When I turned on the telly, I learned warfare had resumed on the border between Sudan and South Sudan, which I was scheduled to visit in ten days. When I went to a beachside bowling alley, no ball fit, and I rolled a 53. And Gulf Air refused to honor its obligation to pay for my hotel and meals.

Some days it truly does not pay to get out of bed. Even if you are in it alone.

The next day I arrived in Ethiopia, where Andrew Doran rendezvoused with me at the airport, in Addis Ababa. But he was not the eager, macho, tough guy I'd known; he appeared tired and confused. He attributed it to jet lag, but it later proved to be something far more serious.

My main objective in Ethiopia was to visit Dinkneh Tamire, a seven-year-old boy I supported through ChildFund International, in his small village 200 km east of Addis. I had arranged, during the preceding ten months, by many international snail mails, to visit him during this trip, and for at least four months ChildFund knew I wanted to buy his family a female goat to get them on the road to self-sufficiency. I chose goat, the "soccer of meats," because it's popular everywhere in the world (except North America) and because it's the easiest to raise and will eat almost anything. It's the least demanding on the environment, requiring only 127 gallons of water to produce a pound of meat, while a pound of chicken takes 468 gallons, and a pound of beef sucks up 1,800.

But had anyone there located a suitable goat or begun to look for one? Of course not.

I met Dinkneh and his mother at his village, which sits astride the discontinued railway to Djibouti. We had a pleasant lunch, joined by our driver, our guide/translator from ChildFund in Addis, and ChildFund's local manager. Andrew had remained in Addis, where we were guests at the Danish Embassy residence. He said he needed to catch up on sleep.

After lunch I announced I was ready to buy Dinkneh the goat.

"But we cannot do that today," apologized the local rep, who was aware that it was the *only* day I could do it. "The livestock market is closed today."

And that, for him, was the end of the matter. No initiative. No creativity. No can-do attitude.

"Look," I said, "about ten minutes before we reached town we passed a flock of sheep and tribes of goats between the road and hills to the north. So let's drive there and buy one. When you want a goat, you go to where the goats are."

"But those goats may not be for sale."

"*All* goats are for sale," I shot back. "They are not children you keep forever. It's just a matter of the price."

Hence, much against the wishes of the driver and the bureaucrats, we piled into the 4×4, drove ten minutes back down the road, turned off onto the dirt track I'd spotted, and within five more minutes were on the tail of a herd of more than a hundred goats.

"Go buy the boy a goat," I told the Addis manager.

"But this man may not own these goats," the city dweller replied.

"Nonsense. You can tell by the way he's treating them that he is the owner."

"But he may not want to sell them," added the local rep.

"You will never know unless you ask."

They came back: "He said he was not yet ready to sell any goats."

"He's just bargaining. Tell him I want a healthy female and will pay 600 birr," I said, quoting a price I knew to be about ten dollars higher than the going rate.

After another conference with the shepherd, they reported back: "He says he will only sell you a male."

No way.

After more dickering, I bought Dinkneh a male and a female for $65, but I was concerned because the male Dinkneh's mother had selected was the year-old son of the female we bought.

I told the translator to tell her she must not breed the female with its son.

All the Ethiopians thought this was a splendid dirty joke and roared with laughter.

This was not funny, I explained. "If you want a goat to give birth to healthy kids who produce a good supply of milk and meat, you never mate mother and son."

Sadly, after more than a thousand years of raising goats, sheep, and cows, and at least a score of years during which the USAID, CARE, and Heifer International had labored to teach Ethiopian herdsmen the basic principles of animal husbandry, they remain ignorant, with inbreeding common and highly detrimental.

When the translator firmly told Dinkneh's mother she must never mate the female with the son, and that when the dam came into heat, she must mate it with a male from a neighbor, she was puzzled. When I told him to explain that it was necessary to expand the gene pool, it got translated that I wanted her to build a large pool where people could swim wearing jeans.

When ChildFund gave me a tour of its schools, I began to understand the cause of the problem: The kids are not taught to think; memorization and recitation fill most of the day. They learn factoids and definitions, math formulas and the periodic table of the elements, but they are not taught to solve problems, to be creative, to look ahead, to think things through.

This disadvantage afflicts many Africans, from the lowliest cart drivers to top government officials. The drivers, for example, fail to realize that when they're driving a dull-colored old vehicle without reflectors and it breaks down at night, other cars are likely to smash into it on the narrow roads unless they provide adequate warning. Yet they uniformly put only two dark rocks on the road about ten feet behind the broken vehicle. The governments also fail to think ahead, as, for example, in their contracts with the Chinese, who are on a rampage across the continent, buying up all the oil, mineral resources, and farmland they can. In exchange, the Africans usually ask for infrastructure projects, but overlook their need to be properly run and maintained. As a result, they are ending up, across the continent, with Chinese-built roads that crumble in three years, railroads whose rolling stock is often sidetracked with mechanical failures, and factories that the locals have not been adequately trained to operate or maintain. This shortsightedness is endemic and easy to understand in a vicissitude-plagued continent whose people have learned, the hard way, that it seldom pays to plan ahead because one long drought, locust invasion, dictator, revolution, tribal feud, or other aleatory event can wipe out a lifetime of savings and planning.

Before I left Dinkneh, I took him to the nearest town and bought him new clothes, although he was intrigued by my heavily taped jungle pants. For several years they'd been threadbare from the knees to the cargo pockets, where I'd mended them repeatedly with massive patches of duct tape, applied inside and out, in the hope of coaxing this one last journey out of them. I was flashing so much shiny metallic tape I looked like RoboCop.

One unanticipated benefit of this decor was that when we were driving back to Addis and I stopped to purchase some produce at a roadside market, the vendors quoted me a price far lower than the typical tourist price. As one woman explained after she sold me eight pounds of tomatoes for less than two dollars at a makeshift market beside a small lake in the Great Rift Valley: "We think that if some *faranji* wears clothes like you, he must be even poorer than we are." The strawberry sellers at the same market were surprised, but impressed, when I insisted—politely but firmly—on getting the one birr (six cents) in change I was owed after a purchase. "We assume," one vendor told me, "all white people are rich and do not care about small change." I don't believe that's a favorable image to impart to poor Africans, so I did my best to dispel it.

At the market I saw in watermelons the results of the same ignorance of basic genetics as with the goats. The melons had so many seeds they were almost inedible. The evolutionary battle of natural selection had been won by those melons that produced the most seeds, and consequently produced the most offspring, not because farmers had consciously chosen their seeds from melons that were tasty and pulpy.

We didn't get to read much about politics in Ethiopia because the country was run by a stern autocrat (who died while this book was being written) and his Marxist-Maoist clique, who are not fans of democracy or freedom of the press. The government had just ousted the reporters for *The New York Times* and *The Washington Post*, with the result that my pal, Peter Heinlein of the Voice of America, with whom I stayed in Addis, was the only fearless and unfettered journalist left in the country, which made him a marked man, and one who would have been booted out or imprisoned years ago were he not married to the powerful Danish ambassador.

After I returned to Addis, I picked up Andrew, who had not left his bedroom during the two days I was gone. We flew to N'Djamena to complete my twice-thwarted attempt to visit Chad.

Andrew and I had not been in Chad for a full minute before the shakedown began, as was to be expected in one of the world's most corrupt countries. An immigration official stamped us in and directed us to one of his colleagues at the far side of the entry hall, where the uniformed officer rubbed his thumb and fingers together and said, "Money, money, money." He asked Andrew for a bribe of "fifty dolla," pay or you stay at the airport. Andrew meekly gave it to the officer without a word of protest, which was way out of character for him.

When the officer demanded $50 from me, I told him, in my most forceful French, I had already paid for my visa.

He looked unimpressed: "Money, money, money."

I told him the Chadian ambassador in the U.S. had assured me I did not have to pay more money to enter Chad.

He looked at me as if I were a simpleton; "Money. Money."

I asked him to show me the regulation that required me to pay.

He looked at me as if I was a troublemaker.

I told him I would pay him only if he gave me a signed receipt.

He choked with laughter and shared the joke with two of his colleagues who were waiting for their cut of the loot.

I flipped over my passport and pointed to the business card that I had, for this very purpose, inserted under the clear plastic protective cover. It bore an engraving of the White House and stated that Albert Podell was Barack Obama's "Presidential Partner." I emphasized that the building—my home base?—was *"La Maison Blanche dans Washington."* (The president had sent me ten of these impressive cards in 2009 to thank me for having been a large and early donor to his campaign, and this was the first time I'd used it for anything other than picking up women.)

The price of the bribe dropped to $15.

I had only a 20, which I gave him, and asked for change. For this I got the biggest laugh of the day and a wave to get-the-hell-out, now.

Corruption like this is endemic in Africa. It is unfair, wearying, invasive, disheartening, and destructive. But it can be turned to good advantage, as we later did.

To secure a visa for Chad, I'd booked our first night at the overpriced Novotel La Tchadienne, one of the few establishments that could provide the letter of invitation required for the application process. The hotel was a mere shade of its glory days, when French tourists thronged to Chad for some fun in the sun and sand. It was French to its core—the room contained a full dozen complimentary condoms of the Prudence brand, with its straightforward slogan, emphatically applicable to this AIDS-ravaged area: "Abstinence, Fidelity, or Prudence."

After we had hobnobbed with the rich and powerful by the Tchadienne's large but freezing pool for a day, we moved into Spartan quarters at a local missionary guesthouse, where my Cornell cohorts Carl and Karen had worked for the past 13 years.

I had chartered a plane from a local flight service to fly Andrew, Carl, Karen, and me down to the edge of Lake Chad, but it turned out to be such a windy, dusty day in N'Djamena that our plane was not allowed to take off. The airport lacked the instrument needed for this kind of weather, and it was not expected to be delivered for three months.

So as not to waste the day, Carl and Karen took us to visit one of their many Chadian friends, Colonel Aran of the Presidential Guard. He graciously received us in a heavily carpeted large tent in his family compound, where his three wives served us glasses of delicious, scalding, sweet mint tea, while several of the younger of his "about 20" children snuggled in his lap and sneaked peeks at the foreigners as the colonel regaled us with his quintessential African story.

Twenty years before, when Aran had been a wild young kid, he joined Idriss Déby's 2,000-man Patriotic Salvation Army (MPS in French), helped him overthrow the government of Hissène Habré, and became a member of Déby's inner circle. He later grew dissatisfied with Déby's administration, defected from it, and joined the United Front for Democratic Change (whose unfortunate French acronym is FUC), an anti-Déby rebel movement operating from Sudan. After two years of rebelling, followed by some delicate negotiations, Aran rejoined Déby's government as a highly placed colonel in his Presidential Guard and actively fought against his former FUC buddies during their attack in early February 2008 (when my plane could not land in N'Djamena). It is not possible to find a U.S. analogy. The closest might be if a member of the Symbionese Liberation Army or Weather Underground joined the president's Cabinet, then defected to the Branch Davidians or the skinheads, then rejoined the government and was appointed deputy director of the Secret Service. But, again, TIA.

The colonel and I managed some quality face time, aided by fluent translations from Carl and Karen, and we bonded as kindred spirits, after which he ardently advised me to "take a wife or two, so you have someone to massage your rheumatism in old age."

He then invited us, and two of his brothers, and two of his children, to travel—all in Carl's 4×4—two hours east of the capital to watch the horse races scheduled for that afternoon in his brother's village.

It was a turn-of-the-century scene, a thousand Arab men—only men—lining the race route, dressed in spotless white cloaks, with white scarves pulled across their noses and mouths to keep out the desert dust and keep alive an ancient tradition. I saw some superb horsemanship during the four races, each about 800 yards along a large oval track of hard-packed dirt outside the village. One rider fell off his horse, one horse fell on his rider, one loser protested the result until the announced winner was disqualified, after which a few fists flew among those who felt wrongly deprived, and a good time was had by all.

Back in N'Djamena, it was evident that Chad was in sorry shape. The capital was utterly listless—little activity, little joy. The people looked traumatized, which is understandable after several decades of rebellions, civil wars, genocide in Darfur, unresponsive governments, distrust, oppression, and widespread corruption. Andrew did not react well to this atmosphere and, after walking only two blocks with me, excused himself and rushed back to the safety of the guesthouse. What the hell was wrong with this tough guy who was supposed to be protecting me?

We eventually needed to avail ourselves of Chad's culture of corruption. The regime—ever wary—required foreigners to register within 72 hours of arrival. We'd arrived on a Thursday and we'd sought to register on Friday, but wherever we went—immigration, the police, the French Embassy, the Ministry of the Interior—no one knew where the rare tourist should go to register. Then all the government offices closed early for the weekend, leaving Andrew and me with glaring gaps in our passports where the immigration police had rubber-stamped a form that was to be filled in when we registered. They had warned us that the penalty for failing to register was severe, including detention. If we were not allowed to fly out on Sunday because of the missing registration, our ongoing itinerary would be a shambles.

On Saturday morning, while we'd been waiting in vain at the airport for the sandstorm to abate, Carl, aware of our problem, had undertaken some reconnaissance and, within ten minutes, had found a senior police officer who offered to meet us at the airport the next day—his day off, he emphasized—to grease some palms and facilitate our departure.

Because Carl is both a good Christian and a guest of the government, he did not resort to outright bribery to secure our freedom, as when you specifically pay an official to achieve a certain result. Instead, using his extensive knowledge of Chadian culture and mores, he conveyed to the cowboy cop, without mentioning money or any amounts thereof, that the cop's intercession on our behalf would be appreciated. "Highly appreciated."

On Sunday morning, with our bags packed and those empty forms burning holes in our passports, Andrew and I and Carl rendezvoused with the cop, who made the rounds of his colleagues for 30 minutes, after which we were whisked through immigration with VIP dispatch as every official in the area pointedly looked the other way. I wouldn't try this technique at JFK, but it's SOP in much of Africa and enabled us to stay on schedule and, via Addis and Nairobi, catch the Midnight Special flying to Mogadishu.

Mogadishu was a blast, but, fortunately, not literally. Although widely deemed "The World's Most Dangerous City," I was pleased to find that, after some 30 years of battling warlords and radical Islamists, it was returning to some form of normality. Two months before, Al-Shabaab had been driven out of all but two northern sections, with so many jihadis killed that they were no longer a match for the 9,000 African Union (AU) and UN soldiers protecting the town.

I visited the spot where the helicopter from *Black Hawk Down* went down and saw some of the heavy parts of the chopper embedded in the clumps of cactus. I walked along dazzling Lido Beach, a world-class strand of wide white sand bordered by war-shattered villas, with not one surviving roof or window in a mile. In the reopened outdoor market in the heart of town I found an authentic Somali-style stool to add to my African stool collection, then at ten. I visited a large IDP (Internally Displaced Person) camp where, despite having nothing but a few pieces of cardboard and plastic garbage bags over their heads for improvised tents, and only getting one meal a day from the refugee organizations, the people—mostly women and children; their husbands and fathers are dead—were exceptionally warm and accessible, eager to pose for photos, and delighted to see their digitized images.

But before you conclude that this sounds like a safe, ordinary, tourist trip, let me note that Andrew and I always had two hired guards walking in front of us with AK-47s locked and loaded, two similarly armed guards walking

Andrew Doran, who accompanied me to the Savage Seven, and is trained in martial arts, sits with three of our six heavily armed Somali guards in Mogadishu. We rode in a bullet-proof window-tinted SUV while the guards both preceded and followed us in pickup trucks, searching for snipers and IEDs. *Andrew Doran*

behind us, plus one guard on each side, all wearing flak jackets, plus two security chiefs beside us, inside this protective square, scanning the roofs and sweeping the alleys with binoculars for killers or kidnappers, all trailed by two specially equipped, bullet-resistant 4×4s that were in constant contact by walkie-talkie, ready to pick us up instantly if any incident unfolded, the entire entourage guarding me and Andrew (at $770 a day) from the second we left our residence to the moment we returned.

Mogadishu was hardly likely to win a Safe Cities award anytime soon, but the expat who headed our security provider optimistically opined that, "Mog is coming back. My construction business is flourishing. Mog might soon be a boomtown. Those wrecked, abandoned houses on the beach may be worth a million bucks in a few years. You can buy one today for next to nothing. You'll see. You'll know we've made it as soon as Mickey Dee, KFC, and the Russian hookers move in."

A representative of the AU Mission, which provided the troops to clear the jihadis out of the country, told me that two of Mog's main markets had just reopened, people were "streaming back" to their homes, roads were being repaved, houses rebuilt, and Mog was "experiencing a resurgence." The prime minister summed it up: After 20 years of competing warlords, pirates, tribal extremists, and religious fanatics, "Somalis are sick and tired of being sick and tired."

But the rest of the nation was not in the control of the government or the AU; it was lawless, with seven million people facing starvation. Their only alternative—making the long, difficult, and dangerous journey to the refugee camps on the borders of Kenya—was not viable because those camps were already filled to over 500 percent of capacity, and the process of getting food to them was rife with corruption. Yet, despite this, the moribund economy was coming to life in a few spots as nomadic Muslim shepherds sold hundreds of thousands of goats and sheep to the northern livestock markets, from which daring Lebanese and Saudi traders exported this prized halal meat to Mecca to feed the annual two million foreign pilgrims.

From Somalia I flew, alone, to Juba, the capital of South Sudan. Andrew had become increasingly weird and paranoid. He declared that, despite our earlier agreement, he would not go with me to South Sudan, but would travel on his own to Kenya and take a "safe" tourist safari with a guide. When I asked him what was wrong, he became angry, insisted he was fine, and refused to disclose more. I had no idea what was causing his atypical behavior, but had no doubt that something was significantly amiss. He agreed, albeit reluctantly, to meet me in Kampala, the capital of Uganda, in ten days, to begin the long journey through guerrilla country.

South Sudan was then in the final stages of the euphoria that followed its independence, still less than six months old, and before the inevitable hangover hits and reality bites, as it must. Wherever I looked, I saw T-shirts and signs proclaiming the glory of freedom and the elation of liberty, but I saw no tangible signs of reconstruction or advancement. Every billboard was tied to independence, from those advertising that freedom meant having a cell phone to those declaring that WE SAY NO TO VIOLENCE AGAINST WOMEN IN OUR NEWLY INDEPENDENT NATION—but those women were the only ones toiling in the heat. And I was shocked when I learned that a larger number of South

Sudanese teenage girls died each year during childbirth than were trying to complete primary school!

Almost every South Sudanese I talked to was enthralled to finally have a state of their own after 57 years of nasty civil war (a peaceful hiatus prevailed from 1972–1982); to have "The People's Own President," the Stetson-wearing lieutenant general who'd led their fight to freedom; and to finally have a government of their own, that cared about them (as the biased Arab/Muslim one in Khartoum never did), in a new nation where they might speak freely, assemble without fear of any secret police, and pursue their dreams. They had hope, ambition, and oil, but they were so impoverished and un-educated, and their land had been so long deprived of funding from Khartoum, and so shattered by the fight for freedom from the North, that experts estimated a best-case scenario would take South Sudan at least ten to 12 years to become a fully functioning and self-sufficient state—and that was only *if* all went well, and *if* Sudan did not attack them, and *if* Khartoum let them use its pipeline to export their oil to earn foreign exchange, and *if* South Sudan's mutually antagonistic Big Men were able to cooperate rather than fight, and *if* the age-old animosity between South Sudan's main tribes did not deteriorate into warfare, and *if* their people dreamed realistic dreams. The world's newest nation was a big *If*.

Numerous problems remained to be solved, high among them the unat-tainable expectations that had accompanied their independence. I met several veterans of the war, some missing an arm or a leg, who proudly—or sometimes angrily—showed me their ID card from the South Sudanese People's Liber-ation Army and expressed dissatisfaction with the high prices, the mass un-employment, and the slow pace of reconstruction and oil development. One of them forced me to put my camera away when he saw me photographing the shabby outdoor market, because he was ashamed of it: "Come back in two years and we will have a city here . . ."

The most flagrant instance of overblown expectations came from a college sophomore I met when deplaning, who helped me find a room at the South Sudan Two Hotel. I treated him to dinner there the next evening—a tasteless buffet of rice, potato chips, macaroni elbows, and scrawny chicken, without a single vegetable, at thrice the price it cost in most of East Africa. He confidently told me that when he graduated in three years he expected to have a starting salary of 300,000 South Sudanese pounds a month, the equivalent of one million dollars a year! I remonstrated with him, told him he was nuts, reminded him that more than 60 percent of his countrymen lived on less than two dollars a day, that even hard-charging minibus drivers, who worked seven days a week, only netted $200 a month. But he bizarrely insisted he was right. And he was majoring in *economics*.

Perhaps this inability to think things through to a wise and valid conclusion is even more prevalent in South Sudan than in most of Africa, because this land had for decades been starved for food, health care, education, communication facilities, and everything else by the harsh regime in Khartoum that despised these non-Arabic Christians and animists. Small wonder that the three most popular shows on Juba TV—as compiled by my own, admittedly unscientific, market research—were patriotic speeches, soccer, and a syndicated wrestling program from the States called *TLC*, in which the combatants fight with tables, ladders, and chairs.

Take that economics major: I'd invited him to meet me at 7:00 p.m. at my hotel to discuss some business, but he came at 6:00 instead and left because he assumed I was out. He later told me he had pushed the door to my room, and when it didn't open, he presumed I was elsewhere. Did he try knocking on my door? No, never thought of that. Did he ask the receptionist if I was out? No, never considered it. Did he wait until our appointed time? You already know the answer. And remember, this kid is one of his country's intellectual elite.

Or consider the wiring in my hotel room: The fan on the wall sported two identically colored cords dangling an inch apart. One was the pull cord to turn it on; the other was a spliced wire for the current. Pull one in the dark and you get cooled; pull the other and you get cooked.

Or when I had to go to the South Sudan One Hotel to use the Internet: The driver dropped me off at 2:00 p.m. and agreed to return for me at 5:00. He never showed. I went to reception and asked them to call South Sudan Two (their downscale branch, where I was staying) to have the van sent back. None of the staff knew the phone number—of their sister hotel! It took three hours to get a ride back.

South Sudan prices were exorbitantly high for everything, as a result of the influx of aid workers from the UN and NGOs, all wanting to do good, but many causing unintended harm to the economy because they imported their Western valuations and spending habits. I've seen this same NGO-induced inflation in other new countries having small populations—Macedonia, Kosovo, East Timor—where the proportion of humanitarian workers was large enough to push up the prices. These aid workers are willing, and able, to spend $60 for a dinner in a land where most folks don't earn that much in a month. Then they plunk down 300 to 400 bucks a night at the few good hotels and further warp the economy. They pay five dollars for a minibus ride that should (and previously did) cost ten cents. They go to the market and pay whatever is asked, no matter how inflated by local standards, because it seems cheap compared to what they paid at home, and they're too busy or too dignified to bargain. But in the process they (and those they hire to cook and work for them) drive up the prices of beans, rice, meat, vegetables, and other staples beyond the purses of the poor locals. The consequence is, inevitably, that the sellers raise their prices to meet what the traffic will bear—and distort the economy for years.

I'm not opposed to those who want to do good—indeed, I donate regularly to many of these organizations—but I wish their workers would be more self-sacrificing and leave at home their insistence on air conditioning, new mattresses, toilets with seats, and fancy food. If they'd live in a more frugal style in these countries, and try to be more sensitive to, and fit into, the established local economy, they'd benefit by not destabilizing that economy and by developing more empathy for the people they're there to help. If you're there to help folks who subsist on two dollars a day, try doing that yourself for a few days. Walk in their sandals, shop from their pockets. You'll be all the better for it. And so will they.

I spent my last two days in Juba preparing to transition from the deserts and dryness of Saudi Arabia, Yemen, Ethiopia, Chad, Somalia, and South Sudan to the wet jungles and moist upland forests of Uganda, Rwanda, and Burundi. I disinfected everything (even the inside of my toiletries kit and the sports soles in my hiking boots) with iodine-pill solution, sprayed all my jungle clothes with pyrethrum to deter mosquitoes, finished off Tom Clancy's nine hundred-page *The Sum of All Fears* so I didn't have to drag it along, delighted the locals with gifts of used T-shirts, and tenderly cut the duct-taped legs off my old jungle pants to turn these faithful friends (who had seen me through some 60 countries in ten years) into shorts. I allocated my stash of dense, high-energy foods—cereal, peanuts, dried figs, dates, and power bars—to each of the remote campsites ahead, where food was scarce, and wrapped my medicine kit in extra insulation. I made an effort to catch up on the sleep I'd previously lost fitfully dozing under airport luggage counters while awaiting dawn flights. I consolidated supplies and containers to lighten my load from 80 pounds to around 70. (I'd left New York with 120.) I did my last wash of the trip (nothing will dry in the jungles), and I traveled six miles to find a cyber café to let my friends know that I missed them and wished them a Merry Christmas.

I informed the taxi driver who brought me from the cyber café to my hotel that I had to go to the airport the next morning at 11:00 a.m. and asked him to come for me. He agreed. But he never showed up. Aware of TIA, I had, as backup, also told the receptionist that I might need the hotel's van to take me to the airport, but when I saw her that morning she had forgotten, and the van was being washed in the Nile and would not return until afternoon. I knew that each of the twin South Sudan Hotels had its own van, so I asked for the other one. They told me it was "broken." When I asked how it was broken, they said, "No gas." I was unable to determine if that meant no gas in the vehicle, no gas in Juba, no gas in the whole country, or no gas between their ears.

I raised my voice—just a bit—and told them I *had* to get to the airport. The receptionist, the assistant receptionist, the guard, and the manager huddled and conversed, but none of them had any idea how I could get to the airport. "Maybe you could wait until tomorrow?"

"Do you have any guests checking out this morning?" I asked.

Yes, they did.

"Well, many of your guests came here in their own cars. There are a dozen in the parking lot. Why don't you ask one of them if they would give me a ride to the airport?"

They were stunned. Transfixed. Stupefied. They had never done this! Never even thought of it. And they could not absorb my suggestion.

Just then a man in a business suit with a large suitcase checked out and headed for a car.

"Excuse me, sir, but if you are going the airport, can you give me a lift?" I asked.

No problem.

I found the attitude of Air Uganda ("The Wings of East Africa") refreshingly realistic and practical. No instructions on door dynamics to us passengers seated by the emergency exits. No preflight safety video. No announcement about what to do if our tired commuter jet crashed in the jungle en route from Juba to Kampala. And no stewardess standing in the aisle pulling life-vest toggles and blowing into inflation tubes, as if we might actually survive an "over-water emergency." This four-year-old shoestring airline knew that if we were going down, we were going *down*. So the crew skipped all that useless salvation stuff.

They did tell us to tighten our seat belts, but that was primarily meant to curtail traffic to the galley for free Tusker on a route where a majority of the passengers seemed determined to set a record for most cans of beer drunk during a one-hour flight, likely inspired by the Tusker billboard at the airport featuring a photo of a well-endowed babe in a bikini embracing the copy line: GOOD BODY GREAT HEAD NEVER BITTER.

Although I seldom venture out at night in an African city, Kampala reputedly had fewer thieves and thugs per capita than most of the continent's capitals, tempting me to consider walking the kilometer from my hotel to catch Midnight Mass at Christ the King Church to see how it stacked up against St. Pat's.

"Is it safe to walk around tonight?" I asked my taxi driver, en route to town from the airport.

"No!"

"But don't the robbers take the night off for Christmas Eve?"

"No. They work extra hard to make a good Christmas for themselves. And YOU will be their Christmas."

Not me, sports fans. I suddenly remembered I was Jewish, and decided to go to bed early and save my ecumenical efforts for daylight.

Before I turned in I got a call from Andrew, who had not shown up at our hotel. He told me he was at the Sheraton, sick, heading home, abandoning our trip, and that, sorry, I'd have to watch my own back. I took a cab to the Sheraton and found him in bad shape.

I have no idea what he ate or drank after we'd separated, but he'd picked up some bad bug and had painful cramps, hourly diarrhea, and other indicia of GI distress. I usually recommend that, if someone gets the tourist trots, they just let nature take its course, with the result that everything will usually come out all right in the end (so to speak). But Andrew had symptoms of amebic dysentery, and he'd soon be stuck in an airplane for many hours, which mandated more active intervention. I gave him Immodium (with a Kaopectate backup) to curtail the toilet trips and a regimen of metronidazole to kill the bugs.

I also finally understood the cause of his recent odd behavior: He was experiencing severe psychological distress from the mefloquine hydrochloride he'd been taking to prevent malaria. Its side effects can include sharp mood swings, paranoia, insomnia, nightmares, anxiety, depression, confusion, hallucinations, irritability, and other semipsychotic effects in about 70 percent of those who take it. "It causes toxic brain injury," said a former Army doctor now at the Johns Hopkins School of Public Heath, and CBS News had summed it up in a report: "In plain language, it can make you lose your mind."

I'd tried it twice, five years before and two years before, and I had to quit each time after just one pill and switch to Malarone. I'd warned Andrew about it a month before we left the States, but he explained that he preferred to use the once-a-week mefloquine to the one-a-day Malarone. Since he was set on using it, I told him to at least test it out for a week or two before he left the States to see if it caused him any psychological problems. I should have realized that Andrew, as an ultra-macho kid, would likely opt to tough it out regardless of the increasing discomfort and disorientation.

Fortunately, the symptoms usually disappear within a few weeks after taking the last pill, so he'd likely be better by New Year's. But the poor kid had a really crappy Christmas. So to speak.

After Andrew headed home, I toured Kampala and became aware how totally different the street life had been in each of the capitals I'd visited on this swing. Their signature characteristics were:

Riyadh—A lot of overweight and often overbearing men in spotless white robes with red-and-white checked head scarves followed, a diffident pace or two behind, by a woman covered from head to toe with a shapeless black robe, of whom only the eyes could be seen—although you are not supposed to look.

Addis—More than a hundred thousand undernourished, skeletal people—mostly withered old men, or women carrying sickly babies—begging, incessantly and insistently, for something to eat in a poor land where upward of seven million are famished at times.

N'Djamena—A plethora of uniformed police and military strutting about, keeping watch, while the populace shrank away.

Nairobi—Lots of upright guys in dark business suits and shiny ties bustling about in the heat, toting briefcases and looking as if they were rushing to important meetings.

Mogadishu—Heavily armed cars with tinted windows, machine-gun nests at many intersections, no traffic lights, few pedestrians, innumerable ruined buildings.

Juba—The women sitting in the sun of the open-air market hawking their tomatoes, carrots, and cucumbers while several hundred unemployed men, former soldiers, sit in the rare shade beside an unpaved road looking slightly stunned that their long-sought and hard-fought independence has not brought instant prosperity.

Kampala—Dozens of enterprising young dudes hanging out beside motorcycles on the corners politely asking if you need a ride to anywhere in the city, whose seven steep hills make Rome look like a landing field.

I hopped aboard one of these rigs for a trip to the Kasubi Tombs of the Buganda Kings, a neglected UNESCO World Heritage site high on a grassy hill at the edge of town, where four of the last kings are buried, the symbol of the political, social, and spiritual state of the ancient tribal nation. I soon feared I was about to join those entombed elders, because it turned out to be the scariest motorcycle ride of my life. The driver plunged through the traffic-clogged streets and hills at full throttle, as if this were a motocross competition rather than a means of transportation. He jumped curbs and cut corners, drove atop raised median strips, scattered pedestrians, dared oncoming traffic to hit us, refused to stop for anything or anyone—and pretended not to hear me repeatedly screaming "Slow down!" And all his colleagues were performing the same stupid stunts in what I later learned was a regular ritual of boredom-breaking, fender-bending, fear-inducing bravado.

For the ride back on his bike—the unacceptable alternative was to walk for two hours down winding hill roads in the heat with his reckless colleagues zooming at me—I reminded myself that I enjoyed a little adventure. When that didn't soothe me, I buried my face in the driver's back, shut my eyes, and pretended I was elsewhere. After that ride, I did my Kampala sightseeing by foot—not out of cowardice, of course, but because I remembered I needed to get in shape for hiking up the volcanoes to the gorillas in the Virunga a couple of weeks down the road.

But first, it was time to buy Amiina the goat I'd promised her.

The drive to her village in southeastern Uganda was completely different from the drive to visit Dinkneh in Ethiopia. That had been a wan concolorous landscape as drab as unbleached linen, where even its main crop of the grain known as teff was the color of sand. But the Uganda through which we passed was 30 shades of green, with every square inch of the lowlands from Kampala to the Nile sprouting sugar cane, rice, bananas, cassava, palms, plantains, and pineapples. Though the rainy season didn't resume until March, I was refreshed by a two-hour tropical downpour, the first drops of rain I'd felt in more than 40 days.

Amiina turned out to be a real charmer, shy and sweet and gentle. Her English was limited to "Thank you very much," but she'd start studying it in school the next year. She wanted to become a doctor, which Uganda can certainly use more of. I'd become aware of her, and had started to support her on an annual basis, through ChildFund International. I decided, after meeting her, to support her until she is 18, to at least give her a fair shot at getting into college instead of being forced to abandon school to make charcoal or bag groceries.

I met her mother and father, who had framed the photo I'd mailed them of me, and who gave me woven mats, and a straw hat, and a small purse made from bark cloth, all of which embarrassed me because I did not want these poor people spending money to get me presents. I also met her aunt and baby brother and took the whole family, and three of the NGO workers, to lunch in Buwenge at an eatery dubiously named the Hunger Clinic. We had a typical, tasteless, super-starchy, Ugandan meal of boiled potatoes, white rice, mounds of mashed plantains, chicken, some bony mystery meat, collard greens, and Orange Fanta. It was Amiina's first meal in a restaurant and she loved it.

I bought Amiina a healthy female goat, which she named Kitabo ("gift"). The price was up to $42 because of the holiday season. I also gave her a bottle of 500 Vitamin Power capsules I'd brought with me, and bought her a pretty dress and a crafts necklace in Jinja, the second largest city in Uganda. I gave her dad several packs of "Camel" cigarettes made in Germany. We then drove in the aid agency 4×4 to the source of the Victoria Nile, where it issues forth from Lake Victoria on its journey across Uganda to merge into the White Nile. Amiina had never seen the Nile before—had never seen *any* river before—and she just stood there for half an hour with her eyes wide and her mouth open.

I was disappointed by my inability to show her Bujagali Falls. We drove there after lunch, 13 km from town, but it no longer existed. Uganda had completed a 750-megawatt power dam on the Victoria Nile two months before, and the once-fearsome series of rapids was now a placid lake. This passes the glory of the world.

I loved playing daddy for a day, but that's probably all the childcare time I'm good for.

I was impressed with how ChildFund allocated the donations it received from the 3,000 of us who sponsor children in Amiina's area. Instead of using the funds to build schools, as did its counterpart in Ethiopia, it sends their kids to the public schools, which it assured me were quite good, and employs the funds for community development. The aid workers showed me a deep water well ChildFund had drilled, and for which it had supplied the pump, saving the villagers hours of walking to fetch safe water. They also showed me a piggery project that taught women how to care for, breed, and sell pigs; and a vocational training facility where adolescents who have little academic ability or inclination learn to be tailors, shoemakers, or beauticians, and become self-supporting.

As we drove back to Kampala, I worried about what kind of a future Amiina would have. Although more prosperous and stable than most African nations, Uganda is still a land of limited economic opportunity. Ugandan girls traditionally marry young, and Ugandan men are notoriously promiscuous. The nation had more than a million people living with AIDS, and more than 1.2 million young children who were AIDS orphans, although a recent educational initiative had curtailed the infection rate. How can I help Amiina avoid this fate when I live 8,000 miles away? Will her education in Uganda public schools be sufficient to enable her to pass the college entrance exams? Will she manage to become a doctor? Or a nurse? Will I still be alive to find out? Do the rest of you who are fathers and mothers worry about your kids every day? Is this what parenthood is like?

(Within a year, Kitabo gave birth to Babiwe, Wayiswa, and four additional kids, and Amiina's family was prospering. As this book went to press, Babiwe also gave birth—to what I think of as my grand-kids.)


When I pack for these trips, I strive to exclude anything I will not definitely use, except antibiotics and pepper spray. I leave home self-sufficient for all but food, water, and detergent so that I'm never required to look for other essentials while traveling. It's sort of a game for me, an entertaining challenge to estimate beforehand exactly how many water purification pills or packets of iced-tea mix I'll consume during the length of the trip. The one exception for this trip was books: I knew I'd need more than the four I'd started with, but I didn't want to lug ten pounds of literature, so I waited until I reached English-speaking Kampala to restock on used paperbacks.

They turned out to be invaluable the next day when our 4×4 got a flat tire on the rocky road to Murchison Falls National Park. The jack the driver found in the back was three inches too short to lift the vehicle high enough to change the tire. Under the jack quickly went two thick books, *The Constant Gardener* and *City of Light*. Up came the car, and off came the tire. (The vehicle also lacked seat belts, working AC, working radio, working windshield washers, and interior lights but, hey, TIA.) The spare tire was, of course, the wrong size, but we managed to limp in to the Red Chili Campsite by dusk on New Year's Eve.

The Eve started out auspiciously from my perspective. I was erecting my tent when two wild warthogs, each the size of a wheelbarrow, ambled through the camp abreast, passed four feet from me, and disappeared into a dense thicket of vines and briars where, I later learned, they'd been making their den for the past year. They can sniff out a biscuit buried in the bottom of a backpack and tear up a tent to get to it, but I'd long ago learned my lesson from the bears at Yellowstone, so all my edibles were hung in plastic bags high in a tree. They didn't attack or threaten anyone, as warthogs are prone to do, but their fearless swagger through the camp revealed they knew that no mere mortal would mess with them and they could be relaxed and (almost) friendly. Just don't try to put a party hat on them.

I turned in after watching ten mated pairs of large marabou storks return to their chick-filled nests in a sprawling ironwood tree thirty yards away, and I fell asleep to the flapping of their wings and the musky scent of the hogs. For me a most Happy New Year.

The high point of New Year's Day was my visit to Murchison Falls, an hour's drive from the camp. These falls are a spectacular sight on the Nile's 6700 km journey to the Mediterranean and are, in the rainy season, our planet's most powerful surge of water, as the mile-wide Nile is compressed into a rock chasm only 23 feet across.

The rest of the holiday was a brutal, bone-jarring, nine-hour ride on rough dirt and rock road out of Murchison, past the shores of Lake Albert, through Queen Elizabeth National Park and the start of the Albertine Rift Valley, and on to Fort Portal, the entry point to some of the earth's most spectacular scenery and wildlife.

I pitched my tent for several days at Lake Nkuruba Community Camp, a charming retreat of monkeys and jacaranda trees set atop a grassy, tree-shaded hill several hundred feet above a photogenic volcanic lake, one of the few bodies of still water in Africa where it's safe to swim because it's not infested with crocs or with snails carrying schistosomiasis, a debilitating parasitic disease that is just behind malaria in its impact on tropical societies and economies.

A troop of a hundred black-faced vervets, who favored the tree on one side of my tent, and a barrel of 25 black-and-white colobus, who favored the other side, cavorted much of the day, playing tag, Capture the Flag, and let's-see-if-Albert-will-give-us-a-banana-as-ransom for his lens cap or his glasses or his baseball hat.

I hiked for several hard hours up a nearby mountain for a view of seven other crater lakes and to start getting in shape for the climb to visit the gorillas a week later.

The following days were a blur of Bigodi Wetland Sanctuary (127 bird species), Semuliki National Park (Pygmies and hot springs), the snowcapped Rwenzori Mountains (aka The Mountains of the Moon —the highest chain in Africa), Bwindi Impenetrable Forest (home to the only mountain gorillas left in Uganda), the Kibale Forest (famous for chimps), the town of Kabale ("The Switzerland of Africa"), where I had booked lodging in the Edirisa Museum, and beauteous Lake Bunyonyi (to which I hiked down and back up a thousand feet, hoping to whip myself into condition).

The future of this paradise, and the entire 920 miles of the Albertine, the western prong of Africa's Great Rift Valley that straddles Uganda, is in doubt. It contains some of the most desirable land on the continent—fecund soil rich in volcanic fertilizer, the highest biodiversity in Africa, sufficient altitude to be pleasantly cool and above the zone of malarial mosquitoes, good rainfall, and valuable mineral deposits—which has made it the target and destination of militias, farmers, cattlemen, and refugees, all grasping and competing for a piece of land, all pushing hard up against the boundaries of the reserves and parks, all at the expense of the wildlife.

When I'd commented favorably that every inch of arable land on my drive to Amiina was filled with crops, I'd failed to consider how that blessing can become a curse where the only remaining land not yet being farmed was in nature sanctuaries. The lack of cultivatable land is so acute in southwestern Uganda and northern Rwanda that families were terracing even the steepest hillsides to grow what they call "Irish" potatoes, often making terraces no more than a foot wide, backbreaking, inefficient labor, but preferable to starvation. (At lower elevations, they grow, in ascending altitude order, bananas, plantains, cassava, corn, sweet potatoes, and tea.)

Eons ago, the Nubian Plate moved westward as the Somalian Plate pulled eastward, rending the earth between them to create one of nature's deepest canyons and several of its fathomless lakes, including most of Africa's Great Lakes—Edward, Albert, George, Tanganyika, and Malawi. This is the region where Uganda, Rwanda, Burundi, and the DRC meet in mist-covered mountains; where Tutsi, Hutu, and Hunde murdered more than a million in the 1973–1974 genocide; where the Great African War (1992–1999) and the still-simmering Second Congo War claimed another five million lives, mostly from starvation and disease; where Ebola and other fatal diseases establish germ reservoirs in the wildlife; where the unsustainable birth-rates range from 4.5 to 6.4 children per woman; where the population will triple by 2050; where an average family of six lives on and farms half an acre; and where the LRA, FDLR, CNDP, RCD, AFDC, and MLC have raped, pillaged, and killed for more than two decades.

Add to this volatile mix the recent discovery of three major oil fields east of Lake Albert, enough oil to soon move Uganda into the big leagues as a producer, and you have a dire situation where Nature loses out. Forty percent of the lions in Queen Elizabeth National Park had been slaughtered by farmers in the past decade to avenge the depredations on their cattle. In DRC's Virunga NP, the first (1925) national park established in Africa, 120 rangers have been killed trying to protect its mountain gorillas from poachers and from timber cutters making charcoal. People who live nearby have petitioned the DRC government to reduce the size of that park by 90 percent. The president of Uganda, ever mindful of the voters, had steadfastly refused to evict any of the thousands of illegal squatters who are living in and burning and farming in Uganda's national parks. And the future is as misty as the tops of those towering volcanoes in the haze of an Equatorial afternoon.

I bused to visit the gorillas at the Parc des Volcans in northern Rwanda, home to 480 of the 786 mountain gorillas remaining on our planet, according to a thorough census in 2010. I joined a burgeoning coterie of ecotourists that had grown from 7,500 in 2003 to 26,500, putting more than $12 million a year of trekking fees into the park treasury, ten percent of which is shared with the locals or spent on such projects as trenches and buffalo walls to protect the crops from destruction by the wildlife. For now, the system is working because the villagers have accepted the notion that the animals have real value. The villagers in the hamlet of Kinigi, where I stayed, abutting the gateway to the park, have so taken the primates to their bosoms that they hold a festive annual ceremony to name the baby gorillas born the previous year, and boast how the park's gorilla population has increased 26 percent in ten years.

Permits must be reserved many months in advance (at $500 a person) and are handed out each morning at 8:00 a.m. to 80 people who are divided into squads of eight, each to visit, for one hour, a different one of the ten major habituated gorilla bands in the park. I got the Hirwa band, of which Lucky was the silverback boss, and which boasted a new set of twins, then seven months old.

In the old days, your group and its ranger trekked blindly through the multiple ridges and valleys of the steep volcanoes to search for its assigned gorilla band. That has changed. Now a ranger stays with each whoop of gorilla until it makes a nest for the night. He then returns to that nest early the next morning and keeps pace with the gorillas as they forage for food (bamboo leaves are a favorite) and informs, via walkie-talkie, the rangers at the base of their location. (For some reason they don't use GPS coordinates, but rely on landmarks.) It took us four hours of difficult hiking, including 2,400 feet of vertical climbing, until we reached Lucky and his delightfully rambunctious family of twelve, including the twins, each the size of a basketball.

The instructions during our orientation forbade us to approach closer than seven meters from any gorilla, but someone forgot to tell that to Lucky and his playful band, who often crawled, rolled, or knuckle-walked to within two feet of where we sat enthralled. I'd been chosen as our group's designated grunter, having won that dubious honor by most closely sounding like a gorilla. Accordingly, whenever Lucky or one of his band grunted at us, I'd return the grunt to show that we were all pals, the verbal equivalent of a dog wagging its tail. It was a rich, fascinating, enlightening, and unforgettable hour, especially when Lucky, roused from a nap by his squabbling younger kids, suddenly leaped up and bounded over our outstretched legs on the way to let those kids know, big time, that Dad needed some peace and quiet. Lucky clearly adhered to the obsolescent concept that you spoil the child if you spare the spanking.

Six thousand miles and more than 200 hundred years after the guns, germs, and steel of the American colonists uprooted the Native Americans who occupied lands sought by ranchers, farmers, and railroads, the Pygmies of Africa are suffering a similar fate because they occupy lands similarly coveted for "white progress," in this case ecotourism. The Pygmies had inhabited the vast Ituru Forest unmolested for a thousand years, until someone noticed they had the unfortunate proclivity of subsisting on bush meat, and had also, from time to time, been known for (or at least accused of) undertaking the contract killing of a gorilla for some mandarin in Hong Kong who wanted a hairy-foot ashtray for a conversation piece.

Whatever the truth, many Pygmies had been forcibly relocated from the forest depths with even less concern and provision than we made for our "Indians" when we dumped them into wasteland reservations. In the DRC, CAR, and Uganda, most Pygmies are now in tourist villages, where vacationers bring them salt, sugar, sewing implements, and cigarettes, while they pose for stiff photos. In Rwanda, they'd been recently relocated onto small patches of farmland, but these hunters had not been taught how to use it. I visited several of their plots of struggling potatoes, where it was clear to this old gardener that they did not understand the rudiments of tilling, planting, mounding, weeding, or watering—and that their crops will not survive. Their children whom I visited were home alone, their parents off getting drunk. Many of these kids were so weak and neglected that they seldom had the energy to attend school. Sometimes the Pygmies tediously plucked chrysanthemum flowers they sold for about two dollars a pound. The buyers turn the flowers into the insecticide pyrethrum; the Pygmies turn the cash into banana beer. If times are really hard, they will pull up their own seed potatoes to sell for alcohol.

Several groups of caring citizens in the countries involved were undertaking efforts to improve the status of their Pygmies, but prejudice persisted against the little folk because they were mistakenly regarded as stupid. But how stupid can you be if you've been able to survive for many hundreds of years in the densest forests with no help from "civilized society"?

Few of the citizens in this region of Africa have faith in their governments. In this entire quadrant composed of Ethiopia, Chad, Somalia, Djibouti, Eritrea, Uganda, Kenya, Rwanda, Sudan, Burundi, DRC, and Zimbabwe, there had been no fair elections, no representative government, no concern for the common citizen. Instead, the citizens were exposed to uncontrolled corruption, stuffed ballot boxes, false vote counts, imprisonment or execution of political opponents on fabricated charges, the muzzling of the press, the murder of investigative journalists, the warping of the judiciary, the cult of the Big Man and, despite solemn election promises, revisions pushed into national constitutions to allow the people who were in power to remain in power. All this has led, in most of these countries, to economic retardation, civil wars, crumbling infrastructure, deep cynicism, famines, starvation, high inflation, high infant mortality, low life expectancy, and a host of other woes. Of the six nations ranked the lowest in the Ibrahim Index of African Governance, five hailed from this region. Ironically, the only country in the region that had held free and fair elections and had a popular government was Somaliland— which is not even a recognized country.

My journey through this quadrant brought me to the front lines of a war—as yet undeclared and underacknowledged—of potentially supervening importance for the hearts and minds, resources and power, of a large swatch of Africa north of the Equator, a war that would have drastic consequences for the rest of the world if it finds fertile ground and escalates.

It's a struggle between militant Islam, on the one side, and moderate Islam and non-Islam on the other, between the deeply devout, proselytizing, and fervent followers of the Prophet Muhammad and those they condemn as infidels or pity as nonbelievers and blame for the "Westoxification" of their homelands. It is the same war Islam almost won a thousand years ago, when the Saracen sword slashed its bloody way to the walls of Madrid and the borders of China, but a war in which Islam today has three formidable weapons—nuclear bombs (in Pakistan and possibly Iran), control of the lion's share of the oil needed by the rest of humanity, and ample funding from some deep-pocket fundamentalists in the Gulf States. It is also a struggle for the soul of the Arab Spring, between that nascent Muslim attempt at representative government, pluralism, and self-expression, and the harsh, hate-filled world of the angry militants and their ultraconservative allies.

I witnessed Islam expanding in Ethiopia, one of the earliest states to convert to Christianity, and long evenly balanced between Christians and Muslims. The Christian areas, in the north and west, remained as they had long been, centered around their large, solidly stone, ornate churches. But the Muslims were moving in. Everywhere I looked—hamlets, villages, fields—they were buying old houses, stores, warehouses, and farms, erecting an adjacent two- or three-story tower to serve as a minaret, and, *voilà!*, they had a mosque sending forth its calls to prayer.

In Chad, I detected further signs of creeping Islamization. As I walked through villages, I heard the chanting of the Koran from madrassas behind high walls, where the Muslims were inculcating the youth, which may shift the balance of power there. The government, sensitive to the issue, announced a rally to celebrate Peace Among Religions Day in the capital's capacious Plaza of the Nation. I was one of the few people to attend.

In Somalia, the radical Islamists of Al-Shabaab still controlled large parts of the country, although neighboring Christian Kenya vowed to oust them. But they had already left their imprint on the citizenry. Somali women had previously been known for wearing the most resplendent robes, shimmering red and iridescent purple embroidered with gold. No more. Under the rule of the Al-Shabaab, which demanded modesty, they'd switched to all black or dull shades with few patterns. When I visited the central cathedral in Mogadishu, it was still a ruin, without steeple, roof, nave, arch, window, or pew, and the diocese had no plans to rebuild it. In contrast, the central mosque, which also had not escaped damage during the years of battle, had been totally rebuilt. It was standing proud, intact, and functioning on its hill overlooking the city— shining, beckoning, ready to do battle for the souls of the people, ready to fill the vacuum a passive Christianity had allowed.

In Kenya, the Islamic warriors have launched terrorist massacres and kidnapped and killed visitors, endangering that country's vital tourist business. Guides and vendors in Nairobi told me tourist traffic was off by two-thirds as a result of the post-election violence and the kidnappings.

Neighboring Tanzania was swept by religious riots during which twelve churches were burned and looted.

In Nigeria, radical Muslims in the northern half were challenging the power of their traditional sultans and emirs and were extending their influence to oppose anything they deemed at odds with their beliefs, including polio vaccinations. During Christmas, three churches were bombed and burned and more than a dozen Christians killed. And a radical Islamic group of killers and kidnappers called Boko Haram vowed to extend its reach to the entire nation, the most populous in Africa, the seventh most populous on the globe.

In Mali, the violent jihadis of Ansar Dine and Al-Qaeda in the Islamic Maghreb murdered a German traveler in Timbuktu and kidnapped his three companions shortly after I left, ruining the tourist trade on which Mali relied for foreign exchange, and began threatening to conquer Mali and turn it into a base for international terrorists. From Mali I also heard the saddest tale of all, impacting the Dogons who'd fled from Islam to the Bandiagara Escarpment. The Dogons are a nature-worshiping, spiritual people who rely on sanctuaries where they store their "spirit symbols" to make those artifacts readily available when a Dogon is feeling lost or depressed and needs to recharge his soul. Two travelers I met coming from Mali told me that radical Islamists had been inducting individual Dogons into their faith, sending them to camps in Saudi Arabia for training, and then ordering them back to their native villages with instructions to burn the spirit houses to shatter the souls and spirits of the Dogons.


Having been refused a visa to Angola, I used that freed week to travel, for two long days each way, to visit Somaliland, a province north of Somalia, whose people, fed up with the constant dangers farther south, had broken away from it 20 years before and established the world's closest entity to a country that is not recognized as a country. It's a pity and a political miscalculation that the Western democracies have kept Somaliland in what its foreign minister called a "twilight zone" by refusing to recognize it as an independent nation, even though it satisfies every requirement of statehood, because the West believes that such recognition will wreck their quixotic attempt to resurrect Somalia to its former borders and maintain the myth that the government in Mogadishu is in control throughout the land.

In Somaliland I heard freedom ring. Although consummately poor, it was a land of joy whose people were pumped and walked about free and proud. They had created a popular parliament that blended democracy with the traditional leadership of clans and elders. The streets resounded with happiness, laughter, bustling business, and exuberance for life. These were not the repressed, downtrodden denizens of the other East African states where Big Men held sway by perverting the political process. The grand arch welcoming me into Hargeisa proclaimed, EQUAL JUSTICE UNDER THE LAW, and these good people walked that walk in every way. Theirs was a government of, by, and for the people, with no corruption, no nepotism, no tribal favoritism, a model for the peaceful resolution of conflict and the construction of democratic institutions that flourished in these infertile soils. If Hitler, Marx, Stalin, and Mao could look upon this scene, they'd understand that their philosophies never had a lasting chance and that the human spirit craves something no dictatorial or collectivist society can offer.

The Somalilanders were so intent on preventing Islamic violence from infecting their country that they did not want to let me leave.

I'd checked out of my hotel in the capital of Hargeisa early, caught a minibus to the car park by the city limits, where the shared taxis waited to head for the border, and found myself in luck—an almost full car with room for one more. It was an old station wagon, and the mite of a room was in the seatless back compartment, where I'd be stretched out perpendicular to three guys who sat on the floor facing the dusty rear window. But at least I didn't have to wait hours for another car to fill up. I slithered in and started to get comfy, when an authoritative guy in a khaki outfit waved me to come out.

What luck! He was going to tell one of the guys in the front seat to yield it to the venerable foreign visitor.

Not.

The guy was a cop who politely, but firmly, asked me to grab my luggage and follow him, which, much dismayed, I did, for 200 yards—to the local police station and jail. No problem, he told me, but he needed to see my identity papers. After a half hour of that he ushered me into a blue police car, and off we went on a ten-kilometer drive to meet the chief of police of Hargeisa. He was equally polite, shook my hand warmly, told me, in a most circumlocutory manner, that he was concerned with general security, asked me a potpourri of questions about my travels and the U.S., looked a little incredulous when I insisted I was an American citizen— Hey, we can't all look like Brad Pitt!—and then told me that the chief of police for the entire district wanted to meet me—just for a short chat, you understand. I had no idea what was going on: Had I forgotten to pay for my hotel? I racked my brains, but could not noodle it out.

So off we went, across town, for a 30-minute ride, to meet two charming, gracious men in blue who welcomed me warmly, assured me I had committed no crime, asked some seemingly innocuous questions about the National League baseball standings (which I had not followed since the Dodgers left Brooklyn), and told me the chief of police for the entire nation of Somaliland wanted to meet me. During all this time I'd tried to explain I had a plane to catch in Ethiopia, places to go, people to see, deadlines to meet, etc., etc. All to no avail.

But if the chief of police for the entire country wanted to have a friendly chat with me about his cousin in Hoboken or whether I thought the Giants could win the Super Bowl, how could I refuse him? So off I went on a 30-minute ride to the military encampments outside of town, where the chief of police shook my hand, took one look at me, and said, "You are free to go," which was my first realization that all this had been more than idle curiosity or a courtesy call. When I pumped the chief, after showing him my Obama Presidential Partner card, he told me they were searching for a large-nosed, pot-bellied, bearded Saudi jihadist recruiter they'd been tracking, and that the police underlings thought I fit the description. Thanks, guys!

My fate could have been much worse: That same day, five European tourists were murdered, and four more kidnapped, in the volcanic wonderland of northeastern Ethiopia, at the *same place and time* I'd planned to visit had I not, at the last minute, opted for the arduous trek to Somaliland.

You just never know when the fickle finger of fate will beckon you, so grab all the gusto you can while you can.

# CHAPTER 29

## Plan X and the Gray-Blue Eyes

Once back in New York, I devoted much of a year to trying, in vain, to obtain a visa to Angola to complete my mission.

But I had run into an even more momentous problem. I had met, started dating, and was falling deeply in love with an amazing young woman named Nadezda Dukhina. She had been a journalist and TV reporter in her native city of Astrakhan on the north shore of the Caspian Sea, and had relocated to the U.S. four years earlier because she perceived far more opportunities for merited and career satisfaction here. She was exceptionally smart, gentle, warm, considerate, beautiful, passionate, realistic, nonmaterialistic, and loving. But there was one huge problem: She was *49* years younger than I was.

I wanted her to share my future, but I knew that was actuarially limited, and I did not want to mess up her life or deprive her of the opportunity to start a family with someone more suitable. I had no idea how to resolve this dilemma. But first I had to get Angola finished.

I concocted five plans for getting there:

**Plan A** was to take courses about diamonds at the Gemological Institute of America to qualify as a buyer of diamonds and enter Angola on a business visa. But, after the first week, it was apparent that my eyes (which had been damaged by Lyme disease) could no more distinguish the color, or clarity, or imperfections in a diamond than they could read a telephone book at forty paces. Abandon A.

Plan B was to ask my British friend Nigel Page, who was in charge of all the African routes for Emirates Air, to "hire" me as an expert on international travel and send me to Luanda, the capital of Angola, to inspect the airport facilities. But Nigel—even though he owed me big time because I had, long ago, parted from my girlfriend Claire, which left her free to become his wife, as she happily did—was too impeccably upright a gent to risk sullying his sterling reputation by aiding and abetting such chicanery. Banish B.

Plan C was to fly to Windhoek in Namibia, rent a 4×4, head north for a day or two, find an unpopulated spot near the Angolan border, and just sneak over, as I had done in Yemen and Equatorial Guinea. But after I read an article on the wretched conditions in Angolan prisons, this no longer seemed a reasonable option. Cancel C.

Plan D was to join a group of bird-watchers on a once-a-year tour of "Angolan Endemics," organized by a well-connected birding company in South Africa. This had serious drawbacks because the company did not guarantee I'd receive a visa, and my further inquiry disclosed that two of the four Americans who'd applied the year before had in fact *not* been granted visas. If I was declined, the birding company would keep $4,200 of my deposit, which I decided was too high a price to pay in view of the odds. Moreover, even if this stratagem did enable me to acquire a visa, I'd have to spend 18 days camped out with a bunch of bird nuts, which my previous experience with members of this species in New Guinea convinced me was an even higher price to pay. Dump D.

Plan E was to sponsor a child in Angola through a charity, and then arrange to visit him. Since I enjoyed my relationship with the kids I was supporting in Ethiopia and Uganda, this seemed like the perfect option. I contracted with SOS Children's Village International to support a young boy in far eastern Angola. But when I later wrote to take SOS up on the offer set forth in their promotional literature, which said they'd gladly arrange for a donor to visit his child, they informed me—without any explanation or rationale—that their policy firmly prohibited them from sending me the letter of invitation I'd need to visit Angola. A bizarre policy and the end of Plan E.

After this year of frustrations and failures, Plan X materialized. It required the cooperation of three Angolan citizens, one Portuguese, and one expat in the Middle East, all of whom splendidly carried out their tasks. After a few fits and starts, and some correctable misunderstandings and delays, Plan X succeeded, and on November 27, 2012, exactly 50 years, two months, and 14 days after I had visited my first foreign country, my TAP Airbus 330 touched down at Angola's Quatro de Fevereiro Airport in Luanda, and I was able to visit my last.

I have pledged not to reveal how this was arranged or the names of those who assisted me, because it would get them in very hot water with the government. But if you apply some of what you've learned in the previous pages about dealings in Africa, you can probably figure it out. (Just keep it to yourself.)

From the touristic standpoint, Angola offered little. There were no breathtaking scenes of natural beauty, just miles of boring fields. The people wore dull Portuguese-style clothing instead of the exotic or brightly colored garments favored in so many other parts of Africa. The food was similarly bland. Most of the animals in the game parks had been killed during the long civil war. And most of the locals were so busy scrambling around in their oil-boom economy that they had little time to fraternize. Luanda was growing so rapidly that everything was under construction or reconstruction, resulting in an unscenic forest of cranes and so many torn-up streets clogged by so many new cars that the traffic jams were the worst and widest-spread I'd ever been caught in, often consuming 15 minutes to drive one block.

The prices were the world's highest because the oil companies paid whatever was asked, with apartments renting for $4,000 to $20,000 a month. A miniscule room in a lowly motel cost at least $200 a night. A one-day round trip to a nature preserve socked you for $500. Wood carvings that sold for $20 elsewhere were priced at $200, and my souvenir shopping was hampered by the take-it-or-leave-it attitude that prevailed among the vendors, who refused to bargain. Fish and chips from a shack cost $25. Most offensive of all, when I asked for a little bag to take home my uneaten food, they charged me three dollars for it. For a doggie bag!

But none of this was of any personal consequence or diminished my feeling of fulfillment.

On 12/12/12, four days after completing my quest to visit every country on earth, I embarked on "life's greatest adventure," by marrying Nadezda Dukhina, a Russian writer and poet who was born twenty years *after* I had already finished my first expedition around the world. *Michael Alden*

On December 9, 2012, with my travel mission accomplished, I landed at JFK, where the glorious Nadezda was waiting for me with open arms. I mumbled a jet-lagged and embarrassingly inarticulate marriage proposal in the middle of the crowded terminal as tears welled into her lovely gray-blue eyes. She pressed her warm and welcoming body next to mine and assured me that—for reasons that to me remain inexplicable but wonderful—she loved this old dude with all her dear young heart and would be filled with joy to be my wife.

Three days later—on 12/12/12—we were married in City Hall and I embarked upon my last—and life's greatest—adventure.

THE END

# CHAPTER 30

## . . . And One More for the Road

When people learn that I've visited every country on our big blue marble, they often ask me one of three questions:

*Q. Which is my favorite country?*

A. The United States of America. Not because I'm chauvinistic or xenophobic, but because I believe that we alone have it all, even if not all to perfection. The U.S. has the widest possible diversity of spectacular scenery and depth of natural resources; relatively clean air and water; a fascinatingly heterogeneous population living in relative harmony; safe streets; few deadly communicable diseases; a functioning democracy; a superlative Constitution; equal opportunity in most spheres of life; an increasing tolerance of different races, religions, and sexual preferences; equal justice under the law; a free and vibrant press; a world-class culture in books, films, theater, museums, dance, and popular music; the cuisines of every nation; an increasing attention to health and good diet; an abiding entrepreneurial spirit; and peace at home.

My favorite foreign countries are, for scenery: Switzerland, France, Canada, New Zealand, Peru, and Nepal. For food: Mexico, France, Italy, China, Thailand, Vietnam, and Lebanon. For the type of women I like: Belarus, Russia, Germany, Ukraine, and the Czech Republic. For tranquility combined with hospitality: Ireland, Burma, Bhutan, Morocco, and most Pa-

Me with the Huli Wigmen in the Central Highlands of Papua New Guinea. All their decorative feathers and cassowary nose quills come from indigenous birds that these so-called "ignorant" tribesmen have harvested for centuries in a sustainable manner.

cific Island nations. For cultural heritage: England, Egypt, India, Cambodia, France, Spain, Italy, and Mali. For unspoiled beauty: Mongolia, Dominica, Costa Rica, the Sahara, and Antarctica. And for wildlife: alas, only Kenya, Botswana, and Tanzania are left.

Q. *Of all you saw, what most concerns you?*

A. Five developments:

1) The increasing evidence that global warming is a fact, and one about which not enough is being done.

2) The spread of a radical form of militant Islam through the Muslim world combined with its hatred toward others. And the increasingly violent schism between the Sunni and the Shia.

3) Schoolyards—in South Korea, Japan, India, China, Singapore, Taiwan, Germany, and Switzerland. Schoolyards filled with kids who show, in their dress, deportment, attitude, and actions, that they (in contrast to American kids) take school and the education it offers seriously, and respect and value

it as the surest path to advancement, a good future, and the opportunity to eat our lunch. I hope our new Core Curriculum will help correct this inbalance.

4) The increasing emergence and virulent nature of epizootic diseases, those that originate in birds and animals but infect humans as they push into the jungles in search of land and bush-meat protein. I am especially worried about those high-morbidity, quick-killing, fast-spreading new viral hemorrhagic fevers—Ebola, Marburg, Machupo, Nipah, and Lassa—all emerging from the forests in recent decades. These are diseases against which humans have no natural immunity, no tested and reliable vaccines or approved medicines, and no adequate public-health systems, enabling them to spread around the world with the speed of a jetliner and potentially devastate the planet with the worst pandemic since the black plague.

5) A band of hard-charging competitors—Asian tigers, African lions, and South American jaguars—increasingly becoming able to dine on our dinner. They have gleaming, efficient 21st-century infrastructure; abundant supplies of, or access to, raw materials; and, above all, citizens who are willing to work diligently, despite lower wages, to have a better and eventually more prosperous life for themselves and their children. If the work ethic I observed in the Western world continues to weaken, and we remain corpulent and complacent, we are history. Ancient history.

The third question most often asked is: *What do I wish had been different on these journeys?* And my answer is always the same: *Nothing.*

I believe you have to take troubles, misfortune, adventures, disruptions, disasters—whatever you choose to call them—as life throws them at you, make the best of them, and, if possible, try to use the accidentally cracked eggs to make a nourishing omelet or a piece of abstract art.

I certainly would have been safer and more comfortable and have fewer gray hairs if many events had not transpired: if Murphy had not visited Kiribati and wrecked my plane connections, if I'd not been nearly lynched in East Pakistan, almost drowned in Costa Rica, detained by the police in Kinshasa and Hargeisa, jailed in Baghdad (for which tale, as for a hundred other adventures, there was no room in this book), attacked by the flying crabs in Algeria, broken my ribs and ripped flesh and torn rotator cuffs in many lands, and if I'd managed to avert or avoid all the other incidents, accidents, break-downs, and derailments described herein.

But, to accentuate the positive, each of these events provided me with new coping skills, prepared me for the next rock or wreck on the road, and increased my confidence that I'd be able to extricate myself from almost any dangerous situation, to endure and survive, and gave me—I hope you agree—some great stories to recount.

Okay, to be totally honest, I would have enjoyed this quest far more if we had not crashed into the pig in Botswana, if I'd not been compelled to eat that poor monkey's brain in Hong Kong, if Steve had not been stricken with cancer, if that college girl in Malawi had not turned me down so effortlessly, if I'd made out better on my final visit to Oz, if . . .

Yet, at the end of the day, I was able to play the cards the world dealt me and survive to 196. Who else can say that?

# COUNTRIES VISITED

## In Chronogical Order

1937    United States of America

1962    Canada

1963    Spain, France

1965    Andorra, Morocco, Algeria, Tunisia, Libya, Lebanon, Jordan, Syria, Iraq, Iran, Afghanistan, Pakistan, Nepal, India, Singapore, Malaysia, Thailand, Cambodia

1966    Japan, Panama, Nicaragua, El Salvador, Costa Rica, Honduras, Guatemala, Mexico

1972    Great Britain / Dominican Republic

1977    Switzerland

1978    Monaco, Italy, Vatican City

1979    Sweden, Norway, Denmark, Germany, Belgium, Netherlands, Luxembourg, Liechtenstein, Austria, Cyprus, Greece

1981    Israel, Australia, New Zealand

1982    Jamaica

1983    Brazil

1984    Antigua

1985    Bahamas

1986    China

1987    Ireland, Peru

# COUNTRIES VISITED

1988   Egypt

1989   Kenya, Tanzania, Barbados, Ecuador

1990   Venezuela

1994   Latvia, Lithuania, Estonia, Russia, Finland

1998   Republic of Korea, Taiwan, Indonesia, Laos, Philippines

1999   Chile, Argentina, Uruguay, Paraguay, Bolivia

2000   Belize, South Africa, Swaziland, Zimbabwe, Cape Verde Islands

2001   Poland, Slovenia, Croatia

2002   Guyana, Suriname, Trinidad, Ethiopia, Eritrea, Djibouti

2003   Togo, Benin, Ghana, Turkey, Iceland, Belarus, Moldova, Ukraine, Romania, Bulgaria, Macedonia, Albania, Central African Republic, Cameroon, Sao Tome & Principe, Gabon, Equatorial Guinea, Georgia, Armenia, Azerbaijan

2004   Czech Republic, Slovakia, Hungary, San Marino

2005   Malta, Serbia, Bosnia, Montenegro, UAE, Kuwait, Bahrain, Oman, Qatar

2006   Senegal, the Gambia, Guinea-Bissau, Guinea (Conakry), Kyrgyz Republic, Kazakhstan, Uzbekistan, Turkmenistan, Tajikistan

2007   Maldives, Sri Lanka, Fiji, New Guinea, Tuvalu, Solomon Islands, Palau, Vanuatu, Marshall Islands, Micronesia, Tonga, Western Samoa

2008   Sudan, Niger, Burkina Faso, Mali, Mauritania, Ivory Coast, Liberia, Sierra Leone, Nigeria

2009   Colombia, Haiti, Cuba, Grenada, St. Vincent, St. Lucia, Dominica, St. Kitts & Nevis, Lesotho, Namibia, Botswana, Zambia, Malawi, Mozambique, Mauritius, Seychelles, Comoros, Madagascar, Democratic Republic of Congo, Congo

2010   Kiribati, North Korea, Mongolia, Brunei, Bangladesh, Bhutan, Burma (Myanmar), Vietnam

2011   East Timor, Nauru, Kosovo, Portugal, Saudi Arabia, Yemen

2012   Chad, Somalia, South Sudan, Uganda, Rwanda, Burundi, Angola

2014   Revisit Yemen and Equatorial Guinea legally

# COUNTRIES VISITED

**COUNTRIES VISITED THAT NO LONGER EXIST**

Czechoslovakia, East Pakistan, East Germany, South Vietnam, USSR, United Arab Republic, Yugoslavia

**TERRITORY: SELF-GOVERNING**

Aruba, Curaçao, French Guyana, Guadalupe, Martinique, St. Maarten, Saba

**TERRITORY: NON-SELF-GOVERNING**

American Samoa, Anguilla, Bermuda, Cayman Islands, Gibraltar, Guam, Hong Kong, Macao, Northern Ireland, Puerto Rico, U.S. Virgin Islands

# I GRATEFULLY THANK

Peter Joseph, my wise, careful, perceptive, knowledgeable, skillful, and patient editor at St. Martin's, who vastly improved my book. While I wrecked his digestion.

Tony Outhwaite, the most positive, passionate, informed, savvy, supportive, and devoted agent any writer could have, for making my dream a reality.

Wolfenden, publishers of the paperback edition of *Who Needs a Road?* for keeping it in print for more than 48 years after its first publication and for permitting me to use material from it for chapters 2 to 7 of this book.

Nan Prener, for her praise of my dispatches from the field, for her early enthusiasm for my doing a book, and for later thrice proofreading the entire manuscript, recommending many constructive changes, and catching many foolish mistakes.

Rick Guimond, my faithful secretary for 30 years, who input my hundreds of corrections and edits on sixteen drafts of the manuscript.

Polly Whittell, for recommending Tony, and for convincing me to cut certain parts of the book that were, believe it or not, far more offensive than those I retained. And the others who helped me search for an enthusiastic agent and a top publisher: Peter Finn, Steve Zimmerman, Harry Petchesky,

# I GRATEFULLY THANK

Larry Sutter, Neil Goldstein, Beverly Hyman, Larry Birnbach, David Hahn, Keven Danow, and Andrew van den Houten.

Harold Stephens, for inspiring me with a love of travel and adventure, for first getting me on the foreign road, for urging me to write this book, and for encouraging me to complete it.

Bob Prener, PhD, and Larry Sutter, J.D., the former for his scientific sagacity, the latter for his lawyerly logic.

David Smith, for a decade of giving me excellent advice on obscure airlines, arcane geography, little-known routes, and potential political problems and dangers along the way.

Professor Jon Surgl, for his painstaking ten-day review and correction of my 13th draft, which almost wrecked our friendship, but vastly improved the manuscript.

Nina Wehner Vitali, without whose vast network of helpful UN connections, I never would have reached 196.

Professor Jose Alvarez of NYU School of Law, for reading and correcting the chapter on what constitutes a country.

Sandy Krinski, one of the best TV sitcom writers, for improving my word usage and polishing my humor.

Melanie Fried, for skillfully organizing and comptently taking care of, a hundred details, from page proofs to photographs.

Paulette Cooper, author of 20 books, for taking time away from *Was Elvis Jewish?* to send me nine single-spaced pages of constructive criticism.

Dr. Todd Linden—for all the vaccinations, prescriptions, admonitions, and treatments that kept me on the road.

Keith Schwabinger, for devoting more than 100 hours to check and correct the facts.

Ira and Sandy Teller for reading my awful first draft and making sound suggestions short of suicide.

All the stalwarts who diligently plowed through drafts 7 to 12 and sent me comments and corrections: Jane Santoro, Stephanie Braxton, Peter Heinlein, John Crowther, Larry Sutter, Keven Danow, Claus Hirsch, Treva Silverman, Miha Loha, Jane Bieger, Chuck Hunt, David Smith, Betsy Brown, Nadezda Dukhina, Sylvia Law, Jeannie Forrest, Don Dunn, Sandy Krinski, and Treva Silverman.

Isaac Simon of UBS and Daryl Weber of Wells Fargo, outstanding investment advisers, for giving me several solid stock recommendations that enabled me to afford these travels.

Those nationals and expats who read and corrected the chapter on their countries:

Australia—Jane Bieger: inveterate traveler, writer, owner of The Rock Shop in Brisbane.

Chad —Karen and Carl Anonymous.

China— Alex Miller: teacher, social media entrepreneur, and husband of Yan.

Ethiopia—Peter Heinlein: fearless correspondent for the Voice of America.

Ghana, Benin, Togo, Mali, and Burkina Faso—Godfried Agbezudor: head of Continent Explorer.

Haiti—Johnathan Haggard: director of Beyond Borders, a charity focused on Haiti.

Mongolia— Balthazar Emke: tour operator and guide.

South Pacific—Tony Wheeler: founder of Lonely Planet and indefatigable traveler.

Russia—Nadezda Dukhina: journalist and writer, recently relocated to the U.S.

Saudi Arabia and Yemen—Ihab Zaki of Spiekerman Travel, Middle East specialist.

Somalia—The owner of the place I stayed in Mogadishu, who has requested anonymity.

Southeast Asia—Harold Stephens, who has lived there for the last 40 years.

Uganda and East Africa—Miha Lohar, who runs the Edirisa hotel in the Gorilla Highlands.

And, most affectionately, Aline, Amy, Anna, Beverly, Carla, Cindy, Claire, Corrine, DeAnsin, Donna, Dori, Eileen, Ellen, Inna, Irene, Jamie, Jodie, Joyce, Lauren, Lora, Lynne, Mary, Nadya, Pamela, Ralitsa, Roberta, Sandy, Sara, Sue, Susan, Svitlana, Veronika, Vickie, and Viktorija, plus Alan, Andrew, Claus, and Dennis, for having the faith and trust to travel with me and for keeping me company on various portions of these otherwise long and lonely journeys.